Difference and Community

Canadian and European Cultural Perspectives

Cross / Cultures

Readings in the Post/Colonial Literatures in English

25

Series Editors:

| Gordon Collier (Giessen) | Hena Maes-Jelinek (Liège) | Geoffrey Davis (Aachen) |

Amsterdam - Atlanta, GA 1996

DIFFERENCE AND COMMUNITY

Canadian and European Cultural Perspectives

Edited by

Peter Easingwood
Konrad Gross
Lynette Hunter

♾ The paper on which this book is printed meets the requirements of "ISO 9706:1994, Information and documentation - Paper for documents - Requirements for permanence".

ISBN: 90-420-0046-5 (bound)
ISBN: 90-420-0050-3 (paper)
©Editions Rodopi B.V., Amsterdam - Atlanta, GA 1996
Printed in The Netherlands

CONTENTS

Gender

Representations of Crisis and Renewal

❧ ❀ ❧

PREFACE

A MONG THE ESSAYS IN THIS VOLUME, certain key words appear: "diversity"; "marginality"; "multiculturalism"; "transculturalism." The immediate subject of these terms of reference is Canada, whose national culture was once invoked by the writer Robert Kroetsch in the statement: "we must confront the impossible sum of our traditions."[1] Certainly Canadians have been aware from the beginning that "Canada" was a highly problematical construct. They have sometimes been regarded as excessively self-conscious on the subject of national identity. The events of recent years have nevertheless shown that there is substantial cause for concern as well as occasion for special interest in the case of Canada, which continues to represent one of the most progressive of the "imagined communities"[2] of our time. The fact that European perspectives are also present or implied in most of these essays may suggest that the relationship between Europe and Canada is still a two-way process, as historically the traffic between them has been: either may have something to offer the other. Europe, too, acknowledges situations today in which "difference" and "community" are hard terms to reconcile.

The essays were given in their original form as papers at a conference held at the University of Leeds in April 1992, organised jointly by the British Association for Canadian Studies and the Association for Canadian Studies in German-Speaking Countries. Many participants attended from Canada and from other European countries apart from those of the organisers. The resulting collection of essays articulates the general themes of difference and community in a suitable variety of approaches and styles. "Difference" may refer to gender, sexuality, race, nationality or language; "community" is the collective understanding which must continually be renegotiated and reconstructed from among these factors. The Canadian–European connection is one in which it seems especially appropriate to explore such circumstances at the present time, for reasons which the contributors themselves consider in detail.

∾ ❀ ∿

---

1 Robert Kroetsch, "Beyond Nationalism: A Prologue," in *Open Letter*, Fifth Series, 4 (Spring 1983): 84.

2 The phrase and the conception of nationalism it implies derive from Benedict Anderson, *Imagined Communities: Reflections on the Origin and Spread of Nationalism* (London & New York: Verso, rev. ed. 1992).

ACKNOWLEDGEMENTS

The editors particularly wish to thank the following individuals and organisations for their support: Shirley Chew, School of English, University of Leeds; Michael Hellyer and Vivien Hughes, Academic Relations Office, Canadian High Commission in London; David Gammage, Foundation for Canadian Studies in the United Kingdom; the Gesellschaft für Kanada-Studien. The editors also wish to acknowledge with thanks the permission granted to use the following paintings: Richard Jack, "The Second Battle of Ypres"; Arthur Nantel, "7 a.m., April 22nd, 1915"; A.Y. Jackson, "A Copse: Evening" (all from the Canadian War Museum, Ottawa), and William Patrick Roberts, "The First German Gas Attack at Ypres" (from the National Gallery of Canada, Ottawa). Finally, it remains for the editors to thank Jens Carstens and Martin Müller–Olm for the technical preparation of the text for this book.

❦ ✸ ❦

ILLUSTRATIONS

Cover illustration: *Anew* (Susan A. Point; serigraph, 1992)

A Note on the Artist

Born in 1952 and resident in Vancouver, British Columbia, Susan A. Point is a Coast Salish Indian artist. She has immersed herself in the study of traditional Coast Salish art, emerging with a language of design that is both attuned to authentic traditions and vibrantly contemporary. Like many Native artists, she uses the form and meaning of traditional art to create innovative work in a wide range of media. In 1980, Susan opened her own studio after studying jewellery techniques, seriagraphy, and painting. To date, she has produced over a hundred limited-edition graphics, including 23-karat gold embossings, woodblocks, prints, serigraphs, glass etchings, handmade paper castings, and textile prints. She has designed and made patterns for cast-iron sculpture as well as concrete bas-relief sculpture, and has explored three-dimensional design in wood and bronze. Many of her works can be found in private and corporate collections in over twenty countries around the world.

> My use of traditional elements has become second nature to me – like an alphabet – helping me to describe any image I wish. When doing contemporary expressions such as acrylics on canvas, I become more illustrative, but I always integrate my ancestral Coast Salish elements into the work. I feel the role of Native art is to evolve continually, to express the cultural beliefs and changes of its community now and in the future.

General Perspectives

The Canadas
of Anglophone-Canadian Fiction 1967–90

FRANK DAVEY

T HIS ESSAY SUMMARISES THE CONCLUSIONS reached in a book-length
study of various constructions of "Canada" offered by sixteen recent
anglophone-Canadian novels. The paper and the study rest on an
assumption that cultural meanings, including those of fiction, are socially
produced; they rest also on my belief that societies function most equitably when
the social nature of their processes of meaning production are acknowledged. I
undertook the study, which is titled "National Arguments: the Politics of
Anglophone-Canadian Fiction Since 1967,"[1] in order to address from the
perspective of textual construction the ongoing political debates on Canada's
confederal institutions. I looked out for novels that were not necessarily the "best"
or most widely circulated of the past two decades, but rather for ones that had
been both critically well-received and socially important to various constituencies
within Canada. I looked for novels that had had an impact on at least one
anglophone-Canadian constituency, had been taught in at least some schools, had
occasioned some kind of critical and cultural discussion, and – equally important –
had offered some portrayal of Canada as a semiotic field.[2] Because of the major
concentration of the anglophone-Canadian population in Ontario, and the
international circulation of the books of a number of novelists, whose work, as
Barbara Godard has noted, is readable "without any regard to [...] Canadianness,"
a selection of merely the most *legitimated* Canadian novels of the period would
have included several each by Atwood, Richler, Findley, Davies, and Ondaatje,
and would have omitted many that were of considerable legitimacy to specific
regions and constituencies within Canada. For my study, I therefore limited

---

1 I use "anglophone-Canadian" here rather than "English–Canadian" because I wish to avoid
both the ethnicity suggestions of "English" and the growing understanding of "English–Canadian"
as signifying Canadians who reside outside of Quebec (much as, in Quebec French, the meaning of
"Québécois" has shifted for many speakers from denoting francophone Québécois to denoting any
resident of Quebec).

2 This criterion excluded some recent novels of considerable importance to Canadian ethnic
communities, such as Nino Ricci's *Lives of the Saints*, M.T. Vassanji's *The Gunny Sack*, and
Rohinton Mistry's *Such a Long Journey*, novels which contain few if any significations of Canada or
of Canadian polity. Such exclusion was not entirely fortuitous, since a Canadian novel's lack of
Canadian reference is itself a political statement.

myself to only one novel per novelist, and sought novels both from the regions of Canada – Pacific, Prairie, Arctic, Ontario, anglophone Quebec, and Atlantic Canada – and from various trans-regional social constituencies that had been discursively prominent within the nation over the past two decades: aboriginal peoples; immigrants from the third world; racial minorities; homosexual communities; varieties of feminism, nationalism and internationalism. These categories of course overlap – Canadian feminism can find a metaphor for itself in the Canadian land and ally itself with nationalism, find a metaphor in the earth and invoke the transnational, or can subdivide into lesbian feminism or lesbian feminism "of colour." Ethnic communities can appeal to models of internationalism and humanism; a specific region can propose itself as a national paradigm.

My focus in the study was not on the explicit politics of the novels studied, but on their implicit politics. I looked particularly at the discourses within the novels' narrations, the array of characters, places, and issues they present, the novels' narrative viewpoints and structures, their selections of imagery, symbol and metaphor, the syntax they award to narrators and characters, and the relative space they give to any of these. I looked not so much for the conscious views of authors as for the socially assumed beliefs encoded in the linguistic, narratological and semiotic conventions they employed. I also attempted to situate the novels within the political discourses circulating generally in Canada – specifically, within the competing discourses of the 1988 "free trade" debate, the 1990 "Meech Lake" debate, and the more recent "Canada Round" of constitutional conferences and negotiations.

The novels I ultimately selected for the study were *The Diviners* by Margaret Laurence, *The Temptations of Big Bear* by Rudy Wiebe, *Slash* by Jeannette Armstrong, *Nights Below Station Street* by David Adams Richards, *Caprice* by George Bowering, *Obasan* by Joy Kogawa, *The Wars* by Timothy Findley, *Joshua Then and Now* by Mordecai Richler, *In the Skin of a Lion* by Michael Ondaatje, *Fifth Business* by Robertson Davies, *The Tent Peg* by Aritha van Herk, *The Biggest Modern Woman of the World* by Susan Swan, *Ana Historic* by Daphne Marlatt, *Heroine* by Gail Scott, *Cat's Eye* by Margaret Atwood, and *Badlands* by Robert Kroetsch.[3] Such a list can, and very likely will, be quarrelled with. Its construction involved the epistemologically dubious procedure of hypothesising positions other than my own, and doing so on the basis of textual evidence that may not circulate well among variously positioned constituencies; other readers almost certainly have their own positions *and* lists. But because of the focus of my study on the signs, discourses, and narrative strategies at work in the novels – and because such textual elements tend to operate in a culture independently of individual speakers, writers or texts, to circulate within communities *across* speakers and texts – I am

---

3 See Works Cited below.

not at all sure that my readings would have been greatly altered by my having chosen, say, a different "arctic" novel from that of van Herk, or an earlier Atwood novel, or by my having included novels from one or two additional constituencies; particular instances of signification would have been different, but the overall array of signs, characters, discourses and narrative structures and strategies might well have been much the same.

What follows is not a summary of all of my readings in this study. I am omitting most of my readings of the extraordinary scepticism toward politics and social action I encountered in all but two of the novels, the tendency in many to rely on transcendent rather than social sources of amelioration and, in many others, to configure a reliable social order as no larger than a family or a single protagonist. All of these, of course, are elements that would certainly seem significant to a moment in Canadian history when the function and survival of any national political system seems to be in doubt. Instead, I will focus on figures, signs and constructions more directly related to an imagining of Canada.

❧ ✦ ❧

Exactly half of the sixteen novels I chose to look at devise their stories as a double narrative, one in which a narrative of inquiry or research frames an earlier narrative which is the target of the inquiry. More than half are narrated under the sign of research, from scholarly research in *Fifth Business* and *The Wars* to personal review and re-assessment in *Heroine* and *Cat's Eye*. Although the novel as a genre has usually operated as a search for coherence and meaning, here both the sign of research and the construction of characters as questers into their owns pasts operate to give the concept of coherence unusual emphasis. For most of the protagonists of the eight double-narratives, meaning resides not in the future but in crucial moments of their own pasts – in a thrown snowball, a family's scapegoating of the mother and consigning her to shock treatment, a rash or cowardly moment on Ibiza, a sexual molestation within sight of the family peach tree. Elaine Risley of *Cat's Eye* creates almost all of her paintings out of events and images she encountered in childhood and adolescence. In *Fifth Business* Dunstan Ramsay's life-long obsession with saints is launched by a woman he knew when he was a youth. In *Badlands* Anna Dawe's spinsterhood begins eleven years before her birth at the moment her father allows the adolescent Tune to die so that the fossil of a "Daweosaurus" may emerge from the Badlands.

Of the other eight novels, five are themselves based on research, offering historiographic re-imaginings of actual events of the Northwest Rebellion (*The Temptations of Big Bear*), nineteenth-century Nova Scotia (*The Biggest Modern Woman of the World*), late nineteenth-century British Columbia (*Caprice*), the First

World War (*The Wars*) and Depression Toronto (*In the Skin of a Lion*). Overall, the sixteen signal a profound uneasiness about the past, a fear that people have been crippled by how it has been remembered, a conviction that new interpretations of it, personal or cultural, may have to be established before the present can be re-engaged. The figure of psychoanalysis hovers throughout, both cultural psycho-analysis in the revisiting of sites of national trauma – Batoche, Ypres, Passchendaele, the Depression, the Japanese–Canadian internment camps – and personal psychoanalysis in the revisiting of private trauma: in *Obasan*, Naomi's loss of her mother; in *The Wars*, Robert Ross's implication in the death of his sister; in *Fifth Business*, Dunstan Ramsay's assumption of guilt for the misfortunes of Mary Dempster; in *Ana Historic*, Annie's complicity in the betrayal of her mother; in *Cat's Eye*, Elaine Risley's nearly fatal persecution by her schoolmates. And the counter-figures of psychoanalysis, neurosis and psychosis, hover also in Naomi and Anna Dawe's solitary spinsterhood, Elaine's deep mistrust of women, Dunstan's obsession with saints, Robert's preference of animals to people, in G.S.'s self-confinement to her bathtub in *Heroine* and in Patrick Lewis's obsessions with surface, form, light and shadow (*In the Skin of a Lion*). Emotionally crippled protagonists, incapable of complex networks of friendships and relationships, survive in solitude, exclusionary pairs, or minimal family units. These signs appear to echo metaphorically not only ongoing Canadian constitu-tional arguments over historical grievances and injustices, but also other signs of disruption that have been at play in the general anglophone-Canadian social text of the Seventies, Eighties and Nineties – provincial rivalry, illegal "cross-border" shopping, profound disagreements on official bilingualism, on multiculturalism, on the "distinctiveness" of Quebec and aboriginal cultures, and on aboriginal "self-government."

～ ❀ ～

> In days of yore
> From Britain's shore
> Wolfe the donkless hero CAME
> (*titters; but what*
> *means* <u>Donkless?</u>)
> (*The Diviners*, 56–57)
>
> The new national flag [...] two red bands and a red maple leaf rampant on
> white, looking like a trademark for margarine of the cheaper variety, or
> an owl-kill in snow. (*Cat's Eye*, 311–12)

One surprise in these sixteen novels is their lack of nationalist discourses and signs, unless ironically deployed. What they offer instead, repeatedly and paradoxically, are various discourses of intimacy, home, and neighbourhood, together with others of global distance and multinational community. Between the local and the global, where one might expect to find constructions of region, province and nation, one finds instead voyages, air flights, and international hotels. Home and family reside not within a nation but as nodes of international travel. *Ana Historic* sends both Annie and Mrs Richards directly from Britain to a Vancouver that almost immediately becomes a metonymy for North America. *Joshua Then and Now* maps Montreal as part of a world whose major sites are Montreal, London, Ibiza and Hollywood, and in which other parts of Quebec or Canada are rarely mentioned and never visited. *Heroine*, despite offering a view of family and politics vastly different from that in *Joshua*, offers a very similar map, in which Montreal is located alongside Morocco, Paris, Cracow and Marienbad, in which Quebec settlements other than Montreal and Quebec City do not exist, and in which Lively, Ontario, and Vancouver, B.C. are sites of naivety or exile.

A general model for this map is provided by the travels of Elaine Risley's brother in *Cat's Eye*, whose interest as a physicist is unified field theory but whose life and discursive efforts are represented as anything but unified. His travels move him with apparent randomness among Germany, Nevada, Bolivia, San Francisco, New York, and the Middle East. His only communications are cryptic notes on postcards: "great particle accelerator"; "interesting life forms"; "got married, Annette sends regards"; "excellent butterflies. Hope you are well" (330– 31). In many of the novels, neither the text nor its protagonists inhabit any social geography that can be called "Canada." They inhabit a post-national space, in which sites are as interchangeable as postcards, in which discourses are deterritor- ialised, in which political issues are constructed on non-national (and often ahistorical) ideological grounds: fascism and materialism, aestheticism, liberal humanism, Christian mysticism, feminism, industrial capitalism. For some, like *The Tent Peg*, *In the Skin of the Lion*, or *Nights Below Station Street*, Canada is an undifferentiatable site in the human condition; the local is finely detailed but situated in a homogeneous human situation – mystic woman, the redemptive power of beauty, fallen humanity – that in turn homogenises other Canadian regions and constituencies and trivialises political argument. For others, Canada is a "world-class" site, part of a global commercial "free-trade" network in which *Badlands'* William Dawe can sell his dinosaurs, Joshua of *Joshua Then and Now* market his writing, Dunstan Ramsay of *Fifth Business* pursue his saints, Anna Swan of *The Biggest Modern Woman of the World* market her height. Here, all Canadian difference except the home-base of the protagonist falls from sight; however, at another extreme, should this global network fail the protagonist, all that can remain is that local base: Dawe drowning in Georgian Bay, Joshua enjoying his Lake Memphremagog garden, Anna Swan's family mourning in Nova Scotia. For still others, Canada is merely part of an overwhelmingly powerful patriarchal order, with virtually no recuperable difference – regional, ethnic, linguistic, or class – within it, and with only extra-social ideologies – mystic feminism, zoological communalism – as alternatives. In nearly all of the novels set outside of Quebec, the transnational mapping appears to eliminate or severely reduce the significance of Quebec as a Canadian sign, as if on a world stage of transnational issues and global significations the presence or absence of Quebec in the Canadian federation were of minor consequence. Even the two novels set in Quebec in different ways oblige this sign to defer to both transnational causes and the protagonist's individual welfare.

Among the sixteen, there are only five which openly resist the transnational. Against the post-national assumptions of Stephen Risley's travels, *Cat's Eye* repeatedly asserts the signs of the local – the details of Elaine's northern Ontario and mid-town Toronto childhood, the specificities of her paintings, and her bridging of far west and central Canada through her Ontario past and Vancouver present. It makes Elaine, who stubbornly works in personal and Canadian images, the marginally "successful" Risley; it kills Stephen for his bland wanderings and lack of attention to detail. But the Canada it portrays is itself following Stephen's model, seeking "world-class" status, buying world-class sweater sets, seeking to create "world-class" New York architecture and art. Elaine's resistance to the transnational is itself portrayed as individual rather than social; she is constructed as incapable of profound affiliations, incapable even of causing one friend or family member to empathise with her paintings. The only symbol of resistance to the transnational the novel can offer is the cat's eye itself – the shining, "crystalline," mysteriously essential self.

In contrast to *Cat's Eye*'s localisms, the models offered by both *The Diviners* and *The Temptations of Big Bear* are to a large extent national, inclusive and incorporating. Both assemble an extensive range of Canadian signs from a variety of classes, regions, ethnicities and interests. *The Diviners*, in particular, repudiates the transnational in Morag's decision not to visit Sutherland, but instead to locate her ancestors "where I was born" (391). In their narrative structures – *Big Bear*'s omniscient narrator, who oversees its action and orchestrates its numerous voices; *The Diviners*' I-narrator, who recalls the other character's stories – these two novels suggest a nation brought together by a generous liberal–humanist imagination that can affiliate itself both with minority perspectives and with environmental process. It is to the sign of harmonising nature that both novels repeatedly appeal – a nature which, like the generous narrator, can reconcile contraries and accommodate difference. This is a sign which, like the sign of the aesthetic or the mystical, attempts to limit social conflict by positing an ultimate and common power external to society itself; paradoxically, of course, such a sign can have profound social power, particularly, in re-directing and re-legitimating certain powerful groups – here white, university-educated liberal nationalists, Margaret Laurence's "tribe" – who may be able to appropriate it. But within these particular texts, it is unlikely that the sign offers any advantage to such marginalised figures as Jules or Piquette Tonnerre, Sits Green On The Earth, Bridie McRaith, Kitty McLean, Eva Winkler, "A Canadian Volunteer," Horsechild, or Christie Logan.

Caprice and *Slash* construct a heterodox and potentially populist Canada, one in which institutions can respond to and perhaps even "belong" to the citizenry, as the B.C. Provincial Police appears to do in *Caprice*, and in which direct social action – town meetings, marches, demonstrations – can effect social change. In *Slash*, this is both a crude though slowly developing actuality on a tribal and inter-tribal level, and an ideal on the national one. It is the possibility of citizenship as an Indian that draws Slash Kelasket out of his arrogant and narcissistic despair, that enables him to be a father and, as the book implicitly constructs him, a story-teller. On a national level it is the idealistic expectation of First Nation people that they may eventually be able to participate in another story-telling, the writing of constitutional and legislative documents, which enables them to envision Canada as a field for their caravans, sit-ins and demonstrations. In *Caprice*, although the transnational signs that mark so many of the novels abound – France, Spain, Germany, the USA, Austria, Italy constitute both the world of Caprice's travels and the first homes of many of Nicola's citizens – it is the Nicola social community and its various institutions that the novel endorses. The village's hospital, Indian tribe, newspaper, brothel, resident capitalist and police force all make generous gestures of support for their Québécoise visitor, and thereby for each other. The transnational signs the novel layers onto this community – Chinese restauranteur, Irish tavern-keeper, Italian labourer, Indian language-teachers, Austrian newspaperman, English horse-breeder, Québécoise visitor – rather than effacing the national, posit Nicola as a metonymy for a cooperating national community of ethnic difference.

◦ ◉ ◦

The Free Trade debate of 1988 of the Canadian Federal Election was argued by various artists and writers, mostly men, and mostly from Ontario, who in the last two weeks of the campaign placed rival advertisements in the *Globe and Mail*, as a debate between two models of anglophone Canada: one a monolithic, Ontario-centred, "caring" society, the other a part of an open postnational arena of unrestrained economic opportunity and world-wide thought. In the sixteen novels of my study, only the second model makes itself powerfully present, although often as something as much to be feared as celebrated, and sometimes, as in *Badlands* and *The Biggest Modern Woman*, as something feared and celebrated in the same text. In addition, implicitly sympathetic with this postnational model are texts that take various humanist positions: *Obasan* with its yearnings for an undifferentiated humanity – for "a land that is like every land"; *In the Skin of a Lion* with its repeated attraction to the aestheticist reductions of light and shadow; *The Wars* with its humanist treasuring of Robert and Rowena's breath. Adding what may be unwitting support to the postnational also are those texts which implicitly construct injustice as residing in politics, education, commerce and other social practices, and represent the good as extra-social: *Nights Below Station Street*, *Fifth Business*, *Ana Historic*, *The Tent Peg*.

Most of the novels construct ambiguous binary models of the postnational culture and its alternatives – models in which the alternative term is often not nation, as both groups of free trade intervenors suggested, but the individual. Such a model should perhaps not be surprising, since the reduction of the significance of national boundaries, the reduction of regulations over travel, trade, and the transmission of information, tends both to increase the range and opportunities of the individual and to strip her of state protections. Anna Swan may be able to become the biggest modern woman *of the world* but she is also vulnerable to being alone in that world, unsupported by family, communal, or national networks. Stephen Risley may be able to become a world-class physicist, and diffidently travel the five continents, but when his life is threatened he is without friends, institutional support, or the effective assistance of his national government. What the conclusions of so many of these novels reveal is not a "caring" society but an isolated protagonist, obliged, in the classical liberal model, to pull herself to wherever by her own bootstraps, or to console herself with visions of transcendence.

Every one of the sixteen novels communicates mistrust, usually profound mistrust, of social and political process. There is often a narrow focus on a particular constituency. The novels' repeated portrayals of individuals left to their own resources, dying unloved and unattended, or subsisting on memory, appear to reflect not so much a preference for individualism as a despair about polity. Similarly, their frequent endorsement of benevolent powers beyond the social order – of some essential humanity, divine power, archetypal femininity, healing natural order, indemnifying will to beauty, or benevolent fortuity – signals a decided lack of faith that human cooperation can address injustice and accommodate difference.

This inability in all but a few instances to imagine a polity reaches out into the novels' construction of the nation and the world. Neither are constructed, except in *Slash*, *The Temptations of Big Bear*, and *Caprice*, as fields for social and political action. The continuities of action are mostly individual, and evolve within a network of discontinuous, interchangeable signs – international cities, famous explorers, chauvinist men, tall prairie grass, phallic guns. Despite the extensive travels of many of the characters, they rarely encounter any sign of international order; none ever applies for a passport, passes through a customs check, or has significant official contacts in the countries visited. The state signs they do encounter tend to be arbitrary and obstructive, like the police Joshua encounters in Falangist Spain, or absurd, like the Queen Victoria who receives Anna Swan. Within Canada, the characters similarly tend to encounter few if any signs of a supportive social structure, or even of Canadian societies beyond their immediate location. In *Ana Historic* the boundaries of British Columbia open onto Britain; in *The Biggest Modern Woman of the World* those of Nova Scotia open onto New York and London; in *Fifth Business* those of Ontario open onto continental Europe.

❧ ❀ ❧

What this array of post-centennial Canadian fiction appears to me most strongly to announce is the arrival of the postnational state – a state invisible to its own citizens, indistinguishable from its fellows, and significant mainly through its position within the grid of world-class postcard cities Stephen Risley flies inattentively among. Specific novels may argue for a humanist Canada, a more feminist Canada, a more sophisticated and worldly Canada, an individualist Canada, a Canada more responsive to the values of its aboriginal citizens; but collectively they suggest a world and a nation in which social structures no longer link regions or communities, political process is doubted, and individual alienation has become normal. Ironically, the strongest will toward community in these novels is expressed in their construction of First Nations peoples – of Big Bear in his efforts to protect a community of his own tribe, its white prisoners, its land and its animals, of the two Indians of *Caprice* who labour to understand white social practice, of the numerous Indians of *Slash* who work toward a pan-Canadian nation of Indian peoples. But for the novels' Euro-Canadians, even for the good citizens of Nicola, "the world [has] started to shrink." *Caprice*'s twentieth-century narrator laments a community of difference that has vanished: "We are all Europeans now" (110), he says.

❧ ❀ ❧

WORKS CITED

ARMSTRONG, Jeannette. *Slash* (Penticton: Theytus, 1985).

ATWOOD, Margaret. *Cat's Eye* (Toronto: McClelland & Stewart, 1988).

BOWERING, George. *Caprice* (Markham, Ontario: Penguin, 1987).

DAVIES, Robertson. *Fifth Business* (Toronto: Macmillan, 1970).

FINDLEY, Timothy. *The Wars* (Toronto: Clarke Irwin, 1977).

GODARD, Barbara. "Canadian? Literary? Theory?," *Open Letter*, Eighth Series, 3 (Spring 1992): 5–21.

HERK, Aritha van. *The Tent Peg* (Toronto: McClelland & Stewart, 1981).

KOGAWA, Joy. *Obasan* (1981; Markham, Ontario: Penguin, 1983).

KROETSCH, Robert. *Badlands* (1975; Toronto: General, 1982).

LAURENCE, Margaret. *The Diviners* (Toronto: McClelland & Stewart, 1974).

MARLATT, Daphne. *Ana Historic* (Toronto: Coach House, 1988).

ONDAATJE, Michael. *In the Skin of a Lion* (Toronto: McClelland & Stewart, 1987).

RICHARDS, David Adams. *Nights Below Station Street* (Toronto: McClelland & Stewart, 1987).

RICHLER, Mordecai. *Joshua Then and Now* (Toronto: McClelland & Stewart, 1980).

SCOTT, Gail. *Heroine* (Toronto: Coach House, 1987).

SWAN, Susan. *The Biggest Modern Woman of the World* (Toronto: Lester & Orpen Dennys, 1983).

WIEBE, Rudy. *The Temptations of Big Bear* (Toronto: McClelland & Stewart, 1970).

❧ ❀ ☙

The North Atlantic Cultural Triangle
The Bermuda Syndrome?

RICHARD COLLINS

"'If we are beginning the European Community all over again', said Jean Monnet, its founding father, 'we should begin with culture'. By linking together European culture and the new technologies, which hold the key to future prosperity and employment, a European television policy is now a major imperative."* 1

"I accept, with no sense of despair at all, a Europe united only in its substructure [...]. If we wish to speak of a single European culture, we shall find it only in a tolerant liberalism which accepts those impulses which seem to be disruptive. National culture has nothing to do with political nationalism [...].We are making an error of logic if we think that political and economic unity automatically signifies cultural unity. Culture is somewhere else."2

S
EVERAL COMMENTATORS³ have recently turned their attention to the homologies and differences between the historical Canadian and contemporary European experiences. (Direct influence, in either direction, of the

* © Richard Collins 1993. The author's research on European Communities' broadcasting policy has been supported by the Economic and Social Research Council, the Council's support under award number R 000232159 is gratefully acknowledged.

1 Commission of the European Communities 1984: 10. The Monnet quotation is interesting; it is frequently cited yet I have found no attribution which has enabled me to identify its origin. It does not appear in Monnet's principal written work, his *Memoirs* (London: Collins 1978). However, the *Memoirs* do record Monnet's conviction that European civilisation is not the exclusive property of Europe. In 1966 he wrote: "We must organise the collective action of our civilisation. How can this be done? Only by uniting in collective action Europe and America, which together have the greatest resources in the world, which share the same civilisation, and which conduct their public affairs in the same democratic manner" (*Memoirs*, 486). In the *Memoirs* Monnet also commented acerbically on the pursuit of a chimera of European identity; "While fifty-five countries were meeting in Lomé or Brussels to seek their common interests, our diplomats were holding pointless debates about a 'European identity'" (*Memoirs*, 499).

2 Anthony Burgess, "European Culture: Does It Exist?," in *European Broadcasting Union Review: Programmes, Administration, Law* 41.2 (March 1990): 21.

3 See *inter alia* P. Gerlach, "Broadcasting in Canada: A Yardstick for Europe?," *European Broadcasting Union Review* 39.1 (January 1988): 20–24; P. Juneau, "Audience Fragmentation and Cultural Erosion," *European Broadcasting Union Review* 35.2 (March 1984: 14–20; Peter Harcourt, "Culture and Communications: The Case of Canada," *London Journal of Canadian Studies* 7 (1990): 14–27.

EC's broadcasting policy and Canada's seems to be confined to advocacy of the Canadian points system for definition of European content.[4]) Peter Harcourt's argument is representative of this current of opinion concerned with the "Canadianisation" of European broadcasting. These commentators have argued that the "American" forces which have (mis)shaped Canadian broadcasting have, and will increasingly, shape European broadcasting.

> The American model [...] [will] increasingly [...] become the European model. Indeed, by 1992, when the European Economic Community becomes a collectively organised, polyglot, but economically homogeneous state, it may well become the British model as well. Now there can some advantages in breaking down the barriers of the European nation states [...] but I would not counter argue, if for individuated vernacular cultures you simply put in place a homogenised cultural commodity.[5]

Many believe that Canada is about to fall apart. Certainly statements such as mine that Canada is "a stable North American state,"[6] "Canada is a remarkably stable and successful state"[7] have now returned to haunt me. At the time of writing we simply do not know how the constitutional crisis in Canada will be resolved; whether a new version of the Conscription Crisis or of 1976 is being played or whether genuinely new divisions of sovereignty will take place in the Canadian polity. And if so, what form these new divisions of sovereignty may take. The new polity/polities might look like Switzerland or Belgium or Ireland or Norway/ Sweden, or India/Pakistan, there are all kinds of constitutional arrangements ranging from the separate and hostile to shared sovereignty with constitutional provision for recognition of cultural and linguistic differences which might obtain. Whatever the constitutional arrangements that eventuate between anglophone (mostly) Canada, Quebec and the native peoples, issues of national culture, national coherence and minority rights will remain, and will be explored in circumstances perhaps no less troubling than those which now prevail.

In the short run there can be no doubt that the rationalist optimism that led me to write "Canada is a remarkably stable and successful state" was overstated (I will not take the opportunities for weaseling that comparisons with disasters like the no longer Soviet, no longer Union offer). In the middle and long term, who knows? As reviewers of my book keep reminding me, the instances of assertive nationalism insisting on the congruence of polity and culture are so evident that

---

4 At the *Assises européennes de l'audiovisuel* held in Paris in 1989 the Group of Experts concerned with Programmes advocated a points system for European content regulation explicitly based on the Canadian model; *Assises européennes de l'audiovisuel: Projet Eureka audiovisuel* (Paris: Ministère des affaires étrangères, République Française/Commission of the European Communities, 1989).

5 Harcourt, "Culture and Communications: The Case of Canada," 22.

6 Richard Collins, *Culture Communication and National Identity: The Case of Canadian Télévision* (Toronto: U of Toronto P 1990): xii.

7 Collins, *Culture Communication and National Identity*, 21.

only the wilfully blind could fail to miss them. They may be right. Certainly the long period of Liberal hegemony and, when a viable Conservative Government emerged, the (as it seemed to me) impossibility of Canada not making a deal on the Meech Lake terms – the least demanding advanced by Quebec for three decades – led me to overstate my hope that indeed Canada was a stable and successful state. And I have recently begun to reflect with more and more curiosity (though so far with no firm conclusions) on the difference in orientation to the national question of me, a white Englishman, and those of others not so firmly bound by discourses of dominance. However, I remain to be persuaded that post-Communist nationalist resurgence east of the Elbe (and south of the Drava) is the same as that east of the Ottawa (or north of the Tweed).

Yet it seems unlikely that the "Canadian questions" of negotiating cultural and national difference, guaranteeing minority rights and reconciling democratic self-government with the interdependence that international trade, pollution control and a host of other imperatives necessitate will be solved by new forms of sovereignty and association. Will they be easier to deal with? And how far did cultural questions contribute to the crisis in the Canadian polity? Do the case of Canada, the actual disintegration on more or less national lines of multinational polities such as Yugoslavia and the former Soviet Union,[8] the unification of Germany, and the possible future nationalist disintegration of the United Kingdom, Czechoslovakia and China suggest that the core nationalist precept, that states can survive only when isomorphic with nations, still holds good?[9] To pose the problem more concretely and more specifically in terms of the audiovisual media: will the two main internationalising pressures exerted by audiences continue? These are to demand productions – particularly drama – budgeted at higher levels than the market of a single state can amortise and for exogenous productions – whether from migrants for "home country" productions or from natives for the diversity which exogenous programming delivers.

To address those questions we have to return to the fundamental theoretical issues which underpin the relationships between culture, politics and community. And, as well as recognising that we live in a period of resurgent nationalism and dissolution of the bonds that have tied transnational unities together, we must also

---

[8] Czechoslovakia, the child of the Versailles Treaty, separated into the Czech and Slovak Republics in 1993.

[9] Here a qualification should be entered; the major disintegrations of transnational states (and German reunification) which we have recently witnessed have communism as a common element. Since the Bolshevik Revolution, European communism and nationalism have been rivals. The Versailles settlement built a Europe of nation-states as a counter-force to the contemporary seductive power of international communism. A good choice by the victorious powers, for, at length, nationalism has proven to be stronger than communism. Whether the cases of disintegration of Canada and the United Kingdom are of the same order seems doubtful.

note that the contemporary era is one of unprecedented *integration* between hitherto sovereign states. The European Communities (hereafter EC[10]) are perhaps the most striking example, but not the only one. Our reflections may be assisted by broadening the terms of reference to the making of comparisons between Canada and other jurisdictions. For the "Canadian questions" are not exclusively Canadian. As the two introductory quotations with which I began this essay suggest, they are, and have long been, European concerns too.

In spite of the notable contemporary efflorescence of nationalism the problems of large scale immigration, integration into transnational markets and building a functioning polity of citizens from diverse ethnic, cultural and linguistic groups which "settler" societies have long encountered are increasingly facing the "core" nation-states; indeed, resurgent nationalism is sometimes a response to forces such as these. Just as the model of the nation-state (generalised from a small number of examples – notably Russia, France, Spain, England, perhaps Turkey and latterly Japan – at a particular time in their history) was exported from the European core and adopted by other societies (including the settler societies which, with varying degrees of success and at varying costs, constructed themselves in the "core" nation-states' image), so now Europe is grappling with the problems of dependence on trading relationships (including cultural trades) with partners who are not subject to Europe's control, of large-scale immigration, and of establishing, exercising and legitimising political sovereignty over diverse populations. However, Europe has given less attention to the experience of settler societies, which had earlier experience of the problems which contemporary Europe now encounters, than settler societies have given to Europe itself.[11]

What, then, has happened, and what might happen, in the European Communities (EC)? Thus far there is scant evidence of homogeneity in EC policy formation or, thus far, outcomes in the audiovisual field. The EC's broadcasting and audiovisual policy has (a Commission official interviewed by the author on 11 November 1991 stated) three foci: establishment of rules – notably through the issue of Directives, promotion of programme production and distribution, and development of the technological and productive capacity of the Communities'

---

10 The plural term European Communities, though pedantic, is correct. Strictly there were three communities, the Economic Community, the Coal and Steel Community and the Atomic Energy Community. Following ratification of the Maastricht Treaty on European Union, the European Community is properly now known as the European Union.

11 I am aware that a generalisation of this magnitude oversimplifies and in important respects misrepresents large-scale and diverse historical processes. In one sense, of course, Europe has dealt with just these problems many times before: by making the boundaries of nations and states coincide, amplifying differences between the "us" sharing a political roof and the "them" outside its shelter, and regularly spilling the blood of those inside and outside boundaries who were designated "them" and not "us."

audiovisual industries. However, these goals are to some extent mutually antagonistic and are not pursued with equal vigour. The EC has as yet lacked jurisdictional power in the cultural field; therefore its measures to promote the production and circulation of audiovisual works have been weak. But the final ratification in 1993 of the treaty on political union concluded at Maastricht in December 1991 significantly extends the EC's powers in the cultural field. Moreover, the interests of the powerful EC aerospace and electronics industries are not the same as those of broadcasters and programme producers. Thus far, the interests of audio-visual production and distribution have been favoured less than other sectors in EC rule-making and industrial policy.

The major achievement of the EC in the broadcasting/audiovisual field has been to establish the formal conditions for a single broadcasting market. The Television without Frontiers Green Paper[12] began a process which resulted in the Community Directive[13] of 3 October 1989, at the time of writing the only major Community requirement in respect of broadcasting until its expiry on 31 December 1991. However, the single market has been described (by Roberto Barzanti, formerly the Chairman of the European Parliament's Committee on Youth, Culture, Education, Media and Sport) as an American Trojan Horse. Barzanti stateS: "The American production and distribution model is best suited to the single market economy. It is better prepared to harvest the economic fruits of the single European market than any other national cultural industry in the Community."[14]

The former European Community Commissioner for the Cultural and Audiovisual sectors, Jean Dondlinger, wrote in similar terms:

> The European film and television industry is among the sectors most seriously endangered by competition from other markets more accustomed to a free and easy diffusion of broadcasts over large areas. The role of the Commission is, of course, that of providing consistent means for policy and coordination at Community level. It is also that of actively supporting a sector little- adapted to purely economic competition.[15]

In the eyes of those such as Barzanti and Dondlinger, the perceived inevitability of market failure has been compounded by the EC's folly in establishing a single audiovisual market. However, due both to the relatively weak institutional

---

12 Commission of the European Communities 1984a.

13 Council of the European Communities 1989.

14 Roberto Barzanti, "Audiovisual Opportunities in the Single Market," in *MEDIA 92: Newsletter of the MEDIA 92 Programme* 09/1990 (Brussels 1990): 1.

15 Jean Dondlinger, "Europe's Media Future," in *Media Bulletin* 6.2 (Manchester: European Institute for the Media, 1989): 3.

position of Barzanti's Committee and Dondlinger's Directorate,[16] none of the European initiatives established to compensate for the perceived failure of audio-visual markets dispose of significant resources. Barzanti has described the Communities' own MEDIA 95 programme (aid to pre- and post-production of European audiovisual works) as insufficient.[17] Other initiatives such as Eurimages (inspired by France and established under the aegis of the Council of Europe by intergovernmental agreement), the Audiovisual Eureka (a "marriage bureau" for European co-productions inspired by France and also established by inter-governmental agreement) have taken place outside the structures of the European Communities. But the ratification of the Maastricht treaty on political union grants the EC new powers which it has hitherto lacked, enabling it to support Community cultural industries.

The seeming absurdity of the EC establishing a single broadcasting market and then seeking powers to roll back the effects of the single market can be best understood in terms of fundamental divisions within the organisation (and, indeed, within the Communities' executive arm, the Commission of the European Communities). Some EC member states have consistently opposed the extension of EC initiatives into the audiovisual and cultural sectors (Denmark and the United Kingdom have been notable here) and some of the Commission's Directorates (its "Ministries") are labelled "ultra-liberal" for their opposition to proactive intervention (whether by Member States or by the Commission itself) in markets. The "ultra-liberal" Directorates for Competition and for the Internal Market (DG III and DG IV) have been much more influential in the audiovisual and cultural spheres than the "dirigiste" Directorates (DG X and DG XIII) for Audiovisual, Information, Communication and Culture and for Tele-communications, Information Industries and Innovation have been.

The Television without Frontiers Directive is a case in point. Sponsored by DG III, the initiative begun in 1984 with the Television without Frontiers Green Paper became Community "law" in 1989. Whereas even the powerful DG XIII has, at the time of writing, not succeeded in securing sufficient support to promul-

---

16 Neither Barzanti nor Dondlinger continues to hold the offices occupied when this paper was first written and delivered.

17 He states ("Audiovisual Opportunities in the Single Market") that the 250m ECU which the President of the Commission of the European Communities, Jacques Delors, had committed to the audiovisual sector at the *Assises de l'audiovisuel* (M. Maggiore, *Audiovisual Production in the Single Market: Commission of the European Communities* [Luxembourg 1990]: 199] were insufficient. The Council's decision reduced this, already notionally inadequate, sum (which had been endorsed by the Economic and Social Committee of the Community) by 20%. The 200m ECU allocated to MEDIA for five years for the whole audiovisual sector (annual sterling equivalent £26.3m) compares unfavourably with the estimated £2,099m spent on programming by UK television in 1990 (*Knowledge Research* 1990).

gate a Directive on satellite broadcasting transmission standards (to replace that promulgated in 1986, which expired on 31 December 1991; this Directive was agreed when satellite television was metaphorically as well as literally a "blue-sky" technology and therefore agreement to Commission proposals was more easily secured than it is now when important vested satellite broadcasting interests to countervail the well-established powers of the aerospace and electronics sectors have become established). Nonetheless, the EC has developed broadcasting and audiovisual policies and practices which have evolved in interesting ways over the last decade, and it is very likely, with the Maastricht ratification, that the inclusion of culture within the Communities' competencies will lead to further proactive Community audiovisual policies – perhaps of a rather Canadian kind.

European Parliamentarians have claimed that, in contrast to most EC policies which have originated in initiatives of the Commission or the Member States, EC broadcasting policy has been initiated by the Parliament rather than by the Commission or Council. Gijs de Vries claims that Parliament has "prompted the Commission into publishing, first the Interim Report, and in 1984, the Green Paper on the Internal Market in broadcasting [...]. Parliament has thus *de facto* initiated legislation."[18] Barzanti (interview with author, 8 November 1991) has described the Hahn Resolution (see below) as the "*première pierre*" in the edifice of Community audiovisual and broadcasting policy. And the Parliament has continued to call "for a comprehensive Community media policy, which not only removes legal and technical barriers to a common market for broadcasting but also supports European audio-visual products."[19] Thus, although the Commission is the most powerful of the Community's institutions, Community audiovisual and television policy cannot be understood solely as a product of the Commission. Nor is the Community's audiovisual policy the product of a single and unified vision of the audiovisual sphere. Rather, it is the result of differing priorities and perspectives among several distinct power centres. Indeed, there are important differences of perspective, and thus of emphasis, between the Parliament and the Commission and within the Commission itself; as officials in DG IV have stated (interview with author, 11 November 1991), "the views and interests of DGs are different." Parliament and DG X have tended to share similar "dirigiste" perspectives opposed to the "ultra-liberal" reflexes of other Directorates. The origins of the EC's proactive audiovisual and broadcasting policies can be found in the Parliament's initiatives in the early Eighties.

In 1982 the Parliament's Committee on Youth, Culture, Education, Inform-ation and Sport produced a report on Radio and Television Broadcasting in the

---

18 European Parliament 1987: ii.
19 European Parliament 1987: 22.

European Community: the Hahn report. The report articulated fears of broadcasting becoming "an article of merchandise in the framework of the Common Market" and that satellite broadcasts would flood "the Community in unlimited quantities as though they were a commercial product."[20] The Hahn report advocated a vision of EC broadcasting based on regulation and proactive initiatives by political authorities in order to achieve desired outcomes which, it was feared, could not be realised through the operation of markets. Indeed, the Parliament's Political Affairs Committee stated that the free operation of a broadcasting market was inimical to the central cultural values of the Community. Its argument, affirming the worth of order as well as of freedom, was framed to counter "ultra-liberal" arguments which appealed to the values enshrined in the European Convention on Human Rights:

> the maintenance of public order is as important to the Member States, in protecting their own fundamental rights and preserving their cultural and political identity, as the principle of a free flow of information. Unrestricted cross-border commercialisation is dangerous [...] regulation should embody the structural guarantees necessary for independence without which a European broadcasting war will inevitably break out which may destroy the cultural values of our Community.[21]

In the mass media, and television in particular, the Hahn report identified an instrument through which its aspirations for a "political community" could be realised, for, it believed, "the instruments which serve to shape public opinion today are the media. Of these, television as an audiovisual means of communication is the most important"– or, more strongly, "Information is a decisive, perhaps the most decisive factor in European integration"; it was judged that this desired European integration was unlikely to be achieved while "the mass media is controlled at national level."[22] However, the new technology of satellite television, as well as *threatening* the broadcasting war foreseen by the Political Affairs Committee in which European culture would be annihilated, also *promised* – if suitably guided – hope to European integrationists. For, the report suggested, "television satellites will lead to a reorganisation of the media in Europe; the new technical facilities will break down the boundaries of the national television networks and enforce the creation of wide-ranging transmission areas."[23] Common to both the pessimistic vision of the Political Affairs Committee and the hopes expressed in the final Hahn report was a profound belief in the power of a new communication technology – satellite television. The Commission's response to the Hahn report (*Realities and tendencies in European Television: Perspectives and*

---

20 European Parliament 1982: 23, 24.
21 European Parliament 1982: 24–25
22 European Parliament 1982: 24–25, 8.
23 European Parliament 1982: 8.

Options) echoes the Parliament's convictions and articulates the twin assumptions of technological and cultural determinism that have underpinned Community audiovisual policy.

> DBS will become a powerful unifying factor. Viewers in one country will be able to share television programmes with viewers in other countries and will thus acquire a new feeling of belonging and involvement. This sharing of pictures and information will be the most effective means of increasing mutual understanding among the peoples of Europe and will give them a greater sense of belonging to a common cultural and social entity. The development of a truly European spirit will therefore become possible in national audiences, who will still, of course, retain their full cultural identity.24

Here the Commission's conception of cultural identity is non-exclusive and plural; European identity can be added to national identity without diminishing either. Yet, if this is so, it is not explained why the presence of an exogenous, non-European, culture is to be feared. If national cultures can non-exclusively coexist with European culture, why is the "invasion" of a foreign culture (to which the report refers on page 11) so much to be feared? Perhaps such questions should not be pressed too far. To demand consistency and rigour in documents which are the outcome of a continuing process of political bargaining and compromise may be tantamount to committing a category error. Nonetheless, the precarious coherence of the assumptions on which policy and policy rhetoric is based is worth noting. Two conclusions may be drawn. First, the theoretical incoherence of the policy rationale testifies to the depth of the sentiments of those who advocate it – were such propositions not firmly believed, it is unlikely that they would be advanced so often and so insistently, for they cannot readily be supported on reasoned grounds. And, second, the absence of a generalised rational basis for such policies means that the processes of exclusion and inclusion which designate some as supporters and others as opponents of audiovisual policies are likely to be very powerful. One is either a believer, or one is not.

In the Hahn report and the Commission's response we see the germination of an enduring theme in the EC's policy discourse: a double notion of determination. First, a *technological* determinism, whereby new communication technologies, notably satellite television, are believed to dissolve long-established relationships and audience-structures which have been based on national mass communication systems and services. Second (and deriving from the first), a *cultural* determinism, whereby the new relationships created by changed patterns of circulation of information and entertainment will necessarily lead to changes in the cultural interests and identities of receivers. From these changed cultural identities it is presumed that new political identities, new presumptions about citizenship,

---

24 Commission of the European Communities 1983: 22.

membership of a polity, will derive. These assumptions lead those who share them
to argue both for European Community initiatives harnessing powerful new communication technologies in order to produce new conceptions of political affinity
and identity in European viewers and listeners and against the circulation within
the Community of exogenous audiovisual productions which will, it is feared,
erode the established European sentiments and consciousness of consumers.

The Hahn committee supported the European Broadcasting Union's proposal
(first canvassed at the meeting of the New Developments Committee in Venice in
1980 by the Head of RAI's International Department, Vittorio Boni), to establish a
European satellite television channel. The first stage of this initiative was an
experiment in 1982; collaboration by five EBU members[25] on Eurikon, an
encoded satellite television service to test the technological, organisational and
programming viability of a transnational European service. Eurikon was followed
by Europa,[26] a satellite-to-cable service which transmitted from 1985 to 1986.
Unlike Eurikon, Europa was actually receivable by European cable subscribers.
However, the expectations of the supporters of these initiatives were not fulfilled;
audience research conducted as part of the Eurikon experiment showed little
enthusiasm for the new service.[27] So, too, with Europa: in 1986, Europa achieved
a 1% share of Dutch television viewing (the Netherlands was where most Europa
viewers were located) whereas the rival commercial Sky Channel achieved a 5%
viewing share.[28]

Hopes that the new technology of satellite broadcasting could be used to
distribute a common European diet of programmes from which – double
determinism again – a common European identity would derive were deceived.
But the political imperatives that gave rise to Eurikon and Europa are now giving
life to a new European television venture: Euronews. This initiative, like Eurikon
and Europa, emanates from the European Broadcasting Union and is inspired by
senior European officials' perception that Europe was excessively reliant on CNN
for its knowledge of the 1991 Gulf War and that no European perspective was

25 The IBA from the UK, ARD from West Germany, RAI from Italy, NOS from the Netherlands and the ORF from Austria (Austria is not a full member of the European Communities).
26 Europa was established by three of the Eurikon partners, NOS, ARD and RAI, who were
joined by RTE (Ireland) and RTP (Portugal).
27 H. de Bock, "Eurikon Considered: The Eurikonsumers' Perspective" (undated, but probably
March 1983); B. Gunter, *Audience Reactions to Eurikon: Evidence on UK Viewer Ratings of a New Pan-
European TV Service* (London: IBA Audience Research Department, 1982); B. Gunter,
"Measurement of Audience Ratings of Eurikon Programming from the First Demonstration Week
(24–30 May 1982): A Report on Three Pilot Experiments and Some Preliminary Research
Findings" (London: IBA typescript, July 1982); RAI (Radiotelevisione Italiana), "Experiment of
the EURIKON Programs Transmitted via the OTS Satellite" (LCMIANUS, typescript, April 1983).
28 W. Bekkers, "The Dutch public broadcasting services in a multi-channel landscape," in
European Broadcasting Union Review. Programmes, Administration, Law 38.6 (November 1987): 34.

available to television viewers in Europe. The extensive evidence provided by the commercial satellite television ventures of the Eighties (as well as by Eurikon and Europa) that the differences rather than the similarities of European television audiences are most notable[29] and the no less extensive evidence that there was no European viewpoint on the Gulf war (several EC states – notably France, Italy and the United Kingdom – were active belligerents, others were not; indeed, Belgium refused to supply munitions to the UK for its Gulf forces) suggest that supporters of Euronews may experience disappointment.

Latterly, the notion of a common European culture and identity has been downplayed in EC policy, for, once the next logical stage in this line of argument is reached, a common European language,[30] the absurdities and disadvantages of the project become evident. In consequence, the European Parliament's response to the Television without Frontiers Green Paper[31] spoke of "the increased importance of radio and television for [...] the emergence of a European consciousness, and the maintenance of Europe's cultural diversity and identity." And Mariano Maggiore, the Deputy Head of DG X's Audiovisual Directorate has said: "We have no interest in promoting a melting pot. We want to preserve European identities."[32] Maggiore stresses the importance of the MEDIA programmes initiatives (notably EFDO[33]) to promote the circulation of works produced in one Community location to consumers in others. The rationale the Community has more recently offered in support of its audiovisual policy has been the promotion of "unity in diversity" – fostering co-productions between partners from different member-states but, even more important, fostering the circulation of works from one member-state to others. However, this policy has not been markedly successful; in general, audiences have not displayed conspicuous enthusiasm for the cinema (or television) of their European neighbours. A representative and particularly pithy commentary was offered by Ryclef Rienstra, the Executive Secretary of Eurimages,[34] who, when asked what was the main pro-

---

29 Richard Collins, "The Language of Advantage," in *Media Culture and Society* 11.3 (1989): 351–72.

30 Eminently practical though one would be. In 1987 nearly 14% of the staff of the European Commission were translators and interpreters (E. Noel, *Working Together: The Institutions of the European Community* [Luxemburg: Office for Official Publications of the European Communities, 1988]: 41). The number of Commission translators and interpreters will increase geometrically as the European Communities grow and further official languages are added to the current nine.

31 European Parliament 1985: 113.

32 In an interview with the author, 11 November 1991.

33 European Film Distribution Office.

34 The European Support Fund for the Co-Production and Distribution of Creative Cinematographic and Audiovisual works (Eurimages) was established (following an initiative of France) on 26 October 1988 in order to develop European cinematographic and audiovisual production (Resolution 15 of the Committee of Ministers of the Council of Europe [1988]). The

blem experienced by Eurimages, stated that "Lack of support from the audience is the biggest problem; I wonder how far we should go in supporting culture."[35]

The evidence suggests that audiences remain obdurately resistant to most of the transnational "European" services conjured into existence in response to production-industry lobbying and the political agendas of European officials. Euronews suggests that the vision of transnational European services is a particularly stubborn ghost and will be difficult to exorcise. But, notwithstanding the continued presence of this phantom, there has been a notable shift in the policy discourse. Rather than a vision of a unified transnational European culture, it is a vision of European culture as a unity in diversity that holds centre stage. However, the notion of unity in diversity makes sense only in terms of those members of the diverse community being differentiated from members of other communities in terms of the absence, in the first diverse community, of the unifying cultures enjoyed by members of the other communities to which they are compared and from which they are differentiated. Diversity of cultural experience clearly distinguishes members of the European Community. So there is unity, too, of a kind, for most members of the European Community share a common tradition of democratic political institutions, Christianity, and post-Enlightenment scientific rationalism. As Burgess[36] suggests, the locus of this unity is in what he calls substructure and what I have variously called anthropological culture or structure.[37] Moreover, the shared elements of the European tradition are not the exclusive property of Europe. Indeed, they are shared with other world communities, notably with inhabitants of the post-colonial societies in North and South America and Oceania which were offshoots of Europe.[38]

Nonetheless, the imperatives remain for a common culture within a particular polity – but more, I believe, because the advocates of a normative culture deem

---

founding members of Eurimages included all EC states (except Ireland and the UK), Cyprus and Sweden; Austria, Finland, Hungary, Iceland, Norway, Poland, Turkey and Switzerland, Ireland and the UK have subsequently joined the Eurimages consortium. The fund was established to encourage the co-production and distribution of creative cinematographic and audiovisual works originating in the member-states of the fund, particularly by helping to finance the co-production of such works and by partly financing the cost of dubbing and subtitling (Council of Europe 1988: 2).

35 In an interview by the author, 17 December 1991.

36 Burgess, "European Culture: Does It Exist?"

37 Collins, Culture Communication and National Identity.

38 The links between Europe's two anglophone states and the Anglo-Celtic diaspora in the United States, Australia, Canada and New Zealand are but the most obvious of many examples. An intriguing testimony to the overseas reach of European culture was given by André Fontaine, the editor of Le Monde, at the Symposium on European Cultural Identity sponsored by the Government of France in 1988. Fontaine said: "je me trouvais plus en Europe, à la limite, à Buenos Aires qu'à Paris, parce qu'à Buenos Aires, il n'y a pas des enseignes en anglais" (SIICE Symposium international sur l'identité culturelle européenne [Paris: Albin Michel, 1988]: 96).

the values of that culture to be superior to the values of exogenous cultures than because a single normative culture is required to maintain the integrity of the polity in question. Rather as those who, prior to the Enlightenment, advocated a state religion as a necessary element in a stable polity ("No Bishop, no King", "*Cuius regio eius religio*") so do some post-Enlightenment intellectuals strive for a *Gemeinschaft* where their values are naturalised as normative (national) and essential to the health of the polity, and thereby are effectively legitimised.

Within the European Communities we can thus see a scenario being played out which echoes familiar motifs in Canadian policy. It is not surprising that there are so many echoes of Canadian themes in European policy-discourse, for the European Communities have the Canadian problem of how to make a multicultural and multi-lingual polity work in unpromising circumstances. Not only do the citizens of the polity's main communities consume little of each others' cultures but, insofar as they share cultural tastes, this shared taste seems to be for exogenous culture.

WORKS CITED

BARZANTI, Roberto. "Audiovisual Opportunities in the Single Market," in *MEDIA 92: Newsletter of the MEDIA 92 Programme* 09/1990 (Brussels 1990): 1.

BEKKERS, W. "The Dutch public broadcasting services in a multi-channel landscape," in *European Broadcasting Union Review: Programmes, Administration, Law* 38.6 (November 1987): 32–35.

BOCK, H. de. "Eurikon Considered: The Eurikonsumers' Perspective" (undated, but probably March 1983).

BURGESS, Anthony. "European Culture: Does It Exist?," *European Broadcasting Union Review: Programmes, Administration, Law* 41.2 (March 1990): 17–21.

COLLINS, Richard. "The Language of Advantage," *Media Culture and Society* 11.3 (1989): 351–72.
———. *Culture Communication and National Identity: The Case of Canadian Television* (Toronto: U of Toronto P, 1990).

COMMISSION OF THE EUROPEAN COMMUNITIES. *Assises européennes de l'audiovisuel: Projet Eureka audiovisuel* (Paris: Ministère des affaires étrangères, République Française and Commission of the European Communities, 1989).
———. "Interim Report. Realities and Tendencies in European Television: Perspectives and Options," in *COM* (83) 229 final. 25.5.83 (Brussels 1983).
———. "Television Without Frontiers. Green paper on the establishment of the Common Market for broadcasting especially by satellite and cable," *COM* (84) 300 final (Luxemburg: Office for Official Publications of the European Communities, 1984).
———. "Towards a European Television Policy," in *European File* 19/84 (Brussels: Commission of the European Communities, 1984).

COUNCIL OF THE EUROPEAN COMMUNITIES. "Directive on the coordination of certain provisions laid down by law, regulation or administrative action in Member States concerning the pursuit of television broadcasting activities," *89/552/EEC. OJ No L 298,* 17.10.1989 (1989): 23–30.

COUNCIL OF EUROPE. "Setting up a European Support Fund for the Co-Production and Distribution of Creative Cinematographic and Audiovisual Works (Eurimages)," in *Resolution* (88) 15 (Strasburg 1988).

DONDLINGER, Jean. "Europe's Media Future," in *Media Bulletin* 6.2 (Manchester: European Institute for the Media, 1989): 3.

EUROPEAN PARLIAMENT. "Audio-Visual Policies of the Community: The Role of the European Parliament; Research and Documentation Papers," *Economic Series* 10.8–1987 (European Parliament Secretariat, Directorate General for Research, 1987).

————. *Report on Radio and Television Broadcasting in the European Community* (Hahn Report). Document 1–1013/81 (1982).

————. *Framework Resolution for a European Media Policy.* OJ C 288 11.11.1985, (1985): 113.

GERLACH, P. "Broadcasting in Canada: A Yardstick for Europe?," in *European Broadcasting Union Review* 39.1 (January1988): 20–24.

Globe and Mail. Daily. Toronto.

GUNTER, B. *Audience Reactions to Eurikon. Evidence on UK Viewer Ratings of a New Pan- European TV Service* (London: IBA Audience Research Department, 1982).

————. "Measurement of Audience Ratings of Eurikon Programming from the First Demonstration Week (24–30 May 1982): A Report on Three Pilot Experiments and Some Preliminary Research Findings" (IBA typescript (July 1982).

HARCOURT, Peter. "Culture and Communications: The Case of Canada," *London Journal of Canadian Studies* 7 (1990): 14–27.

JUNEAU, P. "Audience Fragmentation and Cultural Erosion," *European Broadcasting Union Review* 35.2 (March 1984): 14–20.

KNOWLEDGE RESEARCH. Private Communication to Richard Collins from Knowledge Research Peterborough drawing on research conducted for MERGE (Media Economics Research Group Europe, 1990).

MAGGIORE, Mariano. *Audiovisual Production in the Single Market* (Luxemburg: Commission of the European Communities, 1990).

MONNET, Jean. *Memoirs* (London: Collins, 1978).

NOEL, E. *Working Together. the Institutions of the European Community* (Luxembourg: Office for Official Publications of the European Communities ,1988).

RAI (Radiotelevisione Italiana). "Experiment of the EURIKON Programs Transmitted via the OTS Satellite" (LCMIANUS, typescript, April 1983).

≈ ❀ ≈

National Culture and National Identity
Literature and the Media

DAVID HUTCHISON

I
T IS NOW A COMMONPLACE that nationalism has not proved to be a pre-twentieth-century phenomenon whose fire would dwindle and die during our interdependent age; on the contrary, it is now widely perceived as a force of extraordinary strength and persistence. The ethnic hatreds which have consumed ex-Yugoslavia are an extreme form of the assertion of the right to self-determination which has characterised the politics of nations within nation-states, such as Quebec, for several decades. How the world handles the resurgence of nationalism around the globe has become the overriding question of the post-Communist age.

The survival of nationalism has baffled some commentators such as Isaiah Berlin, and infuriated others such as Eric Hobsbawm.[1] While Berlin seems resigned to the situation, Hobsbawm clearly resents it deeply, and sees it as further evidence of the defeat of "progressive" values. It is of course hazardous to discuss human "essence," but all the evidence does suggest that the need to belong to distinctive groups is a basic requirement – there are several important groups for all of us: our family, our local community, our regional community, our ethnic/linguistic community, our religious community maybe, our national community, and perhaps some supra-national community. In practice we all operate with shifting identities, locating ourselves to different degrees in each, all, or some of these communities at different times. But it does not seem to be open to most human beings to function in some kind of postmodern multicultural situation where the central ethnic or national identity has been dissolved; cosmopolitan intellectuals may find that an easy and attractive option, but they are in the minority.

The national component of identity – the sense of belonging to a nation, which is not necessarily coterminous with a nation-state – appears, then, to be one of the most powerful components of identity in both the political and the cultural sphere, and it is the manifestation of national identity through culture with which this

---

1 Isaiah Berlin, *The Crooked Timber of Humanity* (London: John Murray, 1990); Eric Hobsbawm, "Whose fault-line is it anyway?" *New Statesman and Society* (24 April 1992).

paper is concerned. "Culture," it should be stressed, is used here in the sense of "expressive artefacts" rather than "way of life."

The argument about the relationship between high and mass culture has been a long and difficult one, and has been closely intertwined with the argument about the nature of democracy itself. John Carey has recently mounted a scathing attack on the many philosophers and writers whose reaction to the coming of democracy and mass culture he characterises as a mixture of fear and loathing.[2] Carey's book has not met with universal acclaim, and he has been accused of selective quotation and misrepresentation; but it cannot be denied that writers such as T.S. Eliot, the Leavises and Dwight MacDonald had serious doubts about the cultural values of the mass society in which they considered themselves to live, and felt that the high culture which they valued, and considered to be the finest flowering of the human mind, was under serious threat from the debasing spread of mass culture.[3] Inevitably, their fears focused on America, for it was in that republic that democracy had first appeared in the modern world and there that mass culture became an industry which went on to conquer the rest of the globe. What these commentators were reluctant to admit was that this victory was due not just to the economic power of the USA or the gullibility of the ignorant multitude, but might also owe something to the fact that, for example, the classic Hollywood way of presenting a narrative is a rather impressive approach to telling a story, and the largely Jewish writers of American popular songs do seem to have had the ability to encapsulate basic human emotion and feeling.

Today we are less likely to take the manichaean view of culture espoused by these critics, and we are more tolerant and discriminating in our judgements; but a gulf remains between high culture and mass culture in both production and consumption. Consider literature (not "writing"), on the one hand, and television and cinema on the other. Literature enjoys high status, considerable support from public funds, and is "sanctified" by academic institutions and cultural bodies; however, the economic rewards which accrue to its practitioners are very variable, and it is consumed by a minority of the population. Television and film enjoy variable status, some support from public funds, and are approached ambivalently by academic institutions and cultural bodies; the economic rewards for their practitioners are higher than in literature and they are consumed by the majority of the population.

It can be assumed that teachers of literature, even if they are not unreconstructed Leavisites, take the view that literature is a vital component of national culture, but they might not be quite so sure about television and cinema. They would probably

---

2 John Carey, *The Intellectuals and the Masses* (London: Faber & Faber, 1992).

3 See, for example, Dwight MacDonald, "Masscult and Midcult" in *Against the American Grain* (1962; New York: Vintage, 1965): 3–75.

all argue for the national control of broadcasting, but might wonder about the necessity of a Canadian or, for that matter, a British film industry. They would not, however, question the necessity of Canadian or English (or Scottish or Irish) literature. Yet literature interacts with film and television constantly, whether through adaptation of material from one medium to another, through employment patterns, or by aesthetic cross-fertilisation. The position I adopt is to argue for the necessity of all three media – or, rather, for the necessity of providing circumstances in which they all have the potential to flourish; for it is never possible to guarantee aesthetic development even if the environment is favourable. And the economics of the media mean that in smaller countries it may simply not be possible for both film and television to prosper; what is important is the production of narrative representations in one of these media.

Literature *qua* literature is always going to remain a minority concern, albeit one which enjoys the support of powerful groups; television and film have captured the interest and enthusiasm of the majority. If we accept that the most basic function of literature is to offer people representations of experience, some of which are representations of their own specific experience, and that the absence of such representations means cultural impoverishment, it follows that unless the non-literature-consuming majority are offered on the screen representations of their lives, then there is a serious cultural and identity problem which will not be totally shared by the literature-consuming section of the population, if they have access to indigenous writing. It is therefore difficult to agree with Richard Collins when he argues that it does not matter so very much if English-speaking Canadian viewers do not see a lot of Canadian fiction on television, since Canada exists, regardless of television consumption patterns.[4] Canada most certainly does exist, but the absence of high-quality drama in large quantity on Canadian television screens is a form of cultural deprivation. This is not to deny the force of much of what Collins has to say about the deficiencies of some Canadian television drama output to date, nor is it to argue for a cultural blockade – American television can sometimes, and American film can often, enrich our lives. Indeed, American mass culture can enrich other mass cultures; but these cultures have to exist in the first place for that process of enrichment to take place.

It follows from what has been argued hitherto that there must in any distinct society be policies for the audiovisual sphere as well as for literature, drama or the visual arts. It is sometimes suggested, by contrast, that the audiovisual sphere is better left to the market, or that, whatever might be theoretically desirable, the battle has been lost. The first position is to a significant degree an ideological one

---

4 Richard Collins, "Canada: Nation Building Threatened by US-dominated Media?" in *The Politics of Broadcasting*, ed. R. Kuhn (London: Croom Helm, 1985).

masquerading as pragmatism. The ideology which sees the market system as best suited to supplying most, if not all, human needs has enjoyed much support during the Eighties, but as public and private sector deficits mount, and public facilities crumble and decay in both Britain and the USA, the two countries in which governments have most actively pursued private-sector-oriented policies, the citizenry seem less beguiled by the mantras of deregulation and privatisation than they once were. As to the belief that the battle has been lost, this is an understandable – if not completely accurate – view for a Canadian observer to take, but is not sustainable in the European context.

In the audiovisual sphere during the Eighties there was in Europe, as in North America, more commitment to deregulation than hitherto, but as the decade closed re-regulation appeared to be more likely than further deregulation. In particular, it is worth noting the development by the European Community of a range of policies for the audiovisual sphere, which, although they have a clear economic imperative (the sustenance and development of the broadcast and film industries), are also driven by an explicit cultural argument.

> The commitment of citizens to the European idea depends on positive measures being taken to enhance and promote European culture in its richness and diversity. In this context the European Council considers it essential to consolidate recent achievements and capitalize on the guidelines which emerged from the Audiovisual Conference held in 1989 in order to develop Europe's audiovisual capacity.[5]

Canada, for its part, has a long history of intervention in the audiovisual arena, most obviously in the creation of and continuing support for the Canadian Broadcasting Corporation and Telefilm Canada. But if we compare the audiovisual achievement in English Canada with the development of literature during the period when writers and publishers have enjoyed the support of the Canada Council, and look at the number of Canadian authors who have established themselves both at home and internationally, then we are forced to the conclusion that intervention in the literary sphere seems to have had rather more success.

There is, of course, a danger in taking too deterministic an approach here: all the public finance in the world could not create writers like Atwood, Davies or Munro; on the other hand, public support can make it much easier for authors of talent to find a readership in their own country and to use that as the base for attracting overseas audiences. Why has Canadian intervention in the audiovisual sphere been less successful?

Several reasons suggest themselves. Most obviously, the economics of competing with the American cinema and television industries, which have a huge domestic market and have established dominance in the international market, are

---

5 "Conclusions of the Presidency, December, 1989," in *Community Policy in the Audio-Visual Field* (Brussels: Commission of the European Community, 1990): 9.

daunting. Secondly, Canadian attempts at protection and encouragement of domestic audiovisual culture have always been half-hearted – there might, for example, be government cash to help films get produced, but Canadian administrations tolerate practices in the exhibition and distribution sectors which make it very difficult for these films to be screened. To take another example: high-sounding government declarations of support for CBC have rarely been accompanied by adequate financial subventions.[6] Thirdly, there is the undoubted attractiveness of many American products, and perhaps a certain degree of "miserabilism," an obsession with grim social problems, in Canadian products.[7] There are perhaps other equally important reasons.

It is relatively easy to argue that literature is "a good thing" and needs public support if it is to flourish; there is no thriving mass market in literature (as opposed to writing) which can be pointed to. However, there is a large and thriving mass market in cinema and television, which appears on the surface to be working well. Furthermore, the economic forces ranged against media intervention are extremely powerful, and can draw on populist arguments about giving the public what it has clearly signalled it wants. The forces which would seek to limit Canadian state intervention in support of literature should not be underestimated, either; but it is hard to believe that they are so strong or that they can use similar populist arguments. Even if they tried to do so, they would immediately find themselves up against important groups of citizens – writers, intellectuals, civil servants, even some politicians – who carry considerable clout. But when it comes to mass culture this élite is somewhat ambivalent, for although its members may not share the hostility which characterised much early twentieth-century thought about the media, they may still not be sure whether mass culture is art, commerce, or some hybrid. This phenomenon is not confined to Canada. So it is relatively easy to mobilise the high cultural great and good throughout the world on behalf of a literary cause – witness the outcry against the death-sentence pronounced on Salman Rushdie – but it can be much more difficult to mobilise support for media culture, unless it is unashamedly élitist, like the BBC's Radio Three (which has an extraordinarily low audience-share). The great and the good of Britain, who would happily sign petitions and write letters to broadsheet newspapers if Radio Three were threatened, would be most unlikely to protest if the Corporation decided it no longer intended to produce indigenous soap operas.

The question which must be raised is whether the ambivalent attitude of the relevant élite towards mass culture has had the effect in Canada, at least in English Canada (the situation in Quebec is rather different), of making it difficult to build

---

6 See Manjunath Pendakur, *Canadian Dreams and American Control* (Detroit: Wayne State UP, 1990).

7 Richard Collins, *Culture, Communication and National Identity* (Toronto: U of Toronto P, 1990).

broad public support for the creation of a strong indigenous audiovisual sphere. This is not to deny the support which has been offered, for example, to CBC through such organisations as Friends of Canadian Broadcasting; but there does not seem to have been a willingness to argue forcibly, publicly, and unceasingly for the necessity of intelligent popular television drama. In some countries this might not matter very much: it could be argued that in the UK, for example, the strong theatrical tradition and the controlled competition between the BBC and ITV/Channel 4 have ensured that both sectors have been obliged to produce high-quality soap opera and other forms of popular drama. So successful have these been, that the competition now offered by satellite television has had a limited impact on viewing-habits, with viewers in satellite homes watching the terrestrial services for almost 70% of the time,[8] for the simple reason that BSkyB, although it can offer up-to-date films and re-runs of American series, does not have the resources to present indigenous drama to an audience which has a very large appetite for it. But the situation in Canada is very different: competition has not been controlled, as it has been in the UK, and the proximity of the US television system would have made such control difficult, even if there had been the political will to attempt it.

In this context it would be foolish to claim that the attitudes of a cultural élite could have produced a radically different outcome. However, what can be suggested is that if those individuals who are professionally concerned with representation in literary and theatrical forms, and assert the value of these representations in helping the people(s) of a nation to know themselves, were to take television drama as seriously as they take literature and theatre – and on occasion film – then the situation in audiovisual culture in Canada could only improve. Those of us who see ourselves as literary academics have a responsibility, then, not only to teach literature, and to argue and lobby for appropriate public support for it, but also to direct our scholarly attention and agitational skills to the field of audiovisual culture.

It might be said in response that this is to endorse a kind of glib postmodern "anything goes" approach to the question of value. That is not the intention; but what is being suggested is that the best of film and the best of television drama can enrich people's lives, in the same ways that literature and drama do, and that for such enrichment to be complete it is necessary for there to be good indigenous work. If it is argued that, for there to be a true Canadian nation (or nations), then there must be Canadian literature (or literatures), it must also be argued that for that nationhood to be complete in the contemporary world, there must be sustainable and developing Canadian audiovisual culture/cultures. Academics have an

---

[8] *Satellite TV Finance*, August 1992.

important role to play, and there are those like Mary Jane Miller[9] and Richard Collins[10] who have begun to examine television drama output with a seriousness which can be found in any number of analyses of Canadian literature, and in some analyses of Canadian film, but has yet to take firm root in Canadian analyses of broadcasting output. The sooner it does, the better will be the outlook for television – and film – north of the 49th parallel.

WORKS CITED

BERLIN, Isaiah. *The Crooked Timber of Humanity* (London: John Murray, 1990).

CAREY, John. *The Intellectuals and the Masses* (London: Faber & Faber, 1992).

COLLINS, Richard. "Canada: Nation Building Threatened by US-dominated Media?" in ed. R. Kuhn, *The Politics of Broadcasting* (London: Croom Helm, 1985).

————. *Culture, Communication and National Identity* (Toronto: U of Toronto P, 1990).

"Conclusions of the Presidency, December, 1989," in *Community Policy in the Audio Visual Field* (Brussels: Commission of the European Community, 1990).

HOBSBAWM, Eric. "Whose fault-line is it anyway?" *New Statesman and Society* (24 April 1992).

MACDONALD, Dwight. "Masscult and Midcult," in MacDonald, *Against the American Grain* (1962; New York: Random House/Vintage, 1965).

MILLER, Mary Jane. *Turn up the Contrast* (Vancouver: U of British Columbia P, 1987).

PENDAKUR, Manjunath. *Canadian Dreams and American Control* (Detroit: Wayne State UP, 1990).

Satellite TV Finance, August 1992.

≈ ✹ ≈

---

9 Mary Jane Miller, *Turn up the Contrast* (Vancouver: U of British Columbia P, 1987).
10 Richard Collins, *Culture, Communication and National Identity*.

Alternative Publishing in Canada

LYNETTE HUNTER

C ANADA IS A COUNTRY where many of the political, legal, and social structures are supported by what are still predominantly print-based media. This status raises the question of how the people who have difficulty getting access to print can participate in their society. Canada is a "print society" in the sense that writing, which for various sociohistorical and geographical reasons is the primary mode of communication, is transmitted via print even in the scripts read out during the television news; testable knowledge leading to qualifications for work is acquired through print from libraries, school manuals and in exams; legal and political guidelines are integrated from the printed works of jurisprudence and constitutional issues, and adequate day-to-day existence functions by printed means in shops and hospitals, on insurance forms and breakfast-cereal packets. Print is not the only medium for communication or the most obviously persuasive and engaging medium of culture, but its ubiquity renders it the necessary means for participating fully in society.

A print society begins with education and with literacy, which gives technical training in both "creative" and decorous writing and reading, as well as learning about the value and usefulness of communicating through words. Print society also supports all the aspects of production, publishing, distribution, marketing and sales, as well as the professionalisation of writing, of authorship, copyright and censorship, and the formation of readerships, audiences, patrons, reviews and rewards. The centrality of print and of graphical communication means that many communities are effectively marginalised in society because of difficulty of access to even just one part of the whole complex procedure: whether it be to those parts of production and dissemination of the printed product casually referred to as "publishing" and operating under economic strictures, or to the more subtle strictures on cultural consumption.

Problems of access to print as a producer

The publishing edifice is not at all easy to shift, because it is fundamentally tied into the economic practices of a country, in this case Canada. The economics are based on the bottom-line fact that publishers are not altruistic. Publishing was one of the earliest capitalist ventures and has survived by virtue of a thorough understanding and exploitation of the underlying economic practices of capitalism;

printers simply run factories; booksellers will only stock items they think will sell; and that factor depends on readers with a regular disposable income. The only way to break this central control over production is to publish writing yourself, or print it yourself, or sell it yourself. There are two provisos: first, you have to be sure of an audience; and second, you need to be able to afford the cost of printing.

The history of book production has been closely tied to the ups and downs in the cost of printing. Since the late-fifteenth century there has been a decreasing emphasis on the costs of paper and of printing or the actual costs of production before profit, with more and more of the financial reward going to the publisher and bookseller along with their associated editors, designers, marketers and so on. Yet, in Canada, until the advent of the cyclostyles and mimeographs of the Fifties, access to print in any substantial way was not a possibility for the majority of the population. People could produce items cheap enough for you to buy and read, such as booklets, newspapers and magazines. Individuals could perhaps afford to produce one-off items. But there was no regular access to production, as a means of interacting with a readership or an audience: printing presses, even before the hugely capital-intensive power-driven presses which arrived in the nineteenth century, were simply too expensive. More recently, with photocopying and computer printouts, and now with desktop publishing, access to print is broadening.

Problems of access to print as a consumer

There is no point having cheap, accessible print if there is no writer or audience. In Canada, literacy, or acquired skill in writing and reading, is the central aim of the educational system. This literacy may form the basis for learning in mathematics and science, or for skill in other communicative media, but in its primary focus on writing and reading the educational system is training people in the skills necessary for functioning within its print society. However, literacy is difficult to talk about, and becomes problematical, because desiring literacy presupposes a desire to be part of that society; it takes for granted a community of shared expression and experience that may well not exist. It is estimated that 25% of the adult Canadian population is functionally illiterate.[1] However, included in this number are those who are technically illiterate, and those who are non-literate in that, while they can read and write, they do not recognise or possibly accept that writing/reading is a helpful way of communicating.[2] Accounts offered on the basis of literacy education programmes speak of literacy work as not only providing

---

[1] *Broken Words: Why Five Million Canadians are Illiterate* (Toronto: Southam Newspaper Group, 1988).

[2] Jennifer Horsman, *Something In My Mind Besides the Everyday* (Toronto: Women's Press, 1990).

access to an audience but creating an audience in the first place.[3] Many of those who do not communicate via writing and reading or through the print medium, which is the primary way we disseminate this expression, have no community – but it is a moot point whether they are non-literate because they have no community or whether they have no community because they are non-literate and excluded from access.

In 1959 the federal government of Canada began a programme of funding through the Canada Council for publishers and writers, although they chose not to fund readers directly through subsidy to bookstores. Later, in 1972, the then Multicultural section of the department of the Secretary of State was established, and in 1973 began to fund diverse groups, usually along racial or ethnic lines, for cultural expression.[4] The Canada Council grants encouraged an increasing flow of slim volumes from the emerging public–private presses, many of which derived from initial university sponsorship. Because the grants made it possible to produce these books cheaply, the bookstores were encouraged to take a risk on stocking them.[5] However, access to a market was still restricted: Canadian books still make up only 20% of sales in Canada as opposed to national sales of 90% in countries such as Great Britain or the USA.[6] In addition, the Department of Multiculturalism, as it became, put questions of literacy and training on the agenda. Although there has been considerable worry about the status of multicultural grants, which both writers and publishers often take to indicate second-rate work, this funding has opened up access particularly to communities outside the universities, and increasingly people have begun to take up the opportunity.

Further federal steps which aided the development of publishing work from groups with otherwise marginal access to print were the establishing of the Advisory Council on the Status of Women (1973), and of the Department of Indian Affairs and Northern Development (1967) and the Native Citizens' Directorate of the Department of the Secretary of State (late Seventies). Both sources were eventually able to provide financial aid for the costs in publishing. Provincial developments have been primarily related to educational and literacy programmes, as well as to the establishing of creative writing elements in schooling from primary to tertiary levels of teaching,[7] and some provinces have

---

3 *Women & Literacy*, special issue of *Canadian Woman Studies/Les cahiers de la femme* 9.3–4 (Fall–Winter, 1988); all quotations are taken from this issue and page numbers follow in brackets.

4 See Lynette Hunter, "Writing, Literature and Ideology," in *Probing Canadian Culture*, ed Peter Easingwood, Konrad Gross & Wolfgang Klooss (Augsburg: AV-Verlag, 1991): 52–64.

5 Hunter, "Writing, Literature and Ideology," 52–64.

6 Frank Davey, "Writers and Publishers in English–Canadian Literature," in Davey, *Reading Canadian Reading* (Winnipeg: Turnstone, 1988): 90.

7 A brief look at the "Language Arts" section in the book catalogue for the Ontario Institute for Studies in Education indicates the range of some of this teaching.

also provided support for specific groups through, for example, the Ontario Women's Directorate. Provinces have also been instrumental in funding posts for writers in residence at colleges and universities, for writers in libraries, and for writing instruction in community programmes.[8] An example of one comprehensive programme is that run by the Saskatchewan Writer's Guild, which provides short-term writer residencies in elementary and high schools, in libraries, in communities around the province, and an apprenticeship programme "where a writer with some publications etc is teamed with a senior writer for [...] three months correspondence."[9] The Saskatchewan Arts Board funds the Sage Hills (formerly Fort San) writing school, which offers residential courses for intermediate and advanced writing, and a manuscript reading service.

꧁ ✺ ꧂

The result of these government initiatives to fund both literacy development and access to publishing has been an enormous growth of publications over the last twenty years from groups within the community who have in the past experienced difficulty of access to the written medium and its printed means of dissemination. That growth has highlighted specific aspects of the problem of access which I shall now be examining further. It has also produced, and is continuing to produce, a substantial body of writing that is offering new ways of reading, and new relationships between writer, text and reader, which are starting to shape new genres and communities.

My central concern is with the development of access to publishing and to literacy in Canada since the late Fifties. Also important are the effects of the marginalisation of people from, and the participation of people in, the communities of Canada's print society. It is possible through grant-giving programmes to encourage an easing of economic and cultural restrictions on access, which may loosen the power structures of a dominant ideology. It is particularly possible to ease restrictions on access for writings and readings that understand and accept the aims and limitations of literacy and the print society that underwrites it. However, it is far more difficult to ease restrictions on access for those people who do not fit into, or may actively reject, those aims and limitations: through participation in, for example, oral social media; through disagreement with the ideological implications of the dominant medium; or through lack of opportunity and support. These groups are often represented as being fundamentally ignorant, whereas their

---

8 For example, the Ontario provincial government has funded a Writers in Residence programme for provincial libraries from 1985 onwards.

9 This quotation and much of the surrounding detail has been taken from correspondence with Bonnie Burnard, who works for the Saskatchewan Arts Board.

communication is in effect being repressed. What is significant at the moment is that, while access to production is opening up slightly to these doubly marginalised groups, access to writing and reading/consumption is being complicated by an inability on the part of trained readers in the institution to engage with and respond to writings from the newly literate community.

The first area of focus concerns difficulties of access to production and print distribution in relevant communities; I shall briefly consider some problems of consumption created by language and cultural difference, differences of ethnicity and race, oral communicative culture, sexuality and gender. The discussion will then move on to look at some difficulties of access to production – more specifically, to consumption in a variety of women's communities and in the recently defined area of literacy and women, which describes a high proportion of newly literate writers, or people beginning to engage with Canada's print society.

Research on the relationship between publishing and writing/reading usually refers to periods prior to 1950.[10] In an effort to provide a methodological basis for a relatively new field of inquiry, the research has often been systematic, building comprehensive and coherent structures around available facts.[11] What follows here is, by contrast, analytical of specific observed difficulties. Any such analytical approach must be general rather than abstract, and can only provide marginal commentaries with indications of further sites for study.

Language, culture, ethnicity and race

In Canada, probably the best-recognised groups of writers and readers marginalised from print are those of ethnic immigrants from Europe. Many members of groups such as those from Germany, Italy, the Ukraine or Poland come from cultures firmly literate in a broad Western rhetorical tradition, and are highly educated in their own language and literature. They are used to a culture that

---

10 See Margaret Spufford, *Small Books and Pleasant Histories: Popular Fiction and its Readership in Seventeenth Century England* (Cambridge: Cambridge UP, 1981), which refers to the sixteenth- and seventeenth-century period, or the classic if outdated study by Richard Altick of nineteenth-century British texts, *The English Common Reader* (Chicago: U of Chicago P, 1957). The conference held at the University of Toronto in April 1990, "Discourse Pre-1860," brought together some discussion of the history of Canadian texts, as have the conferences organised by the Research Institute for Comparative Literature at the University of Alberta.

11 Robert Darnton, following the French scholars LeFebvre and Martin, offers an economic system of relationships for British printing in "What is the History of the Book?," in *Books and Society in History: Preconference Papers*, ed. Kenneth E. Carpenter (Sevenoaks: Bowker/Butterworth, 1983); and Milan Dimic & Marguerite Itaman Garstin, following Itamar Even–Zohar, offer a sociohistorical polysystem theory to their Canadian colleagues in "Polysystem Theory," in *Problems of Literary Reception*, ed. Edward Blodgett & Alfred Purdy (Edmonton: Research Institute for Comparative Literature, 1988).

values printed products, if not in all cases a print society which mediates its
ideologies primarily through print, and they understand the acceptance and
authorisation that it permits/conveys to the written word and its author. Over the
last thirty years, as the background lists from the Department of Multiculturalism
indicate,[12] some of these writers have acquired English or French and have passed
their writing on in the form of translated work that can then gain a broader social
audience. Certainly, language is one of the most significant factors in their attempt
to gain access to publishing. But acquiring the official language of the country is
not the only problem of this community in relation to print.[13] The patterns of
immigrant demography indicate that in most major Canadian cities immigrants
with a language in common tend to live near to each other, often acquiring only a
rudimentary or superficial understanding of the majority language.[14] This is particularly common among women who work in the home and among elderly citizens,
neither of which group has to, or can, go outside of a local neighbourhood. The
fact remains that there is also a pressing need for access to publication of work in
their own languages.[15]

A pattern of moving from a beginning in local publishing, which has emerged
in the Italian–Canadian community, is found in several other communities such as
the Ukrainians in the prairies.[16] Many communities have produced mimeographed
or photocopied material for local newsletters carrying stories, poems, letters, local
news and so on. Some people then go on to produce community magazines, or
one-off books of specific interest to the area about family, history, biography or
immediate pragmatic information, which are distributed in church basements,

---

12 The Department of Multiculturalism has published a number of "Preliminary Surveys" to a
variety of immigrant literatures since the late Eighties, including Canadian–Hungarian, Canadian–
Italian, and Canadian–Hispanic. Most of the early publications appear to have been edited by
Michael Batts.

13 Francis Caccia outlines some of the various linguistic needs of a community in "The Italian
Writer and Language," tr. Martine Leprince, in *Contrasts: Comparative Essays on Italian Canadian
Writing*, ed. Joseph Pivato (Montreal: Guernica, 1985).

14 In a collection that frequently refers to patterns of urban habitation of immigrant groups, *Two
Nations, Many Cultures: Ethnic Groups in Canada*, ed. Jean Leonard Elliott (Scarborough, Ontario:
Prentice–Hall, 1979), the article by Alexander Matejko, for example, "Multiculturalism: The
Polish–Canadian Case," notes that among the most important reasons for "preference for living in
an area where most people were of the same ethnic group" were "language difficulties" (243).

15 Such a need, which became clear to me from a number of personal interviews conducted
during August 1989, is formally presented in, for example, "Immigrants and Political Involvement
in Canada: The Role of the Ethnic Media," Jerome Black & Christiane Leithner, *Canadian Ethnic
Studies* 20.1 (1988).

16 Personal communication from Professor Joseph Pivato, who was kind enough to spend considerable time with me during a research trip to Canada in 1989, outlining various areas of
importance to the development of ethnic literatures in Canada from which some of the immediately
following observations are drawn.

local shops, or through advertisements and notices in community and ethnic newsletters. As the producers acquire skills in the publishing process, some go on to form their own publishing businesses; and as the works produced begin to look like books of commercial publishing quality, the writers acquire authorised reputations and may be snapped up by other more established publishers – causing much resentment in the smaller publishers who took the initial risk on them.[17]

But it is clear that language is an important breaking-point. A short bibliography of Italian–Canadian literature produced by Joseph Pivato indicates, in its comparison of the original Italian-language publication with the invariably later English or French-language translation, that it is normally in the translated version that the work finds a commercial publisher.[18] Another form taken by this phenomenon is illustrated by *Ricordi: Things Remembered*, an anthology of short stories about the Italian experience in Canada. Although it has already benefitted from a grant from Multicultural that has made it possible for Guernica to produce it, the two stories in languages other than English (Italian and French) have been translated. This is not to say that commercial publication of Italian- (or other) language books does not happen, but it is comparatively infrequent. A publisher is not going to risk money on a commercial publication which may sell poorly because it is written in a minority language.

A recent interesting development that underscores the problem of language is that of the English-language writers in Quebec, particularly since 1976.[19] Several well-known English-language writers, and publishers who focused on English-language work, left Quebec during the Seventies. Many of those who remained or emerged subsequently often felt obstructed from access to publication. The provincial government gives grants less frequently to other-language than to francophone writers.[20] Both the majority surrounding French-language culture of communication in newspapers, magazines and other media, and even some of the English-language media that might have been expected to provide a forum for reviews and recognition, have been reluctant to do so. Just as reluctant have been the broader

---

17 This, of course, is a common concern for all small presses, which seem to get caught up in a vicious circle of being funded by the government to publish special interest books that major publishers will not pick up, thus establishing themselves as small presses by definition, from which writers wish to move on.

18 This bibliography was contained in a private paper, but a look at the *Newsletter/Bulletin of the Association of Italian–Canadian Writers* 10 (September 1989): 3, provides similar information.

19 1976 was the year during which Bill 101 was passed, making French the only official language in Quebec.

20 For example, it is notable that Gail Scott's *Heroine* (Toronto: Coach House, 1987) acknowledges help from the federal government and from the Ontario Arts Council, as well as from the Ministère des affaires culturelles in Quebec. Indeed, this is partly interesting because it is one of the few English-language books to note such provincial assistance.

English-language media in Canada as a whole[21] – to the extent that Linda Leith, editor of the primarily English-language *Matrix*, states that in interviewing

> dozens of writers, critics, editors and publishers in 1987 and early 1988 I found an overwhelming number of otherwise well-read and well-informed Canadians and Quebecers, French and English, unable to name even one new fiction writer in the English language from Quebec.[22]

There is now an organisation, QUSPEL, which concentrates on raising public consciousness of English-language writers in Quebec. That the cultural politics of Quebec is only to a lesser degree repeating the repressive actions of those it intends to criticise elsewhere in Canada does not make it any easier for these writers or their readers.

Another group marginalised from access to publishing, but also from highly literate cultures, is made up of more recently arrived immigrant groups from the Caribbean, from Central and Eastern Asia, and from South America. Attempts to break into the publishing circle of production follow roughly the same pattern – from photocopied or print-out community newsletters to magazines and special-ised books, and, to a certain extent, to small publishing houses. This movement from newspapers to magazine to book is also the pattern followed in many other parts of the world and at earlier times. Partly due to the intensely local interest of newspapers, which ensures a reasonable number of sales, this medium can have far less risk for the capital investor; and with the cheaper printing methods of today the risk is even smaller.[23] But apart from this rough consistency the immigrant groups have little in common bar their profound cultural differences within the majority society.

There are, of course, often problems of language and translation which exacer-bate publishing problems, particularly in the area of Chinese and Japanese, which have, respectively, pictorial and syllabic alphabets; Chinese has over 48,000 characters, and computers have only recently begun to provide help at an affordable cost. Yet some of the most intense problems stem from Asian and African–

---

21 From personal interview, it was clear that English-language writers in Montreal noted that even the English-language *Gazette* rarely reviewed their work – although, with a new editor at the desk in the Nineties, this may change.

22 Quoted from a typescript copy, but published as: Linda Leith, "Quebec Fiction in English During the 1980s: A Case Study in Marginality," *Quebec Studies* 9 (Fall, 1989).

23 The procedure is outlined in John Feather, *The Provincial Book Trade in Eighteenth-Century England* (Cambridge: Cambridge UP 1985), and has been borne out by a number of case studies, including Lynette Hunter, "Publishing and Provincial Taste," in *Traditional Food East and West of the Pennines*, ed. C. Anne Wilson (Edinburgh: Edinburgh UP, 1991).

Caribbean groups who have received at least part of their education in English.[24] Again, the communities frequently have sophisticated, literate and formally educated members, but the fact that they hold a language and a literary tradition in common with the broader society serves to underscore rather than ameliorate cultural difference. The stylistic play of much of this writing foregrounds radical divisions between the traditions and expectations of the incoming and in-place communities. Because it asks for translation not from one language to another (with the attendant acceptance of any error involved), but for "translation" within one language, there is no escaping the immediate implications for the host culture of the incoming difference.[25] Here again, commercial publishers have been slow to take up writers, but not so much because of a language difference. The reluctance in this case seems to be profoundly cultural and at least residually racial.[26]

From the outside the picture is complex: Multicultural grants aided both writers from ethnic European groups and writers from immigrant groups from the Third World, who would otherwise not be able to publish commercially acceptable products that can be sold in bookshops and kept in libraries. For many, aid from Multicultural is a stepping-stone on the way from local papers and self-publishing to being published by more established presses with aid from the Canada Council or from Provincial Arts Councils. But there is still, within these communities, a substantial gender divide and an insistently rankling race and class divide that the application of such aid has often failed to address.

Oral Communities

A different set of difficulties about access to publishing emerges from the Aboriginal communities. For communities which have a relatively short history of emphasis on media for writing, offering print as a viable medium is not a self-evident path to social participation. Furthermore, the communities are not primarily in the large urban centres of Canada, but are spread over huge distances, and often without a readily disposable financial income. The pattern of self-publishing is similar to those in urban centres, in that many newsletters and newspapers are produced, and a number of bands have started up publishing houses for book production, although some have closed; but what is missing are

---

24 There is also a substantial population that is francophone. For an introductory guide to this field, see Ronald Sutherland, "No Longer a Family Affair: Ethnic Writers of French Canada," given as a paper at the conference on Canadian Literature in Catania, Italy, 1987.

25 See Lynette Hunter, "After Modernism: Dionne Brand, Claire Harris, Marlene Nourbese Philip," given as a paper at the European Association for the study of Commonwealth Literature, in Lecce, Italy, 1990; published in *University of Toronto Quarterly* 62.2 (1992/93): 256–81.

26 See Marlene Nourbese Philip, "Gut Issues in Babylon: Racism & Anti-Racism in the Arts," *Fuse* 12.5 (April/May, 1989): 13.

magazines or other more substantial periodicals.[27] Magazines need an efficient and regular distribution system and an audience with significantly more income to spend than on a newspaper. It may well be that the costs of transport into rural areas and the relatively low sales within what are small communities in any case, simply make this form of publishing impracticable. Radio is a far more sensible medium for distance communication, as would be telephone-linked computer magazines in community/band centres.[28]

Possibly more important is the question of the appropriateness of the written medium at all. Aboriginal linguistic cultures were primarily oral until the twentieth century. The Moravian church missionaries established orthographies for several languages in the late eighteenth century, and in the nineteenth century syllabic systems were introduced.[29] But given the almost insuperable production and distribution problems posed by large distances and poor transport for heavy objects made of paper, and given the non-capitalist economy of the tribal system, when capital is vital to the investment risk and profit-taking of the modern book industry, there would have been little use in employing the graphic systems at all except where fixed records were perceived as necessary.

The concept raises a primary cultural contradiction: on the one side, we have the fact-orientated denotative world of European informational systems, which both rely on, and provide the economic *raison d'être* for, the printed medium, with its associated modes of morphemic and syntactic copyright ownership and subject-based textual authorship; on the other, we have a world of orally transmitted knowledge, with its own modes of narratorial copyright and collective performative production.[30] The contradiction is extended into the controlling financial concept of edition: the fixed text or edition has allowed for the commodification of writing as well as for a broad social access that was impossible in an oral mode of communication before technological media. It has engaged in a positive fight against censorship and information restriction, yet has also often become a tool of control. But if texts are to be produced that are appropriate to the

---

27 For example, of the few publications about an Aboriginal audience stocked by the Canadian Periodical Publishers' Association, even fewer appeared to be for that audience.

28 The efforts of Eugene Steinhauer, a Cree, in this area eventually led to the establishment of the Alberta Native Communications Society in 1968, and by 1984 there were thirteen native communications societies: see Robert J. Rupert, "Native People, Communications," *The Canadian Encyclopedia* (Edmonton: Hurtig, 1985), vol. 2: 1212.

29 This account is now often given in the prefaces to relevant collections of literature such as *Northern Voices: Inuit Writing in English*, ed. Penny Petrone (Toronto: U of Toronto P, 1988), or the series on *Algonquian and Iroquoian Linguistics*, ed. H.C. Wolfart (Winnipeg: Algonquian and Iroquoian Linguistics).

30 See Leonore Keeshig–Tobias, "The Magic of Others," in *Language in her Eye*, ed. Libby Scheier, Sheila Sheard & Eleanor Wachtel (Toronto: Coach House, 1990): 173–77.

contingencies of specific place, occasion and audience, then a fixed medium for the text is not suitable.[31]

This contradiction lies at the heart of a dispute that rumbled during the Eighties throughout the Canadian writing community. Some Aboriginal writers are objecting to the use of Aboriginal stories and even to the portrayal of Aboriginal peoples by non-Aboriginals; others, perceiving the value of at least raising the general social consciousness about Aboriginal communities, particularly in portraying Aboriginal peoples in film or novel, have no such misgivings.[32] But there is a recognisable difference between the arguably racist portrayals of W. Kinsella's stories and the social conscience of Joan Clark's work. The depth of feeling on this issue cannot easily be grasped by people with little notion either of the social responsibility required in the use of stories or of their sacred uses.[33] A close cultural transposition might be effected by suggesting that, just as the appropriation of an individual's words out of context may in Western European countries be considered libellous and defamatory to that person, so appropriation of a group's narrative out of context may be demeaning. The centre of such a translated debate is the context within which appropriateness (or not) is assessed. To insist that the context should be that of the dominant social order is racist. At the Feminist Bookfair in Montreal, June 1988, the question came to an acute point: Lee Maracle, an Aboriginal writer, by saying that no white writer of any kind should use Aboriginal stories, mounted an argument against Anne Cameron, who is white yet married to a Aboriginal and with adopted Haida daughters. Cameron did "move over" from the practice and went on to write about racism.[34]

Nevertheless, participation in Canadian society is predicated upon written skills, and the Aboriginal communities appear to be divided about whether they should be writing at all, let alone writing in English. The situation is compounded by the history of transmission of some texts which have been recently recuperated by Aboriginal writers: stories told orally in Aboriginal languages to nineteenth-

---

31 For an account of some similar cultural problems arising in New Zealand with reference to the predominantly oral Maori culture, see Don MacKenzie, "The Sociology of a Text: Orality, Literacy and Print in Early New Zealand," *The Library*, 6th Series, 6.4 (December, 1984): 333–65. Barbara Godard covers some of this ground in "Voicing Difference: The Literary Production of Native Women," in *A Mazing Space* ed. Shirley Neuman & Smaro Kamboureli (Edmonton: NeWest, 1986): 87–107.

32 See, for example, accounts of Lenore Keeshig–Tobias' accusations of subtle racism in the film *Where the Spirit Lives*, made in 1989 by the non-Aboriginal Keith Leckie yet acted in and supported by many Aboriginal people.

33 A matter all too well underlined by the extent to which it has been taken over by Salman Rushdie's *Satanic Verses*.

34 From an interview with Julia Emberley, who researches Aboriginal writings and attended the bookfair; also now documented in *Telling It*, ed. Telling It Collective (Vancouver: Press Gang, 1990).

century anthropologists and taken down by translation into written English have been translated back into present-day oral Aboriginal languages and then in some cases rendered into written syllabic form and published. The confusion of such transmission possibly achieves a sense of necessary collective authorship, and it also calls into question copyright of any kind. The apparent inadequacy of print to Aboriginal cultures has permitted the federal government to be lax about support for publication, which in turn has excluding effects on social and political particip-ation.[35] But over the last ten to twenty years, with an increasingly book-educated populace, the Aboriginal communities have begun to get more involved in estab-lishing some kind of access. Aboriginal papers such as the *Wataway News*, which is a bilingual English/Cree publication, often include poetry and short fiction as well as the usual news, sport and advertising; and some initially band-connected presses such as Theytus and Pemmican have become commercial publishers. But the problems that the Aboriginal communities have with access to publishing are particularly acute because there is no tradition of privilege for writing or author-ship, which has been the historical bridge between the individual literary communication and social participation.

Sexuality

Although each provides a different focus on the problems of access to publishing, the groups discussed above all have a fairly well-defined community and audience that is recognised by religion, language, colour or race,[36] and which is more or less susceptible to traditional modes of print distribution. But the moment that the location for community becomes nebulous, as in the case of individuals with a sexual orientation outside the socially accepted norms, such as the gay and lesbian communities, questions of access focus on marketing and sales. Many members of these communities are, again, highly literate and formally educated. Language and writing is not the most pressing problem of access, although those factors represent an ideological hegemony which individuals may not want to be part of. The rejection of that hegemony has resulted in the emergence of some magazines focusing on linguistic and literary experiment.[37] However, the massive social rejection of homosexual behaviour in Canada does mean that there are distinct

---

35 For example, Lee Maracle's *I am woman* could not find a commercial publisher and was published by Write-On Press, formed specifically for the occasion.

36 This is probably one of the main factors behind the focus on precisely these communities, of the conference on "Literatures of Lesser Diffusion" held by the History of the Literary Institution group at the University of Alberta, Edmonton, in April 1987. A description of this conference may be found in *Update* 4 (August 1988).

37 For example, see (f.) Lip: *a newsletter of feminist innovative writing*, which is not specifically lesbian, but provides a space for women, lesbian and heterosexual, to explore language.

problems in establishing a focused location for distribution of printed material: in other words, where do lesbians and/or gays meet? And is it possible to sell books in these locations?

For this community there are no necessarily common meeting-grounds in places of religious observance, in distinctive areas of habitation, or in community centres. Furthermore, many commercial bookstores refuse to stock homosexual publications and most certainly refuse to display them as such, often considering them to be pornographic. Mail-order distribution is one solution, if the publisher can purchase a relevant sales list or can rely on swift word-of-mouth information. The fact that magazines rather than local newspapers are more typical of the community underwrites the appropriateness of mail-order sales, which in Canada are favourable to this form of periodical publication. Another avenue which requires considerable capital risk is the setting up of independent bookstores specifically to stock and sell printed material to this community. There are a few bookstores in Montreal, Toronto, Vancouver and elsewhere which have been established to fill this gap in the publishing world and which seem to have found a well-heeled audience.[38] They have come to fill a social gap as well, in providing the urban community with a location or meeting-place for the exchange of news and information, although rural individuals are still extremely isolated. But this response to difficulties of access has not been without trouble. In the early Eighties a Toronto bookstore, Body Politic, had its subscription list as well as much of its stock seized; and there are a number of court cases currently underway involving bookstores and censorship.

Given the social antipathy, which means that few grants are given to gay/ lesbian writers or publishers *in support* of their social difference, it has also been difficult to establish commercial presses, most of which do need initial grant funding to start up. Some presses have emerged from the feminist community concerned with a lesbian agenda,[39] and some have arisen in response to the rather arbitrary censorship that is exercised on imports of printed material from the United States. Customs officers are empowered to seize material considered by them to be dangerous or obscene, even from private individuals crossing the border. Although more research into the implications and results of this policy is

---

38 Among the better known bookstores are Toronto's and Vancouver's Women's Bookstore, L'Androgyne, Ariel, Little Sisters, and Peregrine Books.

39 Press Gang in Vancouver and Ragweed in Prince Edward Island both encourage work from the lesbian community. Press Gang's publicity leaflet specifically states that it is trying to "de-mystify the printing process"; and printing has traditionally been a highly protected trade union activity, see Cynthia Coburn, *Brothers: Male Dominance and Technological Change* (London: Pluto, 1983).

needed, not only with regard to the gay/lesbian community, it seems likely that one effect is to encourage the publication of such material in Canada itself.

Gender

Another group marginalised from the print society by the ephemeral aspects of its community within the current ideology of Canada is that of women. Well-organised responses to access have come from educated feminism and women within other distinctive groups, particularly those differentiated by ethnic origin and colour. In many respects these groups follow the familiar pattern from newsletter through periodical to book publishing. One example among many is the small magazine *Fireweed*, which was started by women who had acquired the necessary credentials to authorise them as publishers.[40] They were university-educated – some in the foreign universities of the United States, which confer even greater credibility than those of Canada. They had gained experience by editing for major commercial publishing houses such as Oxford University Press, or by working on established small magazines in Canada. *Fireweed* emerged into an authorised product through careful tending; it acquired grants and gained access for many writers from 1978 into the Eighties.

Makeda Silvera's introduction to *Fireworks*,[41] which is a selection of essays from *Fireweed*, notes that the aim of the Fireweed Collective was to publish "works by a diversity of women" because "people not of the dominant culture have not had active participation in, or access to, arts journals, whether these have been part of the dominant culture or have emerged from the small presses" (8). But she goes on to say that in earlier issues of *Fireweed* "there were no articles by Native women and that pieces by both immigrant and Canadian-born women of colour were very few in number. Articles addressing the issues of class or by working class women of any colour were also rare" (8). Silvera raises the issue in order to underline the fact that the selection in *Fireworks* will emphasise these areas of omission, and one contribution, "Organising Exclusion," specifically addresses the omissions. The issue is also related to questions of literacy (discussed below). Silvera herself now runs the press SisterVision, which concentrates on publishing writing by women of colour, and has moved to grant-funding from the Canada Council. The quality of production and scale of distribution, visibility for the sisters, and reward, will be substantially extended in the process; and the writers will have far greater ease of access to audience.

The edifice of publishing itself and its complicity in the social fabric is far more difficult to question or shift. When its rules are broken, as they were when

---

40 Most of the following details were taken from personal interview.
41 Makeda Silvera, ed. *Fireworks: The Best of Fireweed* (Toronto: Women's Press, 1986).

the Women's Press (which was specifically established to redress the omissions of the traditional publishers and the elisions of gender) decided in 1988 to drop three contributions to a collection of essays at the last minute, there was objection if not outrage. The reason given for dropping the contributions was that they were racist, although discussion of this difficult and embarrassing topic has been submerged under later discussions on the issue of censorship.[42] However, the shock of the experience for those whose contributions were rejected also lies in the fact that an editorial collective had initially accepted their work, proofs of the material had been printed, and publishers conventionally don't pull out at that stage. In this case, editor–writer relationships, guidelines for which have been in place for at least two centuries, were simply overridden. The Women's Press story is further complicated by the context of collective working and the potentially emotive issues arising from its aims of solidarity and political effectiveness. You may change what you publish, widen your net to include other groups/voices/positions, but change of publishing practices, which in a print society often become naturalised into "rights," is shocking even to the most politically and socially flexible of writing groups.

What distinguishes the responses of these women is a deep understanding of literacy: the fact that reading and writing are the gateway to social participation and can create extended and supportive communities.[43] The larger, currently more disadvantaged group of women with regard to publishing access is that of the newly literate or non-literate – the enormous proportion of the female population which does not communicate in the written medium. If literacy is not just technical reading and writing but also the recognition of the importance of writing and reading in forming, engaging with, and participating in communities, then many women are frequently only marginally literate. There are, of course, other ways of participating in broad social activities and other media for cultural communication, but none so central to the mediation of power in a print society.

Literacy

However, one of the primary reasons for a failure to take up literacy to the extent that other marginalised groups have done is that many women do not know how to break out of the circle of marginalisation: If you don't understand your marginalised position or, more importantly, if you perceive it as necessary, you do not

---

42 Marlene Nourbese Philip, "The Disappearing Debate: Or how the discussion of racism has been taken over by the censorship issue," *This Magazine* 23.2 (July–August, 1989).

43 It is this reasoning that seems to lie behind the West Word and East Word workshops generated by the Women and Words/*Les Femmes et les mots* conference held in Vancouver in July 1983; see *in the feminine* (Edmonton: Longspoon, 1985). The different approaches taken by the various workshops that have since been held needs serious research.

begin to articulate it in any medium and so you remain marginalised. The circle is reduplicated with respect to literacy: if you are not aware of the social possibilities of reading and writing or, again, if you cannot see a way to participating in them, then you do not attempt to use the medium and so you remain non-literate. Breaking the circle is one of the central pursuits of feminism, and much feminist practice has been brought to bear on literacy. On both counts what is needed is consciousness-raising – a painful, lengthy and difficult process for many of us – and support. Given that marginality has been recognised, and that literacy is perceived as a means of addressing its disempowerment, the most urgent problems for this group are often time and money. Most people within this group are working women hard pressed at home, often with children.[44] Few have a readily disposable income that would permit them to enter the publishing world, which is the economic and technological medium through which literacy is currently effected in Canada.

This large group straddles a broad range of socioeconomic strata, and represents the largest single audience for the products of the weekly and monthly commercial periodical market, which have a large after-sales circulation. But while there are many publications produced for this group, there are relatively few printed genres produced by it. Although it is difficult to estimate, the largest genre may be that of the P.T.A. or community newsletter; another important genre is that of the fund-raising recipe book, where women can take the opportunity to share creative variations on changes in food pathways and domestic technology: in other words, what is going into and out of stores selling household products. Other genres that emerge are often related to issues arising out of consciousness-raising groups, such as natural childbirth, domestic violence, child abuse and general social feminist issues. One example here might be *The Midwifery Issue*, from the Midwifery Task Force of Ontario, which throughout the early to mid-Eighties was concerned with creating acceptance for midwifery as a professional body.[45] The newsletter was distributed primarily by mail-order to a membership list, thus reflecting the lack of sales outlets for such special-interest groups. It is interesting that the use of a computer mailing-list was considered highly sophisticated in the mid-Eighties, but by the early Nineties was fairly common among other special-interest group publications. The *Midwifery* newsletter was still firmly part of a pre-desktop-publishing world, and was produced through typed copy and paste-up, unlike many newsletters in 1990 from, for example, the environmental pressure-groups.

---

44 The pamphlet "Let's Talk About Women and Literacy" from the Canadian Congress for Learning Opportunities for Women also cites as a major barrier to progress in this area the threat that "men in a learner's life" may feel when she begins to become literate.

45 The group has been quite successful in achieving its aims. Much of this information was gathered for me by Elizabeth Driver, who contributed to the newsletter.

Publications from groups addressing specific issues are often funded by subscription, and in some cases from private donations. If there is no need for a sale, then one of the most important distribution-points is the local library. Groups with more general interest, although dependent upon subscription, do seem to be able to find distribution in some stores. One example here might be the *Northern Women Journal*, costing $1.50 and collectively produced and published in Thunder Bay, which includes not only news and information but also book reviews, poetry, and short prose. Significantly, a more substantial periodical, *The Womanist*, published from Ottawa, was initially free. It noted in a request for voluntary subscriptions that "We are free because we believe that all women, whatever their economic situation, should be able to get news about women [...] By being free we find that we can distribute *The Womanist* to places where women are, such as laundromats, corner stores, and community centres." Nevertheless, they depended upon advertisements and subscriptions to cover costs.

This relatively recent publication is, of course, selective. If the articles which *The Womanist* prints indicate the breadth of its intended readership, then it is clearly addressed to all women of whatever class, colour or religion who wish to discuss and debate issues arising from a consciousness of women's position in Canadian society. But what is then distinctive about the many publishers and publications advertised in the paper is how few come from groups which identify themselves as white working-class or women concerned with working in the home as a community-forming activity.[46] There are advertisements from publishers and bookstores representing lesbian communities, women of colour, Aboriginal women, women of immigrant and visible minorities: part of each of these communities already recognises the need to participate in the social medium of print. There are also advertisements from feminist organisations and research institutes, which produce valuable material analysing the lives of women in terms of problems and policy, and which aim particularly at those people working on or interested in the interface with disadvantaged and non-literate women; but these books do not appear to be written for those women themselves, and are certainly not written by them.

For many women, difficulty of access to communication through print arises because the difficulty is not recognised as such to begin with. Once recognised as a primary means to social participation, there are problems of finance and problems of time: who will look after the children? But this group has another problem that it shares to a greater or lesser extent with all the other groups: that of literacy.

---

46 These observations are made from issues purchased during the summer and fall of 1989.

It is striking that many of the contributions to an issue of *Canadian Woman Studies/Les Cahiers de la Femme* on "Women and Literacy,"[47] discuss precisely several areas of this newly literate group, as well as including many pieces of writing from people who are emerging from it. This issue presents a valuable collection for literacy studies everywhere, containing as it does scholarly research, bibliographies, commentaries on social and political issues, accounts of programmes in context, and a critical look at contemporary practices. The editorial, by Rita Cox and Leslie Sanders, underlines the importance of reading and writing in a literate society where "the written word is the source of authority and power," and where literacy is needed by women "to function in the public sphere in order to provide for themselves and their children" (3). The editors also note that literacy programmes provide the opportunity for women to gather "on their own behalf," to break their frequent isolation and establish community and support. But they end with a warning that literacy without a "challenge to the status quo" simply maintains faulty social structures. An uncritical acquisition of literacy may lead to uncritical participation in society. As Elaine Gaber–Katz and Jenny Horsman argue in "Is it her voice if she speaks their words," teachers of literacy need to develop a "critical pedagogy" (120) that will alert the reader/writer to the social, political and ideological dimensions of literacy practice.

While a critical pedagogy is important, it is difficult simultaneously to achieve practical skills and a critique of that practice: this process takes time. Further, there is the problem of audience – the fact that too strong a critique may produce writing so unconventional as to lose its potential readership. Practical skills are needed to start with, so that at some point, sooner rather than later, criticism may come. It is important to have the choice to be critical. Not to have that choice is, as Carole Boudrais says, "frightening":

> I was illiterate. Being illiterate is the most frightening thing. It's like being in a prison of your own self. It's one of the deepest secrets that you keep hidden inside, out of shame. Not being able to read street names, medical instructions or menus poses a threat to survival. (72)

Certainly, as the Canadian Congress for Learning Opportunities for Women (CCLOW) notes, illiteracy makes it twice as difficult for women to get a job; and when they do, if they have less than a Grade 8 education, they make only 59% of what men earn compared to the 68% average of more literate women (27). Furthermore, not to have that choice is to be fundamentally isolated – from the social information given by a newspaper about films in cinemas or local events, from the communication possible through use of a telephone book, from the work that children bring home from school. Indeed, a number of personal accounts in

---

47 *Women & Literacy*, special issue of *Canadian Woman Studies/Les cahiers de la femme* 9.3–4 (Fall/Winter, 1988).

"Women and Literacy" note that involvement in a literacy programme began when the woman concerned went to a parent–teacher meeting to discuss her child's work and revealed that she could neither read nor write.

Over the last twenty years literacy programmes have begun to flourish all over Canada, from county and metropolitan councils, from public libraries, from community groups, from colleges, and from pressure groups for the disabled, for recent immigrants, for prison inmates. "Women and Literacy" raises the question of access for a large number of groups, surprisingly omitting the particular problems of the older generations, the senior citizens who suffer from many of the same disadvantages. Less surprising is the omission of the difficult area of children's rights to access, but the collection does point the way back to the problems of access to publishing once literacy has begun for the general community of the newly literate. Literacy programmes will not only provide a way to break the isolation by physically locating people with a common problem in one place where they can weave communities, but, with a critical pedagogy, those communities can also move on to write about their focusing issues and produce material that can be read by others – extending their community by publication and broadening their social participation. What can be difficult at this stage for these groups is entry into the world of publishing. What is usually more difficult is for their writing to find and/or generate appropriate readings – in other words, for some communication to be effected.

Publishing, as indicated earlier, is a high-risk capital venture. To minimise risk, publishers and their editors, who act as ideological censors, produce writing that is acceptable to and desired by as large a market/audience as possible – a majority language, an unthreatening cultural perspective, conventional literary genres. Were publishers the only factor, written culture would have stagnated many centuries ago. It has always been the role of the patron – private or state, and sometimes publisher *as* patron – to support the cultural explorations which effect change. The grant-giving bodies in Canada act in just such a role, but they do apply criteria of evaluation which are rooted in the intensely literate traditions of most of both the early and later immigrant populations. For newly literate writers and readers, there is rarely immediate commercial interest, and there are few sources of financial support.

The writings reproduced in "Women and Literacy" such as "My name is Rose" by Rose Doiron and "My Story" by Olive Bernard are funded by literacy programmes – indirectly, rather than directly by the government. There is no conventional sales and marketing infrastructure for the products, presumably because the audience is perceived to be low-income. The writing does receive some circulation within literacy programmes themselves, but there is little access to engagement with a wider audience. Unlike all the other groups, which get a

helping government hand to make the step from newsletter/paper to small publisher, this group receives at best low-level indirect sponsorship. Certainly, the
writing that is produced is not authorised as "literature."

The Canadian government at federal and provincial level has, over the last
thirty years, been encouraging in a number of ways both to literacy programmes
and to publishing circles. For, whatever benefits to the state might have accrued, it
has at the very least enabled people to choose to participate in society through the
medium of print. For a number of overtly cultural reasons, however, the government remains unaware of the possibilities that are opened up by the writings of
newly literate groups, and needs to address this oversight. One of the more tragic
results of the economic crisis in Ontario has been the radical reduction in literacy
and oral-history programmes since 1991. Unlike some communities with marginal
access to print, which continue to be supported, the community of non-literate
women appears to be being forgotten.[48]

❦ ❦ ❦

Groups with difficulty of access to written communication have a variety of
problems. Those portrayed here relate specifically to the production and consumption of publishing, and to literacy as the recognition of the value of communicating through reading/writing. Canada as a whole is addressing many of these
areas, and one result has been an explosion of writings over the last twenty years,
which has begun to open up new strategies for social discourse. We must hope
that more attention will be paid to the breaks in the literacy-publishing connection
and that the new technologies for producing written material[49] will bridge and
enable rather than obstruct the possibilities for the formation of communities and
their social participation.

---

48 For example, the "Storylinks" project in Toronto organised by Mary Breen is suffering
substantial cutbacks.

49 For example, the Swift Current experiments of Frank Davey and Fred Wah, which use
computer networking technology to provide a forum for writers. Davey's wish to drive a wedge
between the capitalist basis of print technology and the medium of writing outlined in *The
SwiftCurrent Anthology* (Toronto: Coach House, 1988) could easily backfire. While Swift Current II
in particular gives evidence of a new and potentially far more broadly based technology for writing,
it also indicates a potential for different modes of writing, especially the non-linear, and for new
ways of establishing social groupings by way of writing.

WORKS CITED

ALTICK, Richard. *The English Common Reader* (Chicago: U of Chicago P, 1957).

BLACK, Jerome & Christiane LEITHNER. "Immigrants and Political Involvement in Canada: The role of the ethnic media," *Canadian Ethnic Studies* 20.1 (1988).

Broken Words: Why Five Million Canadians Are Illiterate (Toronto: Southam Newspaper Group, 1988).

Newsletter/Bulletin of the Association of Italian–Canadian Writers 10 (September 1989).

CACCIA, Francis. "The Italian Writer and Language," tr. Martine Leprince, in *Contrasts: Comparative Essays on Italian Canadian Writing*, ed. Joseph Pivato (Montreal: Guernica, 1985).

COBURN, Cynthia. *Brothers: Male Dominance and Technological Change* (London: Pluto, 1983).

DARNTON, Robert. "What Is the History of the Book?" in *Books and Society in History: Preconference Papers*, ed. Kenneth E. Carpenter (Sevenoaks: Bowker/Butterworth, 1983).

DAVEY, Frank. "Writers and Publishers in English–Canadian Literature," in Davey, *Reading Canadian Reading* (Winnipeg: Turnstone, 1988).

DIMIC, Milan & Marguerite Itaman GARSTIN, "Polystem Theory," in *Problems of Literary Reception*, ed. Edward Blodgett & Alfred Purdy (Edmonton: Research Institute for Comparative Literature, 1988).

FEATHER, John. *The Provincial Book Trade in Eighteenth-Century England* (Cambridge: Cambridge UP, 1985).

GODARD, Barbara. "Voicing Difference: The Literary Production of Native Women," in *A Mazing Space*, ed. Shirley Neuman & Smaro Kamboureli (Edmonton: NeWest, 1986).

HORSMAN, Jennifer. *Something In My Mind Besides the Everyday* (Toronto: Women's Press, 1990).

HUNTER, Lynette. "After Modernism: Dionne Brand, Claire Harris, Marlene Nourbese Philip," *University of Toronto Quarterly* 62.2 (1992/93): 256–81.

———. "Publishing and Provincial Taste," in *Traditional Food East and West of the Pennines*, ed. C. Anne Wilson (Edinburgh: Edinburgh UP, 1991).

———. "Writing, Literature and Ideology," in *Probing Canadian Culture*, ed Peter Easingwood, Konrad Gross & Wolfgang Klooss (Augsburg: AV-Verlag, 1991).

KEESHIG–TOBIAS, Leonore. "The Magic of Others," in *Language in her Eye*, ed. Libby Scheier, Sheila Sheard & Eleanor Wachtel (Toronto: Coach House, 1990).

LEITH, Linda. "Quebec Fiction in English During the 1980s: A Case Study in Marginality," *Quebec Studies* 9 (Fall, 1989).

MACKENZIE, Don. "The Sociology of a Text: Orality, Literacy and Print in Early New Zealand," *The Library*, 6th Series, 6.4 (December, 1984).

MATEJKO, Alexander. "Multiculturalism: The Polish–Canadian Case," in *Two Nations, Many Cultures: Ethnic Groups in Canada*, ed. Jean Leonard Elliott (Scarborough, Ontario: Prentice-Hall, 1979).

NOURBESE PHILIP, Marlene. "The Disappearing Debate: Or how the discussion of racism has been taken over by the censorship issue," *This Magazine* 23.2 (July–August, 1989).

———. "Gut Issues in Babylon: Racism & Anti-Racism in the Arts," *Fuse* 12.5 (April/May, 1989).

PETRONE, Penny, ed. *Northern Voices: Inuit Writing in English* (Toronto: U of Toronto P, 1988).

RUPERT, Robert J. "Native People, Communications," *Canadian Encyclopedia* (Edmonton: Hurtig, 1985), vol. 2: 1211–12.

SCOTT, Gail. *Heroine* (Toronto: Coach House, 1987).

SILVERA, Makeda, ed. *Fireworks: The Best of Fireweed* (Toronto: Women's Press, 1986).

SPUFFORD, Margaret. *Small Books and Pleasant Histories: Popular Fiction and its Readership in Seventeenth Century England* (Cambridge: Cambridge UP, 1981).

TELLING IT COLLECTIVE, ed. *Telling It* (Vancouver: Press Gang, 1990).

Update 4 (August 1988).

WOLFART, H.C., ed. *Algonquian and Iroquoian Linguistics* (Winnipeg: Algonquian and Iroquoian Linguistics).

Women & Literacy, special issue of *Canadian Woman Studies/Les cahiers de la femme* 9.3–4 (Fall/Winter, 1988).

Ethnicity /
Multiculturalism

From Dialogue to Polylogue
Canadian Transcultural Writing During the Deluge

JANICE KULYK KEEFER

W HAT I'D LIKE TO DO in this paper is to rough out an enormous topic – the current condition of writing in a Canada undergoing a deluge of political challenges, cultural shifts and social changes. Canadian writing now is radically different from what it was during that astonishing literary outburst of the Sixties which first made us familiar with names like Laurence, Atwood and Munro, Godbout and Carrier, Cohen and Ondaatje. What readers of the Eighties and early Nineties have encountered is a no less astonishing and decidedly more varied burst of productivity which I am calling transculturalism, a discourse which comprehends texts that might also be categorized as "ethnic" or "immigrant," "native" or "visible-minority" literature. I will be dealing later with what I consider to be the significant features of transcultural writing in Canada; for the present I simply wish to emphasise the fact that transculturalism has brought to prominence voices that had previously been silenced, or marginalised to the point of virtual neglect. One indication that transcultural has, over the past decade, been acclaimed rather than merely accommodated is the roll-call of recent nominees and winners of the Governor–General's Award, authors such as Czech–Canadian Josef Škvorecký, Trinidadian–Canadian Dionne Brand, Italian–Canadian Nino Ricci, Chinese–Canadians Fred Wah and Sky Lee, and Indian–Canadian Rohinton Mistry, among others.

What I'd like to do in the first part of this presentation is to sketch the problematical context in which Canadian transcultural writing has developed. Before I do this, however, I should acknowledge that the linked phenomena of multiculturalism and transculturalism are to be found in many other countries than my own and often in more problematical form; we all know that in a post-colonial and postmodernist world border-crossings happen in more than a generic or textual sense. When I was in Britain a couple of years ago, newspaper headlines announced the imminent arrival of a "Migrant Invasion" against which Europe would need to "brace" itself. Editorials warned that, with Cold Wars and Iron Curtains a thing of the past, impoverished residents of former Eastern bloc countries would soon be "swamping" Europe and the British Isles. Asians and

Africans in Britain, North Africans in France, Turkish "Guestworkers" in Germany, native peoples from former South American colonies in Spain – these are but a few of the "visible minorities" which the current "West is Best" and "Europe for Europeans" movements have targeted. Yet, whatever the political and socioeconomic repercussions of the "migrant invasion," one thing seems sure – European culture will continue to be enriched and extended by the "ex-centric" perspectives offered by its transcultural artists. Canada, the nation of immigrants, is only one of a group of countries that will have to respond in increasingly flexible and imaginative ways to issues of racial and ethnocultural difference as they affect the question of what makes a nation, a people, a culture.

≈ ✿ ≈

In the past fifteen years or so, Canadian writing has become heterogeneous and polyphonic in ways which suggest that previous distinctions between "main-stream" and "tributary" or even "backwater" have been radically undermined. Not only do we have a remarkable increase in the number of fine writers presently shaping literary discourse in Canada, but these writers have emerged from ethnocultural and racial groups which, as I have mentioned, had previously been either silenced or dismissively "spoken for" by writers of the dominant cultures, British and French. There is a liveliness and exuberance, as well as a highly critical assertiveness, in these new voices making themselves heard today – qualities which may appear puzzlingly out of tune to those familiar with the constitutional mess and economic morass which is contemporary Canada. Why, instead of dirges and elegies or clarion calls for unity, are Canadian writers producing texts which celebrate difference, and demand that otherness be privileged instead of merely tolerated? Could it not be argued that the emergence and significant circulation of texts which foreground not the conventional icon-ography of Canada – for example, snowy or autumnal wilderness – but, rather, Caribbean mountains, isolated Italian villages and Parsi communities in Bombay, have contributed to an erosion of any cohesive sense of place with which we might try to hold together an increasingly fractured land?

Not only "where is here?" but also "who are we?" has again become a primary issue. Given our present constitutional crisis, many Canadians feel that we are in desperate need of a collective and centripetal ethos, a national sense of self which will unite instead of divide. Ironically, just when our newest writers have set out to celebrate difference, to subvert or at least open up a social formation which has for far too long denied any significant form of power to minority groups and the conspicuously other, many Canadian readers are expressing a desire for an atavistic construction of national identity: something coherent and stable, monolithic and monologic. At a recent conference held at the University of Guelph and organized around the topic, "Canada: Break-Up or Restructure," countless speakers from the floor – members of the general public and, most prominently, senior-level high school students – articulated precisely this desire that Canadian artists and academics provide for them a unified, immutably distinctive sense of what it means to be Canadian.

It is true that the Canada of the Eighties and early Nineties finds itself contending not only with Québec separatism, but also with something we could call radical regional fracture. The depth of Prairie alienation is perhaps best signified by the troubling rise of Preston Manning's Reform Party, which has its enthusiasts right across the country. The extent of "the troubles" in the prairie provinces might best be indicated by the alarming dispersal of Saskatchewan's population; it has been calculated that if the current rate of emigration continues unabated there will be no one left in that province by the middle of the next century. As for British Columbia, such is its disaffection from "the centre" that many West Coasters are warming to the concept of "Cascadia," an economic and perhaps political union of provinces and states extending half the length of the Pacific coast of North America. In Atlantic Canada, a region whose economic distress has passed the point of crisis and entered the realm of catastrophe, a parallel concept is in the air and on the tongue: "Atlantia," perhaps uncomfortably close to "Atlantis." The project of some of Canada's native peoples to create the region of Nunavut in the far north, and the impressive drive of other native groups towards self-government, cannot be compared to the disaffection of the regions previously referred to; nevertheless, these phenomena taken together would seem to indicate that Canada's fabled mosaic is not only seriously cracked, but it also appears to be undergoing the political equivalent of continental drift. Perhaps Brian Mulroney, these days, can be heard muttering to himself not "*après moi le déluge*," but "*après moi le centrifuge*."

Nevertheless, it seems to be a peculiar feature of Canadian life that remarkable upsurges of cultural production have coincided with the equally remarkable eruption of national crises, as though political urgency and aesthetic agency were mutually dependent. Our ongoing debate about Canada's identity or lack of it became particularly fierce some three decades ago, when the possibility of a separatist agenda for Québec was finally registered by those in what Canadians of the Nineties have christened ROC, or "the Rest Of Canada." That the Sixties were a watershed in the development of Canadian culture was not, of course, exclusively due to the charged degree of discourse about the future of the country; the development of such institutions as the Canada Council, and the government's commitment to subsidise the arts nation-wide on an ample if not munificent scale, played their parts in creating a climate in which Canada became a *locus standi*, not simply a *terminus a quo*, for those involved in what we now call the cultural industries. Unlike the Laurences and Levines, Richlers and Gallants and Héberts, who, in the Fifties, found the literary air above the 49th parallel very thin indeed, the Atwoods and Munros and Carriers undertook no extended migrations, but proceeded to write and to publish of and at home. Moreover, writers such as George Grant and Northrop Frye made significant and eloquent contributions to extending and developing what we might call the discourse of Canada, advancing myths of origin and dissolution which have profoundly influenced the way successive generations have constructed a "national sense of self," to use Mavis Gallant's term. One of the most prominent strands in the ongoing weave of Canadian discourse in the Sixties was, of course, the need for Canadians to confront what, via Hugh MacLennan, had become known as the "Two Solitudes Syndrome" – the fact that, though Canada had been officially constructed as a bicultural, bilingual state, no effective cultural integration of this state's two "warring" nations had ever been achieved. And while Pierre Trudeau's government devised and implemented that policy of bilingualism which seems still to stick in the craw of large numbers of Canadians living west of Ontario and east of Québec, many of Canada's literary critics, among them Ronald Sutherland, complied with what the age demanded by creating new criteria for judging the authority and validity of cultural production. Literary works could only be authentically Canadian, it seemed, if they manifested an "awareness and sensitivity to fundamental aspects of both major language groups in Canada, and of the interrelationships between these two groups."[1] Those writers who neglected to do so were guilty of succumbing to the view that "Canada, as a nation, is not likely to survive. At least [...] not [...] as anything worthy of being called a nation."[2]

Yet the 1970 Royal Commission on Bilingualism and Biculturalism may be said to have acknowledged the inadequacy of its mandate by the very fact that it published as a volume of its report a text called *The Cultural Contribution of the Other Ethnic Groups*. In 1971 – a year before Ronald Sutherland decreed that the only truly Canadian text was one which acknowledged the bicultural nature of the country – the Trudeau government published a policy statement about the multicultural nature of Canadian society, and although the Canadian Multiculturalism Act did not become law until July 1988, the notion of Canada as a pluralist society continually enriched and transformed by successive waves of immigrants became a commonplace, at least in English-speaking Canada.

One of the corollaries of multiculturalism, of course, is that it has made obsolete our traditional construct of the paradigmatic Canadian difference – that between English- and French-speaking Canadians. The call for dialogue between

---

[1] Ronald Sutherland, "The Mainstream," *Canadian Literature* 53 (Summer 1972): 38.
[2] Sutherland, "The Mainstream," 41.

these two groups has been superseded by the demand for what I would call polylogue – the creation of a discursive arena in which the full range of ethnocultural and racial difference can be meaningfully articulated. One could argue that multiculturalism paid no little role in derailing the Meech express, if one reads as "multicultural" the refusal of Elijah Harper to ratify Meech in the Manitoba legislature, and the dissatisfaction of various premiers with Meech's failure to acknowledge the fundamental contributions of other ethnocultural groups besides the French and English in building the Canadian nation. Moreover, round the time that the various stages of the Meech drama were being performed, some Québécois journalists were expressing strong resentment at the way in which the agenda of multiculturalism had ousted the project of bilingualism and biculturalism in Canada. Some English language journalists have expressed related concerns, notably the redoubtable Barbara Amiel. Defining Canada as having been founded on "the values of [...] essentially Northern European society," Amiel rather staggeringly insists that

> Nowhere in the world since the Third Reich has any country been quite as obsessed with color, ethnicity and religion as Canada. [...] This country was founded on two cultures, both of which have an extraordinary heritage and richness to offer. True, under the schemes of Pierre Trudeau, multiculturalism was brought in to counter Quebec nationalism. In doing so we created this dangerous alienation in which Anglo-Canadians became a minority, while French-Canadians became a distinct and separate entity. This left Canada with no identity at all. [...] What on earth have we done? Our English heritage gave the world the best system of jurisprudence; our French culture contains some of the finest thoughts and values from the Encyclopedists through Diderot to Voltaire. What marvellous roots.[3]

Amiel presumably sees multiculturalism as a "scheme" concocted by the "politically correct" to pull up those roots brutally and plant in their stead who knows what horrid hybrid – one influenced by Black and Asian, or Eastern European instead of Western European culture; one influenced too, perhaps, by the England of Beveridge and Benn, and the France of Foucault and Derrida, not to mention Robespierre.

Amiel is not alone in her distrust of multiculturalism. In *Mosaic Madness*, sociologist Reginald Bibby, an admirer of Allan Bloom, argues that multiculturalism depends upon the concepts of pluralism and relativism – "pluralism establishes choices: relativism declares the choices valid."[4] He goes on to express fears that these twin evils will destroy *all* values and traditions by refusing to concede that *some* are better than others. Multiculturalism can often lead to ghettoisation and intolerance, he declares:

---

3 Barabara Amiel, in *Maclean's*, 27 May 1991: 15.
4 Reginald Bibby, *Mosaic Madness: The Poverty and Potential of Life in Canada* (Toronto: Stoddart, 1990): 10.

> The multiculturalism assumption – that a positive sense of one's group will lead to
> tolerance and respect of other groups – has not received strong support, notes McGill
> university sociologist Morton Weinfeld. The evidence, he says "suggests a kind of
> ethnocentric effect, so that greater preoccupation with one's own group makes one
> more distant from and antipathetic to others."5

It is not, however, just those violently opposed to any projected change to the
status quo who have problematised the nature and working of multiculturalism.
Many transcultural writers have expressed anything from disenchantment to
hostility at the way in which what author M.J. Vassanji has nicknamed "multi-
vulturalism" works in Canada, and the multitude of sins – racism, disempowerment, trivialization of ethnocultural difference – it covers. In an introduction to
Other Solitudes, a collection of what she calls Canadian multicultural fiction, Linda
Hutcheon identifies the gap which exists between the ideology and the ideal of
multiculturalism, acknowledging that many of the authors collected in her
anthology express "views of the stereotyping and ghettoizing tendencies inherent
in multicultural policy and its implementation [that] are testaments to the power of
fear, ignorance, and prejudice that even the most idealistic of ideologies cannot
eradicate."6 Canadian writers of colour might find particularly applicable to their
experience a book entitled *Them: Voices From the Immigrant Community in Contemporary Britain*. As reviewer Tariq Modood summarises:

> The English want you to become like them but they want to treat you differently;
> they do not want to be disturbed by difference but they want to maintain their
> superiority and social distance. However keen they may be to whittle down the rough
> edge of cultural difference, there is always an us and them while there is any hint of
> difference. And whether you are assimilated or culturally distinct, you have to be
> twice as good to be taken seriously. No wonder some immigrant communities take
> little interest in what's on offer.7

And if multiculturalism as government policy is highly problematical, the aesthetic
it impels is no less so. Yet, paradoxically, the more fraught the context in which
today's transcultural writers work, the more dynamic and assured is the polylogue
they have helped to create. It may not have made of Canada a world turned upside
down, its hierarchies and hegemonies exploded, but it has, nevertheless, shaken all
kinds of previously established norms and canons, and in the process given us some
of the most stunning writing we possess: Michael Ondaatje's *Running in the Family*
and *In the Skin of the Lion*; Rohinton Mistry's *Tales from Firozha Baag* and *Such a Long
Journey*; Joy Kogawa's *Obasan*, to name only a few.

❧ ✴ ❧

---

5 Bibby, *Mosaic Madness*, 11.

6 *Other Solitudes: Canadian Multicultural Fictions*, ed. Linda Hutcheon & Marion Richmond
(Toronto: Oxford UP, 1990): 13.

7 Tariq Modood, in *Guardian Weekly* (10 February 1991): 25.

I should now like to make a number of points through which a preliminary definition of both the project and the problematics of Canadian transculturalism can emerge.

1) Regarding my choice of the term transcultural, a few words of explanation are certainly in order. The term "ethnic" – widely regarded as pejorative – has been replaced by "multicultural" in official usage; the consequences of this linguistic shift have been confusing, at the very least. For it makes no sense to speak of a group of people, or of a writer or that writer's work, as "multicultural" – logically, that term can only be applied to a society made up of members of different ethnocultural and racial groups. And while we can speak of a dominant group within Canadian society – a group comparable, in its traditional hold on power and authority, to the American "WASP Ascendancy" – that group, whether its members are of British or French descent, is as much an *ethnos*, or distinctive people and culture, as would be a group of Ojibway or Pakistanis. How can we say that a Josef Škvorecký or a Rohinton Mistry is "multicultural" while an Alice Munro is just "Canadian"? Isn't a Scottish background as "ethnic" as a Czech or Parsi one?

2) Perhaps the most important attribute of the term transcultural is its comprehensiveness. Within the borders of the transcultural (borders which I see as being more like leaky parentheses than strict enclosures) I would include, in no particular order, francophone writers – Franco-Manitobans and Acadians as well as Québécois; Native writers; writers of colour – Black, South/East and West Asian; writers of whatever colour who have emigrated to Canada from the United States; and white writers from ethnocultural groups which have been traditionally and dismissively cast as "other" by Canada's dominant ethnocultural group: white, Anglo-Saxon and Protestant. Members of the traditionally dominant group – those of English and Scottish origin – I would include as well, so that the texts of a Davies and a Munro, for example, could be read as examples of ethnocultural difference rather than as a norm against which the degree of exotic or alarming difference of, for example, Japanese–Canadian or Hungarian–Canadian writing can be measured. If Canada can be defined as a nation of immigrants, then we are all hyphenated–Canadians, to the extent that we preserve our awareness of our ancestral country of origin and the history, traditions, values and prejudices associated with it.

I realise, of course, that I am in danger here not of throwing the baby out with the bathwater but, rather, of packing so many babies into the tub that there is scarcely any room in which to splash. Yet if it is argued that transculturalism is far too heterogeneous or permissive a category to function usefully at all, I would be happy to say: let the category part of it go. For then we would end up with something very close to what Salman Rushdie has termed hotch-potch, or the positive "mongrelization" of cultural forms, whereby exclusionary criteria designed to protect the "purity" of a given canon or tradition would have little force or favour.

3) Transculturalism, of course, did not spring fullgrown from the forehead of the 1971 Royal Bi- and Bi-Commission report, or the 1988 Multiculturalism Act, for that matter. Canada has a long history of writing that is expressive of difference and otherness, whether these qualities be seen in terms of "the immigrant experience" or of ethnicity interpreted as all that which is non-WASP or unassimilable to WASP norms: the racial or religious markers of visible difference. The texts of writers who immigrated to Canada as adults – Frederick Philip Grove and Martha Ostenso, Henry Kreisel and John Marlyn, Ethel Wilson and Walter Bauer, Austin Clarke and Neil Bissoondath, Kristjana Gunnars and Audrey Thomas – and of Canadians who were born into recent or long-established immigrant families, or who came to Canada as young children – Vera Lysenko and Miriam Waddington, Mordecai Richler and Norman Levine, Nino Ricci and Myrna Kostash, Mary di Michele and Ven Begamudré – form an impressive continuum.

4) In an essay on the work of Frederick Philip Grove, and particularly the novel *Settlers of the Marsh*, Robert Kroetsch forwards the idea that the character-istic narrative of what he calls "the ethnic experience" is one involving the story of migration. Characters caught between old and new worlds develop a paralysis expressed by silence, a silence which Kroetsch suggests can be broken by the retelling of old stories, specifically myths of Edenic origin, and by the construct-ing of new story forms adequate to the experience of linguistic, social and cultural as well as geographical translocation. Through the assertion of the narrative of ethnic experience, Kroetsch concludes, silence can find "a way to transform itself into voice."[8]

I would argue that in the period between, let us say, the publication of Grove's *Settlers of the Marsh* in 1925 and the year 1981, when Joy Kogawa published *Obasan*, silence predominated over speech. Even if transcultural voices were speaking out, few ears were tuned to hear them. The decade of the Eighties, however, has heard an extraordinary assortment of transcultural voices – telling stories, true, but also addressing spezialised communities, demanding long-denied rights, and admonishing those in power who have been instrumental or at least complicit in the act of silencing those who had most need to speak out. The fiction of Joy Kogawa is perhaps the clearest illustration of this transition from "coming into voice" to raising one's voice so as to interrogate one's silencers. If *Obasan* deals with the breaking of the stone of silence, a stone whose origins lie not in the nature of things but, rather, in the institutionalised racism which decided the

---

8 Robert Kroetsch, "The Grammar of Silence," in Kroetsch, *The Lovely Treachery of Words: Essays Selected and New* (Toronto: Oxford UP, 1989): 94.

course of Canadian government policy in the Forties, then the recently published sequel to *Obasan*, *Itsuka*, is a sustained throwing of the verbal equivalent of stones at those who obstructed the attempts of Japanese–Canadians to win adequate redress for the extreme suffering so unjustly imposed upon them by their country-people during the last World War.

I could point to numerous other examples of the assertive and insistent mode of transcultural discourse which has propelled what I have called a polylogue on the subjects of difference and belonging in Canada. Dionne Brand's latest and highly political volume of poetry, *No Language is Neutral*, written not for some generalised Canadian audience, but addressed specifically to the Caribbean diaspora in Toronto; Himani Bannerji's declaration to Arun Mukherjee, recorded in *Other Solitudes*: "I want to write about how you and I live here and only insofar as white people impinge on our lives, will they become part of my narrative [...] I don't write for white middle-class readers. I write for you and me."[9] Lenore Keeshig–Tobias' repeated insistence that only Native writers should be permitted to deal with Native issues and culture. Arnold Itwaru's attack, in *The Canadian Imaginary*, upon what he calls the racist nature of certain classic Canadian narratives of immigrant experience. Fred Wah's statement, made at a recent conference organised around the issues of ethnicity and difference, that what he calls "Ethnolit," as opposed to Canlit (the work of Munro, Atwood, Davies and other WASPS, authentic or honorary), projects the anger, fear and alienation which "Canlit" ignores and multiculturalism smooths over by putting "difference" into manageable packages.[10] This is not to suggest that there is now one and only one way of being transcultural in Canada – one need only look at the views expressed by Indian-born Ven Begamudré, who insists that he wants to be read by all kinds of readers irrespective of race or country of origin, or of Icelandic-born Kristjana Gunnars, who has made it repeatedly clear that she wishes to be considered simply as a writer, not as someone whose work is supposed to be "representative" of the Icelandic community in Canada, a group about which she professes to know relatively little. The point is not that the former view is correct and the latter mistaken, or vice versa, but that all are possible, and that contemporary transcultural discourse in Canada is not handicapped but rather energized by being in a state of continual debate and divergence, ferment and flux.

5) The present mode of transcultural writing in Canada is, I would argue, a postmodernist form of the Bakhtinian carnivalesque, combining both the celebratory aspects Bakhtin observes in late-medieval and Renaissance manifestations of "grotesque realism" and expressions of hostility and alienation he connects with

---

9 Himani Bannerji, interview in *Other Solitudes*, ed. Hutcheon & Richmond, 149–52.
10 Fred Wah, Panel Discussion, Alberta Writers' Guild Annual General Meeting, Edmonton, Alberta, May 1991.

what he calls the modernist grotesque. The carnival features of transculturalism are present not only in its rejection of monologic forms of discourse and its preference for polyphony and heteroglossia, but also in transculturalism's interrogating of established social and cultural hierachies, its increasingly insistent transgression of the code of "good behaviour" demanded by the Department of Multiculturalism, a code which, as Kogawa's *Itsuka* shows, demands that "multicul's" sing pretty songs and not make shrill demands for access to political power.

Yet, for all the exuberant energy of its carnivalesque, transculturalism has its own problematic, two aspects of which I will briefly signal: the chasm that is opening between ethnicity and race as mutually exclusive means of situating transcultural subjects; and, as a corollary, the dearth of strategies which transculturalism has devised to allow it to leap across established boundaries and borders, to ensure that the experience of, say, a Ukrainian immigrant family speaks to its Caribbean counterpart, so that ghettoisation, or what we might describe as multiple solipsism, does not become the *terminus ad quem* of transculturalism.

First, then, the growing divide between ethnicity and race. Just as some Québécois tend to conceptualise English Canada as one vast, undifferentiated block of otherness, so writers of colour, by and large, tend to view white Canadians as a monolithic entity, as the dominant group, *tout court*. Speaking as a Ukrainian–Canadian, I would remark that white Canadians of different ethnocultural groups are distinguished by widely varying historical experience, and would point to the fact that among Polish– or Greek– or Italian–Canadians one will find enough different religious views, political affiliations and class attitudes to explode, once and for all, the myth of the white monolith. Surely we need to be wary of lumping together writers from specific ethnocultural groups, assuming that they speak for their community and with one voice. For instance, a writer like Dionne Brand might have far more in common with a white feminist of Ukrainian background like Myrna Kostash than with her fellow Trinidadian, Neil Bissoondath. For, while Brand insists on the importance of writing for and from within her own people, her community of Caribbean–Canadians, Bissoondath insists that he is writing in an international language of exile, as his uncle V.S. Naipaul has done. We also need to be wary of accepting point-blank the revisionings of the literary canon and tradition which some critics of "monoculturalism" insist upon. Thus a writer such as Jane Urquhart, who is presently writing a novel exploring the experience of her Irish forebears, and who has spoken of her delight and fascination with Ethel Wilson's *The Innocent Traveller*, would not for a moment, one assumes, accept Arnold Itwaru's dismissal of Wilson's text as merely racist and imperialist.

In this context it may be necessary to make the point that the supposedly monolithic construct, "English Canada," has long had what Smaro Kamboureli calls "audible" as well as "visible" minorities. And while racism has certainly been directed most often and most conspicuously at Canadians of colour, we should not forget that it has discharged its poisons at white Canadians too. Readers of Mordecai Richler's *Son of a Smaller Hero* will be familiar with the fact that, for example, only a few decades ago, certain beaches in Québec were segregated, signposted as either Gentile or Jewish. Anyone familiar with Mavis Gallant's story "Virus X" will know that, just as all Canadians are hyphenated, so there exists a hierarchy of hyphens: in the Fifties, the period within which the story is set, if it was best to be English–Canadian then it was better to be English– or Scots– than Irish–Canadian, and it was vastly preferable to be German–Canadian than Ukrainian– or Polish–Canadian. But then, there has been a long tradition of revulsion at Slavic "otherness" in Canada. In our recent celebrations of the hundredth anniversary of Ukrainian immigration to Canada we would have done well to remember the comments of the editors of the Belleville *Intelligencer* and the Québec *Mercury* on turn-of-the-century immigrants from what is now Ukraine:

> The Galicians, they of the sheepskin coats, the filth and the vermin, do not make splendid material for the building of a great nation. One look at the disgusting creatures as they pass through the C.P.R. on their way west has caused many to marvel that beings bearing the human form could have sunk to such a bestial level [...].
>
> Mr Sifton's Galicians have not parted with any of the usages which mark them off from the rest of mankind [...] There are some Indians in the Northwest who are pretty low down in the scale of humanity, but they appear to be above associating with the kind of Galicians Mr Sifton has introduced.[11]

Finally, if, as Catherine Simpson urges, literature can help us to defuse and contain fear of difference by teaching us "about the ineluctability of the differences among us and about the moral, political, and psychological wisdom of generously admitting those differences into consciousness and feelings,"[12] then that literature must reach as wide and diverse an audience as possible. The insistence of Himani Bannerji, for example, that she writes only for those born into her particular racial, cultural and linguistic community, will thus need to be challenged or resisted by writers and readers outside that community. Equally importantly, the claim Kristjana Gunnars makes in *The Prowler* – that Icelanders are the white Inuit – must not be barred from the field of transcultural discourse, as some would urge, but must be permitted to perform what it sets out to do: to leap across closed borders, trespass on private property, and encourage lively debate – polylogue – among us.

---

11 Jaroslav Petryshyn, *Peasants in the Promised Land: Canada and the Ukrainians, 1891–1914* (Toronto: James Lorimer, 1985): 100.
12 Catherine Stimpson, "Are the Differences Spreading? Feminist Criticism and Postmodernism," *English Studies in Canada* 15:4 (December 1989): 368.

What we must emphasise and enable, in other words, is the "trans" in transculturalism. For it seems to me that only by sharing our differences can we discover unexpected similarities which we will not erase or occlude painful and problematical articulations of otherness. And only by recognising and celebrating the increasingly diverse and mutable nature of Canada's sociocultural formation can we hope to approach what Bakhtin saw as the laudable – indeed, imperative – goal of the carnivalesque: "to consecrate inventive freedom, to permit the combination of a variety of different elements and their rapprochement, to liberate [us] from [...] conventions and established truths, from clichés, from all that is humdrum and universally accepted. This carnival spirit offers [us] the chance to have a new outlook on the world [...] and to enter a completely new order of things."[13]

WORKS CITED

BAKHTIN, Mikhail. *Rabelais and His World*, tr. Hélène Iswolsky (Bloomington: Indiana UP, 1984).

BIBBY, Reginald. *Mosaic Madness: The Poverty and Potential of Life in Canada* (Toronto: Stoddart, 1990).

HUTCHEON Linda, & Marion RICHMOND, ed. *Other Solitudes: Canadian Multicultural Fictions* (Toronto: Oxford UP, 1990).

KROETSCH, Robert. "The Grammar of Silence," in Kroetsch, *The Lovely Treachery of Words: Essays Selected and New* (Toronto: Oxford UP, 1989): 84–94.

PETRYSHYN, Jaroslav. *Peasants in the Promised Land: Canada and the Ukrainians, 1891–1914* (Toronto: James Lorimer, 1985).

STIMPSON, Catherine. "Are the Differences Spreading? Feminist Criticism and Postmodernism," *English Studies in Canada* 15:4 (December 1989): 364 82.

SUTHERLAND, Ronald. "The Mainstream," *Canadian Literature* 53 (Summer 1972): 30–41.

❧ ✦ ☙

---

13 Mikhail Bakhtin, *Rabelais and His World*, tr. Hélène Iswolsky (Bloomington: Indiana UP, 1984): 34.

"Home Ground / Foreign Territory"
Transculturalism in Contemporary Canadian Women's Short Stories in English

CORAL ANN HOWELLS

"NOW I AM ON MY HOME GROUND, FOREIGN TERRITORY," is, as you recall, the narrator's statement of her own position in Margaret Atwood's *Surfacing*.[1] It is this special metaphor of estrangement that I take as my starting-point, though I intend to use it to describe rather different social and psychological spaces than the ones that Atwood constructs. In fact, a different Atwood quotation would have provided a more explicit gloss: "We are all immigrants to this place, even if we were born here."[2] I want to highlight one particular area within the contemporary discourse on Canadian multiculturalism, by discussing some short stories written in English by women born in Canada of ethnic immigrant parents or grandparents, for these stories seem to represent a particular condition within multiculturalism, which might more accurately be described as "transcultural" than as "multicultural." My thinking about this topic emerges from some work I did on contemporary immigrant women's writing in Canada,[3] when it occurred to me that the writing by Canadian-born women represented a significantly different area of the multicultural phenomenon.[4] To be Canadian-born and of ethnic origin is to be in a peculiarly nuanced situation, where ethnicity as the mark of separateness from a majority culture is in the process of being superseded by a more hybridised condition of slippage both ways across two cultures. These stories register a series of discrete but sequentially related moments within the dynamics of the transcultural scenario in Canada.

My use of the term "transcultural" needs some explanation and grateful acknowledgement. It comes out of some lively conversations I had at the University of Guelph with Janice Kulyk Keefer, Constance Rooke and Diana

---

[1] Margaret Atwood, *Surfacing* (1972; London: Virago, 1980): 11.

[2] Margaret Atwood, *The Journals of Susanna Moodie* (Toronto: Oxford UP, 1970): 62.

[3] Coral Ann Howells, "Canadian Signatures in the Feminine" (London: Canada House Lecture Series, 47, 1991).

[4] I have not included Native writing here, though clearly I could have/should have, because that too is produced out of a situation of two cultures in contact.

Brydon, all of whom lent it their own inflections.[5] Since then, Janice's excellent essay "From Mosaic to Kaleidoscope" has appeared in *Books in Canada*, where she makes many of my points for me.[6] That essay is subtitled "Out of the Multi-cultural Past comes the Vision of a Transcultural Future," suggesting the ideal of an evolving culture, while she also stresses the importance of the individual within the multicultural phenomenon. While Canadian society may be multicultural, any individual is far more likely to exist between two cultures (a heritage culture, and a mainstream culture into which she has been educated), so that "transcultural" accurately denotes both the condition of the individual writer and also the discursive positions the protagonists are negotiating within these fictional texts.

In addressing the question of the representation of the transcultural female subject in writing, many of the issues are the same as those in feminist theory, though given a sharper edge. The relation between the subject and discursive structures, for instance, becomes even more problematical when the subject herself happens to be constructed through more than one social and linguistic discourse. How can her position be defined within such doubled discourse, when she herself has become the site where different cultural perspectives coexist? Mercifully, such a static model as the word "site" suggests is transcended by human agency. As Rita Felski puts it, "Human subjects are not simply constructed through social and linguistic structures, but they themselves interact with those structures" in a complex dialectic of modification and revision.[7]

It is this concept of human agency which provides the crucial ingredient in the dynamic (not to say ambiguous) condition of transculturalism, and which in turn urges the need for a critical engagement with the paradigm of marginality so often used in discussions of multiculturalism. The binary oppositions implied by this model cannot account for the individual's interaction with the two existing cultural frameworks within/between which she is situated. It is this area of trans-action that needs to be investigated in transcultural stories. These stories written by women from a variety of ethnic backgrounds – Chinese, Russian Mennonite and French Catholic, Russian Jewish, and Polish–Ukrainian – represent a heteroglossia of different voices haunting the English texts. But the stories are not allegories of selfhood; they are representations of the transcultural condition in writing. They construct a variety of individual subject positions through a range of

---

5 See Jean Lamore, "Transculturation: Naissance d'un mot," in *Métamorphoses d'une Utopia*, ed. Jean–Michel Lacroix & Fulvio Caccia (Paris: Presses de la Sorbonne Nouvelle, 1992): 43–48. First published in *Vice Versa* 21.

6 Janice Kulyk Keefer, "From Mosaic to Kaleidoscope," *Books in Canada* (September 1991): 13–16.

7 Rita Felski, *Beyond Feminist Aesthetics: Feminist Literature and Social Change* (Cambridge MA: Harvard UP, 1989): 57. I am indebted to Felski's theorising on subjectivity in my discussion of the transcultural female subject.

fictional discourses that include realism, fantasy and dream, in texts that are themselves indeterminate, unresolved. Transculturalism is, of course, only one of the elements through which these female subjects are constituted. Other elements include age, sexuality, and desire, so that I run the risk here of oversimplifying – except perhaps in Miriam Waddington's non-fictional essay, where ethnicity is the main element in her autobiographical construction.

❧ ✿ ☙

To begin my series of moments within the transcultural scenario, I shall be looking at Lesley Lum's story "Old Age Gold," which is very close to represent-ations of immigrant experience and its crises of unbelonging, for it focuses on one woman's attempt to construct an acceptably "Canadian" identity.[8] It is the story of old Mrs Chiang's Canadian Citizenship hearing, which takes place after thirty years of her living in Vancouver. It's an ironic situation: Mrs Chiang wants her Canadian citizenship so that she can get her old-age social security benefits in order to leave Canada and return to live with her daughter in China: "They gave to Canadians, only to Canadians. Were they giving this time?" (170). Ironically, it's a hearing where nothing is heard, for Mrs Chiang does not understand English, and the Canadian official cannot hear Mrs Chiang, who is presented throughout the story as a silent subject undergoing a private crisis which might be said to be brought on by her confrontation with the English language.

Structured inside a frame of official questions and Mrs Chiang's silent answers given in her indirect interior monologue, the story has a double focus. There's a dominant discourse of the Canadian white male official, juxtaposed with the old Chinese woman's counter-discourse, which is interpreted for us by the narrator. Two cultures are shown in confrontation, and when the gap is finally collapsed through the benevolent paternalism of the official, a rift has opened up in Mrs Chiang's own mind which will make her forever homeless, even though she will indeed have her Canadian citizenship papers.

The story turns on language and silence, where, lost in alien official discourse, Mrs Chiang is excluded as a speaking subject. Mrs Chiang, who has never learned to speak English in her rooming-house in Vancouver's Chinatown, is not really an immigrant who lives between two cultures at all. She lives in a particular Canadian expatriate version of Chinese culture in a pocket outside time: "The new immigrants laughed at the old ones. They said they had kept the old customs of old China. There was no such China now" (171).

---

[8] Lesley Lum, "Old Age Gold," in *The Last Map Is the Heart: Anthology of Western Canadian Fiction*, ed. Allan Forrie, Patrick O' Rourke & Glen Sorestad (Saskatoon: Thistledown, 1989): 162–72.

Of course, English does not accommodate Mrs Chiang's experience, either. Indeed, the questions on the Citizenship form do not even allow her to state her name as she wishes:

> Surname last, these funny westerners, surname last as if it did not matter at all, hidden behind the sound of given name. And surname must be given of husband, not father, another complication. How very contrived, a mystery these westerners and their logic were. (162)

Faced with Mrs Chiang's value judgements, we experience a series of reversals of perspective, so that we too begin to wonder Who's on Whose Margins?[9] Mrs Chiang has no great interest in the English language; she might even be said to have a contempt for it: "English, language of the barbarians, for Canadian-borns and westerners. English, not needed in her neighbourhood" (164).

The final irony in this cross-cultural encounter is that the Citizenship hearing does change Mrs Chiang's life, though not in the way she had expected. Under the gaze of the "White Bear" official, Mrs Chiang's sense of unbelonging in Canada extends towards another more disturbing realisation of unbelonging: "The white bear looked at Guy Mo Chiang. Guy Mo Chiang watched China disappear [...] China, after thirty years, why had she even thought of it. She could never belong" (172).

Belong where? That is the question, and one which remains unanswered even when she is granted her Canadian citizenship by the white bear ("Such a nice man"). The official happy ending masks Mrs Chiang's private sense of dereliction as her story refigures a familiar trope, the shattering of the immigrant's dream of return to the homeland: "Perhaps Guy Mo Chiang would go down to visit her son in San Francisco, now that she had her Canadian citizenship and Old Age Gold. China was so far away" (172).

It is Russia that is so far away for the young narrator in Sandra Birdsell's story "Flowers for Weddings and Funerals,"[10] which traces a Canadian-born adolescent girl's painful attempts to negotiate the gap between her family's ethnic traditions and the ethos of the prairie town where she is growing up. The transcultural condition is emblematically presented from the beginning as the narrator moves physically between two worlds, riding her bicycle along the dirt road out of town to her grandmother's cottage with an order for flowers: "I am the messenger." In the end she rejects the world represented by her Russian Mennonite grandmother and turns towards Laurence, the boy from the town with whom she is in love, though even as she chooses him she can see in her mind's eye her grandmother

---

9 Sneja Gunew, "Migrant Women Writers: Who's on Whose Margins?" in *Gender, Politics and Fiction: Twentieth Century Australian Women's Novels*, ed. Carole Ferrier (Brisbane: U of Queensland P, 1985): 163–78.

10 Sandra Birdsell, "Flowers for Weddings and Funerals," in Birdsell, *Night Travellers* (Winnipeg: Turnstone, 1982): 91–98.

waiting for her: "I can see Omah rising to search the way I take, and she will not find me there" (98).

Within the conventions of an adolescent love-story, there is enacted a more complex scenario of choice and betrayal, of failures in translation across the gaps of generation and culture, in a confrontation between the discourses of duty and desire, so that the narrating subject is positioned at the raw edges and forced to choose between two worlds, haunted by lack and facing both ways.

For Birdsell's protagonist, slippage between cultures becomes traumatic defection, though I would recommend Miriam Waddington's autobiographical essay "Outsider: Growing Up in Canada,"[11] which provides a more optimistic representation of the transcultural condition from the perspective of a Canadian-born woman writer of Russian–Jewish parents who grew up in Winnipeg in the mid-Twenties and early Thirties:

> Even in the life of one person like myself, living in a raw provincial city like Winnipeg, you can find the presence of duality and paradox that is so characteristic of Canadian life. I moved from the permissive atmosphere of the Yiddish school to the English Fabianism of the summer camp, and then finally into the structured, rigid, conservative school system, without an apparent crack in my wholeness. I stepped without much consciousness from the uniculture of the Yiddish home to the multiculture of a very mixed social group. These two cultural aspects – Yiddish and English–Canadian – did not come together in me for many long years. They simply existed side by side, and I devised two codes of behaviour, one to fit each world. That's why I also had to create a third world, my own invented one, where I could include the elements I chose from the other two. (38)

This beautifully precise model of the transcultural subject's fragmented construction occurs within an essay that insistently radiates outwards from autobiography to become representative. In her need to find a "third world, my own invented one," Waddington prefigures Janice Kulyk Keefer's attempts to find her position as a writer: "I think that a great part of my sense of myself as a writer, an artist in words, comes from my early awareness of being caught in various linguistic traps, of having my identity fragmented by language."[12]

Janice Kulyk Keefer, with her Polish–Ukrainian background and her Toronto upbringing, shares Waddington's condition of divided loyalties; though she has moved a step further than Waddington from her ethnic inheritance, being brought up in English with Ukrainian as a second language. She has written stories about East European immigrants in Canada, but the one I've selected, "The Grey

---

[11] Miriam Waddington, "Outsider: Growing Up in Canada," in Waddington, *Apartment Seven: Essays Selected and New* (Toronto: Oxford UP, 1989): 35–44.

[12] Janice Kulyk Keefer, in *Multiple Voices: Recent Canadian Fiction*, ed. Jeanne Delbaere (Sydney/ Mundelstrup: Dangaroo, 1990): 34.

Valise,"[13] subsumes Keefer's ethnic heritage under another construction of difference within identity, being the story of a middle-aged WASP Canadian woman from New Brunswick who goes to Italy on a secret journey, only to find that this trip into "foreign territory" uncovers hitherto unrecognised territory much closer to home.

This story, which begins with a passport photograph of the Travelling Lady Mrs Fanshawe, ends with a postcard image of an Italian saint, suggesting a subtle dismantling of self-definition within Mrs Fanshawe herself. Proceeding by a series of arrangements and disarrangements, the story traces her unwilling journey to Italy to scatter her late husband's ashes, according to the terms of his will, above the village of Fermio, where he had been sheltered during the Second World War. While the travel arrangements are quite clear, the disarrangements occur within Mrs Fanshawe's psyche, where, confronted with the otherness of Italy, suppressed memories and conflicts flood her consciousness. Language itself breaks down/ breaks up, for her stiff, grudging Italian turns out to be useless when she's sitting opposite her kindly host at the Albergo Rustico. Asked the reason for her visit, she finds herself speaking in neither Italian nor English but in German, "though it had been some forty years since she'd even heard German spoken." And next day, when she unlocks the grey valise to scatter her husband's ashes on the hillside, she discovers she has released another voice – through the silence she can hear her husband speaking from beyond the grave:

> What a fool she'd been. She, with her flair for languages never being able to hear what Digby had to say to her [...] What if it was simply this – that he hadn't wanted to come back to her at all [...] had wanted to disappear into the arms of a peasant girl from Fermio and end his days sitting in a dusty courtyard pungent with the odour of geraniums. (234)

After this moment of revelation (or is it translation?) Mrs Fanshawe returns home to Canada, but there is one trace of her secret journey – the postcard of the patron saint of Fermio, Santa Livia, who has the same name as herself, which she keeps "tucked inside the frame of her dressing-table mirror" (236). This postcard, with its picture of a girl surrounded by flames and a man with a sad gentle face pointing at her, is in a curiously doubled way a framed portrait of herself, where Santa Livia, Olivia Fanshawe and the girl from Fermio in Digby's wartime photograph are fused in one composite image.

The grey valise has been emptied of its ashy contents and thrown away at Rome airport. There is the greyness of irrecoverable loss, but there is also another kind of grey area suggested in the final image of Mrs Fanshawe asleep, "about to utter some exclamation, whether of pain or pleasure, or some shifting mix of both,

---

13 Janice Kulyk Keefer, "The Grey Valise," in Kulyk Keefer, *Travelling Ladies* (Toronto: Random House, 1990): 214–35.

it would be impossible to tell" (236). The story carries the strong suggestion that fixed identity is maintained only by suppressions and secrets, which are finally acknowledged, if only in dreams, and that "foreign territory" is no more slippery a terrain than what we have fondly constructed as "home ground."

≈ ❀ ≈

Identity is a more shifting concept than we conventionally assume and trans-cultural fictions highlight the indeterminacies, hidden agendas and slippages within any concept of identity. These stories offer representations of identities under construction/deconstruction/reconstruction, from a variety of subject positions. Yet, taken together they seem to construct a sequential narrative which might be seen as moving towards a redefinition of Canadian identity in culturally hybrid terms. Canadianness has always included cultural, ethnic, and regional diversity; this has now become a politically and socially sensitive issue as well as a significant aesthetic one. In these women's fictions, being "at home" in Canada means an active engagement with cultural diversity. The stories would seem to be emblematic of the multiple voices and the interchange between those voices which mark Canada's evolving national literature.

WORKS CITED

ATWOOD, Margaret. *Surfacing* (1972; London: Virago, 1980).

BIRDSELL, Sandra. "Flowers for Weddings and Funerals," in Birdsell, *Night Travellers* (Winnipeg: Turnstone, 1982): 162–72.

GUNEW, Sneja. "Migrant Women Writers: Who's on Whose Margins?" in *Gender, Politics and Fiction: Twentieth Century Australian Women's Novels*, ed. Carole Ferrier (Brisbane: U of Queensland P, 1985): 163–78.

HOWELLS, Coral Ann. "Canadian Signatures in the Feminine" (London: Canada House Lecture Series, 47, 1991).

KULYK KEEFER, Janice. "From Mosaic to Kaleidoscope," *Books in Canada* (September 1991): 13–16.

———. "The Grey Valise," in *Travelling Ladies* (Toronto: Random House, 1990): 214–35.

LAMORE, Jean. "Transculturation: Naissance d'un mot," in *Métamorphoses d'une Utopia*, ed. Jean–Michel Lacroix & Fulvio Caccia (Paris: Presses de la Sorbonne Nouvelle, 1992): 43–48. First published in *Vice Versa* 21.

LUM, Lesley. "Old Age Gold," in *The Last Map Is the Heart: Anthology of Western Canadian Fiction*, ed. Allan Forrie, Patrick O' Rourke & Glen Sorestad (Saskatoon: Thistledown, 1989): 162–72.

WADDINGTON, Miriam. "Outsider: Growing Up in Canada," in *Apartment Seven: Essays Selected and New* (Toronto: Oxford UP, 1990): 35–44.

≈ ❀ ≈

Henry Kreisel's "The Almost Meeting"
An Intertextual Reading
of Jewish Writing in the Canadian West

WOLFGANG KLOOSS

A FEW YEARS AGO, I had the opportunity to spend some time in the Library Archives of the University of Manitoba (Winnipeg) looking at the papers of two prominent Canadian men of letters. Among the texts that attracted my immediate attention was a small piece of juvenile poetry, entitled "Perhaps," which was composed on 9 September, 1940 and reads as follows:

> When I, one afternoon in May,
> Was led out of the cell
> Where first I lost my freedom,
> I saw a girl standing there.
> She looked up, and as she did,
> My eyes met her's and her's met mine.
> And as she looked at me, she smiled.
> And I smiled back,
> And then was led away and lost her.
> I was a prisoner, a prisoner!
> Perhaps, I thought,
> She does not think of you as such,
> Perhaps she thinks that you are
> What you are:
> A boy so young,
> A boy who did no harm to anyone.
> Perhaps – Perhaps.[1]

Similarly, I was fascinated by a rather cryptic note, very different in mode, written many years later, whose handwriting seemed unbalanced, almost bouncing beyond the margins of the page, full of mysteries and uncertainties, and yet signalling some meaning:

> Unlikely as it seems, the road that took me back to Regina, the city where I spent my youth, began in a small fishing village [...] on the Costa del Sol in Spain. [...] more often than not as I walked around the stony fields and through the olive groves near our house on the mountain-side or looked across the red hills to the Mediterranean I found myself brooding about the years I had lived in Saskatchewan, in the drought-stricken town of Estevan [...]. At the time I didn't understand the obsession, nor do I

---

[1] Henry Kreisel, "Perhaps," *Internment Notebooks*, n.p., n.d.

fully understand it now, but whatever its cause it convinced me I ought to go back to the prairies. And so in 1974, my wife Ann, and I travelled across the south-west of Saskatchewan and I began the book which eventually, with Ann's photographs, became *Out of Place*, a series of medidations on perception, memory, and region, lost past and mythicized home. [...] It was as if I were writing myself into a new kind of existence, each step leading to another, each marking out the impossible road back.

Half a page later the narrative continues with a question that receives no definite answer:

"Why in the world would you want to spend a year in Regina?" I remember my Toronto friends asking me. And the first days back I kept asking myself that question. Ten years in Toronto had changed me. Now I felt the appalling loneliness of a prairie town, the sense of emptiness around me, spaces unfilled, quiet streets, muted pastel colours, the abstractness of autumn, the places *between* objects.[2]

Another text which I came across more recently offers itself for an intertextual dialogue complementing some of the previous messages:

There was the sky. Always the sky. Not just to look up to, that blue in the dominant, but to look round at, yes, down at even, from the precarious shelf of prairie to look down at an underlying horizon [...] Here you hang in the sky with only the soles of your feet glued to earth, flies on the ceiling of the universe. Breadth and depth of sky, uncompromising stretch of prairie, leading on like the endless dream, the dream of becoming a writer someday [...] of discovering whether, if you go far enough, sky and sod will meet and be reconciled.[3]

This leads directly to my final quotation:

I used to dream of living in Israel, but after a few exploratory visits, the overwhelming presence of American culture, the pluralism of cultural backgrounds, and the complexity of the political picture – as well as my own prejudices and limitations – have made me think twice. [...] Although I once wrote in one of my poems that I don't know anymore where home is, here or in Jerusalem, as time goes on I do know that my organic physiological home is Canada – the wintry Manitoba prairie, to be specific. But my spiritual and cultural home is at least partly in Eastern Europe and partly in Jerusalem, metaphorically speaking.[4]

A summary of the uncertainties and ambiguities conveyed in these citations could be easily subsumed under notions such as "dislocation" and "displacement," "decentering" and "marginality," "multi-faceted" or "transient identities," "sacrifices" and "betrayals," "other countries" and "almost meetings," "driving home," yet "out of place," "voicing voicelessness," or just "silent-speaking words."

---

[2] Eli Mandel, "The Road to Regina," undated MS no. 18, box 40, folder 11.

[3] Adele Wiseman, "A Brief Anatomy of an Honest Attempt at a Pithy Statement about the Impact of the Manitoba Environment on My Development as an Artist," *Mosaic* 3.3 (1970): 98–106.

[4] Miriam Waddington, "Outsider: Growing Up in Canada," in Waddington, *Apartment Seven: Essays Selected and New* (Toronto: Oxford UP, 1989): 41.

As most readers are quite aware, some of the notions inscribed here appear either directly or indirectly on the title pages of a body of lyric and prose texts that have become important markers on Canada's literary landscape. As most readers have immediately discovered, of course, the two writers who opened themselves up to me in the Library Archives in Winnipeg are Henry Kreisel and Eli Mandel, just as the supplementary comments have been provided by Adele Wiseman and Miriam Waddington.

Inasmuch as these four writers stand for difference in gender, genre and cultural background, they share in a common Jewish heritage. Furthermore, their constant shifting between an uprooted European past and the Canadian present, their overwhelming urge to reconcile the two, to rewrite deserted homes and lost traditions into existence, places Jewish–Canadian literature right in the middle of any focus on Canada and Europe.

Usually associated with the works of Mordecai Richler, Irving Layton, Norman Levine, Matt Cohen, Leonard Cohen, and, above all perhaps, A.M. Klein, the Jewish voice in Canada sounds male and urban, definitely eastern, especially echoing the polyphonic city-life of Montreal. As Richler, for instance, recalls in *The Street* (1969), a collection of autobiographical short stories, Montreal's Main

> was a poor man's street, it was also a dividing line. Below, the French Canadians. Above [...] the dreaded WASPS. On the Main itself there were some Italians, Yugoslavs, and Ukrainians, but they did not count as true Gentiles. Even the French Canadians, who were our enemies, were not entirely unloved. Like us, they were poor and coarse with large families and spoke English badly. [...] Actually, it was only the WASPS who were truly hated and feared. [...] – if the Montreal *Canadiens* won the Stanley Cup it would infuriate the WASPS in Toronto, and as long as the English and French were going at each other they left us alone: *ergo*, it was good for the Jews if the *Canadiens* won the Stanley Cup.
>
> We were convinced that we gained from dissension between Canada's two cultures, the English and the French, and we looked neither to England nor France for guidance. We turned to the United States. The real America.[5]

In other words, the exiled home of Richler, Cohen and Layton is essentially the world of the ghetto between Canada's two solitudes.

At the same time, Henry Kreisel, Eli Mandel, Miriam Waddington and Adele Wiseman, like Robert Currie, Jack Ludwig or Seymor Mayne, demonstrate in most of their works that Jewish Canada extends far beyond the limits of eastern townships. Their affiliation with the prairies is so strong that Winnipeg's North End, small prairie communities like Estevan, or Alberta's metropolis Edmonton take their place alongside New York, Chicago and Montreal in sharing a rather similar mindscape, or, as Michael Greenstein claims, "in offering a unique

---

5 Mordecai Richler, "The Street," in *Other Solitudes: Canadian Multicultural Fictions*, ed. Linda Hutcheon & Marion Richmond (Toronto: U of Toronto P, 1990): 35, 36, 37–38.

perspective for Jewish experience in North America."[6] Accordingly, Tom
Marshall in a study of A.M. Klein goes even further, observing that "as an
unusually stable and cohesive group related to larger cultural entities both inside
and outside of Canada, the Jews are, in a sense, the most Canadian of Canadians."[7]
Regardless of its geographical location,

> Jewish culture is the record of a continually displaced people attempting to find a
> home for themselves in a hostile environment. [...] In a country where every
> individual is a member of an ethnic group [...], the Jew becomes a kind of Everyman
> – a stranger trying to fit into an alien geography and culture.[8]

It is the unsettled mindscape, migrating from west to east and east to west, from
Canada to Europe and centre to periphery, which requires further investigation.
The following attempt at a decoding of some of the most obvious as well as
hidden messages encoded in Jewish–Canadian literary expression focuses on
Henry Kreisel's short fiction, in particular on his highly acclaimed story "The
Almost Meeting."

Born in Vienna in 1922, Kreisel, in his later years, has stimulated the intellectual and textual scene in Canada enormously. Although his œuvre is closely
connected with western Canada, its psychological as well as linguistic and artistic
scope reaches far beyond the prairie region, thus blurring geographical borderlines, regional shapes and topographical signifiers.

Kreisel belongs among those refugees who, as Richler recalls in his story,
brought about considerable changes within the Jewish community:

> These men, interned in England as enemy aliens and sent to Canada where they were
> eventually released, were to make a profound impact on us. I think we had conjured
> up a picture of the refugees as penurious *hassidim* with packs on their backs. We were
> eager to be helpful, our gestures were large, but in return we expected more than a
> little gratitude. As it turned out, the refugees, mostly German and Austrian Jews,
> were far more sophisticated and better educated than we were. They had not, like our
> immigrant grandparents, come from *shtetls* in Galicia or Russia. Neither did they
> despise Europe. On the contrary, they found our culture thin, the city provincial, and
> the Jews narrow. This bewildered and stung us. But what cut deepest, I suppose, was
> that the refugees spoke English better than many of us did and, among themselves,
> had the effrontery to talk in the abhorred German language.[9]

Although Kreisel does not stay in Montreal, but moves on to Toronto, he fits the
pattern well. He had already acquired a decent command of the English language

---

6 Michael Greenstein, *Third Solitudes: Tradition and Discontinuity in Jewish–Canadian Literature*
(Montreal: McGraw–Hill Ryerson, 1989): 206.

7 Thomas Marshall, "Introduction" to *A.M. Klein*, ed. Marshall (Critical Views on Canadian
Writers; Scarborough, Ontario: McGraw–Hill Ryerson, 1970): x.

8 "Introduction" to *The Spice Box: An Anthology of Jewish Canadian Writing*, sel. Gerri Sinclair &
Morris Wolfe (Toronto: Lester & Orpen Dennys, 1981): viii.

9 Richler, "The Street," 39–40.

during his brief exile in Leeds, where he had fled the *Anschluss* in July1938. The first impressions on his arrival in England are recollected in an autobiographical narrative entitled "Two Streets (A Phantasy)":

> In the North of England there is a town called Leeds. Not a very beautiful town, not a town that is famous for its buildings, not a town famous for musical events, a town whose chimneys and smoke never in the past have, to my knowledge, inspired a great poet or composer to write about it.
>
> It is a typical industrial town, populated by half a million souls, and dominated by factories and chimneys and smoke.
>
> There arrived in this town one day in July at midnight a young boy of sixteen, who came from Vienna. He was tired from the journey and could hardly keep his eyes open. He only dimly recorded that people had come to fetch him from the station, that these people were his relatives, that he was put into a motorcar and driven through the town. He dimly recorded that he came into a very brightly-lit room, that many people were there and that they all shook hands with him.
>
> "I can speak English," he announced proudly. He then started to speak English and the people in the room smiled, for he spoke with a queer accent and made many mistakes.
>
> And then he went to bed, forgetting that he was a refugee who had fled Hitler, only knowing that he was tired and wanted to sleep. He fell asleep quickly.[10]

In addition – and this is not without irony – he had been exposed to the highly sophisticated ideas of a remarkable Jewish intelligentsia during his eighteen months of internment as an enemy alien in Camp "B" near Fredericton, New Brunswick.[11] Looking back at this time, Kreisel admits that

> the internment camp experience [...] was central to [...] my own development. Suspended in a kind of no man's land [...], I could look back at the horrendous events of the 1930s and see them in some kind of perspective, and [...] I could prepare myself intellectually for the tasks I wanted to undertake in the future [...] I learned and absorbed a lot. It was not until many years later that I finally realized that I had a liberal education in many ways more remarkable than the article available in universities.[12]

However, at the beginning of his future career as an academic, critic and writer, Henry Kreisel cannot escape the fact that he is, linguistically speaking, still exploring a borderland situation. Like so many of his Jewish contemporaries, he has "lost one language to find his voice on the edge of another."[13] This may account for his adopted kinship with Joseph Conrad, whom he discovers as his

---

10 Kreisel, "Two Streets (A Phantasy)," in *Another Country*, ed. Neuman, 93–94.

11 Among Kreisel's fellow prisoners were Max Stern, Peter Oberlander, Ernst Deutsch, Walter Hitschfeld, Gregory Baum, Ernest Reinhold and numerous others, all of whom were later to hold prominent positions in Canada's academic and artistic life.

12 Kreisel, in *Another Country: Writings By and About Henry Kreisel*, ed. Shirley Neuman (Edmonton, Alberta: NeWest, 1985): 23, 24.

13 Greenstein, *Third Solitudes*, 170.

"patron saint."[14] Likewise, in his search for a new poetics, he joins with other Jewish writers and comes across A.M. Klein: namely, his seminal short novel *The Second Scroll* (1951), which in the beginning serves as a model and a guideline.[15] This can hardly surprise, as Klein not only locates home within the physical geography of exile, ie defines place as (mental) space dominated by a sense of loss and absence, thus establishing the psychological paradigm for the Canadian Diaspora, but tries to come to terms with this genuine dilemma. In view of the contrast between religion as an ethnic demarcation line and its potential for abolishing group definitions altogether, he moves in his novel "in these two directions simultaneously, a paradox that [...] reflects his own struggle to maintain a cultural heritage divorced from racial definition."[16] Subsequently, he employs a cosmopolitan perspective which "expands the scope of the Canadian imagination, extending its formerly ingrown concerns to those of Everyman."[17]

In this way, Northrop Frye's paramount "question about Canadian identity – where is here? – becomes compounded by [the] Jewish question – where was there?"[18] Cut off from their European roots and cultural traditions, and neither quite at ease with, nor adequately recognised beyond, the new-found home abroad, the writers of Canada's "third solitude" not only remain caught in marginality, but also suffer from obscurity, or, as Leslie Fiedler puts it: the Jewish writer in Canada inhibits a "No-man's land, the Demilitarized Zone", where he is "invisible from South of the Border as well as from the Other Side of the Atlantic."[19] Marginality, by the way, is employed here not as a social category referring to the writer's class position, but as a marker distinguishing "the way in which verbally inventive authors [like A.M. Klein] need time to acquire a fit audience." In terms of social and economic status, however, "Jewish class positions have generally been higher than other non-Anglo racial groups [in Canada]."[20]

Inasmuch as this obscurity applies to Klein, who in his struggle for acceptance is eventually silenced by the burden of displacement and, even more so, by neglect

---

14 Kreisel, *Another Country*, 22.

15 Cf, for example, Seymour Mayne and Miriam Waddington, who are among those who have honoured Klein with poetic tributes as well as other creative and critical works.

16 Terrence Craig, *Racial Attitudes in English–Canadian Fiction 1905–1980* (Waterloo, Ontario: Wilfrid Laurier UP, 1987): 124.

17 Craig, *Racial Attitudes in English–Canadian Fiction*, 125.

18 Greenstein, *Third Solitudes*, 12. Cf Northrop Frye, "Conclusion to a Literary History of Canada," in Frye, *The Bush Garden: Essays on the Canadian Imagination* (1965; Toronto: Anansi, 1971): 220.

19 Leslie Fiedler, "Some Notes on the Jewish Novel in English," in *Mordecai Richler*, ed. G. David Sheps (Critical Views on Canadian Writers; Scarborough, Ontario: McGraw–Hill Ryerson, 1971): 101; quoted from Greenstein, *Third Solitudes*, 3.

20 Reinhold Kramer, "'I Am Not More than a Thing Which Thinks': Scatology and Representation in the Canadian Novel," doctoral dissertation, University of Manitoba (Winnipeg, 1992): 101.

"in a conservative Canadian mosaic,"[21] some of his successors make deliberate efforts to reinvestigate their ambiguous existence between vanishing traditions and an unsettled metaphoric in order to gain fresh idioms from their marginality. Discovering contemporary critical theory and linguistics they adapt to post-structuralist notions of aesthetics which pave the way for a deconstructive understanding of the Canadian Diaspora. It is here that Henry Kreisel's contribution to Jewish literature in Canada is especially instructive.

As is already evident even in a fugitive piece like "Perhaps," for Kreisel a life in limbo yearns for dialogue:

> When I, one afternoon in May,
> Was led out of the cell
> Where first I lost my freedom,
> I saw a girl standing there.
> She looked up, and as she did,
> My eyes met her's and her's met mine.
> And as she looked at me, she smiled.
> And I smiled back,
> And then was led away and lost her.
> I was a prisoner, a prisoner!
> Perhaps, I thought,
> She does not think of you as such,
> Perhaps she thinks that you are
> What you are: A boy so young,
> A boy who did no harm to anyone.
> Perhaps – Perhaps.

While the invisible fence surrounding the prison camp, which the reader writes into the text, symbolises the invisible paradox inherent in the simultaneity of proximity and distance, it is the uncertainty encoded in this (early) almost meeting which reconciles the seeming opposites. In other words, the notion of "perhaps" operates on the basis of undecidability (a key term in contemporary theory), as it signals openness in either direction. Since indirection is essentially a transient notion, positioned outside of any referential system of clear-cut truths, it creates spaces for speculation, fantasy, imagination, for paralysis as well as hope, thus eventually allowing for both distortion and appeasement of the mind. In this respect, Kreisel's internment poem already anticipates aesthetic principles which emerge more fully in later prose texts such as the two novels *The Rich Man* (1948) and *The Betrayal* (1964), or short fictions such as "Homecoming: A Memory of Europe after the Holocaust" and "The Almost Meeting." Moreover, it is certainly no accident that traces of Kreisel's dialogic imagination, his sense of ambiguity as well as of incompatibility and paradox, come also fully to bear in those writings which contain a unique prairie perspective.

---

21 Greenstein, *Third Solitudes*, 5.

Kreisel's regional affinity is probably most explicitly developed in "The Broken Globe," a short story which was first published in 1965. Here the scientific perception of a young Albertan geophysicist who now lives in a top-floor apartment on the London Embankment where he can sense the feeling of lost space, collides with his father's prairie-based belief in the fundamental flatness of a non-rotating earth. Since there is no chance for a reconciliation of such opposing views it takes a mediator figure, who, upon the request of his scholarly friend, visits the old farmer on his land somewhere southeast of Edmonton. Exposed to the prairie landscape for the first time, the visitor from Europe has to admit to himself that "there was a strange tranquillity" and that "all motion seemed suspended."[22] In this way, the occasion comes at least to an almost meeting of two antagonistic modes of seeing which also symbolises the gap between an "immigrant generation and its assimilated offspring,"[23] or between a metaphysical past and scientific present, scriptured history and visible geography.

It is interesting to register the enormous impact which Kreisel's own prairie experience has had on his literary perception, especially on works which contain a distinctly Jewish perspective. In his classic essay "The Prairie: A State of Mind" (1968), Kreisel eagerly points out that the imagery unconsciously used in "The Broken Globe" corresponds exactly to the imagery employed by other prairie writers before him – for instance, Martha Ostenso, Frederick Philip Grove, or Sinclair Ross. While they depict the prairies as desert and as barren sea, in his novel *The Betrayal* Kreisel moves even further and links prairie topography with the Arctic. The implication here is that the prairie as a topographical entity inflicts itself upon the mind, evoking a particular consciousness which finds its literary expression in a specific set of metaphors. The unlimited space of the prairies "brings to the surface anxieties that have their roots elsewhere and thus sharpens and crystallizes a state of mind."[24] Physical geography is thus also transformed into a landscape of the artistic imagination.

It is certainly no accident that for Kreisel this landscape is characterised by its marginality, its "lonely and forbidden spaces [which] combine to a form of metaphorical modern wasteland, a moral wilderness devoid of signposts and heedless of individual identity."[25]

I think that it is precisely at this point that Kreisel's regional determination can be identified as a major source for his deconstructive understanding of the

22 Henry Kreisel, "The Broken Globe," in Kreisel, *The Almost Meeting: The Collected Short Stories* (Edmonton, Alberta: NeWest, 1981): 139.
23 Michel Greenstein, "Close Encounters: Henry Kreisel's Short Stories," in *Another Country*, ed. Neuman, 341.
24 Henry Kreisel, "The Prairie: A State of Mind," in *Contexts of Canadian Criticism*, ed. Eli Mandel (Patterns of Literary Criticism; 1968; Toronto: U of Toronto P, 1971): 260.
25 Robert Lecker, "States of Mind: Henry Kreisel's Novels," *Canadian Literature* 77 (1978): 83.

Canadian diaspora. This I would like to explore a little further now by looking at his brilliant story "The Almost Meeting" (1981), which is technically by far the most advanced of Kreisel's short stories and which, from a theoretical point of view, can be read as a fictionalised poetic manifesto.

In merely thematic terms, this story describes a near-encounter between a promising young writer of fiction, Alexander Budak, and the highly acclaimed poet and novelist David Lasker, whom Budak admires. Lasker has written an encouraging letter to Budak in praise of his first novel, and the younger man now tries to contact his idol during a visit to Toronto. Through Budak the reader is informed that Lasker

> had given a voice to the immigrants who had come to Canada in the early years of the century. His first book of poems presented a marvellous gallery of the Jewish immigrants, the men and women of [Budak's] parent's generation, but then he had gone beyond his own community and had written some wonderful things about the immigrants who had come to the city after the second world war – the Greeks and Italians and the people from Eastern Europe [...] Often in his writing people of different nationalities came together and almost touched, only to find themselves pulled apart again. [...] when it seemed to Alexander Budak that Lasker might hold out the hope that solitudes could touch and interwine, he had fallen silent, had drawn into himself, and apart from a few enigmatic utterances, had published nothing.26

Kreisel's Lasker is apparently modelled on A.M. Klein, just as Budak resembles Kreisel, who almost met with the older poet, so that this short prose work is not only another literary tribute to Klein, but also invites a biographical reading (which, however, I shall not pursue here).

The almost meeting between Budak and Lasker functions as a frame-story that is disrupted by the plot of Budak's novel, which, doubling the external narrative, centres on a boy in search of his father Lukas. Lukas, an immigrant, "had first gone to Ontario, and then had drifted West [...] to Edmonton", where he married his wife Helena against the will of her family. "The family [had come] from the same border region as Lukas, but they belonged to a different nationality, and they brought with them all the hostility and all the ancient enmities that were endemic in the border region."27 Deeply infected by the religious prejudices of the Old World, Helena's father disowns his daughter and two grandchildren, but they are reconciled when Lukas, who can no longer stand the racial pressure, abandons his wife and children. Torn between the love for his grandfather and the need to fight the absence of his father, the boy begins his search. He follows Lukas's trails, which take him across North America, from Alberta's Edmonton, to Yellowknife, to the east coast and to the west coast, from Canada into California. Budak's protagonist almost comes to the end of his quest on two occasions, "only to have

---

26 Henry Kreisel, "The Almost Meeting," in Kreisel, *The Almost Meeting*, 12.
27 Kreisel, "The Almost Meeting," 13.

[his father] vanish [again] before he [can] meet him face to face."[28] What got lost in the Old World cannot quite yet be redeemed in the New World.

At this point, Kreisel returns to the external narrative by reference to Lasker's letter, which contains an inscrutable comment on both the boy's quest for his father and Budak's vain attempt at a personal encounter with his own poet–father:

> The letter, written in that strange hand-writing that looked like the intricate web spun by a long-legged spider, was brief.
> "I salute you," Lasker had written. "How sad. How sad. How we torture each other. I sense a bitterness in your hero because he cannot find his father. Let him not despair. An almost meeting is often more important than the meeting. The quest is all."[29]

Upon his subsequent request to meet Lasker, Budak receives another letter which consists only of a one-word sentence, the adverb "perhaps"; another uncertainty.

What makes "The Almost Meeting" such fascinating reading is the poetic device underlying the narrative. Kreisel's obsession with obscure forms of dialogue is entirely based on textuality, ie on textual intercourse. Budak and Lasker never get to see each other, yet they meet through and in their writing. In Lasker's case, it is the word which moves continually into the foreground, while the poet becomes more and more detached from it, until he is finally invisible behind his work. This seeming paradox of, at the same time, writing oneself out of bodily and into textual existence makes it particularly evident how strongly Kreisel relies on intertextuality as a constructive principle for his story.

If intertextuality is the prime artistic device employed in "The Almost Meeting," the argument would also need to be taken beyond the immediate text, including the reader as well. And indeed, Kreisel – and this recalls the reader's active participation in his short prison-camp poem – makes a special effort to invite the reader to become a writer. In this sense, Kreisel is also telling a story about the invention of the subject as a writer, a notion which manifests itself internally in the story of Budak as well as externally in the reading-process. The reader is challenged to create a whole text out of the sparse information provided by Kreisel's brief plot-summary of Budak's novel. If the reader masters this challenge, this is possible because of imaginative interplay between the actual narrative and the pretexts surrounding it. Since the number of pretexts, however, is infinite, since there is no ultimate authorised version of story, "every manifestation of text is undercut by its inherent equivocation as the 'trace' of a previous text which we never track down."[30] Thus, even the meeting of texts is reduced to an almost meeting, or, to use different terminology, Kreisel's short story offers

---

28 Kreisel, "The Almost Meeting," 17.
29 Kreisel, "The Almost Meeting," 18.
30 Stephen Scobie, "On the Edge of Language," in *Another Country*, ed. Neuman, 346.

itself as an ongoing narrative, meandering between constant reinventions. Since "The Almost Meeting" is presented in a highly realistic mode, it can additionally be read as an almost encounter of conventional mimetic writing and postmodern narrative.

The intertextual practice encoded in the formal arrangement of the work corresponds thematically to Budak's fictionalised quest for a father-figure who can bridge the gap between the irritations of exile and those meaningful traditions that got lost during the transatlantic voyage. Kreisel's answer to this holds true for all exiled intermediaries. He concludes his story with Lasker's final words:

> "It was impossible for me to see you, [...]. You wanted to ask me things. I have no answers. But you are in my heart. Let me be in your heart also. We had an almost meeting. Perhaps that is not much. And yet it is something. Remember me."[31]

A more sophisticated reading would suggest that Kreisel tries to subvert the appeal of established (literary) authorities. In the context of the Canadian diaspora, which by definition is a situation void of definite referents, the emphasis is on the writer's struggle for an idiom that would suit his liminal position, his borderland position, between two incompatible worlds. Moreover, an intertextual approach towards Kreisel's narrative would disclose that this subversion of authority goes hand in hand with a deconstructive understanding of marginality, the result of which is a reversed positioning of centre and periphery. By decentering ethnic hierarchies, the Jew as an archetypal figure of displacement would then no longer be an inhabitant of the periphery, but would become the central paradigm for an immigrant society that is composed of numerous minorities.

WORKS CITED

CRAIG, Terrence. *Racial Attitudes in English-Canadian Fiction 1905–1980* (Waterloo, Ontario: Wilfrid Laurier UP, 1987).

FIEDLER, Leslie. "Some Notes on the Jewish Novel in English," in *Mordecai Richler*, ed. G. David Sheps (Critical Views on Canadian Writers; Scarborough, Ontario: McGraw–Hill Ryerson, 1971).

FRYE, Northrop. "Conclusion to a Literary History of Canada," in Frye, *The Bush Garden: Essays on the Canadian Imagination* (1965; Toronto: Anansi, 1971): 213–51.

GREENSTEIN, Michael. "Close Encounters: Henry Kreisel's Short Stories," in *Another Country*, ed. NEUMAN, 338–42.

——. *Third Solitudes: Tradition and Discontinuity in Jewish–Canadian Literature* (Montreal: McGill–Queen's UP, 1989).

KRAMER, Reinhold. "'I Am Not More than a Thing Which Thinks': Scatology and Represent-ation in the Canadian Novel," doctoral dissertation, University of Manitoba (Winnipeg, 1992).

KREISEL, Henry. "The Almost Meeting," in Kreisel, *The Almost Meeting*, 11–21.

---

[31] Kreisel, "The Almost Meeting," 21.

——. *The Almost Meeting: The Collected Short Stories* (Edmonton, Alberta: NeWest, 1981).

——. "The Broken Globe," in Kreisel, *The Almost Meeting*, 135–47.

——. "Perhaps," *Internment Notebooks*, n.p., n.d.

——. "The Prairie: A State of Mind," in *Contexts of Canadian Criticism*, ed. Eli Mandel (Patterns of Literary Criticism, 1968; Toronto: U of Toronto P, 1971): 254–66.

——."Two Streets (A Phantasy)," in *Another Country*, ed. NEUMAN, 93–94.

LECKER, Robert. "States of Mind: Henry Kreisel's Novels," *Canadian Literature* 77 (1978): 82–93.

MANDEL, Eli. "The Road to Regina," undated MS no. 18, box 40, folder 11 (Winnipeg, Manitoba: Library Archives of the University of Manitoba).

MARSHALL, Thomas. "Introduction" to *A.M. Klein*, ed. Marshall (Critical Views on Canadian Writers; Scarborough, Ontario: McGraw–Hill Ryerson, 1970): vi–xxv.

NEUMAN, Shirley, ed. *Another Country: Writings By and About Henry Kreisel* (Edmonton, Alberta: NeWest, 1985).

RICHLER, Mordecai. "The Street," in *Other Solitudes. Canadian Multicultural Fictions*, ed. Linda Hutcheon & Marion Richmond (Toronto: U of Toronto P, 1990): 33–48.

SCOBIE, Stephen. "On the Edge of Language," in *Another Country*, ed. NEUMAN, 345–47.

SINCLAIR, Gerri & Morris WOLFE, sel. *The Spice Box: An Anthology of Jewish Canadian Writing* (Toronto: Lester & Orpen Dennys, 1981).

WADDINGTON, Miriam. "Outsider: Growing Up in Canada," in Waddington, *Apartment Seven: Essays Selected and New* (Toronto: Oxford UP, 1989): 36–44.

WISEMAN, Adele. "A Brief Anatomy of an Honest Attempt at a Pithy Statement about the Impact of the Manitoba Environment on My Development as an Artist," *Mosaic* 3.3 (1970): 98–106.

❦

Homelands and Habitations
in the Fiction of Bharati Mukherjee

SUSAN SPEAREY

I N A REVIEW OF THE FILM *BRAZIL*, Salman Rushdie succinctly sets out the conditions which attend the migrant experience. He writes:

> The effect of mass migrations has been the creation of radically new types of human being: people who root themselves in ideas rather than places, in memories as much as in material things; people who have been obliged to define themselves – because they are so defined by others – by their otherness; people in whose deepest selves strange fusions occur, unprecedented unions between what they were and where they find themselves. The migrant suspects reality: having experienced several ways of being, he understands their illusory nature.[1]

Rushdie's summary provides an apt introduction to the fiction of Bharati Mukherjee, a writer who, over the years, has evocatively depicted the migrant experience at its most celebratory and – more often – its most sordid extremes. Rushdie's observations raise several pertinent questions which furnish logical avenues for investigation of Mukherjee's writing. First, his proposal that the migrant is more deeply rooted in ideas than in places suggests that it is an alteration in consciousness rather than in physical situation that characterises the migrant condition. Following this line of reasoning, migrancy of necessity entails much more than a straddling of two or more cultures, or a transition from one location to another; what it involves fundamentally is a reshaping of worlds and world views. How does Mukherjee choose to explore such transformations, and what narrative strategies does she adopt to render them in writing? A second and related concern is that of the role of memory. Is identity more a function of memory and its inevitable distortions for the migrant, whose history is in all likelihood not evidenced in and by his or her immediate surroundings? How does memory influence the role that history plays in the migrant's world? And how, in turn, do memory and history influence the migrant's relationship to his or her homelands, both native and adopted? Conventional considerations of national or cultural affinities can reductively divide migrants into categories of "backward-looking" emigrants who constantly orient themselves in relation to their ancestral lands or "forward-looking" immigrants for whom the adopted habitation provides

---

[1] Salman Rushdie, "The Location of Brazil," in *Imaginary Homelands* (London: Granta, 1991): 124–25.

a more immediate focus. "Topocentricism" is the term attributed by Leon Surette to such geographical orientations. Surette contrasts Zionist claims on Palestine, which are based on historical lineage, to Canadian topocentricism, in which historical considerations are less pronounced. He notes that "instead of holding that the soil of England, France, Scotland, Germany, Italy or wherever is sanctified ground to which we are forever mystically linked, we [Canadians] argue that *our* spiritual constitution is to some degree formulated by the soil and climate of our immediate environment."[2] How does Mukherjee orient the migrants about whom she writes, and how do their memories and histories inform the worlds they inhabit?

Rushdie's third point engages directly with the issues and problems of difference and community. Mukherjee has written at length about her own experiences on this count. A constant lament during her fourteen-year residence in Canada – a country she describes as one which "proudly boasts of its opposition to the whole concept of cultural assimilation"[3] – was her inability to find acceptance in any community, social or literary. Refusing to conform to the "aggressively nationalistic" stance of many Canadian writers, or to to be converted into a token figure advocating "Brown Power," Mukherjee found what she describes as her painful visibility as a citizen matched by an equally painful invisibility in the Canadian literary world.[4] In her 1974 book, *Days and Nights in Calcutta*, she outlines the resulting situation as follows:

> Reviewers claim that my material deals with Indians usually in India, and because my publisher is American, my work is of no interest to Canadian writers and readers. In Canada I am the wife of a well-known Canadian writer who "also writes", though people often assume it is in Bengali [...]
>
> And so I am a late-blooming colonial who writes in a borrowed language (English), lives permanently in an alien country (Canada) and publishes in and is read, when read at all, in another alien country, the United States.[5]

A consideration of difference and community might at first be seen to point ominously towards Mukherjee's unwilling election of the former term at the expense of the latter, as the only possible angle from which to approach the subject of migrancy. She claims to have seen in V.S. Naipaul a literary model, whose lead she chose to follow in adopting a "mordant self-protective irony" as the means of best addressing her own situation and those of her various characters, and as a way of exploring what she terms "state-of-the-art expatriation" (*D* 2).

---

2 Leon Surette, "Creating the Canadian Canon," in *Canadian Canons: Essays in Literary Value*, ed. Robert Lecker (Toronto: U of Toronto P, 1991): 23.

3 Bharati Mukherjee, *Darkness* (Markham, Ontario: Penguin, 1985): 3. All subsequent references to this book will be indicated in the body of the text by the initial *D*.

4 Bharati Mukherjee, *Days and Nights in Calcutta* (co-authored by Clark Blaise; Garden City NY: Doubleday, 1977): 169–70.

5 Mukherjee, *Days and Nights in Calcutta*.

This latter term was enlisted to describe her specific circumstances because she, like her characters, retains "sentimental attachments to a distant homeland but no real desire for permanent return" (*D* 2). Her 1980 emigration to the USA, according to her own accounts, signalled a turning-point in her life and career, whereby she was able to overcome this feeling of exclusion and alienation and instead to embrace the immigrant condition, which she describes as "singing in the seams even of the dominant culture" (*D* 3). Mukherjee's statement suggests a liberation deriving both from a sense of identification with the American immigrant community and from the accompanying shift in her mode of apprehending the world and her place within it. Yet it would be an over-simplification to advance the argument that her treatment of the migrant condition in its many manifestations can be divided along the line of the Canadian experience in which difference prevails, and the American years in which a sense of community is discovered and developed. Her writings, both fictional and non-fictional, certainly suggest that a much more complex set of relations obtains in the migrant's experience. Difference and community, moreover, are terms, like habitations and homelands, which are neither oppositional nor mutually exclusive, and which are open to a proliferation of interpretations and appropriations. "Difference" can be cause for celebration, or for segregation, can be invoked as evidence of diversity, of isolation, or of "authenticity." Similarly, "community" can be read as a source of solidarity, as a connection, or a network of affiliations, as a link with the past, as the root of communalism, as ghetto, as constraint. How are these concepts formulated and negotiated by Mukherjee and her characters? How is otherness perceived, and, if at all, mobilised as a technique of survival?

The fourth point which Rushdie raises is crucial to the thesis he is advancing: the migrant is a "radically new type of human being" precisely because of the breaks with the past and with tradition which accompany any change in situation. He or she is a hybrid, a product of those "strange fusions" of past history and present location, fusions which may or may not be acknowledged or understood. How are these breaches of tradition accounted for and accommodated, by the migrant, by the ancestral culture, and by the adopted society? And, in the light of the fact that every society demands a certain degree of conformity, to what extent are these transformations allowed to be played out? These questions lead nicely to Rushdie's final point – that notions of reality, which often depend on predict-ability and conformity to an established world-view, are regarded with scepticism by the migrant. How does Mukherjee treat such ontological plurality and flexibility, both as formal and as thematic considerations?

≈ ❀ ≈

The American "melting-pot " theory furnishes an interesting case study of the dynamics of migration, one that endeavours dialectically to accommodate notions of both continuity and breach of tradition.[6] It holds that America's immigrants, old and new, perpetually combine the best of all world cultures to produce what amounts to a Super-Race. Hybridity and innovation are posited as the constituent features of its ongoing tradition and as the very foundation of national strength. Each newcomer, in theory, wields the power partially to re-invent the nation in which he or she arrives. Yet critics of American culture would be quick to point out that the American Dream encourages very specific behaviours and values, and permits innovation only insofar as it occurs in accordance with the rules governing dominant ideologies. This latter perspective admits much less power to newly arrived Americans in determining the shape and texture of a national ethos.

In "Orbiting," a story from the 1988 collection entitled *The Middleman*, Mukherjee examines the mutual play of people and the places they inhabit as the myth of the melting-pot theory is explored and teased out. Michel de Certeau's distinction between *place* and *space* provides a useful means of approaching the revisions which are charted as the story unfolds. According to de Certeau, a *place* "delimits a field" and "is ruled by [...] an orderly contiguity of elements in the location it defines." A *space*, on the other hand, is "not the substance of a place but the product of its transformation [...] Space occurs [...]":

> "In short, [says de Certeau], space is a *practised place*. The street defined by urban planning is transformed into a space by walkers; and, in the same way, an act of reading is a space produced by a written text ('a place constituted by a system of signs')."[7]

De Certeau's formulation opens to question the implications of America's claims as a nation of immigrants to foster assimilation. Does America the *place* transform its "huddled masses yearning to breathe free" into identifiable American citizens? Or do the *spatial* practices of these same newcomers continually redefine what it is to be American? Or both?

The story is set in New Jersey, which each character can in some sense claim to call home, while at the same time being able to trace roots with ease back to other cultures and continents. It is peopled by Italian–Americans of various generations and degrees of assimilation, an El Salvadorean neighbour, a "rebellious" son of Amish parents, and a refugee from Kabul, most of whom are in the process of celebrating that all-American tradition of Thanksgiving. Each has purposefully

---

6 Again, I am indebted to Leon Surette's essay "Creating the Canadian Canon," in which tradition is discusssed in terms of models of continuity and breach.

7 Michel de Certeau, *The Practice of Everyday Life*, tr. Steven F. Rendall (Berkeley: U of California P, 1984): 117ff., cited in Meaghan Morris, "At Henry Parkes Motel," in *Cultural Studies* 1.2 (January 1988): 37.

negotiated the extent to which he or she has chosen to adhere to or to reject the traditions of the ancestral land; the relation of each to America has been formulated to a much lesser degree. A stark contrast is set up between the present and former lovers of Rindy deMarco, the first-person narrator, in which can be found the first indication of the unsettling of fixed notions of place and reality. Both male lovers are engaged in the "orbiting" of the story's title, although for one the action is centrifugal and for the other centripetal. Vic Riccio, Rindy's former lover, is an Italian–American who, in her own words, has "tak[en] off for outer space" in his efforts to transcend the mundane existence of mainstream American life. New Jersey for him is seen as regulated, prescriptive and highly claustrophobic, and he seeks release first in a sampling of alternative life-styles and later in literal movement away from the centre. It is precisely this world into which her current lover, Ro, a Kabuli refugee, hopes eventually to touch down, having spent the better part of his recent life in transit from one international airport to another in search of asylum. New Jersey for him may also be seen as regulated and normalising, but the stability and security afforded by an engineering qualification from New Jersey Institute of Technology is precisely the condition he seeks to attain.

Although both men are on some level rooted in ideas, and their movements governed by the ease with which these can be expressed and practised, Vic appears ultimately to view place as overdetermining, its fixed form as something to be escaped by perpetual movement and uprooting. Ro is more aware of the potential to transform place into space, through political activism, through resistance to oppression, through gestures such as the conversion of airport lounges into prayer rooms. Although he is and has been literally confined by place, having hidden in an underground tunnel for four months, then having been incarcerated, and currently having to hide in the back room of Mumtaz's Restaurant with the other "illegals," his world is shaped by his Islamic principles and his political commitment, and with these ideas he endeavours to reshape the places in which he finds himself. He belongs simultaneously to the Afghanistan of his father's garden estate and of his student protest groups; to the life of Mumtaz's Restaurant and of the detention centre of "Little Kabul;" and to Rindy's Clifton; Vic, on the other hand, tenaciously pursues his desire to be grounded nowhere, living, as a result, in a state of "permanent isolation."[8]

The depiction of both men through Rindy's narrative voice is revealing; despite the interruptions in her account when she contemplates with horror the ways in which her father, Brent, Franny and Ro must be constructing the encounter, she does not self-consciously acknowledge the constructedness of her own version. She chooses to interpret the differences between the two men in terms of Vic's self-

---

8 Bharati Mukherjee, *The Middleman* (London: Virago, 1989): 57. All subsequent references to this book are indicated in the text by the initial *M*.

sufficiency and Ro's dependency, a view which enhances her own role, places her at centre stage, and echoes the posture adopted by America towards its immigrants. The recounting of her own family story – her father's "rescuing" of her mother from the sweatshop – gives some indication of the tensions at play between "established" Americans and arriving immigrants. Rindy explains,

> Mom's a Calabrian and she was born and raised there. Dad's very American, so Italy's a safe source of pride for him. I once figured it out: *his* father, Arturo deMarco, was a fifteen-week-old fetus when his mother planted her feet on Ellis Island. Dad, a proud son of North Italy had one big adventure in his life, besides fighting in the Pacific, and that was marrying a Calabrian peasant. He made it sound as though Mom was a Korean or something, and their marriage was a kind of taming of the West, and that everything about her could be explained as a cultural deficiency. (*M* 58–59)

Rindy's comments demonstrate not only that regional chauvinism survives the transatlantic crossing, even after two generations, but also that her father is grounded as much in American as in North Italian culture, which leads to an ambivalent orientation towards the transcultural encounter. On the one hand, his adoption of a superior – if gracious – attitude to newly-arrived immigrants conforms to a long-standing tradition through which established Americans welcome newcomers, forgive them their cultural "inadequacies," and help them to find their feet. On the other hand, he clings to Italian traditions and societies while resisting changes brought about by other migrant communities. He feels, for example, that "an Italian–American man should be able to live sixty-five years never having heard the word [*halal*]" (*M* 69). These ambivalences are echoed in Rindy's own attitudes; although she allows Ro a cosmopolitanism which she sees her family as lacking utterly, and cringes with embarrassment at each display of ignorance or misinformed judgement on their part, she detects in Ro's posture, his choice of clothing, and his Kabuli prep-school manners an incapacity which is within her power to rectify. What she views as Ro's dependency is for her something of a triumph, in that it enables her to perpetuate her family tradition by encouraging him to abandon his own. Just as her father had "saved" her mother from the sweatshop, so she too has the capacity to put the world to rights. In her own words,

> I realize all in a rush how much I love this man with his blemished, tortured body. I will give him citizenship if he asks. Vic was beautiful, but Vic was self-sufficient. Ro's my chance to heal the world.
> I shall teach him how to talk like an American, how to dress like Brent but better, how to fill up a room as Dad does instead of melting and blending but sticking out in the Afghan way. In spite of the funny way he holds himself and the funny way he moves his head from side to side when he wants to say yes, Ro is Clint Eastwood, scarred hero and survivor. (*M* 74–75)

Significantly, although Rindy equates Ro's difference with inadequacy, on the grounds of his alien aspect within American culture, the archetypal "scarred hero" she evokes to describe him is an all-American Hollywood idol. She assumes responsibility for the reshaping of Ro's character, basing her authority on the power she wields to grant or withhold citizenship. Rindy enumerates clearly the ways in which she feels her lover falls short of the American ideal, allowing for "improvements" of her own making. Her focus on Ro's "tortured, blemished" body as opposed to Vic's "beauty," however, serves two purposes. Not only does it sustain this perceived relationship in which she nurses him to social health, but also – insofar as each scar tells a story – it also provides him with a history which he literally embodies.

Ro's recitation of his history from beneath the makeshift dining-room table leads Rindy to observe: "Dad looks sick. The meaning of Thanksgiving should not be so explicit" (*M* 73). In spite of her stance as perpetrator of cultural assimilation, Ro's presence transforms the significance and rituals of the deMarco's Thanksgiving celebrations. Rindy recalls the story of Grandma deMarco preparing two Thanksgiving meals, one with the full American fare, the other with Grandpa's favourite kinds of pasta. The Italian component of the ritual is eventually dropped, but the extended family continues to sit down to a fresh turkey dinner every Thanksgiving. This year, the dinner is pot-luck and the turkey is frozen, but, more notably, it is carved by Ro, with an Afghan dagger which has seen him through many a clandestine adventure in his efforts to escape Kabul, and is currently used to gut chickens in Mumtaz's back room. Rindy is not unaware of the ways in which he has reshaped her America. Her membership in Amnesty International, which she had formerly viewed as merely a legacy of her relationship with Vic, in keeping with his interests in feminism, macrobiotics and theories of yin and yang, takes on new meaning in the light of Ro's scars and stories of torture. And when Ro mentions his efforts to dissuade his cousin Abdul from embarking on a hunger strike, Rindy exclaims:

> "A hunger strike! God!" When I am with Ro I feel I am looking at America through the wrong end of a telescope. He makes it sound like a police state, with sudden raids, papers, detention centres, deportations, and torture and death waiting in the wings. (*M* 66)

Again, place is revealed not as static and overdetermining, but as potentially transformable, either through social practices such as hunger strike or negotiation with authority, or through the adoption of a different code for the interpretation of "reality." The America Mukherjee evokes is not without its paradoxes and contradictions, but is nonetheless a nation in which rituals and traditions can be transformed or can accrue new meanings through the spatial practices of its immigrants, past and present.

The transmutation of place, both through social practices and through the adoption of alternative visions of "reality," has long been a focus of Mukherjee's fiction, although it has been approached from a variety of angles. In an earlier story from the *Darkness* collection, entitled "The World According to Hsu," she probes with subtlety the nature of such ontological and epistemological indeterminacy. The story in this instance is set on an island off the coast of Africa, which unexpectedly proves to be in the throes of revolution. It is recounted by a third-person narrator whose ironic tone and patterning of motifs also gesture towards the existence of multiple and mutable realities. For example, political upheavals described as "especially ferocious" are attributed to "*melancholy* students and *ungenerous* bureaucrats"; the discrepancy in the import of the descriptive adjectives alerts the reader to the dangers of reading the narrative as mimetically realistic – at least two possible interpretations are suggested by the narrator's comment (*D* 37, emphases added). We are also told that "coups and curfews visited with *seasonal regularity*," and that the protagonists "had wanted an *old-fashioned* vacation on the shores of a *new* ocean" (*D* 37; 38, emphases added). The curious combination of social and political practices with natural processes prefigures the tropes upon which the story is built, while at the same time, particularly in the second example, signalling the incongruity of the time-scales which frame the metaphor. Further, the island enjoys an enduring reputation among travel-agents for "langour and spices," is virtually unknown to the world press, and is obviously perceived in very different terms by the various political and ethnic communities that reside there (*D* 37).

In addition to the variety of possibilities contained in language are the distinctive visions which are a function of perspective. The subjective nature of reality is perhaps most clearly illustrated by the divergent world-views of the story's protagonists. Ratna Clayton, a Calcutta-born freelance journalist living in Montreal, sees her life, which up until recently has been "manageably capricious," as bearing testimony to the unpredictable and protean nature of reality (*D* 37). Graeme, her English–Canadian husband, views the world from a vantage-point she cannot share. His perceptions of reality are underpinned by a conviction in the existence of order, stability and permanence. He sees the chaotic beauty of the island as something to be tamed, from which "definitive order" can be "extracted," and it is with this end in mind that he carefully photographs its wildlife, its quotidian curiosities, all apparent evidence of its current political upheaval, later to organise his observations into a comprehensive slide presentation framed by an explanatory commentary for the benefit of his friends and colleagues (*D* 38). This manner of cataloguing and description conforms to the tradition of the "anti-conquest" practices of eighteenth-century Linnaean scientists, as outlined by Mary Louise Pratt in *Imperial Eyes*. According to Pratt,

> [...] the eighteenth-century systematizing of nature [was] a European knowledge-building project that created a new kind of Eurocentred planetary consciousness.

> Blanketing the surface of the globe, it specified plants and animals in visual terms as discrete entities, subsuming and reassembling them in a finite, totalizing order of European making.[9]

As a psychologist, Graeme's mandate encompasses both natural history and social history, and the twentieth-century knowledge-building project is Western rather than specifically European; these differences aside, the project remains the same. Graeme's photographs and commentary answer directly to the drawings, written descriptions, and collected samples of the Linnaean scientists, through which classification and clarification of a given and enduring world is ostensibly achieved. The Coal Sack and the Southern Cross, constellations which have fascinated humanity since the beginning of time, are perhaps exemplary of this enduring order, and for Graeme provide the principal appeal of the island to which he and Ratna choose to travel. Pratt emphasises the visual nature of the anti-conquest narrative to which Graeme's perceptions conform, which tacitly posits surface appearance as the outward manifestation of deep structures and essential properties. Although reality in his eyes is neither multifaceted nor subjective, but rather an *a priori* condition, it is something to be experienced and understood in varying degrees. Ratna notes that for her husband, romance "[is] not the opposite of reality; it [is] more a sharpening of line and color, possible only in the labs or on a carefully researched, fully cooperative, tropical island" (*D* 40). The heightened experience afforded by the holiday, in other words, provides for Graeme an intensification of a given reality, rather than an alternative to it or variation on it.

Ratna is less concerned with, or confident in, the existence of enduring order. For her, the fascination of the island lies precisely in its juxtaposition of seemingly random or incompatible elements, and in the state of upheaval in which she finds it, which further confirms her world-view. In contrast to Graeme's linking of surfaces with deep structure, Ratna is acutely aware of their deceptive nature. Her own unmistakably Indian appearance is a case in point; beneath it, her "Europeanness lay submerged like an ancient city waiting to be revealed by shallow-water archeology" (*D* 44). In the same vein, the story's narrator observes, "continents slide, no surface is permanent" (*D* 37–38). The theory of plate tectonics, which Graeme introduces at the dinner table as a "respectably scientific" topic of conversation, for Ratna serves as an apt analogy for the mutability of surfaces that constitute the migrant's world, all of which subtly shift, slide, create friction, collide or drift apart. She marvels at the "human deposits" of various eras in the island's history – the "Peruvian-looking Africans" who are virtually Parisian in manner (and beside whom she suspects Montrealers would appear "nothing but wonderstruck Americans, accidental French-speakers with Quebec fleurs-de-lis

---

[9] Mary Louise Pratt, *Imperial Eyes: Travel Writing and Transculturation* (London & New York: Routledge, 1992): 38.

sewn on their bulging hip pockets"); the king's band, which has waited for centuries for the monarchical régime to resume; the counter-revolutionary soldiers and sentinels who serve as a reminder of Africa's proximity; the Lutheran churches which predominate as a result of the endeavours of nineteenth-century Swedish missionaries; the looted Indian shops which speak both of past migrations and present hostilities; the road which is described as an "untidy gash, an aid-project miscalculation" which suggests the intervention of "First World" agencies (*D* 46; 49). These deposits speak neither of a cumulative and linear progression of development within a singular place, nor of its isolated or auto-nomous history. Rather, they provide evidence of the interaction of a multitude of forces, of alterations both spatial and temporal, and of the continual combination and confrontation of seemingly incongruous elements. Among such disjointed and disjunctive faces of the island, and despite the incoherence, divisions and dis-ruptions they indicate or anticipate, Ratna feels safer than she could in a Toronto subway, and more at home than she will ever feel again. For her, "home" is not necessarily determined by a the presence of community, but by her recognition of an exemplary world in transition which coincides with and confirms her own sense of reality.

As Graeme reads aloud from his issue of *Scientific American* an article by Kenneth Hsu, both his own and Ratna's perceptions are affirmed. He is fascinated by the time-scale of continental drift, by the methods of its calculation, and by the advancement of knowledge which has facilitated an understanding of the pro-cesses involved. For Ratna it is the *effects of the process* which are of greater and more immediate interest. Although he fails utterly to see the relevance of the geo-logical analogy to their present circumstances, the poignancy is not lost on Ratna:

> "Did you know, according to ... [Hsu] ... that six million years ago the Mediterranean basin was a desert? And it took the Atlantic a million years to break through and fill it again? Gibraltar for a million years was the most spectacular waterfall the world will ever see. The old sea was called Tethys and it connected the Atlantic with the Indian Ocean."
> At the table to her right a German communications expert was teaching an English folk song to three Ismaili-Indian children.
> "Row, row, row your boat," the children shouted before collapsing in giggles.
> "In the last Ice Age the Black Sea was a freshwater lake. They have fossil crustaceans to prove it."
> The children's father, a small handsome man, scraped his chair back and said, "Watch me. Here is Bob Hope playing golf." The children giggled again. How, Ratna wondered, how in the world had they seen or heard of Bob Hope? Or golf? Or had they? Or did it matter? It struck her as unspeakably heroic, gallant.
> Graeme asked her if she was crying. (*D* 52)

In the dining room of the Hotel Papillon, cordoned off by the curfew and only yards away from the exchange of sniper bullets, seated amongst a "collection of

Indians and Europeans babbling in English and remembered dialects," Ratna revels in the "strange fusions of self" and the shifting of surfaces which have enabled her to gain a fleeting understanding of the word "home" (*D* 56).

In the third story I want to look at, Mukherjee's narrative technique enacts similar shifts, collisions, unexpected juxtapositions and slippages. "The Management of Grief," which is the final story in the *Middleman* collection, deals with the effects of the 1985 bombing of an Air India jet, bound from Toronto to Bombay, on the surviving relatives of the flight's victims. Here Mukherjee examines with painstaking care and sympathy the extreme difficulties of straddling two heterogeneous and constantly changing cultures in the face of unforeseen and catastrophic circumstances. The narrative consists of a series of accounts relating to the aftermath of the terrorist attack as experienced by Shaila Bhave, who has lost her husband and two young sons in the tragedy. Its basic structure is chronological if open-ended, moving from the moment that Shaila learns of the plane's disappearance to the point at which she chooses a path to follow after her return to Toronto. The shifts in physical location correspond roughly with the temporal changes charted in the story, following a course from the interior of the Bhave's Toronto home to Ireland, where the bodies of the deceased are identified and claimed, on to an odyssey around India, and back to Toronto, ending – or beginning again – in a park in the city's centre. Stylistically, the narrative moves between interior monologue and dialogue, and between observation of minute details in the immediate physical surroundings to reflective assessment of the situation, to projection into less tangible worlds. On another level, the story charts Shaila's confrontation and negotiation with friends, neighbours, fellow relatives of the flight's victims, bureaucrats, family and larger social groupings, as she endeavours to explore and rethink notions of community and to define a system of beliefs which can provide her with a sense of purpose.

Noting that the family members surviving the victims of the attack have come to be known as the "relatives," Shaila assesses: "we've been melted down and cast as a new tribe" (*M* 191). This process is evidenced repeatedly in the story, as newfound affinities are forged, and older foundations of common ground are either called into question or broken down completely. The trope varies only slightly from that of plate tectonics, sustaining the notion of the constant reconfiguration of seemingly permanent forms. The Indo-Canada Society, to which the Bhaves belong, at first appears to provide an integral community, a point of contact for those Indian families who have "made it big in Toronto," but the diversity within the community and the looseness of the ties which hold its members together become readily apparent in the aftermath of the bombing (*M* 181). The onset in Canada of the communalism and political contention from which many of the society's members had sought release in emigration precipitates just such a realignment of affiliations. Shaila admits, "as much as I try not to, I stiffen now at the sight of beards and turbans. I remember a time when we all trusted each other in this new country, it was only the new country we worried about" (M 193). And yet, she partially reasserts this former sense of community when Judith Templeton takes her to the apartment of an elderly Sikh couple who have also lost their sons in the bombing. In spite of her involuntary hostility towards Sikhs, and her profound difference in background, language, religion and life-style from the Punjabi couple, Shaila claims cultural affinities with them. Her description of the locale in which their apartment building is situated speaks strongly of difference, even foreignness, especially when details about her own home and neighbourhood are recalled, and she notes that "inside the building, even I wince a bit from the ferocity of onion fumes" (M 193). Yet, once inside the apartment, she hears "the most familiar sound of an Indian home, tap water hitting and filling a teapot," and she becomes noticeably more receptive to their laments, and less comfortable about her "alliance" with the government agencies represented by Judith (M 193). Although Shaila struggles to convey to the couple the reasoning behind the government's interest in them, she understands their resistance to the help offered. When Judith later expresses her exasperation, Shaila's mental response indicates an assertion of common ground with the Punjabis: "I want to say, *In our culture, it is a parent's duty to hope*" (M 195; emphasis added).

New divisions and connections are also evidenced within the Hindu community, both in India and in Canada. Some of these are a function of generation, but all ultimately boil down to differences in degrees of conformity to tradition, and, in the case of the migrant, in the ways in which cultural hybridity has variously manifested itself. Kusum's elder daughter Pam is ostracised for "dat[ing] Canadian boys, and hang[ing] out in the mall, shopping for tight sweaters" – pursuits presumably ill befitting a young Hindu woman, regardless of her cross-cultural upbringing. (M 181). Shaila is acutely aware of the ways in which she herself has been altered by emigration, particularly in the light of her more assertive and less demure behaviour, and is caught between regret, on the one hand, at never having challenged tradition by calling her husband by his first name or expressing her feelings for him, and remorse, on the other, at dealing with widowhood in a manner out of keeping with Hindu custom. When Judith commends her for her exemplary grief-management, Shaila replies:

> "By the standards of the people you call hysterical, I am behaving very oddly and very badly, Miss Templeton." I want to say to her, *I wish I could scream, starve, walk into Lake Ontario, jump from a bridge*. "They would not see me as a model. I do not see myself as a model." (M 183)

Although she acknowledges these ambivalences, the location of her allegiances and obligations remains elusive. She shares with Kusum the experience of bereavement, but cannot follow her friend's example of committing her future to seeking "inner peace" in an ashram, which to Shaila would constitute a form of escapism. Nor does her return to India provide for her a consolidated sense of community; the world from which she hails is divided not only by communalism and feuding between religious groups, but also, within the Hindu community, by such divergent modes of knowledge as rationalism and the extremism of religious orthodoxy. Oversimplifying divisons between new-world heterogeneity and old-world homogeneity are averted by Shaila's account of her own family history, which also leaves her adrift and in doubt as to where her sense of community and commitment lies:

> My grandmother, the spoiled daughter of a rich *zamindar*, shaved her head with rusty razor blades when she was widowed at sixteen. My grandfather died of childhood diabetes when he was nineteen, and she saw herself as the harbinger of bad luck. My mother grew up without parents, raised indifferently by an uncle, while her true mother slept in a hut behind the main estate house and took her food with the servants. She grew up a rationalist. My parents abhor mindless mortification.
>   The *zamindar's* daughter kept stubborn faith in Vedic rituals; my parents rebelled. I am trapped between two modes of knowledge. At thirty-six, I am too old to start over and too young to give up. Like my husband's spirit, I flutter between worlds. (*M* 189)

Despite the particulariy of her circumstances, this sense of being trapped between modes of knowledge is not unique to Shaila. The widowers similarly find themselves caught between the desire to grieve and honour the memory of the dead and the call of custom extolled by fathers and elder brothers who exert pressure upon them to remarry and to return to Canada with new families. Dr Ranganathan's resolution not to give way to such expectations marks a rebellion such as that of Shaila's parents. Curiously, the sway of the tradition observed by her grandmother, in which the widow is viewed as a harbinger of bad luck, frees Shaila from the more pressing choice faced by the men; the less immediate nature of her decisions exacerbates the sense of limbo which she describes. As breaches of tradition abound, and differ vastly in their nature and import, community appears ultimately to be determined as much by contingency and circumstance as by commitment to a shared tradition or to common goals for the future. The multifarious nature of hybridity, although but one of the ways in which the continuity of tradition is broken, renders conviction and commitment all the more difficult to formulate.

The metaphor employed by Shaila of fluttering between worlds is appropriate not only with regard to the negotiation by individuals of a sense of community; it takes on further associations in the light of its relevance to Mukherjee's narrative strategy in the story. As I mentioned earlier, the narrative moves between concise detailing of event and location to reflective assessment of the situations treated, to projection into less tangible worlds. The temporal and locational divisions of the narrative seem to suggest both a logical order and a sense of continuity and development, but these ordering devices exist in constant tension with the breaks, which are less obviously being affected thematically and structurally. The transitions required by these breaks, in other words, leave the reader, if unwittingly, "fluttering between worlds," or at least between models of inter-pretation. Shaila's communing with her deceased husband and sons offers perhaps the most obvious case in point. Where is the reader left during and after the following account? It is interesting to note the way in which the incident is so precisely set up:

> Then, on the third day of the sixth month into this odyssey, in an abandoned temple in a tiny Himalayan village, as I make my offering of flowers and sweetmeats to the god of a tribe of animists, my husband descends to me. He is squatting next to a scrawny *sadhu* in moth-eaten robes. Vikram wears the vanilla suit he wore the last time I hugged him. The *sadhu* tosses petals on a butter-fed flame, reciting Sanskrit mantras, and sweeps his face of flies. My husband takes my hands in his.
> *You're beautiful*, he starts. Then, *What are you doing here?*
> Shall I stay? I ask. He only smiles, but already the image is fading. *You must finish alone what we started together*. No seaweed wreathes his mouth. He speaks too fast just as he used to when we were an envied family in our pink split-level. He is gone.
> In the windowless altar room, smoky with joss sticks and clarified butter lamps, a sweaty hand gropes for my blouse. I do not shriek. The *sadhu* arranges his robe. The lamps hiss and sputter out.
> When we come out of the temple, my mother says, "Did you feel something weird in there?"
> My mother has no patience with ghosts, prophetic dreams, holy men, and cults.
> "No," I lie. "Nothing." (*M* 190–91)

If the reader has been lulled into a ready acceptance of the veracity of Shaila's account by the precise and evocative manner in which its descriptions are rendered, her occasional forays into realms of the spiritual or supernatural, and the ambiguous way in which the physical and metaphysical are juxtaposed, might prove somewhat unsettling. The detail of the groping, sweaty hand, particularly, sows a seed of doubt as to the nature of Shaila's experience, and the light in which she interprets it. These "digressions" can be accommodated either by abandoning the category of "mimetic realism" and thereby altering one's expectations of the narrative account, or by discounting familiarity as the criterion for realistic representation on account of cultural difference, and in so doing, granting it a wider jurisdiction. In this latter option lurks the danger of subscribing to Orientalist views of Eastern mysticism, which are given the lie by Mukerjee's deptiction of Shaila's parents. In either event, expectations have been unseated, and narrative convention foregrounded. The reader is forced to reconsider his or her own point of entry into the story, the light in which the narrator is regarded, and perhaps the point of the story itself. What I am suggesting is that the breaks resulting from shifts in narrative tone and focus, and the juxtaposition of mundane detail with other-worldly presences, affect in readerly terms a sense of dislocation or disorientation highly appropriate to a text which is very much concerned with states of limbo, and with the accompanying battle to establish or reassert foundations. Shaila assesses her resulting situation (or, rather, her lack of situation) as follows:

> A wife and mother begins her new life in a new country, and that life is cut short. Yet her husband tells her: Complete what we have started. We, who stayed out of politics and came halfway around the world to avoid religious and political feuding have been the first in the New World to die from it. I no longer know what we started, nor how to complete it. (*M* 196–97)

With Shaila's determined and decisive embarkation on a journey which is spurred by her last documented communication with her family – a moment which notably also marks Mukherjee's exit from the story and from the collection – the reader is similarly cut off from the narrator, no longer knowing exactly what was started, nor how to complete it. Both are set adrift, unsure of which connections to make; yet both wield the power to transform place into space.

Mukherjee's short fictions, with their focus on spatial, temporal, epistemological and ontological flux, gesture towards the often destabilising and always disorienting condition of migrancy, at one and the same time critiquing politically forces which render "otherness" a negative category, enacting textually the dislocations described, and celebrating in both senses the transformational possibilities afforded by the migrant experience.

WORKS CITED

CERTEAU, Michel de. *The Practice of Everyday Life*, tr. Steven F. Rendall (Berkeley: U of California P, 1984).

MORRIS, Meaghan. "At Henry Parkes Motel," in *Cultural Studies* 1.2 (January 1988).

MUKHERJEE, Bharati. *Darkness* (Markham, Ontario: Penguin, 1985).

———. *The Middleman* (London: Virago, 1989).

——— & Clark Blaise. *Days and Nights in Calcutta* (Garden City NY: Doubleday, 1977).

PRATT, Mary Louise. *Imperial Eyes: Travel Writing and Transculturation* (London & New York: Routledge, 1992).

RUSHDIE, Salman. "The Location of Brazil," in *Imaginary Homelands* (London: Granta, 1991).

SURETTE, Leon. "Creating the Canadian Canon," in *Canadian Canons: Essays in Literary Value*, ed. Robert Lecker (Toronto: U of Toronto P, 1991).

✌ ❀ ✌

The Weight of Cultural Baggage
Frank Paci and the Italian–Canadian Experience

LEON LITVACK

"You come telling me you going to Canada as a' immigrant? To be a
stranger? Where Canada is? What is Canada?" (Austin Clarke, "Canadian
Experience")
"We are all immigrants to this place, even if we were born here."
(Margaret Atwood, *The Journals of Susanna Moodie*)

T HE WORD "MULTICULTURALISM" emerged in Canada during the
Sixties to counter the word "biculturalism" as used in the terms of reference
of the Royal Commission on Bilingualism and Biculturalism.*[1] By 1971,
when the term was officially adopted by the federal government to describe a policy
enclosed within a bilingual (English and French) framework, it enshrined three
distinct meanings. It was (1) the social policy of encouraging retention of group
heritages and full participation in Canadian society; (2) the philosophy or ideology
of cultural pluralism; and (3) a measure of ethnic diversity within a society. As a
government policy, multiculturalism has both proponents and critics. Among the
latter, some have declared it misdirected, divisive, patronising, and even a cynical
political ploy. Nevertheless, as a description of Canadian society and as a public
policy, multiculturalism has been adopted into our vocabulary, and has affected,
both consciously and unconsciously, many areas of Canadian life.

Multiculturalism has been embraced on a political level in a number of ways. In
the Canadian Constitution of 1982, clause 27 stated that the *Charter of Rights and
Freedoms* shall be interpreted in a manner consistent with the preservation and
enhancement of the multicultural heritage of Canadians. In 1985 a House of
Commons Standing Committee on Multiculturalism was established. In 1988
Parliament passed the *Canadian Multiculturalism Act*, which was committed to four
distinct areas:

i)   Race Relations and Cross-Cultural Understanding;
ii)   Heritage Cultures and Languages;

---

* I am grateful to Dr J.R. Barta, University of Guelph, for his assistance in gathering materials
for this essay.
1 For this summary on the development of Canadian multiculturalism I am indebted to the
"Minister's Message" in *Together* 1.1 (Winter 1990): 2–3.

iii)   Community Support and Participation; and
iv)   Cross-Governmental Commitment.

In the same year the Prime Minister announced the creation of a new Department of Multiculturalism and Citizenship, devoted to promoting Canadian pluralism, and encouraging an active and informed citizenry. More specifically, the Minister of Multiculturalism and Citizenship is mandated to promote among all of Canadian society an understanding of the values inherent in Canadian citizenship, and to encourage participation in the social, cultural, political and economic life of Canada, as well as to promote a greater awareness and understanding of human rights, fundamental freedoms and related values.

While these are all laudable aims, we must be aware that we are far from achieving the desired goals. The problems are familiar ones: racism, segregation, language barriers, cultural stereotypes, cultural confusion, the class system, and religious conflict. Multicultural writing in Canada treats these issues with great insight, and draws immense strength from looking to cultural roots for inspiration. Despite the sometimes "other-worldly" nature of their experience, these writers are also Canadian (a term which becomes increasingly deconstructed and numinous with each passing generation), and their writing provides an arena for dialogue about reconciling different aspects of their identities. Ethnocultural diversity is now an integral part of the Canadian experience; the ways in which this phenomenon has added to Canadian writing – and its effect on our ideas of canonicity – are not fully understood. One cannot generalise about the experience of "hyphenated" Canadians: questions of gender, class, religion, race and education affect the lived experience and literary productions of writers in fundamental ways. Thus, although Frank Paci cannot be said to speak for a monolithic Italian–Canadian experience, his writing about this duality (which he says played a "large role" in shaping him) casts some light upon the attempt to come to terms with two – or more – identities. As Paci admits, writing "seemed the only way to find out who I was and why I was on earth."[2]

Paci was born in Pesaro in 1948; in 1952 his family emigrated and settled in Ontario, the destination for over half of the post-World War II immigrants to Canada. In general, Italian–Canadians have gravitated towards urban centres, undergoing a transition from being peasants in an underdeveloped rural economy to becoming proletarians in an urban industrial economy.[3] They have been involved in many important industries: construction, transport maintenance, smelting, as well as in more traditional crafts, such as terrazzo, mosaic, and

---

2 Frank Paci, interview with Joseph Pivato, *Other Solitudes: Canadian Multicultural Fictions*, ed. Linda Hutcheon & Marion Richmond (Toronto: Oxford UP, 1990), 231.

3 For a fuller consideration of conditions in Italy prior to immigration, see the chapter on "Southern Italy and its Immigrants" in Franca Iacovetta, *Such Hardworking People: Italian Immigrants in Postwar Toronto* (Montreal/Kingston: McGill–Queen's UP, 1992): 3–19.

Venetian glass-blowing. They have also encouraged the spread of vineyards in Ontario and British Columbia and thus the growth of a Canadian wine industry.[4] The relative youth of Italians as an immigrant population, combined with their preparedness to work hard in order to secure a better future for their families, has contributed to their marked impact on the development of unions and of the labour movement in Canada. This process was assisted by the preservation of extensive networks of family and *paesani* (co-villagers), acting as buffers against the more alienating features of urban industrial life. Thus value systems, cultural rituals, and old-world institutions were often preserved – if not intact, then at least in a modified form – in the new country.

In terms of population, Italian–Canadians number more than half a million, and are the fourth-largest ethnic group in Canada.[5] Yet, because of the dominant bicultural divide, there has been a tendency to view their situation – and that of other ethnic groups – as a "third solitude," or an "other solitude," reflecting the multiracial, pluri-ethnic nature of the country. The first generation in particular belongs to an ethnic culture outside the mainstream, and many wage a battle for preservation of the familiar "old-world" identity, which necessarily involves segregation of various kinds. This strong desire to cling to pre-migration traditions and values is understandable, particularly because many of these immigrants come from agrarian villages and towns. Confusion or bewilderment concerning goals or expectations is not uncommon, because these individuals are faced with a choice which was not always easy to make: on the one hand, they believe that acceptance of a changed economic order leads to increased prosperity; on the other, they are fearful or hesitant because of unfamiliarity with North America and its capitalist economy, and as a result many prefer a retreat into customary ways of work and life.[6] Their descendants' situation is complicated by many additional factors, including education in the "new world," and there is a tendency towards an abandoning of cultural and linguistic signposts in favour of varying degrees of assimilation into the larger "mainstream" culture, with accompanying destabilisation and crisis of identity. This is the background to Paci's fiction, and in the five novels he has written to date, *The Italians* (1975), *Black Madonna* (1982), *The Father* (1984), *Black Blood* (1991) and *Under the Bridge* (1992), there is a

---

4 In Paci's novel *The Father* one of the characters exclaims: "Back in our village in the Abruzzi [...] learning to make wine is more important than going to school. A man is known by the quality of his wine" (*The Father* [Ottawa: Oberon, 1984]: 62).

5 George Woodcock, *Canada and the Canadians* (Toronto: Oxford UP, 1970), 91. They are surpassed by the French, Germans and Ukrainians.

6 For further information see Kenneth Bagnell, *Canadese: A Portrait of the Italian Canadians* (Toronto: Macmillan, 1989); *Arrangiarisi: The Italian Immigration Experience in Canada*, ed. Roberto Perin & Franc Sturino (Montreal: Guernica, 1989); and *The Italian Immigration Experience*, ed. John Potestio & Antonio Pucci (Thunder Bay: Canadian Italian Historical Association, 1988).

common *terminus a quo*: the old defend their language and their lives; the young the right to be young, and to be "Canadian" in some numinous sense. There develops a shifting pattern of coping strategies, in which the novelist defines the identity of his characters, and the reader is invited to reflect on the problems presented. In each case a way forward is adopted; a pattern of development in terms of the solution proffered may be observed in contrasting two of the novels, *Black Madonna* and *Black Blood*.

Black Madonna is largely set in Sault Ste. Marie, Ontario, where Paci spent his formative years. The novel deals with the theme of cultural adaptation, and with the sub-themes of conflict between generations and the formation of ethnic identities. The plot is stark and tragic, focusing on the pervasive degeneration of the interpersonal relationships in one Italian–Canadian family. The novel opens with the death of the patriarchal bricklayer Adamo Barone, known affectionately as Babbo. He has left behind a widow, Assunta, and two children, Joey and Marie. With the husband gone, Mrs Barone becomes a Black Madonna, one of the retinue of Italian widows, perpetually clad in black mourning, who have profound difficulties in coming to terms with their loss, and find strength and meaning only in religion and in the "old-world" traditions of Italy. The narrator says of them: "All peasant women like his mother, they had brought their old-country existence with them" to the New World.[7] Paci depends upon familiar images: the woman dressed in black who does the weekly grocery shopping, brings the children to and from school, understands little English, and is a constant attender at church. For over a quarter of a century Assunta has raised her family in a predominantly immigrant neighbourhood in Sault Ste. Marie's West End; but despite her long sojourn in Canada, she clings tenaciously to her Italian customs and language, to the shame and embarrassment of her two children, especially her university-educated daughter, Marie, who becomes angry when she recalls the burden which she feels her mother represents:

> How can she be my mother when she never had the slightest idea of who I was? [...] We've never spoken the same language even. How can she be my mother? She never had the least comprehension of what I was doing in school or what I wanted in life. All she did was cook and wash for me. And hit me a lot when I was a kid. There are no two people so different as we are. She's like a fossil. She's in the wrong time and the wrong country. (*BM* 17)

With the death of her husband, the Black Madonna loses her bridge to the outer world and to her children. She is suddenly a helpless victim of her unadapted immigrant life. Yet the peculiar and puzzling behaviour that she assumes becomes the very catalyst which forces her son and daughter to come to terms with their

---

[7] Frank Paci, *Black Madonna* (Ottawa: Oberon, 1982): 12. All subsequent quotations will appear in the text as *BM*.

italianità, their Italianness. The son, Joey, endures the day-to-day withdrawal of his mother, her incessant television-watching, her newly-acquired slovenly habits, her self-administered butcher haircut, her silent and dazed stares. He is forced to rely upon his own resources, and to evaluate his own life. He wants more than anything to become a professional hockey player. His goal is scoffed at by his parents, but the game is in his blood (a key word for Paci). The quest for fame in hockey becomes part of Joey's quest for a Canadian identity. He plays for the Steelmaking team in an industrial league with his friend Donny "The Cat" Belsito, "an inspiration to every kid who had laced on a pair of skates" (*BM* 45) because of his having played for one season for the Detroit Red Wings in the National Hockey League. With their comrades Tubby Minelli and Boofy Pagnotta, they take on all comers in an arena which seems to dominate their life. For them, the historical landmark of nationhood is the memorable 1972 Canada–Soviet hockey series, in which Paul Henderson scored the last goal in the last game, played in the Soviet Union, to give Canada the overall victory. Yet, in the course of the novel, as a result of musing on Donny's injuring himself, being dropped to the farm team, treated like a commodity, and thus being forced give up professional hockey in disillusionment and sorrow, Joey comes to terms with his dream of hockey fame. Donny tells him:

> "When you play a game for a long time [...] you tend to remain a kid for a long time [...] In some deep part of you there's that twelve-year-old kid hollering and screaming in the cold wind of the outdoor rink. And you never want that kid to grow up or change because, somehow, he's the best part of you [...] that kid has something that can't be shared with anyone else, something that was his alone and makes him different from everyone else [...] I was never as alive as I was then." (*BM* 130)

At this point Donny retires from the game, and, at age 46, loses that part of his identity – his Canadian identity – which was so central to his life. Joey too retires from hockey, and assumes his father's role as he finishes laying the bricks for an unexplained pyramid in the garden. He has found the proverbial fresh meaning and start in life; but there is an implication that, because of the accompanying sense of loss, this is also a kind of death.

The daughter, Marie, reflects on her struggle for independence and freedom, and savours her victory over her mother and her mother's way of life from the safe distance of Toronto. Married to the Anglo-Canadian Richard, and teaching high-school mathematics in an immigrant area, she has ostensibly overcome her Italian origins (although, as the narrator is careful to point out, "her Italian background had definitely proved instrumental in getting her the job"; *BM* 138). Yet the ties of family are too strong to break. Marie recalls her father's words: "No matter what you are, what you become, Maria, she had you in her belly. How can you fight the blood in you, ignoranta!" (*BM* 116). In the end the spell is too strong to break: Marie undergoes a miraculous transformation. After the inevitable death of

Assunta, in an eerily symbolic ceremony that stretches the bounds of credibility, Marie – alias Maria – literally dons the black peasant dress of her mother and in so doing becomes her mother, a Black Madonna, and sets off for Italy in search of her roots.

The act of reverse migration to discover one's roots is an important journey for Paci, who forces his character to re-examine the past, and in the process to correct her errors and reconcile herself to the ghosts. When asked by Joseph Pivato about the act of return, Paci recalls:

> I was four years old when my parents emigrated and I went back for the first time when I was twenty-four, in 1972. I was the first in my family to go back. For twenty years I had been nurtured away from Italy in a house that I took to be representative of Italy. It was as if I had been asleep for twenty years. I woke up. I saw that Italy was in my blood; I came to see my parents more clearly and to appreciate them for the first time. Before, I little understood or respected them. The trip made me see them from a different angle. I saw the soil they came from, and, from a larger perspective, the grandeur and age of a culture that made Canada rough and dark by comparison. Don't get me wrong, though. I'm much more Canadian than I'll ever be Italian. From that trip I realized that I had to write from the deepest roots of my being, from the concretely felt experiences of the family.[8]

The reader can clearly see that, though Marie too considered herself to be "Canadian," Italy was in her blood.

In documenting the Marie–Assunta relationship, Paci has made a commendable effort to explore one type of mother–daughter liaison in Italian immigrant families, albeit with some excesses. For instance, there is the disgusting scene at Christmas dinner, during which Maria becomes physically ill as a result of her mother's persecution by pasta. Joey says:

> "Marie, why don't you make her happy for once and just eat a little more. It won't kill you. You look like you can even use a little more."
>
> She turned to face him, feeling her blood start to boil.
>
> "It won't kill me, will it? Just look at you, Joey. And for the life of me I've never been able to understand why she's always tried to push the food down our throats while she eats nothing herself."
>
> Joey made a sour face. "Maybe she's just trying to be a mother in the only way she knows how."
>
> Assunta was fuming at her.
>
> "You can't speak to me anymore?" she said in *dialetto*. "You come into my house and you don't eat my food and you can't speak to me, your mother? You go to a big school and read many books and you act like this? An ingrata you are. A stranger you are. How can you be my daughter?"
>
> [...]
>
> "You want me to eat your food, Ma?" she said icily. "I'll eat your food. I'll show you how to eat your food."

---

⁸ Paci, interview, 232.

> And with that she reached her hand into the bowl of ravioli, grabbed a handful of the hot slippery pasta, and quickly stuffed it into her mouth. Assunta stared at her with mouth agape. Joey made an exclamation of disgust and turned his head away.
> [...]
> Her mind was blank. She could feel the sauce flowing down her throat and onto the collar of her muslin dress. She munched on the thick gooey pasta with her cheeks puffed out wide. It took much effort to swallow. The food had an immediate effect. Her head felt it was lolling on an unsteady ship. She felt nauseated. Through a distorting mist she saw her mother's pained incredulous expression. put more food into her mouth before her father could stop her. Her stomach began to heave. Before she could grab a napkin she spewed some pasta onto the table in a fit of coughing.
> Giving her mother one last look she rushed upstairs to the bathroom. (*BM* 102–103]

More laudable than this crude display of protest is Paci's portrayal of an Italian–Canadian daughter's need to assert her own independence and pursue her desire for achievement. However, in Marie's case, her ultimate goal (a doctorate) is not achieved, and she becomes the victim of severe emotional and physical imbalances which betray her lack of adjustment to the two cultural influences in her life – the Italian more clearly defined than the "Canadian." As she recalls the ravioli incident later in the novel, she feels sick again, and looks at herself in the mirror:

> Her face was worn and ravaged. It was as if her mother were staring back at her.
> "Mamma," she said. "Mamma, I'm sorry." (*BM* 117]

Like her mother, Marie is maladapted to her Canadian milieu.

Overall, the novel is somewhat unsatisfactory and immature. This is demonstrated not only through the overplaying of incidents like the Christmas dinner, but also in the character of the Black Madonna. The novel is written in the past tense, and the reader develops a sense of sympathy with the characters; yet the writer never allows for the possibility of identifying with them. Assunta's presence infiltrates the story as it does her children's lives; but, like her children, the reader never gets to know her. She remains hidden behind the stereotype.

Black Madonna clearly outlines the tensions experienced by many immigrant families, arising from the contrast between the old ways of the parents and the new ways of the children growing up in the adopted country. A decade has passed since the publication of this novel, and Paci has recently taken the dilemma of the immigrant into new dimensions. In *Black Blood*, published in 1991, Paci employs a first-person narrator to explore more fully the formative years of second-generation Italian–Canadians. The protagonist, Marco Trecroci, relating the story at thirty years' distance, constructs a narrative which follows the lives of him and his friends through primary school in Sault Ste. Marie in the Fifties. The children experience various rites of passage in their communal existence, including first communion, and first sexual experience; the boys in particular participate in a bonding ritual of blood brotherhood, which cements their lives together.

This novel differs from previous ones in several ways. First of all, the perspective provided by the retrospective child's point of view means that there are fewer entrenched attitudes to deal with, and also much that is either incomprehensible or misunderstood in the generational tensions. Also, there is a much heavier overt emphasis on Catholicism. The entire novel is set within the framework of a confession, enunciated in the opening lines ("It's been 25 or 30 years since my last confession").[9] Marco Trecroci, who – significantly – was born in Italy and brought to Canada as a child, develops a fascination with religious ritual and liturgy, and by the end seems to have defined for himself a vocation for the priesthood. Ironically, it is he who first experiences the "other" culture in a direct, physical manner at age five, when ten-year-old Anglo-Canadian Judy Hiller fumblingly seduces him. The coupling with "Canadian" culture on a sexual level sets the tone for the work, and clearly marks out characters' stances on the potential to become part of the dominant (in this case Anglo-Saxon) tradition.

Marco's friends include Rico Stocco (another recent immigrant), Maria Fera, Susan Orletti, an Irish girl called Katie O'Gorman, and Perry Garson, whose father is an Anglo, but whose mother is Italian. It is clear from the outset that the focus of the narrative will be on Perry, the half-breed, the product of a mixed marriage, the cultural freak – but also, perhaps, the hope for the future. Together these characters play and grow, engaging in activities common to children in their situation, with this exception: they are all acutely aware of their parents' foreignness. The Italian children are particularly singled out and teased because of their "Dee Pee" (Displaced Person) status – which applies more to their parents than to them, but (as many who are from ethnic backgrounds are aware) stereotypes are difficult to overcome.

As in *Black Madonna*, there is the dream of "making it" as a hockey player, and the Esposito Brothers, Phil and Tony, who excelled in the National Hockey League, are held up as a shining example of what could be achieved by local boys. There is also a sense of distance from the Old Country, expressed by Marco early on in the novel:

> I developed a strange curiosity about my parents. The only evidence I had to help me shed light on their dim past were the old photographs they kept in a shoebox [...] Even the clothes they had worn in the pictures were there, either packed in plastic wraps or still worn. Throwing anything away for my mother, was like hacking off a limb. Especially the few items she had been able to bring with her in her trunk.
> [...]
> The smell and the feel of the clothing added to the sight of the photographs gave me a glimpse of a past that I could only recreate in my imagination. (*BB* 41)

---

9 Frank Paci, *Black Blood* (Ottawa: Oberon, 1991): 3. All subsequent references will appear in the text as *BB*.

The alien nature of these images (some depicting himself) is heightened as Marco pores over them and decides that those photographed "look at the camera like aborigines caught for the pages of the *National Geographic*" (*BB*, 43). He comes to think of his parents "no longer" as "bulwarks against the outside world – or safe havens for me to return to in times of trouble" (51).

Marco and his friends try to fight against their *italianità*, both within their family units and in a strange episode concerning the Stone Garden, a walled enclosure owned by old Mr Sforza. It is a symbolic fortress against the New World, where the owner has tried to re-create a little piece of Calabria. The interior is a lush, Edenic landscape in miniature, a "dense luxurious oasis with fruit trees and sculptured hedges and gravelled walkways and beautiful flowers" (*BB* 69). The holy ground is desecrated by the children, who steal fruit and vegetables, and narrowly escape being devoured by guard-dogs. In clambering back over the wall, Marco scrapes his forehead against a low-lying branch (*BB* 71), thus echoing the mark of Cain in Genesis 4:9–16, and mitigating his banishment to the land of Wandering. Despite the fact that Marco has committed a sin (and the fruit he eats is described as being the best he ever tasted in the world; *BB* 74), he is marked out in a way which will become significant later in the novel.

A recurring phrase in *Black Blood* is "*la merda di Dio*", the shit of God (*BB* 64), used to describe the rich, black earth not only of this garden, but of all fertile places, both in Canada and in Italy. It is an expression used by Marco's father, who is from an agricultural background, a *paisan*, who has obligations and allegiances to all his Italian brothers, and therefore must not desert them – ever. The same is true of the boys, who engage in a momentous bonding-ritual involving Marco, Rico and Perry, from which the novel takes its name:

> [Rico] made a long cut on Perry's thumb, then mine, then his own,. It hurt like hell. The blood popped out and down our hands. I was surprised it all looked exactly the same.
>
> We joined our three thumbs, mashing the blood together. Rico took out a piece of string from his pocket and tied it around the three thumbs.
>
> "*Siamo fratelli*," he intoned. "Real brothers. Brothers of the blood. Sons of Italy."
>
> "But I'm only half Italian," Perry said.
>
> "That's all right. Be your better half. I want you to swear something."
>
> And then in unison, following Rico's lead, we said, "I swear to make this hand strong, three fingers but one hand of the same blood. We are Brothers of the Blood."
>
> I didn't know where Rico got the words of this oath. It seemed just a game to me, something that could've come out of a comic book or a movie – something that I didn't realize the full importance of until it was too late. (*BB* 96)

The incident which shakes this seemingly indissoluble fraternity involves growing up, and replacing hockey with awakening feelings of sexuality. Rico (who has a greater awareness of his *italianità* than the others) excels at making out with the girls. Marco, who has been described as a "saint" (*BB* 87), and is more interested in Catholicism than in worldly matters, is the observer, the mediator, who tries to be a friend to all. Perry, who feels that Rico's new interest is jeopardising the brotherhood, is angry, and discovers that Rico has been taking girls to the boys' secret place, the place where they swore the blood-oath. The problem is complicated by the fact that both Rico and Perry are interested in Maria, a member of the old gang, and it is this dilemma in particular which sparks the crucial row which brings the novel to its climax. The two fight, and Perry is knocked unconscious, as Marco ineffectually declares, "'We weren't supposed to fight each other, remember? [...] We're blood brothers'" (BB 168).

The rising anger and frustration are not only a symptom of rivalry between two friends, but also of growing up in an environment where the key cultural icons are John Wayne, Charlton Heston, Gary Cooper, Rita Hayworth, Pat Boone, Marilyn Monroe and Jayne Mansfield. Marco voices their concerns when he says:

> These and so many more, the heroes I'd study so carefully to learn how to talk and act [...] someone I could look up to and love, someone who would help me define myself. (BB 165)

In the end, Rico and Marco cope with the changing situation more effectively than Perry, the half-breed, the lost soul, caught between a juvenile Italian brotherhood bond and an adult world in which the key symbols and rituals are alluring, but at the same time frightening. The indecision and resentment come to a head after graduation, when the gang prepare to separate and begin new chapters in their lives. The anger inside Perry continues to build, and he challenges his rival Rico to walk, as if on a tightrope, on the guardrails of the international bridge which links the Canadian and American sides of the Sault. Rico accepts, and, in a scene filled with terror, Perry plunges to his death in the river below. Marco, the mediator, affirms that he could have stopped them, that he "had their futures in the palm of my hand" (BB 188); but he does not, thus evoking Paci's belief that choices must be made by those in cultural dilemmas. In the aftermath Marco says, "How could I explain black blood, when it was still a vague notion inside me?" (BB 190). He does not know whether words will make a difference; in an address to the reader he says:

> More and more words until the reality is buried in words and you sit stupefied, as if your whole world has collapsed like a stack of cards. You try to reach into the silence for the meaning behind the words, but it's no use. The pain is unbearable. The sense of loss. It can't be taken back. Like an arm ripped from you before you know it. You're shocked. Stunned. You don't feel a thing. It makes no sense. Which is the easy time before the pain comes like a knife twisting inside your gut. (BB 190)

Marco comes to recognise that he had to allow Perry to make up his own mind, to face his own challenges, to fight his own battles. He addresses his dead friend in the closing pages:

> You died so young. Who knows what you could've become. A doctor. A lawyer. A tinker. A tailor. A soldier. A sailor. A great hockey player, skating his way into the Canadian Dream. A fighter pilot. An astronaut daring to conquer the stars. A sky-walker. You could've done it so easily – as if you had been born to it. Others have done it since.
>
> But you died so young – and now are only a faint reminder of all our broken dreams. We who had been raised in the mining and industrial towns and cities of the northern bushlands – all displaced persons in limbo seeking the golden lights to the south. (*BB* 198)

By "the south" Marco means southern Ontario, the power-base, the place where all promising junior hockey players go to make it in the big leagues, the place where there is greater possibility of breaking free from the ties of family, blood, and perhaps *italianità*. However, if the example of Marie in *Black Madonna* is anything to go by, Paci is saying that it makes no difference whether one stays at home or not.

Paci's narratives dwell on the past; yet they are not nostalgic. The past is approached with a sense of foreboding, and with a feeling of "homage to the sacrifices of the first-generation immigrant parents," for these have not been in vain. The writer draws strength from these experiences, and uses them to make sense of the present.[10] His work underscores the fact that for some time to come we shall remain a society of immigrants, of Dee Pees, as Marco realises himself to be at the end of *Black Blood*. No ready solutions are offered. The novels speak for the European immigrants to Canada, which Paci endows with a "simple" state of consciousness,[11] and for their children, telling of their struggles, which are sometimes with the language, values and traditions of the old society, and at other times with the pressures and problems of the new. Paci is particularly good at exploring the inhibited nature of his characters, and their struggle to contact each other – and the world outside – in a meaningful way. In *Black Madonna* Assunta Barone is almost voiceless; Paci asks us to consider why this is so. The narrator in *Black Blood* is aware of the inadequacy of words to express the instinctive bonds that hold individuals together, and which form part of their cultural burden, but may also contribute to their salvation. Paci still has some way to go in maturing as a writer; yet as he develops he merits reading, for the problems he evokes are important ones in the ongoing attempt to define and endorse the culturally diverse nature of Canadian society.

❧ ✦ ❧

---

[10] Paci, interview, 232.
[11] Paci, interview, 234.

WORKS CITED

BAGNELL, Kenneth. *Canadese: A Portrait of the Italian Canadians* (Toronto: Macmillan, 1989).

IACOVETTA, Franca. *Such Hardworking People: Italian Immigrants in Postwar Toronto* (Montreal/ Kingston: McGill–Queen's UP, 1992).

PACI, Frank G. *Black Blood* (Ottawa: Oberon, 1991).

———. *Black Madonna* (Ottawa: Oberon, 1982).

———. *The Father* (Ottawa: Oberon, 1984).

———. Interview with Joseph Pivato, in *Other Solitudes: Canadian Multicultural Fictions*, ed. Linda Hutcheon & Marion Richmond (Toronto: Oxford UP, 1990): 228–34.

PERIN, Roberto & Franc STURINO, ed. *Arrangiarsi: The Italian Immigration Experience in Canada* (Montreal: Guernica, 1989).

POTESTIO, John & Antonio PUCCI, ed. *The Italian Immigration Experience* (Thunder Bay: Canadian Italian Historical Association, 1988).

WEINER, Gerry. "Minister's Message" *Together* 1.1 (Ottawa: Multiculturalism and Citizenship Canada, 1991): 2–3..

WOODCOCK, George. *Canada and the Canadians* (Toronto: Oxford UP, 1970).

❧ ✿ ❧

The Ethnic Other in Quebec Cinema

IAN LOCKERBIE

I T IS GENERALLY ACKNOWLEDGED that, in the past, and for good historical reasons, Quebec was a relatively enclosed society. To find support for such a view one need look no further than Quebec literature itself. One of the recurring themes of the Quebec novel is that of *le survenant*, the mysterious stranger who comes into a local community from the outside and shows up its closed mentality. The unsettling effect is achieved even if the stranger is not markedly different from the local people, as in the classic novel *Le Survenant* by Germaine Guèvremont. One can imagine, therefore, how much greater the sociocultural clash might be in the case of a totally foreign outsider.

An example of such a situation can be found in Quebec cinema on the eve of the *Révolution Tranquille*. The film *L'immigré* (1959) by Bernard Devlin, from a script by Clément Perron, depicts the xenophobia unleashed in a small rural town by the arrival of a German immigrant. The German is eventually forced to leave by the pressure of intolerance. The repetition in the final scene of the laconic exchange between two characters which opened the film – "*Quoi de neuf? Rien!*" – marks the triumph of the status quo over the intruder. Here, as in many other Quebec films, including several written or directed by Perron,[1] Quebec is seen as enshrouded in *la grande noirceur* and the resulting narrowness of outlook is denounced.

It was the historic accomplishment of the *Révolution Tranquille* to dissipate the darkness and transform Quebec into a dynamic modern nation. Among other aspects of openness and modernity that now characterise Quebec society is its growing multi-ethnic, multicultural nature. Three decades and more of immigration and social development have produced a society well on the way to creating that ethnic and cultural mosaic which is held to be an ideal of Canada as a whole and of many other liberal western democracies.

This social evolution has not taken place without tensions, insofar as it has had to interact with the overriding public concern to maintain French language and culture as the signs of the distinctiveness of Quebec society. Many other countries whose language and culture are under no particular threat have had difficulty in

---

[1] Clément Perron wrote the script of *Mon Oncle Antoine* (Claude Jutra, 1971) and was the director of *Taureau* (1973) and *Partis pour la gloire* (1975), among others. My attention was drawn to *L'immigré* by Yves Lever's excellent *Le Cinéma de la Révolution Tranquille* (published by the author, 1991).

accommodating themselves to increasing ethnic heterogeneity. How much more problematical the task must be for a society which is trying to cope with changes of this kind, while simultaneously seeking to defend itself against linguistic and cultural erosion.

Some commentators have seized on these difficulties of adaptation to allege that Quebec has been an unwilling participant in the move towards a more mixed society and remains locked in an ethnocentric mentality. Such charges multiplied during the Meech Lake constitutional imbroglio, often in a style and form that seemed far from dispassionate.[2] Fuel was added to the flames by the appearance, at a delicate point in the political debate, of a television documentary, *Disparaître*, which took a pessimistic view of the survival of Quebec as a French-speaking society, and seemed to attribute much of the blame to excessive immigration. It is important to note, however, that Quebec critics were foremost among those repudiating *Disparaître*. It was generally judged to be unnecessarily alarmist, inaccurate in its statistical data, and uninformed on the extent to which Quebec language-policies are successfully converting immigrants from all sources to French.

Nevertheless, the question of how open Quebec is to other cultures and those from other ethnic backgrounds is one that deserves investigation. The cinema is a relevant field for enquiry, since, like all the arts, it is a revealing mirror of social attitudes. Often unconsciously, films will uncover the norms and values in the public mind at a given moment, and show the interaction of behaviour and deeply held convictions.

The evidence that cinema can yield on such a topic, however, is not all of equal status. There are countless current-affairs documentaries and films of a quasi-official nature which deal, as a matter of course, with subjects like race relations, colour prejudice, and immigration. This kind of production is important in creating enlightened public opinion on such topics, and there are no grounds for doubting that public attitudes towards the idea of a mixed society in Quebec are liberal and sincere. But this type of film does not tell us about the subtler area of private feeling. To test more deeply held attitudes towards the ethnic other[3] one has to turn towards the fiction cinema, which, to be successful, has to appeal not simply to the civic sense but, more profoundly, to its audience's elusive subjectivity. Equally important is the "personal" documentary, which, unlike the current affairs type of film, is the work of a creative personality, and deals with complexities and nuances of attitudes in a way comparable to that of the fiction film.

---

2 Mordecai Richler's *Oh! Canada! Oh! Quebec! Requiem for a Divided Country* (Markham, Ontario: Penguin, 1992) is a particularly prominent example.

3 There is occasional dispute about the concept of ethnicity. In this article the term "ethnic other" and related expressions are used to refer to people from different races and from distinct language and cultural groups.

The vastness of the field makes it impossible to undertake a fully comprehensive survey. The aim will rather be to sample the main areas in which the cinema has looked at the ethnic other, in order to take the pulse of current sensitivities.

Pride of place among communities to be represented goes not to immigrants but to the indigenous other – the native peoples of Canada, both Inuit and Amerindian. This may seem surprising to the casual or unsympathetic observer who remembers the highly publicised clashes between Indian groups and the Quebec authorities at Oka in the summer of 1990. It is the case, however, that the native peoples have grievances about territorial and ancestral rights throughout Canada and North America, and conflicts similar to those in question have occurred elsewhere in the past and in all probability will do so again. They cannot reasonably be taken as evidence of a state of friction that is specific to Quebec.

What is certain is that, from the earliest days of the *Révolution Tranquille*, there has been a cinematic concern with native history and peoples that is almost invariably liberal in nature. Some well-known films of the early Sixties re-examined the myths of the origins of French Canada and rejected the traditional view of the Indians as ignorant and bloodthirsty savages. Denys Arcand's revisionist *Champlain* (1964) presents them, on the contrary, as the rightful possessors of North America and as a people with natural dignity and an evolved culture. The same view is pressed further in Fernand Dansereau's first fiction film, *Le festin des morts* (1965), an ambitious historical reconstruction of the Jesuit missions of the early seventeenth century. The film secures the audience's sympathy for the missionaries by replicating the traditional hagiographic images of their death by torture, and by making Père Brébeuf the embodiment of humanity and charity. But it also presents the value-system of the Indians as being in some respects as valid as that of the Jesuits and allows Indian spokesmen to expose the ambivalences of the missionary project, articulating a natural wisdom which seems more attractive than the Jesuits' religious doctrines.

Since then, Amerindians or Inuits have appeared in a number of mainstream feature films, notably by Gilles Carle, usually as sympathetic and sometimes dignified characters, if not always as aesthetically convincing ones. Jacques Dorfmann's *Agaguk* (1992) eliminates certain negative elements in Yves Thériault's original novel to ensure that the main impression given of Inuit life is one of romantic grandeur and beauty, albeit a somewhat stereotypical one.

The place of the native peoples is even greater in the creative documentary. Over the last twenty-five years many films, including substantial contributions by major directors like Arthur Lamothe, Pierre Perrault and Maurice Bulbulian,[4] have given exemplary first-hand accounts of the life, traditional culture and con-

---

4 For filmographies, see *Le dictionnaire du cinéma québécois*, ed. Michel Coulombe & Marcel Jean (Montreal: Boréal, rev. 1992).

temporary problems of the native peoples. The spirit in which the films of Lamothe and Bulbulian are made is not that of traditional ethnographic filming. There is, rather, a passionate commitment to the whole way of life of the native peoples, especially the Amerindians, who are seen to represent values, a community ethos, and even a spiritual message for contemporary Western man. The dedication with which the film-makers adopt the world-view of the Amerindians is reflected in the very form of the films. The techniques of Direct Cinema, originally associated with an aesthetic of realism, are pushed further in order to render the different tempo and outlook of Amerindian life. Through long-held shots, slow rhythm and sparse editing, the viewer experiences a different social and value-system with a particular quality of close attention.

What emerges from all of these films is that many of the characteristics associated with the native peoples are also central to Quebec history and self-consciousness, to the extent that Amerindians (especially) and Inuit can become metaphoric extensions of the Quebec people themselves. The symbolic association takes place at two different levels. Insofar as the Québécois sense of identity involves a feeling for the past, nature, and the vastness of the land, the films identify naturally with those whose way of life is an exemplary representation of these values. Insofar as these original founding peoples have been dispossessed by history, the identification is through a shared sense of victimisation and oppression.

When these alternative images are placed in a context relating to contemporary industrial society, a complex discourse can result. This is the case with the notable film *Le dernier glacier* (1984) by Jacques Leduc and Roger Frappier, a feature-length documentary with fictional strands concerning the closure of the mining town of Schefferville in the far north of Quebec. The primary thrust of the film is one of anger at the callous treatment of the workers, thrown into unemployment and made virtually homeless by multinational industrial conglomerates. The closure not only of a workplace but of an entire town which was wholly dependent on the mine seems the ultimate symbol of the malfunctioning of the industrial order.

Yet a contradictory discourse is introduced by the recognition that the territory belonged in the first place to the native peoples who will now re-inherit it. On-camera time is given to native spokesmen to make the case about their ancestral rights to the land. Sequences showing native hunters and fishers going round their animal traps in a crisp snowy silence, contrasting with shots of gigantic bulldozers and other mining equipment abandoned in empty landscapes, suggest the defeat of noisy, destructive intruders and the reversion of the land to its pristine origins. The pathos of the end of a dream for the white incomers is kept alive throughout the film, however, and the possibility of Québécois sharing in the Indians' new beginning is held out when the wife of the fictional couple decides to remain behind in Schefferville when her husband goes south to look for work.

The plurality of discourses is increased when the disconsolate husband on the train south is linked to the lonely figure of an Amerindian migrant also heading south (presumably in search of industrial work, a hint that the natural wilderness is not totally a paradise). The film ends with the husband listening to the Amerindian's sad song of commiseration as the train remorselessly bears them away from Schefferville. In the final sequence, it is therefore the metaphor of Québécois and Indian as brothers in distress and dispossession which predominates, without displacing the earlier symbolism of a kingdom restored.

On a similar but smaller scale, tension of discourses is to be found in Maurice Bulbulian's *Dans nos forêts* (1971). This is a more straightforward documentary on the exploitation of forestry workers and the misuse of natural resources on the part of timber companies. But it is prefaced by a sequence in which the forest is presented in mysterious, highly stylised images, on which is superimposed the head of an elderly Indian chanting a shaman-like incantation. Clearly this is another evocation of a pre-existing natural order, held in trust by the native peoples for whom the forest is a sacred place. The idea never recurs, however, either in the imagery or the argument of the film. At best, it remains in the experience of the viewer as a disturbing memory to suggest that the timber companies, over and above the precise accusations levelled at them, are guilty of a more profound violation of spiritual origins. Yet if such an argument were clearly articulated and followed through, it could well conflict, at least partly, with the film's defence of the forestry workers' rights.

These tensions should not be seen as representing an ambivalent position on the part of the film-makers. They represent, rather, competing sympathies, without which the films would be less rich in both form and content. Above all, they testify to a strong and enduring regard for the native peoples, which is to the honour of Quebec cinema.

When one turns to other ethnic communities who occupy a place in Quebec cinema, one difference is apparent. Whereas the films about the native peoples are never made by them, since they have virtually no involvement in the film industry, other ethnic groups are increasingly represented in the ranks of film-makers. Rather than simply being spoken about, the ethnic other, in many cases, is the one who speaks.

This obviously has important consequences for the authenticity of representation of the other, and for the greater openness of cinema to the whole spectrum of society. However, it does not fundamentally change the status of the films concerned as social signifiers. The ethnic other as film-maker does not stand outside Quebec culture, but is intimately bound up in the film-making community and its relationships with audiences. In effect, his or her very presence springs from a cultural affinity which audiences recognise and are tacitly prepared to explore further.

From this point of view it is interesting to note the fairly strong representation of films about, and made by, immigrants from meridional countries. The original waves of immigration into Quebec were from the Mediterranean countries of Europe, and in various ways the presence of Greek, Portuguese and Italian communities has helped Quebec culture to rediscover or reinforce its Latin roots. Not only in cinema but, more strongly, in literature, one can discern a progression by which Quebec sensibility develops from defining itself in terms of winter towards an instinctive affinity with summer, the sun, and a meridional set of values. More recently, this tendency has been reinforced by a growing interest in the Caribbean and South America, initially through tourism but also increasingly in intellectual and cultural terms.

The Caribbean and South America thus loom larger in cinema than one might have expected. A number of South American film-makers live in Quebec and make films in which the encounter between their latinity and the apparently different character of the host culture is the central theme. Beyond the surface differences deeper affinities are clearly being discovered, leading Quebec directors to take an interest in South America. Thus André Melançon's children's film *Fierro, l'été des secrets* (1989), set as it is on the Argentinian pampas, responds to a very Québécois sense of space.

Les noces de papier (1990) by Michel Brault, one of Quebec's major directors, is on a more serious theme. It concerns a political refugee from one of the totalitarian South American régimes who undertakes an arranged marriage with a Quebec woman in order to stay in the country. A useful reminder that exotic cultures of the sun are not exclusively paradises, its most important feature is that the refugee develops from being an object of pity to a human being whose specific South American otherness is an attractive characteristic rather than a distancing one. Although simple, the difference is essential to a genuine openness to the other.

It is worth noting that there is also a more lighthearted, lucid side to Quebec's response to the Caribbean and South America. What it keys into is the atmosphere of exuberance, fantasy and fiesta in these cultures which appeals to the extrovert and Dionysian strand in the Quebec temperament.[5] The enthusiastic reaction to Carlos Ferrand's *Cuervo* (1989), a burlesque adventure story set in Cuba, illustrates how readily Quebec audiences warm to this strain of sensibility.

---

[5] In *Les Québécois* (Paris: Seuil, 1974), the sociologist Marcel Rioux makes a classic distinction between the Dionysian/extrovert and the Apollonian/introvert strands in the Quebec character, asserting that the former is the more fundamental.

Among Mediterranean immigrants, neither the Greek nor Portuguese communities have featured much in cinema.[6] The Italian community, by contrast, forms the backdrop to a number of films from Gilles Carle's *Dimanche d'Amérique* (1961) to the present day, and almost always is given meridional connotations of colourful exuberance and good humour. (The Italian mafia of Hollywood films although it makes a brief appearance in Paul Tana's *Caffe Italia*, is as unthinkable in Quebec cinema as the theme of criminal violence itself.)

The tendency to present the Italian character as invariably warm-hearted and boisterous may seem limiting, but one only has to look at Jean–Claude Lauzon's *Léolo* (1992) to see how much real seriousness may underlie such a stereotype. Opening with as farcical an evocation of the Italian connection as one could imagine, the film then deploys a yearning for the light and beauty of the Sicilian countryside as an expression of the adolescent hero's aspiration to escape social confinement. The theme of a liberating *ailleurs* is a constant in Quebec culture, and has never been more poignantly expressed than through the Italian dream in this film.

The films of the Quebec director of Italian extraction Paul Tana are almost the reverse image of *Léolo*, since he is concerned to chronicle the real hardships experienced by the immigrants from Italy to Quebec in the early years of the century. For them, the movement was from Léolo's dream to the harsh urban environment of Montreal. Nevertheless, first in a fictionalised documentary, *Caffe Italia* (1988), and then in a feature film, *La Sarrasine* (1992), Tana articulates a philosophy of biculturalism (Italian and Québécois in this case) which is one of the finest examples in cinema of the dialogue between Quebec and the other.

In *La Sarrasine* the prejudice and hostility encountered by the first Italian immigrants are not hidden, but the film works towards a large-scale reconciliation of the immigrant and host communities, in the character of a young Sicilian wife who stays on in Canada after her husband's conviction for an unintended murder. Revealingly, in the final scene of reconciliation, the two cultures have a meeting point in the sense of nature. Sicily is defined by its peasant earthiness, Quebec with its vast landscapes – its land. There is a veritable apotheosis as the young wife contemplates a snow-covered landscape to the accompaniment of an ethereal singing voice, suggesting an almost mystical union of north and south.

Although Tana has regretted that his characters have to be thought of as immigrants rather than Québécois who also happen to be part-Italian, it is, in fact, his choice of subject which so defines them. His own position, as a Québécois who has recovered his Italianness through making his films, and the position of many other members of the Italian community who are active in the arts in both

---

6 Interestingly, however, the Chilean Marilù Mallet, one of the most important of the South American film-makers, has devoted two films to Portuguese immigrants: *Les Borges* (1978), and *Chère Amérique* (1990).

languages,[7] represent a considerable degree of successful integration of Italian otherness to the benefit of Quebec culture as a whole.

The meridional qualities of warmth, sensuousness, light and colour have never been better embodied than in the creative, semi-autobiographical documentary by Michka Saäl, *L'arbre qui dort rêve à ses racines* (1992). It is the story of two young women immigrants, one an Arab from the Lebanon and the other (the film-maker herself) Jewish from North Africa, who become friends in Quebec and who, despite barriers to their integration, find happiness and fulfilment in their new country. The whole film has a sensuous beauty and an atmosphere of friendship and laughter, but it is about more than simple conviviality. The organic metaphor of the title suggests that there is a deep and vital spiritual nourishment which comes from the Mediterranean origins of both young women, and which, through interaction, will enrich the host community. As in Tana, the connection with Quebec is made through the elemental and the natural – in this case, the trees invoked by the title, which have a strong tactile and textural presence in the film. In a key scene, the young women crouch among the tree-trunks as they exchange their most intimate memories and secrets. Like the trees, they are growing from their hidden roots but, if the source is elsewhere, the maturity into which they grow is formed and fashioned by the host environment.

An interesting feature of the film is that it shows friendship transcending the divisions between Arabs and Jews. Even more strikingly, it substantially reconstructs the traditional Western stereotype of Jewishness, and in this it contributes to a dialogue with one of the principal ethnic others in Quebec in a way that is markedly different from that adopted by other contemporary films.

Although, like all Western societies, Quebec has a long-established Jewish population, they have until recently featured little in Quebec cinema. In the few cases where they appear, the tendency has been to construe them as a community with a religion and social values which give them a perceptible distinctiveness within Quebec society. This was the thrust of an early film by Fernand Dansereau: *La Communauté juive de Montréal* (1956), a respectful and sympathetic attempt to explain orthodox Jewishness to a wide audience.

The emphasis in *L'arbre qui dort*, by contrast, is to dissolve the barriers of otherness by interpreting Jewishness as synonymous with openness, colour, happiness and flamboyance. A scene in the film shows a wedding in a Jewish synagogue which ends in a communal dance. The two young women, who had been observing from behind a screen, are invited into the dance and swept into its

---

7 The work of the Italian-born dramatist Marco Micone, who writes in French, and of those writers who direct the bilingual review *Vice-versa*, are notable examples of a successful biculturalism. A prominent member of the Italo-Quebec intellectual community is the historian Bruno Ramirez, who has been Tana's principal collaborator on his films.

swirling colour and rhythm in a style that would not have been out of place in an operatic film, or even a musical comedy. The viewer is given no indication of the religious meaning of the dance or any other part of the ceremony, but is simply left with an impression of beauty and vitality. The film thus constructs Jewishness as an essential expression of those life-enhancing Dionysian values, integrative rather than separating, which have a profound appeal to contemporary Quebec sensibility. This notion, implicit throughout, is articulated explicitly in an interview with a male friend of the film-maker, who evokes the cosmopolitan character of Jewishness and defines it as being above all *disponible* – open, adaptable, sociable and responsive to its local environment.

Nothing could be more different from the image offered by the Hassidic Jewish community, which is a noticeable presence in certain areas of contemporary Montreal. Black dress, severe uncommunicativeness and total withdrawal from neighbourly relations are the perceived characteristics of this community, making it an extreme example of the traditional stereotype and one that in everyday life attracts occasional unfavourable comment in the Quebec press and media.

Faced with such an extreme assumption of otherness, Quebec film-makers could have been forgiven for avoiding the subject. What is interesting is that, on the contrary, the attempt has been made not simply to understand the social and religious basis of this otherness, but also to engage the sympathies of Quebec audiences for their apparently remote neighbours. Garry Beitel's scrupulously liberal documentary *Bonjour! Shalom!* (1991) seeks to explain and interpret the Hassidic faith and way of life with the same appeal to the viewer's intelligent understanding as Dansereau's film twenty-five years earlier. Michel Brault, however, goes further in *Shabbat! Shalom!* (1992) by dramatising one of the main sources of conflict between the two communities – the buying-up of domestic houses for conversion to synagogues – in such a way that common humanity triumphs. That emphasis is even stronger in the short film *Moise* (Howard Goldberg, 1990), in which a Hassidic couple bring up in their faith a baby found abandoned on their doorstep, but broken-heartedly hand it back to its rightful Québécois mother when she reappears. Brault indulges in more clichés and simplifications than Goldberg, but in both cases a Québécois audience cannot but identify with the Hassidic characters as human beings sharing common feelings.

Neither of these films can change the principles of non-cooperative cohabitation laid down by the Hassidic community itself, as Beitel's documentary makes clear. But they do demonstrate a willingness to treat the withdrawn or recalcitrant other with dignity and respect. While it seems natural that Quebec audiences will respond with much more enthusiasm to Michka Saäl's seductive image of Jewishness, the Hassidic films undoubtedly set an irreproachable standard of decency in inter-community attitudes.

Other "visible minorities" in Quebec have not so far occupied a great place in the cinematic *imaginaire*. The black population of Montreal can be glimpsed occasionally in the new wave of lively urban documentaries which ushered in the *Révolution Tranquille* in cinema. The girlfriend in Claude Jutra's *A tout prendre* (1963), one of the key films of the new wave, was black, a choice that was obviously far from accidental. Since then, any black presence has been marginal, but this may well change. It is more than likely that the black Haitian community, native French speakers who are already contributing to Quebec literature, as well as being the subject of one or two films,[8] will soon make its voice more clearly heard. In the case of the more recently arrived Asian groups, and the very self-sufficient Chinese community, the time-scale might be longer. While Law 101 has been very successful in converting immigrants to French, linguistic assimilation is fully achieved only with the second generation. In addition to an inevitable time-lag, the willingness of these communities themselves to mix culturally with the host country is an imponderable factor. In many comparable situations Chinese communities have remained remarkably faithful to their own culture and impermeable by that of their hosts.

Whatever happens in the future, there seems nothing particularly abnormal concerning the current absence of these communities from the cinematic scene. Such is not the case with the anglophone community. The virtually total absence of the other "founding people" of Canada from contemporary Quebec cinema (as well as from most other arts) does call for special comment, and is indeed a recurring cause for controversy. If complaints about ethnocentricity are heard, they are usually from the Quebec anglophone community and concern their own absence as subjects from the arts.[9]

This situation has not always been the case, but is the outcome of an understandable evolution. In the new wave of the Sixties, the English language and English-speaking characters were perceptible elements in both documentary and feature films. In one of the most important films of the decade, Gilles Groulx' *Le chat dans le sac* (1964), the young hero has an anglophone Jewish girlfriend. As in Jutra's *A tout prendre*, the intimate relationship with the ethnic other is essentially a foil for the discovery of self, but for Groulx self-identity is a cultural problem more than a personal one: "*Je suis Canadien Français donc je me cherche.*" Claude, therefore, does not so much reject the intimate other as grow away from her as he becomes more conscious of his own sociocultural situation as a French-Canadian.

---

8 See especially Tahani Rached, *Haïti-Québec* (1988) and *Ban pay a! Rends-moi mon pays* (1986), and *Taxi sans détour* (M. Landry and G. Beitel, 1989).

9 In *Le Devoir* (17 February 1990), Connie Tadros, the editor of the now-defunct *Cinema Canada*, published an article denouncing Quebec cinema for its failure to include anglophones.

Here the evolution is neither hostile nor strongly politicised, but part of a slow growth of consciousness. In the more polemical Seventies, however, the anglophone appears in cinema in one guise only – that of the overbearing figure of authority to be denounced and repudiated. Among others, two of the major films of the decade, *Mon Oncle Antoine* (Claude Jutra, 1971) and *J.A. Martin, photographe* (Jean Beaudin, 1976), have scenes which are classic statements of the power-relationship between bawling anglophone bosses and resentful francophone workers who understand the message but not the actual words being shouted at them. The historical reality of this type of situation is beyond dispute. The understandable feeling of humiliation and anger which it left in Quebec consciousness is memorably expressed in Michèle Lalonde's poem "Speak White" and many other literary texts of the Seventies.

The progressive disappearance of anglophone characters from the cinema has therefore to be seen as a necessary stage in a cultural evolution. What it represents is the elimination of a negative and constraining stereotype. In the Eighties, Quebec sensibility reached a position where it freed itself from a traumatising image of subordination; it can now explore its own concerns without being haunted by an oppressive other. Whether this stage will or should be followed by a final one in which intimacy and cultural exchange are established is an open question. To expect it to happen automatically might be to take too mechanical a view of the evolution of consciousness. It seems just as persuasive to see cultural maturity in terms of self-sufficiency, in which two neighbouring indigenous cultures can be appreciated for their characteristic differences rather than be expected to pursue artificial forms of interchange.

A glance at anglophone cinema in Canada is revealing in this respect. Although anglophone consciousness has not had to overcome any historical experience of disadvantage vis-à-vis francophone culture, it is, with minor exceptions, remarkably innocent of references to French Canada. The silence is particularly striking in the case of English-speaking cinema produced in Quebec itself. Two of the outstanding Canadian films in recent years are *Train of Dreams* (John Smith, 1988) and *Company of Strangers* (Cynthia Scott, 1991). Both were made by film-makers resident in Quebec, yet neither takes any cognizance whatsoever of the French character of the society in which they are supposedly set, and in this they are entirely typical of Anglo-Quebec cinema.

Train of Dreams is about a juvenile delinquent in Montreal who falls into the hands of the police and ends up in a Montreal jail. But in the whole film there is no visual sign of French in the streets, shops and cafés, and even the police and prison officers are native English speakers. The actual social reality of Montreal could not have been more radically deleted. *Company of Strangers*, set as it is in the countryside and dealing with an isolated group of characters, is less blatant in its deletion of a French presence, but, judged from the standpoint of inter-community dialogue, it is equally oblivious of the realities of its social environment.

Yet the unrepresentative character of these films was not an issue for discriminating francophone viewers. Both films won the Grand Prize in the annual Quebec film festival of their respective years, against distinguished francophone competitors. This amounted to a recognition that, rather than being gratuitously indifferent to the French language community, Smith and Scott were simply creating works from their own social and cultural experience which happened to be entirely anglophone. Such a reaction is obviously truer to the nature of works of art than one which would see them as accurate identikit portraits of their social background.

One could conclude that there is no necessary and rigid connection between the openness of a society to the other in its midst and the extent to which that other features in its cinema or elsewhere in art. A host of different social and cultural factors can influence the process of representation and deflect the mirror-image. Nevertheless, the very special nature of the anglophone case should not mislead us. In most circumstances it would be abnormal for a mixed society to show no trace of heterogeneity in its culture. One can legitimately look for some signs of awareness of the other, and a recognition of the enrichment that a mixture of different cultural traditions can bring to a host society.

Quebec cinema surely meets this test, probably as well as that of any other Western society. It would be easy to enumerate cases and situations where openness to the other has not gone as far as it might, but the same could be said of the cinemas of most Western nations. In general, it has moved far beyond the closed world of Devlin's *L'immigré* thirty years ago. Against the sense of closure and introversion which marks the end of *L'immigré* one could set the openness to the other that is conveyed by the end of Denys Arcand's *Jésus de Montréal* (1989). When the actor who plays Christ dies, Arcand skilfully finds a secular version of the Christian message through the donation of Daniel Coulombe's heart and eyes to immigrant patients in urgent need of a donor. There is thus a gift of self to the ethnic other from which new life and fulfilment will spring. In this symbolic action, the film represents modern Quebec's movement outwards towards others in a spirit of hope and communion.

WORKS CITED

COULOMBE, Michel & Marcel JEAN, *Le dictionnaire du cinéma québécois*, rev. ed. (Montreal: Boréal 1992).

RICHLER, Mordecai. *Oh! Canada! Oh! Quebec! Requiem for a divided country* (Markham, Ontario: Penguin, 1992).

RIOUX, Marcel. *Les Québécois* (Paris: Seuil, 1974).

❦

Robbed Graves, Whiteshamans and Stolen Stories
(Re-?)Appropriations of Native Cultures

HARMUT LUTZ

I
N THIS PAPER I WOULD LIKE TO SHARE some ongoing thoughts and ideas about cultural appropriation that I have pondered, on and off, for over a decade. I cannot come up with final answers and conclusions, but perhaps I can help to refocus a discussion that is very important to Native peoples and that raises central questions regarding our present-day European attitudes towards peoples that were colonised by our ancestors. For years I've been intrigued by the uses and misuses of Native culture, history, literature by dominant society, and I've been puzzled by the general displacement of Native origins of some cultural practices in the dominant academic and public discourse, particularly in North America.[1] The armed conflict at Oka in the summer of 1990, for example, provided a telling example of the painful truth that a collective forgetting or displacement of history will lead to repetitions of past mistakes, because, as Native American writer and critic Geary Hobson has stated, "those who do not know their history, acknowledging and accepting it for what it is, are then doomed to repeat it – all good intentions to the contrary."[2]

Besides such ideological and historical implications, there are other aspects to the question of displacing cultural appropriations, pertaining to material cultures as well as culture's intangibles.

Stolen Artifacts

On July 5, 1991, our local newspaper in Osnabrück, the *Neue Osnabrücker Zeitung*, published an article by Ayhan Bakirdögen, "Who Owns the Winged Sphinx? Renewed Conflict Between Officials from Turkey and Museums in East-Berlin" (*"Wem gehört die geflügelte Sphinx? – Neuer Streit zwischen türkischen Behörden und Ostberliner Museen"*). On November 12, 1991, eleven months before the quin-

---

[1] "Regional Culture, Ethnicity, and the Displacement of Indian Heritage in the United States Academia," *Englisch Amerikanische Studien* 8.4 (1985): 648–59.

[2] Geary Hobson, "The Rise of the White Shaman as a New Version of Cultural Imperialism," in: *The Remembered Earth: An Anthology of Contemporary Native American Literature*, ed. Geary Hobson (Albuquerque: Red Earth, 1979): 107. All subsequent quotations will appear in the text.

centennial of Columbus' discovery (of America? by Arawaks?), the Community College (*Oberstufenkolleg*) of Bielefeld hosted a conference on that fateful event, including a panel discussion about the "Return of Stolen Indian Cultural Objects" (*"Rückgabe der indianischen Kulturgüter"*). In 1992 "medico international" mounted a campaign for the "Return of Stolen Artifacts from Third-World Countries" (*"Rückgabe der geraubten Kulturgüter der 'Dritten Welt'"*). These are some examples of a post-colonial discussion about intercultural relations and colonial appropriation. Third- and Fourth-World peoples demand the return of at least some of the artifacts from their traditional cultures that were appropriated by the colonisers and that now fill showcases and archives of ethnological collections in European and European-derived states.

The return of tangible artifacts makes sense to many. But the matter becomes more complicated when the intangibles of cultures have been appropriated, such as parts of a nation's *Weltanschauung*, philosophy, music, or stories. And yet, a similar discussion about the appropriation of Native culture has been going on in Native America for at least two decades. The current discussion about the re-patriation of stolen artifacts exhibits some striking parallels with the US debate in the Seventies about whiteshamanism, and the present Canadian discussion about the theft of Native stories. All three debates raise questions about who owns whose culture, and what the relationship is between the present owners of Aboriginal artifacts and the people whose ancestors produced them. In terms of literature, the debate also addresses problems of plagiarism, copyright, and the borderline between Western individual artistic freedom and conventions of "censorship" imposed upon most oral traditions of tribal cultures.

To demonstrate the issue of the re-appropriation of stolen artifacts I would like to share with you four concrete examples – out of at least ten which I have myself witnessed during the last decade or so.

1) On March 9, 1980, Jerry Antone, a Papago student I had worked with at DQU, showed us around a very isolated burial site near Vamori on the Papago Reservation in Southern Arizona. In the sand on the desert level were the Christian graves of both his parents and most of his brothers and sisters, but on the rock surfaces of surrounding cliffs, there were traditional graves of stones and heavy logs heaped around and piled over the bodies that had once been laid out on the cliffs in the dry desert air. All of these graves had been opened, and they were empty except for a few bones. "Opened by archaeologists?" I asked. "No, Indians, who sell the stuff, who need the money," Jerry replied.

The example shows clearly that even without the physical presence of archaeologists or hobby excavators, the integrity of Native cultures is severely jeopardised if the larger society sees Indian artifacts as commodities marketable for cash value to public museums or private collectors. In this case, the situation is further aggravated by other effects of colonialism. Many Papago people have learned from their Franciscan missionaries to despise the non-Christian culture of their ancestors. Given unemployment figures of about ninety percent on a reservation that is hit terribly by the drug trade and affected by alcoholism, robbing graves has become a convenient source of revenue.

2) False face-masks are carved by Iroquoian carvers from living elm-trees. They are alive and powerful, and they are used in healing ceremonies. Their keepers feed them regularly with tobacco and administer the appropriate ceremonies. You can find Iroquoian false face-masks in almost every Indian museum. Besides, you can buy replicas at Indian traders throughout North America.

The Oneida Nation Museum on the (Iroquoian) Oneida Reservation near Green Bay, Wisconsin, houses several such masks behind a free-standing glass panel that sections off part of a display area which is left tastefully in semi-darkness with indirect lighting. The curator of the museum is an Oneida person, trained by non-Native ethnologists. The Longhouse traditionals, led by the clan mothers, have given him three official warnings to remove the masks and to desist from displaying sacred objects.

On October 1, 1982, I was taken to the museum by Louis T. Webster, an Oneida–Menominee musician and flute maker, and my host, Professor Ric Glazer Danay, the Mohawk painter and art historian. While Professor Danay stayed in the reception-area with the curator, Mr Webster took me to the room displaying the masks. Standing with his back to them, and avoiding looking at them, he said: "They are powerful. They always give me the shivers. You see the tobacco?" Sure enough, all around the masks, and particularly on the ground before them, there were shreds of tobacco and bits of broken cigarettes, which visitors had thrown over the glass partition to feed the masks.

The second example shows that differing attitudes about how to treat appropriated artifacts may cause serious friction between the more traditional and the more "progressive" members of Native communities – *divide et impera!* It also shows that for Aboriginal people the proper caretaking of artifacts may imply much more than right temperature, moisture and lighting, and that expertise in the material aspects of preserving museum-pieces alone may be far from adequate when seen in a traditional perspective.

3) Sherry and Calvin Racette are Métis cultural nationalists working as folk-art specialists with the Gabriel Dumont Institute in Regina, Saskatchewan. In an interview on February 13, 1991, Calvin Racette spoke about their trip to museums in Ireland, Scotland and England, during which they catalogued and photographed Métis quill-works and other artifacts, returning with 1,400 slides and a years' work of entering their information into their database. He said there seemed to be millions of Métis artifacts in European archives. In a dungeon-like cellar of an

Edinburgh Museum, preserved by a few mothballs, they found hanging on ordinary coat-hangers more beautifully decorated Métis coats than have remained in the whole of Canada. Often, documentations were incorrect or used racially obscene language like "squaw" or "half-caste." On the curator level of European museums, he said, they met open ears for repatriation, whereas an official of the famous Glenbow Museum in Calgary was appalled by the idea of "lending, repatriating or selling back" any of the Métis artifacts in their anthropological "warehouse" – not even to a projected Métis museum to be owned and operated by Métis people in Canada.

This final example demonstrates that, today, many Native people have acquired the skills demanded by anthropological museums to care for and preserve artifacts made by their ancestors, whereas, despite protestations to the contrary, many European museums simply do not have the facilities required to preserve the loot. It also shows that geographical distances between countries of origin and countries now housing the appropriated materials make it impossible for most Native people to ever see them.

The discussion about whether or not to reappropriate or repatriate cultural objects to Third- or Fourth-World people is an ongoing one. While those who advocate a return tend to point out that these objects were stolen, often robbed from graves, and that most of them are mouldering away in archival collections inaccessible to descendants of those who created, preserved, and often worshipped them, those directors and curators who are opposed to a return tend to repeat arguments from the following cluster:

First, the question of property and possible profits. It is claimed that until the possession of each artifact can be judicially defined once and for all – "theirs" or "ours"? (according to whose laws?) – they cannot be returned. Besides, if artifacts are repatriated the new/old proprietors would only sell them to the booming private market of collectors of exotica.

Secondly, the educational public interest. The exhibition of artifacts in museums "here" serves the important educational function of fostering understanding and appreciation of overseas cultures. Therefore, it is claimed, all artifacts must stay "here."

Thirdly, the question of appropriate accommodation. Third-World countries and Fourth-World nations in particular, it is put forth, are generally impoverished, hence too ill-equipped to house these very precious, often highly perishable objects.

And fourthly, the question of scholarly expertise. University-trained ethnologists and scholars of anthropology, through a century of research and experience, are the specialists best equipped to handle, analyse, discuss and disseminate information about the objects in question.

I am not going to respond to these claims here. The above examples indicate that the issues are indeed complicated. Gert von Paczenski and Herbert Ganslmayr, in their study of 1984, *Nofretete will nach Hause*[3] ("Nofretete wants to go home" –Nefertiti: a famous bust of an Egyptian queen, housed in a Berlin museum), demonstrated convincingly how untenable such positions are. I've heard the same arguments myself from the famous American ethnohistorian James Axtell. After a lecture at Carleton University in Ottawa, October 1989, about "The Art of History: Methodological Debates Concerning the Presentation of Scholarly Research in Non-Scholarly Forms," he came out strongly against a return of bones or artifacts to Indian people: "No way! I have the money, I have the museum, I have the expertise. Those people don't. No way would I give those things back to them!"

"There" "we" are!

"Whiteshamanism" in the USA

In the United States during the Seventies, a discussion started about the appropriation and misuse of non-tangible aspects of Indian cultures, mainly in religion, philosophy and literature. Criticism was directed both against mainstream authors who used Native spirituality out of context in their works, and against authors who claimed part-Indian ancestry and did basically the same. Dan Cushman's *Stay Away Joe* (1953), while liked by many Native readers, came under attack for racial and sexual stereotyping. Hyemeyohsts Storm's beautifully written and sweetly illustrated cult-novel, *Seven Arrows* (1972), was accused of distorting Cheyenne religious philosophy and stereotyping cultural practices. Gary Snyder's "shamanist" poetry was attacked for similar reasons, though Native critics acknowledged his greatness as a poet and centered their attack more on later "shamanist poets" of the Seventies. Carlos Castaneda was accused of fabricating a false Yaqui mythology for the cash of New Age freaks. Ruth Beebe Hills' *Hanta Yo* (1979) loosed a storm of protest, mainly from Lakota people, who felt their culture had been denigrated, besmeared and ridiculed by a book which, quite contrary to the author's claims, was a fabrication written for a booming market interested in noble savages and their religious and sexual practices. Published in the year when *The Remembered Earth* demonstrated clearly that Native American writers and critics not only could but would speak for themselves, this historical novel was hailed as an Indian *Roots*, "filled with the music of mysticism [...] the Indian novel of our era" (blurb from the *Cleveland Plain Dealer*, printed on the back cover of the novel). The book was carefully launched as a bestseller, with

---

3 Gert von Paczenski & Herbert Ganslmayr, *Nofretete will nach Hause* (Munich: Bertelsmann, 1984).

exuberant reviews in daily newspapers and a positive one in the most prestigious ethnological journal in the United States, the *Smithsonian*. But Native intellectuals retaliated with carefully argued and well-researched reviews of their own, most notably Bea Medicine's "*Hanta Yo*: A New Phenomenon,"[4] and Victor Douville's "*Hanta Yo*: Authentic Farce."[5] Unfortunately, these reviews never reached the large numbers which Warner Brothers' campaign had activated. So, Lakota elders and cultural activists (Jo–Allyn Archambault, Darrel Standing Elk, Marla Powers) and sympathetic non-Natives took over the campaign on a national level. The battle included hundreds of Lakota people and their supporters, who passed resolutions, sent their protests to producer David Wolpers, and staged press conferences throughout North America, stalling the filming of the book for years. By May 1980, a year after its first release, no fewer than nine Sioux tribal councils, fifteen colleges and national Indian organisations, and the National Education Association had passed resolutions against the film project.[6] At first, Ruth Beebe Hill and her Native collaborator, Chunksa Yuha, alias Lorenzo Blacksmith, tried to dismiss as "Pop Indians" busloads of Medicine people, elders, intellectuals and political activists who confronted her at readings in the Plains and along the West Coast. However, their adamant resistance forced Warner Brothers off all Indian reservations and reserves in the United States and Canada, and the series was finally shot in Mexico under the title "Mystic Warrior," and on release was a flop.[7]

To date, the *Hanta Yo* campaign of 1979–80 remains the largest of its kind, although there have been sporadic events staged against bestseller author Lynn Andrews, also known as the "Beverly Hills Shaman." Andrews was criticised for her untenable claim to have been initiated by a Cree medicine woman into an "Indian" ideology catering to the New Age interests in shamanism of white middle-class "feminists."

In this heated debate, Cherokee–Chickasaw critic, poet and scholar Geary Hobson coined the term "whiteshamans" for non-Native authors like Snyder, Storm, Castaneda and others.

> These are the apparently growing number of small-press poets of generally white,
> Euro-Christian American background, who in their poems assume the persona of the

4 Bea Medicine, "HANTA YO: A New Phenomenon," *Indian Historian* 12.2 (Summer 1979): 2–5.

5 Victor Douville, "HANTA YO: Authentic Farce," *Sinte Gleska College News* (April 1980): centre-fold.

6 I have a folder of resolutions, newspaper clippings and lists of organizations which supported that struggle, given to me by Darrel Standing Elk, University of California at Davis, or gleaned by myself during a year at Davis and DQ University as an ACLS fellow in 1979–80.

7 For a discussion of the HANTA YO-campaign in the larger context of Indian literary stereotyping, see Hartmut Lutz, *"Indianer" und "Native Americans": Zur sozial- und literarhistorischen Vermittlung eines Stereotyps* (Hildesheim: Georg Olms, 1985).

>Shaman, usually in the guise of an American Indian medicine man. To be a poet is
>simply not enough; they must claim a power from higher sources. (102)

In his discussion, Hobson already uses the term "appropriation" (101), and he draws parallels between colonial land-grabbers, ethnologists, buffalo-hunters and would-be shamans, because they are all collectors who believe "that this body of knowledge and consciousness, like the land and water and the sky itself, now belongs to them by dint of appropriation."

The term "whiteshamanism" stuck. The first scholarly reactions by Native critics were published in 1979 in Hobson's *The Remembered Earth: An Anthology of Contemporary Native American Literature*, in which both he and Laguna novelist and poet Leslie Silko addressed the issue in separate articles. A few years later Hopi–Miwok poet, critic and anthropologist Wendy Rose addressed the issue again in her famous talk "Just What's All This Fuss About Whiteshamanism Anyway?" She states clearly:

>[...] it is apparent that a pattern exists. European-derived Americans consider
>themselves to be uniquely qualified to explain the rest of humanity. Coupled with
>this bizarre notion is the idea that *natives* of a particular culture are inhibited from
>being able to articulate themselves in a cultural context, or are merely superstitious
>when they try.[8]

While approaching the problem from different angles and addressing different authors, the three essays draw attention to recurrent patterns. They attack the tacit assumption of European-derived Americans that they are innately superior to Native specialists, be they linguists, writers or archaeologists. Native stories and/or artifacts, the Native scholars insist, are *not* public property but were *stolen* from Native people, and the publication of works by white shamans in turn obliterates Native writers from the public view. Hobson sees whiteshamanism as another form of cultural imperialism, "such as the theft of homeland by treaty" (101).

The two women critics, Silko and Rose, also go into the motivations that seem to lie behind the need of non-Natives to appropriate Native spirituality. Other than economic greed, spiritual appropriation may be understood as an expression of the lack of roots from which most Euro-Americans seem to suffer. Besides, such appropriation may constitute an attempt, via some mythic identification, to deny the guilt many of them feel towards Native Americans on whose continent they have made their homes. Finally, Wendy Rose also addresses the question of artistic freedom versus cultural restraint. In the European notion, she explains, art is free, and the artist is at liberty to use anything he or she likes. Traditional Native

---

8 Wendy Rose, "Just What's All This Fuss About Whiteshamanism Anyway?" in *Coyote Was Here: Essays on Contemporary Native American Literature and Political Mobilization*, ed. Bo Schöler (Aarhus: Seklos/The Dolphin/English Department, 1984): 15. All subsequent quotations will appear in the text.

notions about "art" differ. For Native people art has always been part of everyday
life-practices, and it is governed by rules that ensure the common benefit of the
whole community of which the artist is an integral part. This leads to many
restrictions for the individual artists, which a traditional tribal person, however,
would not perceive as such. If a non-Native person appropriates Native art, he or
she is generally not aware of the restrictions that are attached to it, and most
whiteshamans break such rules constantly. Rose stresses that Natives are not
"trying to dictate subject matter and form," nor are they "staking a claim as the
sole interpreters of Indian cultures, most especially that which is sacred." But
since credit should be given where credit is due, she states that "the problem with
'whiteshamans' is one of integrity and intent, not of topic, style, interest, or
experimentation." She thus clearly states that the problem is one of professional
ethics. Referring to Lynn Andrews, she says:

> There is a world of difference between the white woman who expresses her feelings
> and perceptions about Native spirituality honestly, stating that they are *her*
> perceptions, and a white woman with the delusion of having been appointed as a
> "bridge" between the two cultures through initiation as a medicine woman [...] (22)

Finally, Wendy Rose asks that wherever non-Natives use material that "is sensitive or belongs to another person" they do so "with permission" (22). Like Geary
Hobson, she puts the whole discussion into the larger cultural and political context
of colonialism.

> The individual "whiteshamans" are not the enemy so much as is ignorance and a
> culture history steeped in theft. The enemy resides within the continuing colonial
> relationship that has co-opted Indian cultures and possessed them for entertainment
> and wealth. (23)

"Theft of Native Voice" in Canada

While there are many parallels with the "whiteshamanism" discussion in the
United States, the debate in Canada about the appropriation of the Native voice by
non-Native writers also shows some differences.

Adolf Hungry Wolf, a Swiss- or German-born Blackfoot living on the Blood
Reserve in Alberta, has since 1970 continued to publish *Good Medicine* books
about the people his wife Beverly Hungry Wolf was born into. In the process, he
has become a sort of Native "guru" for many non-Native people in Europe. For
years, W.P. Kinsella has published novels set on the Hobemah Reserve in Alberta,
using Indian characters, which, while enjoyed by many Native readers, present
Native people as stereotypes of big-hearted drunkards and sexually licentious
women. Novelist Rudy Wiebe's *The Temptations of Big Bear* (1973) uses the
persona of the famous Cree Chief, and, in *The Scorched-Wood People* (1977), he
adds what has been understood as a unique Métis voice to the history of the

Manitoba Struggle and the Rebellion of 1885 in Saskatchewan.[9] Anne Cameron's *Daughters of Copper Woman* (1981) and other books from the Oral Tradition of West Coast Native women, were published for a growing market interested in woman's history and power. Barbara Smith, whose Cherokee ancestry has come under suspicion, has published a New Age ecological fantasy, *Renewal*, in two parts, *The Prophecy of Manu* (1985) and *Teoni's Give Away* (1986). In public appearances she has assumed the role of Indian feminist shaman. Again, Lynn Andrews is criticised for claiming initiation by a (non-existent) Cree medicine woman from Manitoba. All of these writers have come under attack for cashing in on Indian culture and reaping publicity and recognition in Canada which Native authors themselves ought to enjoy.

Even more so than in the USA, the discussion about cultural appropriation and the struggle against it was initiated and carried through by Native women.[10] It started at the Third International Feminist Book Fair in Montreal in June 1988 with West-Coast Métis Lee Maracle asking Anne Cameron to "move over." It continued with Anishinabeg Lenore Keeshig–Tobias addressing a panel at the Writers' Union of Canada Annual General Meeting in the Spring of 1989, asking writers to "Stop Stealing Native Stories." The following year also saw the publication of Maria Campbell's and Linda Griffith's *Book of Jessica*,[11] the most poignant document of a transcultural literary and dramatic cooperation. It traces

---

9 For the most comprehensive discussion of the portrayal of Métis people in Canadian literature, see Wolfgang Klooss, *Geschichte und Mythos in der Literatur Kanadas: Die englischsprachige Métis- und Riel-Rezeption* (Heidelberg: Carl Winter, 1989).

10 See also: Lee Maracle. "Moving Over," *Trivia: A Journal of Ideas* 14 (Spring 1989): 9–12; Henry Mietkiewicz, "Native Calls Canadian Film Racist," *Toronto Star* (September 16, 1989); Bronwyn Draine, "Minorities go toe to toe with majority," *Globe and Mail* (September 30, 1989): C1; Lenore Keeshig–Tobias, "Stop Stealing Native Stories," *Globe and Mail* (January 26, 1990); Brian D. Johnson et al., "Tribal tribulations: Debate grows over who owns native culture," *Maclean's* (February 19, 1990); Loretta Todd, "Notes on Appropriation," *Parallelogramme* 16.1 (1990): 24–32; Marie Baker, "Stealing Native stories," *Briarpatch* (March 1990): 29; Allyson Dandie, "Native people must start telling their own stories," *Leader–Post* (Regina; April 19, 1990): B6; Margaret Hryniuk, "They have taken our land, now they want our words," *Leader–Post* (Regina; April 19, 1990): B6; Lynne Van Luven, "NeWest anthology draws Saskatchewan writers' fire," *Edmonton Journal* (May 12, 1990); Jeannette Armstrong, "The Disempowerment of First North American Native Peoples and Empowerment Through Their Writing," *Gatherings: The En'Owkin Journal of First North American Peoples* 1.1 (1990): 141–46. A broader discussion of the whole issue by both Native and non-Native authors was published in *Books in Canada* 20.1 (1991): 11–17. Additional statements about appropriation and intercultural relations between Natives and non-Natives by Maria Campbell, Lee Maracle, Emma LaRocque, Lenore Keeshig–Tobias, Beth Cuthand, Daniel David Moses, Basil Johnston and others are included in Hartmut Lutz, *Contemporary Challenges: Conversations with Canadian Native Authors* (Saskatoon: Fifth House, 1991).

11 Maria Campbell & Linda Griffith, *The Book of Jessica: A Theatrical Transformation* (Toronto: Coach House, 1989).

through recorded conversations the love–hate relationship evolving from the white actress' appropriation of Maria Campbell's life story. In 1990–91 the Saskatchewan Aboriginal Writers' Group, led by Annharte (Marie Baker) and Sue Deranger, tried in vain to halt non-Native editors' Jeanne Perrault and Lyndia Vance's anthology of Native Women's works, *Writing the Circle*.[12] While Lee Maracle and Lenore Keeshig–Tobias are the best-known voices in the debate, most Native writers support their arguments and address the issue individually, while others – and this includes several of my friends at the SIFC, some of whom are writers themselves – feel that whoever writes best should write down Native stories. The debate is ongoing.

While I was interviewing about twenty Native authors in Canada in 1989–90, most of the arguments I heard resembled those put forth in the whiteshamanism debate. Native writers resent the fact that appropriators cash in profits made by disseminating Native stories as if they were their own. They state strongly that Native stories are *not* public property, and that nobody should speak on their behalf without authorisation, or use their stories without permission. They insist on a Native "copyright system based on trust" (Alexander Wolf). Again, the question is an ethical one.

Besides, they criticise the lack of expertise on the part of white writers who tell Native stories. Lenore Keeshig–Tobias, in particular, states that without "equity between First Nations people and Canadians" there can be no sharing or meaningful dialogue about the issue. So, again, the conflict is seen also as a political issue, resulting from the colonial disempowerment of indigenous cultures.

Before dealing with Native peoples' identities, it is felt, non-Natives have to come to terms with their own conflicting identities as imperialist land-grabbers and/or rejects from Europe's poor. What makes the discussion different in quality from the one a decade earlier is the insistence on the unique quality of contemporary Native writing as coming from the Oral Tradition, ie from the land. Nearly all the writers I interviewed told me that they came from a strong storytelling tradition, and they relate their modern texts to it.

In the oral tradition the spoken word carries power it does not have when written down. Besides, the exact verbatim rendering of certain myths is the only safeguard against cultural loss. Non-Native users of Native myths do not generally know or master the appropriate methods of rendering such texts without destroying them. Once an unauthorised or faulty version becomes ossified in print, Native story-tellers can no longer control its effects.

More importantly, the oral tradition is tied to the land, to the tangible and intangible givens of a specific region or place, and the language, Native or

---

12 *Native Women of Western Canada: Writing the Circle; An Anthology*, ed. Jeanne Perrault and Sylvia Vance (Edmonton: NeWest, 1990).

English, has to reflect that uniqueness, whether it is called "home"-space or even, as Maria Campbell and Beth Cuthand explain it, the "voice of the Mother." English, Maria Campbell was told, "lost its Mother a long time ago,"[13] and her task as a Native story-teller is to put the Mother, which can only partially be explained as being the spirit of the land, back into it (which, incidentally, she does by using "village English"). In her perception, European immigrants only come from half a place, only see half of the world, and unless they come to see and acknowledge the other half too, they are incomplete at best, unable to "interpret or tell" a Native story.

Different Reactions in the USA and Canada

In the United States the whiteshamanism discussion remained restricted almost hermetically to the Native community, to scholars and students of Native literature, or to those having access to the "moccasin telegraph." The campaign against the filming of *Hanta Yo* gained much media attention, but it remains an isolated phenomenon. Few mainstream writers except those attacked ever acknowledged or addressed the issue, and scholars tend to write about Gary Snyder or Carlos Castaneda seemingly without being aware of the Native reactions to these authors.

In Canada the situation is markedly different. Owing in part to the ideal of multiculturalism, Native issues in Canada generally receive better media attention than in the USA. Mainstream authors and publishers reacted widely, especially after the appropriation discussion in 1990 coincided with crucial political events that brought the Native plight to the public attention, eg, the failure of Meech Lake and the military standoff at Oka. Moreover, Canada's creative writers are well organised in their writers' union, and there is much discussion among writers throughout the state. In 1990 the provincial annual meetings in Alberta and in Saskatchewan – probably elsewhere as well – hosted panels discussing the appropriation issue. The same year, the Vancouver International Writers' Festival dedicated many events to Native literature. Even the triennial conference of the Nordic Association for Canadian Studies in Oslo, Norway, in August 1990, at which there were nine Euro-Canadian authors present, chose the appropriation issue as the main topic for their panel discussion, at the suggestion of Rudy Wiebe. In the discussion, reactions differed greatly. While Heather Spears asked, "Would it be alright for a German writer today to write about the holocaust in the voice of a Jewish victim?" Betty Jane Wylie, a former writer's Union president, spoke out strongly against "Indian censorship," thus trying to wipe the whole debate off the agenda without addressing the issues it raises – a particularly interesting form of "censorship," given the hegemonic structure that exists be-

---

13 Maria Campbell, "Maria Campbell (Interview)," in Lutz, *Contemporary Challenges*, 49.

tween most mainstream authors and Native writers. *Books in Canada*, in its January–February 1991 issue, published a debate "Whose Voice *Is* It, Anyway?" in which Native and non-Native critics controversially discuss the topic – and there have been various articles, pro and con, elsewhere. There are also more practical moves to atone for past or present injustices. Maria Campbell received an honorary doctorate from the English Department of York University. In 1991 she was invited to give the keynote lecture to the Canadian Writers' Union annual conference. Individual writers have also reacted. Anne Cameron has moved over, Margaret Atwood, Rudy Wiebe and others support Native writers as best they can. Lynn Andrews continues her shamanism, after having admitted that her books are sheer fantasies following Castaneda but having the feminist market in mind.

On the institutional level, Native people themselves are becoming ever more ready to counteract the appropriation process. In Toronto, Lenore Keeshig–Tobias, Daniel David Moses and Tomson Highway have established the Committee to Re-Establish the Trickster. In Ontario, Joy Asham Fedorick single-handedly started a computer-based Native writing and publishing programme for Ojibway language texts. In many provinces, Native writers have formed their own associations and direct their own workshops. Small outfits record and release Native poetry and that of other People of Colour and put it to music on tapes, which young people like to listen to. Today, there are at least two Native-owned and -operated publishing houses, Theytus Books in Penticton, B.C., and Pemmican Press in Winnipeg, Manitoba, and there are several other small presses also disseminating the Native voice. More importantly, there is an International School of Native Writing, also in Penticton, the only one of its kind in the world. Directed by novelist, poet and cultural activist Jeannette Armstrong (Okanagan), the centre trains Native students to become creative writers, scriptors, editors and publishers. So: Native writing is alive and exuberant.

In an 1987 interview, non-Native author Aritha van Herk, referring to the silencing of women writers in general, laughingly quoted Canadian author Audrey Thomas, who said, "The best revenge is writing well."[14] Some Native writers seem to react in exactly this way, and they are getting published more than ever before. In their stories and poems, some of them also address the appropriation issue, often with great humour. Emma Lee Warrior, a Peigan (Blackfoot) herself, in her short story "Compatriots"[15] writes about Hilda Afflerbach, a German student, who has come to the Blood (Blackfoot) reserve to meet some real Indians, and who is taken to the tipi of "Helmut Walking Eagle," obviously a fictional

---

14 "Aritha van Herk im Gespräch mit Hartmut Lutz," *Zeitschrift der Gesellschaft für Kanada-Studien* 9.2 (1989): 109–15.

15 Emma Lee Warrior, "Compatriots," in *All My Relations: An Anthology of Contemporary Canadian Native Fiction*, ed. Thomas King (Toronto: McClelland & Stewart, 1990): 48–59.

version of Adolf Hungry Wolf. In her poem about Christopher Columbus, Jeannette Armstrong talks about "the mob" that burst "Out of the belly of Christopher's ship / [...] Running in all directions / Pulling furs of animals."[16]

There are hundreds of "Indian hobbyists' clubs" in Germany and other European countries, emulating Indian clothes and lifeways on weekends. Novelist, short-story writer, critic and scholar Thomas King promised me a short story for publication in *OBEMA*, the bilingual series of Third- and Fourth-World authors. The story will be about a small Blackfoot boy who is so fascinated with German culture that he sets up a German Club on the reserve, collecting brass music, beer mugs, lederhosen, and all the stereotypically German artifacts.

A final example: the Saskatchewan Indian Federated College at the University of Regina is the largest Indian institution of higher education in North America and the only of its kind in Canada. Its Native Studies Department is the largest at the college. Director Dave Miller, himself a non-Native ethnologist, is preparing the implementation of training courses in Museum Science for Native students, so that First Nations communities will be ready for the 2,000 Indian skeletal remains, and hopefully many artifacts besides, that the Smithsonian Institution in Washington DC is considering giving back to Native people.

WORKS CITED

ARMSTRONG, Jeannette. "History Lesson," in *Seventh Generation,* ed. Heather Hodgson (Penticton: Theytus, 1989): 54–55.

CAMPBELL, Maria. "Maria Campbell (Interview)," in Hartmut Lutz, *Contemporary Challenges: Conversations with Canadian Native Authors* (Saskatoon: Fifth House, 1991): 41–65.

———— & Linda Griffith. *The Book of Jessica: A Theatrical Transformation* (Toronto: Coach House, 1989).

DOUVILLE, Victor. "HANTA YO: Authentic Farce," *Sinte Gleska College News* (April 1980): centrefold.

HOBSON, Geary. "The Rise of the White Shaman as a New Version of Cultural Imperialism," in *The Remembered Earth: An Anthology of Contemporary Native American Literature,* ed. Geary Hobson (Albuquerque: Red Earth, 1979): 101–108.

KLOOSS, Wolfgang. *Geschichte und Mythos in der Literatur Kanadas: Die englischsprachige Métis- und Riel-Rezeption* (Heidelberg: Carl Winter, 1989).

LUTZ, Hartmut. *"Indianer" und "Native Americans": Zur sozial- und literarhistorischen Vermittlung eines Stereotyps* (Hildesheim: Georg Olms, 1985).

MEDICINE, Bea. "HANTA YO: A New Phenomenon," *Indian Historian* 12.2 (Summer 1979): 2–5.

PACZENSKI, Gert von & Herbert GANSLMAYR. *Nofretete will nach Hause* (Munich: Bertelsmann, 1984).

---

16 Jeannette Armstrong, "History Lesson," in *Seventh Generation,* ed. Heather Hodgson (Penticton: Theytus, 1989): 54.

PERRAULT, Jeanne & Sylvia VANCE, ed. *Native Women of Western Canada: Writing the Circle: An Anthology* (Edmonton: NeWest, 1990).

ROSE, Wendy. "Just What's All This Fuss About Whiteshamanism Anyway?" in *Coyote Was Here: Essays on Contemporary Native American Literature and Political Mobilization,* ed. Bo Schöler (Aarhus, DK: Seklos/The Dolphin/ English Department, 1984): 13–24.

VAN HERK, Aritha. "Aritha van Herk im Gespräch mit Hartmut Lutz," *Zeitschrift der Gesellschaft für Kanada-Studien* 9.2 (1989): 109–15.

WARRIOR, Emma Lee. "Compatriots," in *All My Relations: An Anthology of Contemporary Canadian Native Fiction,* ed. Thomas King (Toronto: McClelland & Stewart, 1990): 48–59.

❧ ✦ ❧

Gender

Gentle-Women in the Wilderness
Self-Images of British–Canadian Pioneer Women

BARBARA KORTE

B ETWEEN THE 1780S AND THE 1920S, women came from different
countries and different social classes to settle in Canada; their pioneer
experience was shaped by a variety of Canadian environments.* Prairie
women around the turn of our century were of another cast than the women who,
like Susanna Moodie and Catharine Traill, had "roughed it" in the Ontario bush of
the 1830s: Nellie McClung admired her mother as an ideal pioneer woman, "calm,
cheerful, self-reliant, and undaunted."[1] Georgina Binnie–Clark and Elizabeth
Morris welcomed homesteading as an opportunity for a self-determined life.[2] But
it is the gentlewomen of earlier phases of settlement who most impressed the
Canadian imagination, with Moodie and Traill as the principal culture heroines.[3]

These gentlewomen came to Canada straight from the British Isles and as the
appendage of impoverished husbands (officers on half-pay or gentry without land)
to whom emigration provided the only alternative to a loss of caste. Canada
attracted a high percentage of (upper-)middle-class immigrants, of whom a first
wave, between 1825 and 1835, preferred the proximity of Lake Ontario; those of a
second wave, with its climax in the 1870s, settled in Eastern and Western Canada.

This paper focuses on women's autobiographical writings: journals and letters,
memoirs, and emigrant manuals based on the writer's own experience.
Contemporary feminist criticism argues that these genres display a less conventional view of a woman's life than does the fiction written by either men or
women.[4] However, none of the texts to be considered here is free from (self)-

---

* An earlier German version of this paper was published in *Zeitschrift für Kanada-Studien* 22.2
(1992).

[1] *Clearing in the West: My Own Story* (Toronto: Allen Lane, 1935): 82.

[2] Binnie–Clark, *Wheat and Woman* (1914; Toronto: U of Toronto P, 1979); Morris, *An English-
woman in the Canadian West* (London: Simpkin Marshall, 1913).

[3] See, for example, Robertson Davies' play *At My Heart's Core* (1950), Margaret Atwood's *The
Journals of Susanna Moodie* (1970), Margaret Laurence's *The Diviners* (1974), or Carol Shields'
Small Ceremonies (1976). Also cf Eva–Marie Kröller, "Resurrections: Susanna Moodie, Catharine
Parr Traill and Emily Carr in Contemporary Canadian Literature," *Journal of Popular Culture* 15.3
(1981): 39–46.

[4] Cf *The Private Self: Theory and Practice of Women's Autobiographical Writings*, ed. Shari Benstock
(London: Routledge, 1988); *Life/Lines: Theorizing Women's Autobiography*, ed. Bella Brodzki &
Celeste Schenck (Ithaca NY: Cornell UP, 1988); *Women's Autobiography: Essays in Criticism*, ed.

censorship and the silencing of self-statements that would have violated traditional decorum. Moodie's *Roughing It in the Bush* (1852) and *Life in the Clearings* (1854)[5] as well as her sister's *Canadian Settler's Guide* (1855)[6] were written for a general audience; Traill's *The Backwoods of Canada* (1836)[7] is based on family letters whose more personal sections were edited out when the book was published for the general reader. Even letters and journals unpublished in their writers' lifetime used to be dispersed among a wider audience than their nominal addressee. In all instances, the female self speaks only from a sub-text, from below the facts of colonial life in which the texts' overt purpose consists. There is no feminist concern as in the book of a famous traveller in Canada, Anna Jameson;[8] the Strickland sisters and other gentlewomen tended to conform to the gender norms with which they grew up. Nevertheless, their writings reveal that emigration meant a deconstruction and reconstruction of their former self-image and understanding of themselves as women. It is the indirection of this self-presentation, the double-voicedness of self-statement and self-denial, which makes the accounts interesting from a textual perspective.

Many gentlewomen stress the learning process entailed in pioneer life. Frances Stewart, a friend and neighbour of the Traills, wrote that emigration had placed her in situations "in which [she] could hardly have been[,] had [she] lived three lives at home."[9] Susanna Moodie, in *Roughing It*, is even more explicit:

"You have much to learn, ma'am, if you are going to the woods," said Mrs. J—.
"To unlearn, you mean," said Mr. D—. (263)

Of course, emigration meant a redefinition of life for men and women of all classes. But, for genteel immigrants, the new world was not a promised land with the possibility of upward mobility; they left a culture which, had there been an

---

Estelle C. Jelinek (Bloomington/London: Indiana UP, 1980); Estelle C. Jelinek, *The Tradition of Women's Autobiography: From Antiquity to the Present* (Boston: Twayne, 1986); Sidonie Smith, *A Poetics of Women's Autobiography: Marginality and the Fictions of Self-Representation* (Bloomington/Indianapolis: Indiana UP, 1987); *Women's Studies International Forum* 10.1 (1987; Special Issue: Women's Autobiographical Writings, ed. Dale Spender); *The Female Autograph: Theory and Practice of Autobiography from the Tenth to the Twentieth Century*, ed. Domna C. Stanton (Chicago: U of Chicago P, 1987).

5 *Roughing It in the Bush: Or, Life in Canada* (Toronto: McClelland & Stewart, 1989); *Life in the Clearings versus the Bush* (Toronto: McClelland & Stewart, 1989).

6 Traill, *The Canadian Settler's Guide* (Toronto/Montreal: McClelland & Stewart, 1969); first published as *The Female Emigrant's Guide* (1854).

7 *The Backwoods of Canada: Being Letters from the Wife of an Emigrant Officer, Illustrative of the Domestic Economy of British America* (Toronto: McClelland & Stewart, 1989).

8 *Winter Studies and Summer Rambles in Canada: Selections*, ed. Clara Thomas (Toronto: McClelland & Stewart, 1965).

9 *Our Forest Home: Being Extracts from the Correspondence of the Late Frances Stewart*, ed. E.S. Dunlop (Montreal: Gazette Printing, 1902): 112.

adequate income, would have been their ideal habitat. The "equalizing system of America"[10] upset the class foundation of the gentlefolk's self-image. Gentility at home was based on an education which exempted men and women from the necessity of physical labour; the gentlemen and gentlewomen in the bush were obsessed with how they could preserve their rank while performing the menial duties of an inferior class.

The idea of having to "work" must have been more alienating for gentle*women* than for their husbands. Female in contrast to male gentility was associated with gentleness – delicacy, softness, timidity, weakness and other attributes of "femininity" that incapacitated the woman for strenuous activity. For gentle-women, pioneering was incongruous not only with notions of class, but also with a gender-stereotyping identified with this peculiar class.[11]

In contrast to their wives, British gentlemen received an education which incorporated the notions of achievement, activity and adventure. The word *adventure* occurs in the titles of men's accounts of settlement life,[12] but never (to my knowledge) in the titles of those written by women. Samuel Strickland, the brother of Mesdames Moodie and Traill, begins his reminiscences with a sentence that emphasises activity: "A preference for an active, rather than a professional life, induced me to accept the offer made by an old friend."[13] In a later passage he claims that "the amusements of shooting and fishing, riding and exploring excursions, quickly make newcomers much attached to the country" (319). For men, even genteelly educated ones, pioneer life had its attractions and was not unprepared-for – a fact which is stressed by the women, who had not been equipped with a comparable physical and mental makeup: "Many young men," writes Susanna Moodie in *Life in the Clearings*, "are attracted to the Backwoods by the facilities they present for hunting and fishing" (11). "But in none of these can their sisters share," Traill added to an almost identical statement in *The Backwoods of Canada* (13). Education in the early nineteenth century recommended physical exercise as beneficial for pre-pubescent girls, but after puberty the public pursuit

---

10 Traill, *The Backwoods of Canada*, 103.

11 In her *Autobiography* (3rd ed., London: Smith, Elder, 1877), Harriet Martineau comments on the restrictive quality of her family's gentility, which prevented her from becoming active and useful. The family's "pecuniary ruin" after the father's death in 1829 meant a gain of personal liberty: "I, who had been obliged to write before breakfast, or in some private way, had henceforth liberty to do my own work in my own way; for we had lost our gentility" (vol. 1: 142).

12 Cf *Life in the Woods: A Boy's Narrative of the Adventures of a Settler's Family in Canada*, ed. John C. Geike (Boston MA: Crosby & Ainsworth, 1865); J.W. Dunbar Moodie, *Scenes and Adventures, as a Soldier and Settler, During Half a Century* (Montreal: Lovell, 1866).

13 *Twenty-Seven Years in Canada West or The Experience of an Early Settler*, ed. Agnes Strickland (1853; Edmonton: Hurtig, 1970).

of sports and games was considered unsuitable for a lady.[14] In 1826, six years
before her own emigration, Catharine Strickland wrote a children's book, *The
Young Emigrants*, in which the prospective women pioneers are worried about the
waste of an education in which music, drawing, and French featured prominently.
A brother tries to console the girls, but his words point to the uselessness of such
accomplishments in the new world. There, "more active pursuits" await the
women, and their "more elegant attainments" will only "serve as a pleasing
relaxation."[15]

The idea that the gentlewoman-as-pioneer had to transcend the boundaries of
genteel femininity seems to have been a common one. On the other hand, the
stereotypical view of a gentlewoman's proper sphere was imported unmodified
from the mother country and propagated in the colonial press. A newspaper article
of 1849 contrasts the "Parallel Qualities of the Sexes" in a way that entirely
neglects conditions in the new world:

Man is strong	woman is beautiful,
Man is daring and confident	woman is diffident and unassuming,
Man is great in action	woman is suffering,
Man shines abroad	woman at home,
Man has judgement	woman sensibility,
Man is a being of justice	Woman an angel of mercy.[16]

The lady pioneer had to adopt all the attributes in the left-hand column and frequently suppress those in the right. This process may be envisaged as a migration
of gender-traits from the "masculine" to the "feminine" side of the stereotypical
spectrum. It has also been referred to as one of androgynisation,[17] but this term
implies a more radical change of the feminine self-image than that which can be
traced in the pioneer women's texts. A more adequate term is the "gender ambiguity" which Shirley Foster observes for another type of nineteenth-century
gentlewoman, the Victorian globetrotteress.[18] As migrant in the margins of the
British Empire, both the gentlewoman as pioneer and as traveller had a chance to

---

14 See Deborah Gorham, *The Victorian Girl and the Feminine Ideal* (London: Croom Helm, 1982): 71–72.

15 *The Young Emigrants or Pictures of Canada* (New York: Johnson Reprint, 1969): 12.

16 Cited from *Pioneer and Gentlewomen of British North America 1713–1867*, ed. Beth Light & Alison Prentice (Toronto: New Hogtown Press, 1980): 222.

17 See Marian Fowler, *The Embroidered Tent: Five Gentlewomen in Early Canada* (Toronto: Anansi, 1982): "The wilderness introduced them to what I have chosen to call the 'androgynous' ideal [...] The androgynous ideal constitutes an escape from the shackles of gender-stereotyping into a wide-open, freely chosen world of individual responses and behaviour" (10). Cf also Carol Shields's even more extreme view of Moodie's "sexual reversal" in *Susanna Moodie: Voice and Vision* (Ottawa: Borealis, 1977).

18 *Across New Worlds: Nineteenth-Century Women Travellers and Their Writings* (Brighton: Harvester Wheatsheaf, 1990): 11.

transgress the gender-stereotyping of a patriarchal culture. However, public opinion and the women's own conditioning made the addition of allegedly "masculine" traits to the "feminine" personality appear dubious or even outrageous, so that most women in their writing played down their new "unfeminine" components. Although Moodie and Traill praise Canada as a land of freedom and hope in *general* terms,[19] they hesitate to spell out the implications of these freedoms for their own lives. Like other female writers of their time, they overtly conform to a conventional view of women's lot, with apologetic and self-deprecatory phrases that disturb the modern (female) reader.[20]

"Man is great in action – woman is suffering." The myth which first evolved from such gender-stereotyping was that of the "reluctant" female pioneer, the obedient spouse who is brought into the new land against her will. It is Susanna Moodie, or rather the persona through which she dramatised herself in the first half of *Roughing It*, with whom the image of the reluctant pioneer is most frequently associated. Moodie wants it to be understood that the decision to emigrate was not one in which she shared, but one to which she consented: "My husband finally determined to emigrate to Canada" (72); "I had bowed to a superior mandate, the command of duty" (194). The passive woman also emerges from the writings of Traill, who is generally considered the more cheerful and adaptable of the Strickland sisters: here, too, "the master of the household" makes the decision to leave his native land (*The Canadian Settler's Guide*, 1). The travel sections in the accounts of both sisters, too, contain strong images of "suffering," passive and confined femininity. When Moodie's ship collides with another vessel on the St Lawrence, Susanna "patiently" sits the danger out in the cabin, the enclosed space reserved for her sex, and admonishes the other women to follow her example instead of hindering the men's active rescue operations (*Roughing It*, 44–45). Traill, during her voyage across the Atlantic, seems to identify with her captain's tame bird:

> "It is all one to him whether his cage is at sea or on land, he is still at home," said the captain, regarding his little favourite with an air of great affection, and evidently gratified by the attention I bestowed on his bird. (*The Backwoods of Canada*, 17)

Ellen Moers has pointed out the special significance of the caged-bird image in women's fiction: "Of all creatures, birds alone can fly all the way to heaven – yet

---

[19] "Canada is the land of hope; here every thing is new" (Traill, *The Backwoods of Canada*, 210); Moodie's *Roughing It* begins with a poem the first line of which runs "Canada, the blest – the free."

[20] Cf phrases like "womanly propensity of over-much talking" (Traill, *The Backwoods of Canada*, 145); "my husband, who is better qualified than myself, to give a more accurate account of the country" (Moodie, *Roughing It*, 206); "I leave statistics for wiser and cleverer male hands" (Moodie, *Life in the Clearings*, 59).

they are caged."[21] Like her captain's bird, Traill is shipped across the ocean in a cage, trapped in a gender-role that confines her to the "home" as woman's proper sphere – whether on the old or the new side of the ocean.[22] On Canadian ground, too, Traill occasionally presents herself as the helpless female: "wrapped in my cloak, I leant back against the supporting arm of my husband" (68). With obvious irony, the journal of Mary O'Brien, who emigrated to Upper Canada in 1829, reveals the conventional pose in such behaviour. After her engagement to her husband, the latter's arm

> seemed quite necessary to prevent my slipping on the icy road though I had passed the same road in the morning alone in perfect safety. This shows the helplessness consequent on resigning our independence.[23]

If the gentlewoman was to become a successful pioneer, delicate helplessness could only be preserved as an occasional pose. Once she arrived at her destination in the wilderness, the angel in the house had to get her wings dirty, although her education had prepared her for the supervision rather than the performance of household work. There are, as is to be expected, many complaints about the active pursuit of tasks one had been used to supervise in a former life. "I am becoming a perfect working machine," Letitia Hargrave wrote in one of her letters from York Factory, whither she had accompanied her husband in the 1840s.[24] Many women emphasise their initial failure and clumsiness in (supposedly) unfamiliar housekeeping chores. Susanna Moodie's first Canadian loaf of bread is an inedible affair, burnt outside and raw inside.[25] However, there is reason to believe that Moodie and the other women present themselves as more helpless in the kitchen than they actually were: middle-class women received a fair amount of practical household training and many of them were more active in the house than was deemed appropriate for a gentlewoman.[26] The gentlewoman's clumsiness in the pioneer household seems to be a signifier of conventional, gentle femininity.

On the other hand, most writings of the gentle pioneers also convey excitement and joy in their new-found activity, as well as pride in what they could achieve despite the public image and self-image with which they had grown up. Traill in particular became a paragon housewife and chief promoter of active

---

21 *Literary Women* (New York: Doubleday, 1976): 250.

22 For an extensive investigation of images of imprisonment and escape in nineteenth-century women's fiction, see also Sandra M. Gilbert & Susan Gubar, *The Madwoman in the Attic: The Woman Writer and the Nineteenth-Century Literary Imagination* (New Haven CT: Yale UP, 1979).

23 *The Journals of Mary O'Brien 1828–1838*, ed. Audrey Saunders Miller (Toronto: Macmillan, 1968): 91.

24 *The Letters of Letitia Hargrave*, ed. Margaret Arnett Macleod (Toronto: Champlain Society, 1947): 126.

25 *Roughing It*, 121.

26 Cf Gorham, *The Victorian Girl and the Feminine Ideal*, 11.

womanhood,[27] whose books leave no doubt about her own expertise in cooking, weaving, tailoring, gardening, managing poultry and dairy-cows, as well as more exotic colonial exploits like candle-, soap- or sugar-making. "Now I am doing work to which I never was accustomed [...], and I am able for all," Frances Stewart was pleased to announce.[28] After a whole day's scrubbing of her brother's house, Anne Langton, who came to Canada in 1837, felt "a strengthened conviction of the importance of woman."[29] Doing it herself gave Langton a sense of self-esteem which emerges even more clearly from another passage of her journal:

> As long as the lady is necessarily the most active member of her household she keeps her ground from her utility; but when [...] the delicacies of her table, and the elegancies of her person become her chief concern and pride, then she must fall, and must be contented to be looked upon as belonging merely to the decorative department of the establishment and valued accordingly. (154)

What made household activity so gratifying was its importance for the success and the survival of the pioneer family. By becoming useful – if only in the house – and taking pride in it, gentlewomen in the colonies realised the ideal of Mrs Ellis's educational bestseller of the nineteenth century, *The Women of England*.[30] And they escaped the boredom and invalidism to which the later Victorians condemned their gentlewomen. Although the pioneer men tended to regard their wives as helpmates,[31] the women actually were, and presented themselves as, their

---

27 See, amongst many examples, the following quotations from *The Backwoods of Canada*: "an *active* and cheerful partner" (12); "our sugar-making, in which I take rather an *active* part" (129); "a settler's wife should be *active*, *industrious*, ingenious, cheerful" (149) (my emphases).

28 *Our Forest Home*, 58.

29 *A Gentlewoman in Upper Canada: The Journals of Anne Langton*, ed. H.H. Langton (Toronto: Clarke, Irwin, 1950): 99.

30 Sarah Stickney Ellis, *The Women of England: Their Social Duties, and Domestic Habits* (London: Fisher, 1839). Ellis's views are an odd mixture of conservatism and progressivism. Although she considered women inferior to men ("and it is right that it should be so," 223), she propagated female usefulness for women of the middle class: "the humblest occupation, undertaken from a sense of duty, becomes ennobled in the motive by which it is prompted" (350). Also cf the favourable comment on female industry in the pioneer and travel books of Frances Beavan, *Life in the Backwoods of New Brunswick* (1845; St Stephen, New Brunswick: Print's Press, 1980): 79; Mrs Edward Coplestone, *Canada: Why We Live in It, and Why We Like It* (London: Parker, Son & Bourn, 1861): 71; Lady Harriet S. Jephson, *A Canadian Scrap-Book* (London: Marshall Russell, 1897): 101.

31 In a didactic allegory of pioneer life, Joseph Hilts described the ideal companion of his hero John Bushman: "There are three kinds of women in relation to life's duties and its burdens. There are those who help their husbands; there are those who hinder him by making him spend his time in helping them; and there are those who are like a handful of clean chips in a pot of soup – they do neither good nor harm. Mary Bushman was among the first class, and, consequently, she was one of the best"; cited from Joseph H. Hilts, *Among the Forest Trees or, How the Bushman Family Got Their Homes, Being a Book of Facts and Incidents of Pioneer Life in Upper Canada, Arranged in the Form of a Story* (1888; Toronto: Toronto Reprint Library of Canadian Prose and Poetry, 1972): 106. Anne Langton's father wrote about a pioneer neighbour's wife: "Daniel's spouse is a capital helpmate for a backwoodsman" (*A Gentlewoman in Upper Canada*, 60).

husbands' partners. Increasingly, they seem to find their identity not in their husbands' perceptions of them, but in their own achievements.

In the wilderness women had to do a man's outdoor work when no male help was available for their husbands, and men performed their wives' duties when the latter were ill. Most gentlemen could *not* put up with this reversal of gender-roles unless it was motivated by force of circumstance. Anne Langton's brother found that

> there is something absurd in the very inconveniences which we are exposed to. The idea of Billy and me having to cook, milk the cows, etc., and attend upon two men, five women, and three children, all more or less ill of ague and fever, has a good deal of the ludicrous in it.[32]

The words "absurd" and "ludicrous" indicate that the writer wanted this reversal of gender roles to be considered exceptional. In his journal of the late 1830s, the gentleman immigrant John Tidey recorded with anger and frustration that his wife preferred outdoor work to being his ministering angel:

> Now this is exceedingly trying – three days she assisted me in logging off a piece of Ground – a part of two days she helped me in the Hay field – & parts four days in reaping Oats & Wheat. She worked some in planting in the Spring but that was altogether unnessessary [*sic*]. Her own choice & against my will.[33]

Quite obviously, Tidey had the impression that his wife was trespassing on forbidden ground. The writings of the Canadian gentlewomen, too, impart an awareness of gender trespassing.

Juliana Horatia Ewing was not a pioneer proper and, as an officer's wife, spent a few comfortable years in Fredericton in the late 1860s; but for her, too, life in the colony meant that she could become active in "masculine" domains. She enjoyed papering the drawing-room as much as shutting up her husband's perplexed orderly with "'*I'm* the man that's going to paper, Hartney'."[34] Her discovery that she was a much better carpenter than her husband made her wonder about the justification of gender-roles:

> I often think our *hands* are a curious fact. His so rough & strong looking you would think him a born carpenter, & very ill adapted to the execution of fine arts. Mine *look* very like harp playing or anything elegant – & not useful. Whereas on most fine evenings his fingers are bringing the tenderest tones & most exquisite renderings of Mendelssohn out of the harmonium, & mine are, I flatter myself, not inefficiently

---

[32] *A Gentlewoman in Upper Canada*, 234–35.

[33] Cited from Light & Prentice, *Pioneer and Gentlewomen of British North America*, 123. In a sketch of his *Reminiscences of a Canadian Pioneer for the Last Fifty Years [1833–1883]* (1884; Toronto & Montreal: McClelland & Stewart, 1968), Samuel Thompson describes another woman (though not a gentlewomen) who prefers felling trees to household chores. In the end this "Amazonian chopper" (40) is struck dead by a tree – in punishment for her unwomanly behaviour?

[34] *Canada Home: Juliana Horatia Ewing's Fredericton Letters 1867–1869*, ed. Howard Blom & Thomas E. Blom (Vancouver: U of British Columbia P, 1983): 218.

> carpentering, digging, knocking in nails & taking up twitch grass, whereas they
> lumber about on the notes like so many logs in a strong current!!! (172)

For Juliana Ewing, although she had little money at her disposal, carpentering was
primarily a leisure pursuit. The reversal of gender roles does not seem to have
caused severe disorientation, and it is rendered as a curiosity to her family back
home.

The *pioneer* woman was faced with a life in which such a role transgression
was of a permanent and thus more disconcerting nature. Anne Langton repeatedly
emphasises the "unfeminine" quality of some of her chores, like wielding a
cleaver when a quarter of beef has to be cut up.[35] Such activities, as well as her
active participation in sailing and rowing, aroused bewilderment concerning her
gender identity:

> I am sometimes reminded of my early years and companionship with boys only;
> perhaps you would think my feminine manners in danger [...] but don't be alarmed;
> [...] my woman's avocations will always, I think, more than counterbalance them. I
> said I was often reminded of my early years. I have caught myself wishing an old
> long-forgotten wish that I had been born of the rougher sex. Women are very
> dependent here, and give a great deal of trouble; we feel our weakness more than
> anywhere else. (72–73)

Despite its brevity, this discourse is clearly disruptive, incoherent, and contradictory, and it conveys a very strong sense of double-voicedness. An unconventional voice speaks of the woman's nostalgia for pre-pubescent life and the wish to
belong to the other sex.[36] But this thought seems to be perceived as a sinful
violation of gender boundaries, and its emergence is thus immediately stifled by a
conventional voice affirming woman's basic difference from man and her status as
the weaker sex. Langton's confusion about her gender identity is also obvious in a
another passage of her journal. During a walk in the snow, she wonders whether
her footsteps, alongside those of her brother's, can still be recognised as a
woman's imprint:

> I looked back at our own tracks, and wondered whether mine would be recognized as
> that of a woman, enveloped as are my feet in two pair of stockings, a pair of socks,
> my house moccasins, and another pair over them. (95)

This is not just a factual or anecdotal detail of Canadian winter life. Women's
apparel, to a far greater extent than that of men, is a signifier of her conventional
gender-role, and it is significant that Langton reflects on her gender identity in
connection with her clothing. The Victorian woman, properly dressed, was clad in

---

35 *A Gentlewoman in Upper Canada*, 94.

36 Cf Moers, *Literary Women*, 130, on the significance of the tomboy in women's literature: "For
in every age, whatever the social rules, there has always been one time of a woman's life, the years
before puberty, when walking, running, climbing, battling, and tumbling are as normal female as
they are male activities."

several layers of clothes – except her feet, which (like her waist), were expected to exhibit dainty femininity. In the Canadian winter, this gender-symbol is virtually buried under multiple layers of "unfeminine" socks.

The pioneer accounts of Moodie and Traill were intended for publication in Britain, and it is understandable that their statements about the porousness of gender boundaries are more muted than Langton's comparatively private observations. Both sisters seem to have been more capable pioneers than their husbands, one of whom had a physical, the other a psychic handicap. As Marian Fowler shows in *The Embroidered Tent*, Traill developed "masculine" qualities, but then attempted to hide them behind close-up descriptions of Canadian fauna and an extreme focus on the "legitimate" domain of household activity. But even Traill's panegyric to housekeeping in the bush, *The Canadian Settler's Guide*, conveys an unmistakable sense that the wilderness set free in women an energy supposedly reserved for men – while the latter are seen as "indolent" and "inactive":

> I have marked with astonishment and admiration acts of female heroism [...]. Sometimes aroused by the indolence and inactivity of their husbands or sons, they have resolutely set their own shoulders to the wheel, and borne the burden with unshrinking perseverence [sic] unaided; [...] showing what can be done when the mind is capable of overcoming the weakness of the body. (24)

A later passage in the book gives an example of this female energy. A young officer's wife, when her husband is ill, brings in the farm's first harvest. Traill's comment on the consequences of this display of female heroism is remarkable: "Possibly this very circumstance gave a tone of energy and manly independence of spirit to the children" (115). The text is vague about the sex of these children: "energy" and "independence" appear not to be restricted to the family's sons. It seems that, for the next generation, stereotypical gender-boundaries fall more naturally than they did for their parents.

Moodie's *Roughing It* implies something similar. After a period of accommodation, Moodie learns to appreciate what made pioneering attractive for men in the first place – hunting and fishing expeditions, during which her sense of partnership with her husband is particularly strong and all sense of a split gender identity seems to have disappeared: "Oh, how I enjoyed these excursions on the lake; the very idea of *our* dinner depending upon *our* success added double zest to *our* sport!" (356, my emphasis). Occasionally, Moodie is joined by her daughter: "By the time she was five years old, my little mermaid could both steer and paddle the light vessel, and catch small fish, which were useful for soup" (357). Moodie's daughter seems to grow up with a different sense of activity and usefulness than her mother; however, this statement about a change of gender-role is slightly muted by Moodie's use of the mermaid image – a traditional and romanticised view of beautiful, otherworldly femininity, which has little to do with paddling a boat or catching one's supper, and which contradicts the gender transgression that is at the core of the description.

Significantly, these last quotations are from the second half of *Roughing It*, in which Moodie dramatises herself less and less as the delicate, "reluctant" pioneer and emerges, through her actions, as the woman who successfully copes with life in the bush. It is in this half of *Roughing It* that the act of self-creation implied in autobiographical writing becomes obvious.[37] For the first time, Susanna helps her husband in the field and takes pride in her achievement (352–53); she behaves most rationally and courageously when her house is on fire (390–92). However, Moodie's self-representation in these passages is not free from traces of her former double-voicedness. When her husband comes to his family's rescue in the fire episode, Moodie shows herself as a woman who no longer needs to be brave and feels "giddy and faint" (392); when she is "reported to have done prodigies," she immediately "apologizes" by ascribing her achievement to a state of unconsciousness: "I was unconscious, both to the cold and the danger" (394). She was also unconscious, one might add, of traditional cultural expectations of a lady's proper behaviour.

It is through the action of Susanna the character rather than in her own narrative discourse that Susanna the narrator reveals a new self; the split between the experiencing and the narrating self is taken advantage of as a means of doubling a "new" self and a conventional "voice." Another means of indirect self-statement is a series of androgynous images of other characters in *Roughing It*, most of which are to be found in the book's second half; here, Moodie seems to project her own gender transgression onto other characters. The old servant Jenny is a he-woman and brave enough to help Mr Moodie frighten away a bear. The boy John Monahan is only one of the Moodies' helps who, apart from doing a man's work, seems to enjoy women's work and displays a womanly tenderness:

> To little Katie he attached himself in an extraordinary manner. [...] Of a night, he cooked her mess of bread and milk, as she sat by the fire, and his greatest delight was to feed her himself. (149)[38]

The chapter entitled "The Outbreak" (407–28) is the climax of Moodie's development as it unfolds in the second half of her book. Overtly, the chapter heading

---

37 Cf Smith, *A Poetics of Women's Autobiography*, 45.

38 For other examples, cf the servant Jacob who "baked, and cooked, and churned, milked the cows, and made up the butter, as well and as carefully as the best female servant could have done" (325), and John E. who does his own washing and tailoring and even knits (397). In *The Young Emigrants*, Traill, too, describes a Canadian boy who can knit and does not consider this occupation unmanly: "'It is by no means an uncommon thing in our country,' said Gordon. 'We try to live, as much as possible, on the produce of our own farms [...]. And let me ask you, my dear Sir, why should a boy be unmanly, because he employs his hands, in the long winter evenings, in contributing to the comfort of himself and his family?'" (79–80).

refers to the Mackenzie Rebellion of 1837, but Moodie has far more to say about herself than about the political event. This might be seen as an acknowledgement that the public sphere of politics was not considered one in which a woman was expected to venture. But, in her private sphere, Susanna carried out her own rebellion: the "Outbreak" chapter contains some of the rare passages in gentlewomen's pioneering accounts where the woman is self-assertive beyond the occasional statement of her efficiency. With her husband away for almost a year to fight the rebels, the new Moodie has her coming out,[39] and Moodie as self-narrator is – at least temporarily – bold enough to spotlight her. The chapter's accumulation of the first-person singular, immersed with a self-confident sense of selfhood, is remarkable:

> I actually shed tears of joy over the first twenty-dollar bill *I* received from Montreal. It was *my* own; *I* had earned it with *my* own hand; and it seemed to *my* delighted fancy to form the nucleus out of which a future independence for *my* family might arise. *I* no longer retired to bed when the labours of the day were over. *I* sat up, and wrote by the light of a strange sort of candles [...] (417)
>   By lending *my* oxen for two days' work, *I* got Wittals, who had no oxen, to drag *me* in a few acres of oats, and to prepare the land for potatoes and corn. (421)

Moodie, in her husband's absence, considers herself as *pater familias*; her strong sense of owning the farm, in an age when a woman's property became her husband's as soon as she got married, is quite exceptional.

Susanna manages the farm most effectively and enhances the family income by selling painted fungi and, as she claims, by earning her first Canadian money as a writer. She also writes the petition which finally gains her husband the position that brings the family out of the bush. Arguably, this is Susanna's most drastic violation of her traditional gender-role,[40] and one for which she is careful to note that it got a man's (her brother-in-law's) approval. *In nuce*, the "Outbreak" chapter exemplifies the narrative strategy which underlies the whole second half of the book: more and more, faster and faster, Susanna unfolds a story of personal achievement and personal development. It seems that in writing about the period of greatest personal freedom in her life, Moodie the narrator becomes more daring than in other passages of her book, takes more liberties in constructing the tale of her self. She even condenses in this chapter what actually took several years to achieve. As Moodie's correspondence reveals, she earned her first money as a writer almost one year after her husband's first absence during the Mackenzie

---

39 As Fowler, *The Embroidered Tent* (123ff) has shown in detail; see also Wayne Fraser, *The Dominion of Women: The Personal and the Political in Canadian Women's Literature* (Westport CT: Greenwood, 1991): 25–29.

40 Cf one of the "Instructions for the Married" which were published in the *Niagara Herald* in 1828: "A wife may have more sense than her husband, but she should never seem to know it"; cited from Light & Prentice, *Pioneer and Gentlewomen of British North America*, 219.

Rebellion.[41] The fact that she backdates the event in *Roughing It* may be considered a polishing up of an already resplendent self-image.

That Moodie no longer visualises herself as a conventional gentlewoman is implied in a chapter following the "Outbreak" one. A character's relation to other characters is an essential means of fictional and dramatic characterisation, and it is through this means that Moodie, in constructing her narrative, states that she has changed. In "A Walk to Drummer," Moodie contrasts herself with other women of her class: ie, she sees herself in a new relation to her class and its conception of femininity. With another officer's wife she embarks on a charity mission to relieve a helpless gentlewoman who has been deserted by her husband. After the strenuous walk through the bush, it is her companion who is exhausted, not Susanna: "Emilia went immediately to bed, from which she was unable to rise for several days. In the meanwhile I wrote to Moodie an account of the scene I had witnessed" (463).

Finally, the change in her self-image is obvious in Moodie's rendering of her departure from the bush. When her husband summons her to join him in Belleville, Moodie looks back on her life in the wilderness and records the change that this life has effected; the paragraph starts with a description of her outward appearance:

> For seven years I had lived out of the world entirely; my person had been rendered coarse by hard work and exposure to the weather. I looked double the age I really was, and my hair was already thickly sprinkled with grey. (476)

Although no mirror is mentioned, the passage evokes an impression of Moodie investigating her mirror image and taking account of herself. In Lacanian psychoanalysis, the mirror-stage is the very base on which identity rests. Nineteenth-century patriarchal society held up a mirror to women in which they saw not themselves, but a male-created ideal of woman – or, in Lacanian terms, saw themselves through a screen of patriarchal conventions of femininity. For Moodie, at the end of her wilderness years, this screen seems to have disappeared; she now sees a woman shaped by an unconventional life, and although she seems prematurely aged, the unconventional image is only superficially presented as a negative one. The very next sentence asserts that Moodie hates to leave the environment in which her new image developed ("I clung to my solitude. I did not like to be dragged from it"). The reluctant pioneer is now a reluctant returner to civilisation, as she emphasises in a later passage:

---

41 See Carl Ballstadt, "Susanna Moodie: 'The Embryo Blossom': Susanna Moodie's Letters to Her Husband in Relation to *Roughing It in the Bush*," in *Re(Dis)Covering Our Foremothers: Nineteenth-Century Canadian Women Writers*, ed. Lorraine McMullen (Ottawa: U of Ottawa P, 1990): 139.

> It was the birthplace of my three boys, the school of high resolve and energetic action
> in which we had learned to meet calmly, and successfully to battle with the ills of
> life. Nor did I leave it without many regretful tears, to mingle once more with a
> world to whose usages, during my long solitude, I had become almost a stranger, and
> to whose praise or blame I felt alike indifferent. (480)

Moodie seems to head this passage with a reference to a conventional female attribute, a mother's sentimental attachments. There is also, however, a sense of the mother's partial identification with her boys and their upbringing in the wilderness. In this respect, the passage is a parallel to Anne Langton's reminiscences of pre-pubescent life in the company of boys. It is as if Moodie had got a second chance to learn about life as a boy. She then proceeds to speak openly about the "masculine" qualities of "resolve and energetic action" which she has learnt in her wilderness school. The word "battle," too, points to the fact that Moodie has adopted qualities traditionally associated with the male, and it matches the "female heroism" of which her sister speaks in the passage quoted above.

Women's accounts of pioneer life, in particular those of the Strickland sisters, have been considered in the tradition of the female (Canadian) *Bildungsroman*[42] – although none describes a development as extreme as that of the female protagonists in Margaret Atwood's *Surfacing* or Marian Engel's *Bear*. None of the women considered here, although some of them were professional artists and thus exceptional women of their class, would have openly rebelled against accepted notions of femininity; none freed herself entirely from her traditional, middle-class conditioning. The gentlewomen's writing is frequently double-voiced and betrays a considerable confusion about the newly developed self-image. But it is undeniable that this image did develop. The conditions of pioneer life almost naturally undermined stereotypical middle-class notions of gender difference and provided a context which provoked and encouraged a re-negotiation of woman's role and her conception of self. Feminist and post-colonial criticism draw a parallel between the situation of women and that of former colonial countries.[43] For the gentlewomen pioneers of the nineteenth century, however, the concepts of "double marginalisation" or "double colonisation" seem not to apply. De-centred in the margin of the British Empire, they were able to transcend the gender stereotyping which marginalised women in the culture of the Imperial Centre. And auto-biographical writing as a form ephemeral to the established literary canon provided them with an opportunity to express their new, de-marginalised self-image.

---

[42] See Coral Ann Howells, *Private and Fictional Words: Canadian Women's Novelists of the 1970s and 1980s* (London: Methuen, 1987).

[43] See *A Double Colonization: Colonial and Post-Colonial Women's Writing*, ed. Kirsten Holst Petersen & Anna Rutherford (*Kunapipi* 7.2–3; Aarhus, 1985).

WORKS CITED

BALLSTADT, Carl. "Susanna Moodie: 'The Embryo Blossom': Susanna Moodie's Letters to Her Husband in Relation to *Roughing It in the Bush*," in *Re(Dis)Covering Our Foremothers: Nineteenth-Century Canadian Women Writers*, ed. Lorraine McMullen (U of Ottawa P, 1990): 137–45.

CLINE, Cheryl. *Women's Diaries, Journals, and Letters: An Annotated Bibliography* (New York: Garland, 1989).

CONRAD, Margaret. *Recording Angels: The Private Chronicles of Women from the Maritime Provinces of Canada, 1750–1950* (CRIAW Papers 4; Ottawa: Canadian Research Institute for the Advancement of Women, 1982).

CORDASCO, Francesco. *The Immigrant Woman in North America: An Annotated Bibliography of Selected References* (Metuchen NJ: Scarecrow, 1985).

COWAN, Helen I. *British Emigration to British North America: The First Hundred Years*, rev. ed. (Toronto: U of Toronto P, 1961).

DUNAE, Patrick A. *Gentlemen Emigrants: From the British Public Schools to the Canadian Frontier* (Vancouver/Toronto: Douglas & McIntyre, 1981).

EATON, Sara. *Lady of the Backwoods: A Biography of Catharine Parr Traill* (Toronto/Montreal: McClelland & Stewart, 1969).

FAIRBANKS, Carol. *Prairie Women: Images in American and Canadian Fiction* (New Haven CT: Yale UP, 1986).

—— & Sara Brooks SUNDBERG. *Farm Women on the Prairie Frontier: A Sourcebook for Canada and the United States* (Metuchen NJ: Scarecrow, 1983).

FRASER, Wayne. *The Dominion of Women: The Personal and the Political in Canadian Women's Literature* (Westport CT: Greenwood, 1991).

HAMMERTON, A. James, *Emigrant Gentlewomen: Genteel Poverty and Female Emigration, 1830–1914* (London: Croom Helm, 1979).

HELLERSTEIN, Erna Olafson, Leslie Parker HUME & Karen M. OFFEN. *Victorian Women: A Documentary Account of Women's Lives in Nineteenth-Century England, France, and the United States* (Brighton: Harvester, 1981).

HOWELLS, Coral Ann. *Private and Fictional Words: Canadian Women's Novelists of the 1970s and 1980s* (London: Methuen, 1987).

JACKEL, Susan, ed. *A Flannel Shirt and Liberty: British Emigrant Gentlewomen in the Canadian West, 1880–1914* (Vancouver: U of British Columbia P, 1982).

JOHNSTON, Jean. *Wilderness Women: Canada's Forgotten History* (Toronto: Peter Martin, 1973).

JONES, Dorothy. "Ladies in the Bush: Catharine Traill, Mary Barker and Rachel Henning," *SPAN: Newsletter of the South Pacific Association for Commonwealth Literature and Language Studies* 21 (1985): 96–120.

LIGHT, Beth & Veronica STRONG–BOAG. *True Daughters of the North: Canadian Women's History: An Annotated Bibliography* (OISE Press/Ontario Institute for Studies in Education, 1980).

MAZUR, Carol & Sheila PEPPER. *Women in Canada: A Bibliography 1965–1982* (OISE Press/Ontario Institute for Studies in Education, 3rd ed. 1984).

MORRIS, Audrey Y. *Gentle Pioneers: Five Nineteenth-Century Canadians* (Toronto/London: Hodder & Stoughton, 1966).

MYERS, Sandra L. "Victoria's Daughters: English Speaking Women on Nineteenth-Century Frontiers" in *Western Women: Their Land, Their Lives*, ed. Lillian Schlissel et al. (Albuquerque: U of New Mexico P, 1988): 261–81.

NEEDLER, G.H. *Otonabee Pioneers: The Story of the Stewarts, the Stricklands, the Traills and the Moodies* (Toronto: Burns & MacEachern, 1953).

NEUMAN, Shirley & Smaro KAMBOURELI, ed. *A Mazing Space: Writing Canadian Women Writing* (Edmonton: Longspoon/NeWest, 1986).

PETERSEN, Kirsten Holst, & Anna RUTHERFORD, ed. *A Double Colonization: Colonial and Post-Colonial Women's Writing* (*Kunapipi* 7.2–3; Aarhus, 1985).

PRENTICE, Alison et al. *Canadian Women: A History* (Toronto/New York: Harcourt, Brace Jovanovich, 1988).

ROUSLIN, Virginia Watson. "The Intelligent Woman's Guide to Pioneering in Canada," *Dalhousie Review* 56 (1976): 319–35.

SKELTON, Isabel. *The Backwoodswoman: A Chronicle of Pioneer Home Life in Upper and Lower Canada* (Toronto: Ryerson, 1924).

STICH, K.P. ed. *Reflections: Autobiography and Canadian Literature* (Ottawa: U of Ottawa P, 1988).

THOMAS, Clara. "Happily Ever After: Canadian Women in Fiction and Fact," *Canadian Literature* 34 (1967): 43–53.

———. "Journeys to Freedom," *Canadian Literature* 51 (1972): 11–19.

———. "The Strickland Sisters," in *The Clear Spirit: Twenty Canadian Women and Their Times*, ed. Mary Quayle Innis (Toronto: U of Toronto P, 1966): 42–73.

THOMPSON, Elizabeth. *The Pioneer Woman: A Canadian Character Type* (Montreal/Kingston: McGill–Queen's UP, 1991).

☙ ❀ ❧

The Twinkling of an "I"
Subjectivity and Language
in Alice Munro's Friend of My Youth

KIT STEAD

I N ALICE MUNRO'S *LIVES OF GIRLS AND WOMEN*, the narrator, Del Jordan, says of her mother:[1]

Inside that self we knew, which might at times appear blurred a bit, or sidetracked, she kept her younger selves strenuous and hopeful; scenes from the past were liable to pop up at any time, like lantern slides, against the cluttered fabric of the present. (73)

Munro is fascinated by the possibilities not only of other selves, but of other worlds. Her narratives probe the gaps between "reality" (or the ideological code which we have learned to recognise as "reality") and what lies beyond. Her acute character portrayal attracts enthusiastic recognition from those who approach her work from a classic realist angle. W.R. Martin claims Munro for the "great central tradition of English literature," making "the whole world kin."[2] Conversely, Linda Hutcheon puts Munro firmly on the list of Canada's "postmodern metafiction writers," whose recordings are "not fixed, closed, eternal and universal."[3] These contradictory evaluations indicate the textual complexity of Munro's apparently straightforward narrative style.

Her strategy is to approach her stories via an investigation of the shifting subject or "self." She is intrigued by the idea of former selves, future selves, and of the self in relation to others. The Anglo-American "object-relations" feminist Nancy Chodorow distinguishes between a "true self," which is developed during the child's ideally harmonious early relationship with its primary caretaker, and another relational ego which is defined through differentiation from others.[4] A useful way of looking at Munro's treatment of her characters is to meld the Lacanian idea of the self as being in a constant state of process from one stage to the next, with Chodorow's valorisation of relationships in the formation of the

---

[1] Alice Munro, *Lives of Girls and Women* (1971; Markham, Ontario: Penguin, 1987). Page references are to the Penguin edition.

[2] W.R. Martin, *Alice Munro: Paradox and Parallel* (Edmonton: U of Alberta P, 1987): XIV, 206.

[3] Linda Hutcheon, *The Canadian Postmodern* (Toronto: Oxford UP, 1988):46.

[4] Nancy Julia Chodorow, "Gender, Relation and Difference in Psychoanalytic Perspective," in *The Future of Difference*, ed. Hestes Eisenstein & Alice Jardine (1980; New Brunswick NJ: Rutgers UP, 1988): 10.

subject. It is apt, in view of the importance that the feminist revisionists of traditional psychoanalytic theory have given to the mother's role in relation to the
child, that Munro has dedicated *Friend of My Youth* – which is the particular focus
of this paper – "to the memory of my mother."

The first story in the book, which also bears the same title, has two strands.
The "outer" narrative is the story of the narrator's relationship with her mother,
who died some years before of a paralysing illness. The main text is a story that
the mother tells the narrator of a strange *ménage à trois* on a farm she stayed at as a
young schoolteacher. There are several versions of "my mother" within the story.
There is the mother in the narrator's dream

> looking quite well – not exactly youthful, not entirely untouched by the paralysing
> disease that held her in its grip for a decade or more before her death, but so much
> better than I remembered that I would be astonished.[5]

There is the "mother" that the narrator had remembered as a "bugbear in my
mind" before encountering the "reality" of this dream. The use of the word
"reality" in connection with the dream does not undermine the narrator's revision
of her mother, but casts doubt on whether any of the "incarnations" presented
could possibly be the "real" woman.

There is also the mother who indirectly narrates the main story about the
Grieves family. She is, the narrator says, "a young woman with a soft, mischievous face and shiny, opaque silk stockings on her plump legs" (4). The narrator guarantees the verisimilitude of this description by adding: "I have seen a
photograph of her, with her pupils." In *Running in the Family*,[6] Michael Ondaatje
uses real photographs to illustrate his text, and Linda Hutcheon has pointed out the
constant use of photographic and film imagery in the work of contemporary
writers. Hutcheon attributes this interest to the way in which photographs can help
to invoke the absent object, and yet, paradoxically, that the presence of a photo
refers to the absence of that to which it refers.[7] I would add that photographs also
invoke the absent subject and offer a way of "pinning down" that subject at one
moment in time. Their spuriously "real" representation seems to offer a way of
capturing the "true self." What they do not show is more revealing than what they
do, and they therefore serve as a useful metaphor of postmodernism.[8]

The narrator interprets the photograph for the reader. The sibilant alliteration
of "soft," "mischievous," "shiny silk stockings," with the contrasting, but by no
means harsh, sounds of the *p* in "plump" and "opaque" is pleasing to the inner ear

---

[5] Alice Munro, *Friend of My Youth* (Toronto: McClelland & Stewart, 1990): 3.

[6] Michael Ondaatje, *Running in the Family* (Toronto: McClelland & Stewart, 1982).

[7] Hutcheon, *The Canadian Postmodern*, 46.

[8] The camera can also serve as a metaphor for sexual and social power, and this is how Margaret
Atwood uses it in *Surfacing* (1972; London: Virago, 1980).

and inclines the reader to like this young woman, even while perhaps not taking her very seriously. Photographs of women within our patriarchal discourse are generally to do with faces and legs (at the very least), and the important subject is the gazer rather than the "gazee." The narrator actually diminishes the reader's perception of her mother by referring to the photograph and thus triggering off reactions in the reader which have already been implanted by the photographic discourse so prevalent within our culture.

Later in the story we see the mother as a newly married woman. She has moved into a different social discourse and is unable to communicate with Flora without painful misunderstanding which almost totally ruptures their relationship. In addition, there is the mother's own awareness of latent selves within her: "If I could have been a writer – I do think I could have been; I could have been a writer – then I would have written the story of Flora's life" (19).

This never happened; but the narrator, who was created by the mother, is now telling the mother's story through the mouthpiece of "mothers" created by herself. We also perceive the narrator as a series of "selves": towards the end of the story, she confesses feelings of dislike towards her sick mother:

> I felt a great fog of platitudes and pieties lurking, an incontestable crippled-mother power, which could capture and choke me. There would be no end to it. I had to keep myself sharp-tongued and cynical, arguing and deflating. Eventually I gave up even that recognition and opposed her in silence. (20)

The pleasant p's of "plump" and "opaque" have shifted into the sinister p's of "platitudes," "pieties," "power" and "opposed." The narrator describes her mother's power as incontestable, but recounts her apparently successful opposition to it. The paradox of "crippled-mother power" is clear and should undermine its potency as an image, but because we are all imbued with the idea of the good, strong mother, it is powerful and unsettling. Del Jordan, in *Lives of Girls and Women*, also silently turns against her mother in adolescence: "Suddenly I could not bear anything about her" (79). She adds, revealingly: "I myself was not so different from my mother, but concealed it, knowing what dangers there were" (80).

Helen Deutsch describes the psychological process which girls use to effect their individuality and independence, often becoming very critical of their mothers, and defining themselves as "I am what she is not."[9] The familiarity of this situation and Munro's narrative strategy with its intimations of psychology leads the reader to sympathise with the narrator. Then comes the surprise, as the narrator deconstructs her own statements: "This is a fancy way of saying that I was no comfort and poor company to her when she had almost nowhere else to turn" (20). But it is the narrator's present self who makes this judgement on her

---

9 Quoted in Nancy Chodorow's *The Reproduction of Mothering: Psychoanalysis and the Sociology of Gender* (Berkeley: U of California P, 1978): 137.

younger self; the "truth" of the earlier description still stands, but it is now accompanied by a parallel "truth."

The story ends with the narrator's feeling of anger towards the dream-mother:

> My mother moving rather carelessly out of her old prison, showing options and powers I never dreamed she had, changes more than herself. She changes the bitter lump of love I have carried all this time into a phantom-something useless and uncalled for, like a phantom pregnancy. (26)

The "prison" is not just the physical prison of paralysis, but the prison of the narrator's memory of her mother. In producing a new self for the narrator, the mother challenges the narrator's own sense of ego and unsettles the nature of the relationship between them. The "lump of love" is an unusual combination of words, which plays on the association with "a lump in the throat," indicating both emotion and a difficulty in speaking, which the mother (for physical reasons) and the narrator (for psychological reasons) experienced in their relations with each other.

The image of a "phantom pregnancy" links the narrator with the unhappy Ellie Grieves, who, after countless fruitless pregnancies, finally succumbs to a malignant growth inside her. The name of the Grieves family with its resonances of "grief," "grievances" and "graves" signals the sorrow in store for them in their sexual and romantic relationships. The narrator's mother, shortly to be married, is counterpoised against Flora's spinsterhood and Ellie's botched life as a wife and mother. The language used to describe her nuptial preparations is reminiscent of romantic novels and popular magazines:

> The lilacs came out, the evenings lengthened, the birds were back and nesting, my mother bloomed in everybody's attention, about to set out on the deliciously solemn adventure of marriage. (15)

This description stands in marked contrast to Ellie's "hurry-up" marriage to Robert and the physical and mental ruin which follows. Casting a further shadow behind the romantic clichés, and effectively undermining their impact, is the reader's prior knowledge of the future unhappiness to come to the narrator's mother.

The characters within the story shift according to the perspective of the teller. The narrator's mother sees Flora as having variously "the air of a comedian" or looking like a "gypsy queen." The mother would like to re-write Flora as a "Maiden Lady," while the narrator's younger self sees her as a witch, and then later, and most improbably, re-creates her as a permed shop assistant with painted nails. But this "notion that I can know anything about her" (26) is a false one. The division in the Grieves' house signals the split between Flora and Robert, but also the splits within Flora herself as a constructed subject. One side blank, the other painted, it encodes her possibilities.

Munro uses the phenomenon of the house as a metaphor for its inhabitants in the story "Wigtime." When she is a child, Margot's house is crowded and confused. Ducks are made ready for market in the kitchen:

> There were feathers in the milk jug and a horrible smell of feathers burning on the stove. Blood was puddled on the oilclothed table and dripping to the floor. (246)

This intrusion of the outside world is not allowed when Margot creates her own home as a grown woman. Again Munro ironically uses the overblown and clichéd discourses of women's magazines to undermine her own description:

> The kitchen was done in almond – Anita made a mistake, calling it cream – with teal-green and butter-yellow trim. Margot said that all that natural-wood look was passé. They did not enter the living room, with its rose carpet, striped silk chairs and yards and yards of swooping pale-green figured curtains. They admired it from the doorway – all exquisite, shadowy, inviolate. (245)

The first kitchen is dirty, smelly and chaotic, but the blood and milk that are found there are symbolic of sexuality and maternity – the raw matter of life itself. While the feathers in the milk represent a rude intrusion of the farmyard into the domestic scene, Margot's new house, by contrast, is virginal, untouched – "exquisite, shadowy, inviolate" – to be admired from afar. Margot has re-created her disordered personal life through it. The house is a "self" that Margot can identify with. It is a signifier, and she is the signified; indeed, the house represents Margot to such an extent that she expends effort to make it beautiful in her eyes, while neglecting her own physical appearance. She scorns aids to diguise her middle-aged physical shortcomings, yet relishes the hyperbolic advertising discourse that represents the colour cream as "almond," elevating it from the ordinary and, incidentally but importantly, revealing the ignorance of those like Anita who are not "in the know." Anita's mistake over the colour is described in reported speech by the narrator, and the irony is clear. It is not really a "mistake" to describe as cream a colour that falls into the wide spectrum of shades between white and yellow, but it is clear from the context that Margot quickly corrects Anita's simplification. The right words are important to Margot in order to keep her carefully built "self" intact. Anita's verbal slip betrays her ignorance of the decor discourse and, for perhaps the first time in their lives, Margot can feel superior towards her. However, it also reminds Margot that there is a world in which her precious "almond" is really "cream" and betrays the precariousness of her constructed image. Despite Margot's desperate attempt to alienate herself from the past, she cannot completely evade something that is an integral part of her – the ducks are still getting into the kitchen, albeit within the colour *teal*-green.

Margot uses emotional blackmail to force her husband to buy the house after she catches him having an affair. In order to spy upon him, she disguises herself with a wig and bright, tight clothes that she would not normally wear. Paradoxically, the clothes, designed to attract male attention, give Margot the anonymity she needs at the campsite by the beach where her husband has taken their teenage babysitter.

The old minister, Austin, in "Pictures of the Ice" also uses clothes to create a new self. Apparently he is going to be married and live in Hawaii, and the new life in the sun with a vivacious widow seems to explain his investment in new, colourful clothes and his unexpected appreciation of coarse jokes. But Austin is playing a double bluff. While he leads his family and friends to believe he is about to enter a paradisiacal retirement, he is actually preparing to begin a new existence as minister in a tiny community on the shore of a northern lake in the wilderness.

The narrator tells us in the very first sentence of the story that Austin has drowned, and the knowledge of the destruction of his physical self is a counter-point to the text, as it deals with his imaginary self. The pictures of the ice that he takes before leaving on his fateful journey are symbolic on several levels:

> Sheets of ice drop from the burdened branches of the willow trees to the ground, and the sun shines through them from the west; they're like walls of pearl. Ice is woven through the wire of the high fence to make it like a honeycomb. Waves have frozen as they hit the shore, making mounds and caves, a crazy landscape, out to the rim of the open water. And all the playground equipment, the children's swings and climbing bars, have been transformed by ice, hung with organ pipes or buried in what looks like half-carved statues, shapes of ice that might be people, animals, angels, monsters, left unfinished. (151)

The downward slip of the ice from the "burdened" trees echoes the downward slide of Austin's body – a slipping and a flow which has left "dry channels, deep lines" (146). The "walls of pearl" are not very far removed from the "Pearly Gates" that Austin will presumably pass through after his death by drowning in water, whose force overcomes him, just as he is overcome by the power and beauty of the ice. The half-carved statues symbolise the incompleteness of any "text" and of the images that we have of even those we seem to know well. Ice is transparent, but gives a distorted image if peered through. The ice-pictures which Austin takes and which Karin sends to Megan, Don and Brent after his disappearance represent a code which is less easy to crack than the ice. Karin instinctively feels that they hold a key to the mystery that is Austin: "she gets the feeling that he is in them, after all. He's a blank in them, but bright" (155). The oxymoron of a "bright blank" is a startling image which reinforces the idea of a potent subjectivity, whilst emphasising the endless possibilities behind and within it. Austin has been reduced to silence by his death, but the photographs which he took make up a polysemic cipher that "speaks" for him.

A photograph is just one key to the protagonist in "Meneseteung." Almeda Roth (her surname, which sounds similar to "wrath," is a signal of the turmoil within her) is presented to us as a series of selves. She is the author of the preface to her book of poetry, who laconically describes the sudden deaths of her siblings and parents. She is the poet and the child within the poems, who suddenly finds herself lost and alone when her brother and sister disappear. She is the woman described in the local newspaper, the *Vidette*, first with a hint of irony as "our poetess" and a "literary lady" and, later, after her senile dementia and death, as "a familiar eccentric" and "a figure of fun."

The narrator foregrounds the fact that she is creating "Almeda." In describing her photograph, the narrator uses words like "seem," "may," "probably," "might," "makes me see," "indicate" and "perhaps." These qualifying words counterbalance the narrator's affirmations of what Almeda's character may be, but the narrator then slips into the omniscient mode to recount Almeda's deeply significant encounter with the drunk woman and Jarvis Poulter's subsequent approach. It is only at the end of the story that the narrator admits her fallibility: "I may have got it wrong. I don't know if she ever took laudanum. Many ladies did. I don't know if she ever made grape jelly" (73).

The effect of this is to unsettle retrospectively the relationship between reader and text. The reader is forced to reassess her reactions to the narrative and to "Almeda." If "Almeda" is a construct, then what must be made of the other characters in the story? It seems that, on the one hand, they can be seen as extensions or possibilities of Almeda herself, and that, on the other, they can also be seen as constructed subjects themselves:

> One thing she has noticed about married women, and that is how many of them have to go about creating their husbands. They have to start ascribing preferences, opinions, dictatorial ways [...] Almeda Roth cannot imagine herself doing that. She wants a man who doesn't have to be made [...] (60)

But there is no such thing as a fixed subject, and Almeda can't escape her own unconscious desires. Her fantasies about Jarvis merge him into memories of her father. For his part, Jarvis can only see Almeda as a possible wife when she has been degraded by association – that is, when he has seen her next to the half-naked, beaten and drunk woman in the street at the back of her house. The woman's abased, brutalised state and Almeda's "indiscretion" and "agitation" reaffirm his innate feelings of male superiority. He sees a new "Almeda." Almeda bears within her a self that is a sister to the drunken woman. Poulter only senses the possibilities, but it gives him the courage to *tell* Almeda (rather than invite her) to walk with him to church.

Almeda also subconsciously recognises the connection between herself and the woman, but this has the opposite effect on her, turning her away from Poulter rather than towards him. Her menstrual bleeding is an image which echoes the blood on the battered woman. Nature, in the metonymic form of the grape-juice plopping slowly through the cheesecloth into the basin and onto the floor, reinforces the idea of blood, of stains, of something out of control, of a patriarchal view of biological womanhood – far removed from Poulter's "masculine" world of figures and finance.

Marianne Hirsch tackles the question of biological determinism in *The Mother/ Daughter Plot*,[10] arguing that it is a "discomfort with the body" which leads many Anglo-American feminists to keep the definition of the feminine within the cultural. (She claims that the French feminists' discourse of the female body appears essentialist, but is, rather, metaphorical.) Sherry B. Ortner puts forward a convincing argument, in her essay on women's position in society, that the pan-cultural secondary status of women has come about because women are seen as closer to nature than men, and that "all begins of course with the body and the natural procreative functions specific to women alone."[11]

Almeda walks through the grape-juice after realising that she has begun to menstruate, and

> walks upstairs leaving purple footprints and smelling her escaping blood and the sweat of her body that has sat all day in the closed hot room. (71)

Almeda has become an image of Woman in Nature. The grape-juice, originally and cosily intended for jam for Christmas presents, and, as such, presenting an image of orderly domesticity, is now spilling onto and spoiling the floor, "and the stain will never come out" (70). The drunken woman spilled over the boundaries of social decency and discourse, and the "stain" can never come out of Almeda. She is a decent spinster, but the maenad coexists within her. Just as her house has a respectable front view, and overlooks the brutal poverty of the swamp at the back, so Almeda recognises that she and the woman are blood-sisters, connected in a way that she and Poulter cannot be.

Almeda/the narrator escapes biological mysticism and determinism by adding that she doesn't mistake anything for reality, "and that is how she knows that she is sane." In other words, the "reality" of Almeda is not even a sum of her "selves," but a consideration of them all, plus the recognition that the subject extends beyond that, like a series of paper dolls in a chain streching to and beyond the horizon, their "bright blank" surfaces signalling their endless permutations.

---

10 Marianne Hirsch, *The Mother/Daughter Plot: Narrative, Psychoanalysis, Feminism* (Blooming-ton: Indiana UP, 1989): 166. Susan Rubin Suleiman is concerned by what she calls the "fetish-ization of the female body in relation to writing" which can arise from the codification of women's writing in relation to her biological essence. Susan Rubin Suleiman, "Writing and Motherhood," in *The (M)other Tongue: Essays in Feminist Psychoanalytic Interpretation*, ed. Shirley Nelson Garner et al. (Ithaca NY: Cornell UP, 1985): 371.

11 Sherry B. Ortner, "Is Female to Male as Nature Is to Culture?," in *Women, Culture and Society*, ed. Michelle Zimbalist Rosaldo & Louise Lamphere (Stanford CA: Stanford UP, 1974): 73.

Barbara Johnson claims that "if human beings were not divided into two bio-logical sexes, there would probably be no need for literature."[12] It is true that most, if not all, stories are based upon human relationships; but those relationships do not have to be heterosexual or even primarily sexual, and we must bear in mind the great extent to which our notions of "gender" are constructed by the ideology within which we exist, just as our subjectivity is also constructed. However, we can accept these proposals without destroying the mystery of what it is that makes a person uniquely herself or himself. Each person carries within a series of past, present and future "selves," each one of which can be interpreted and deconstructed in different ways by those who interact with them. This is the area in which Munro is telling her stories. She describes the Ottawa Valley as "a scrambled, disarranged sort of country with no easy harmony about it" (*Friend*, 4–5). This is the kind of narrative country in which we find ourselves when con-sidering her work. The "easy harmony" is not to be construed as a comment on her narrative style, which is straightforward; it refers, rather, to her approach when considering the human condition. In "Oh What Avails," the protagonist, Joan, for a nightmarish moment, sees the sunlit street turn to rubble; and Munro is definitely a writer who sees "the skull beneath the skin." Her work can be compared to a hall of mirrors, sometimes reflecting "accurately" a "reality" that we can recognise, and sometimes creating new perceptions by distorting what we are accustomed to take for granted. Paradoxically, by opening up the frontiers between fact and fantasy, they enable a new and useful vision to be achieved.

WORKS CITED

CHODOROW, Nancy Julia. "Gender, Relation and Difference in Psychoanalytic Perspective," in *The Future of Difference*, ed. Hestes Eisenstein & Alice Jardine (1980; New Brunswick NJ: Rutgers UP, 1988).
———. *The Reproduction of Mothering, Psychoanalysis and the Sociology of Gender* (Berkeley: U of California P, 1978).
HIRSCH, Marianne. *The Mother/Daughter Plot: Narrative, Psychoanalysis, Feminism* (Bloomington: Indiana UP, 1989).
HUTCHEON, Linda. *The Canadian Postmodern* (Toronto: Oxford UP, 1988).
JOHNSON, Barbara. *The Critical Difference: Essays in the Contemporary Rhetoric of Reading* (Baltimore MD: Johns Hopkins UP, 1980).
MARTIN, W.R. *Alice Munro: Paradox and Parallel* (Edmonton: U of Alberta P, 1987).
MUNRO, Alice. *Friend of My Youth* (Toronto: McClelland & Stewart, 1990).
———. *Lives of Girls and Women* (1971; Markham, Ontario: Penguin, 1987).
ONDAATJE, Michael. *Running in the Family* (Toronto: McClelland & Stewart, 1982).

---

12 Barbara Johnson, *The Critical Difference: Essays in the Contemporary Rhetoric of Reading* (Baltimore MD: Johns Hopkins UP, 1980): 13.

ORTNER, Sherry B. "Is Female to Male as Nature Is to Culture?," in *Women, Culture and Society*, ed. Michelle Zimbalist Rosaldo & Louise Lamphere (Stanford CA: Stanford UP, 1974): 67–87.

SULEIMAN, Susan Rubin. "Writing and Motherhood," in *The (M)other Tongue: Essays in Feminist Psychoanalytic Interpretation*, ed. Shirley Nelson Garner et al. (Ithaca NY: Cornell UP, 1985).

❦ ✾ ❧

"Just Scribbling"
FICTION/THEORY in Nicole Brossard's *Mauve Desert* and Daphne Marlatt's *Ana Historic*

MARION WYNNE-DAVIES

W HEN I BEGAN BEFORE.... I had a set of notes tracing over the page – this page, any page – in which my language and her language mixed with writing and rewriting, the interweavings of text. My focal points were *Mauve Desert* by Nicole Brossard and *Ana Historic* by Daphne Marlatt....[1] Here I should like to take a breather in my narrative, a quick gulp of the air of conventional criticism, and point out that these are the two works (is it possible to delimit generically, to say "novel" or "poem"?) that I shall concentrate on in this essay – though I have no intention (will rather than ability) to remain within these initially formulated B. O. U. N. D. A. R. I. E. S.

My Notes: two excerpts

BROSSARD: *Mauve Desert*

Lorna Myher: retelling of narrative – this is from Lorna's viewpoint; she is BODY.

Kathy's voice: "her grave and melodic voice, a voice which, when no attention was paid to the words, could bring to mind a motet. Each vibration of the vocal chords gave the impression of a sound originated in multiple mouths.... She would choose her words for the length of the vowels, the mimic of the lips that could, if the breath, if the tongue sort to, reproduce the maddest laments and imitate, this being the case, her sense of worry" (89). A mother's voice: SEMIOTIC.

MARLATT: *Ana Historic*

Male voice on correct way to write and use notes (use quote to start essay) – "but what are you *doing*? i can imagine Richard saying, looking up from the pages with that expression with which he must confront his students over their papers: this doesn't go anywhere, you're just circling round the same idea – and all these bits and pieces thrown in – that's not how to use quotations.

---

[1] Nicole Brossard, *Mauve Desert* (Toronto: Coach House, 1990); Daphne Marlatt, *Ana Historic* (Toronto: Coach House, 1988).

irritated because i can't explain myself. just scribbling, i'll say [...] but this is
nothing, i imagine him saying. meaning unreadable. because this nothing is a
place he doesn't recognize, cut loose from history and its relentless progress towards some end. this is undefined territory, unaccountable. and so on edge" (81).

Scribbling.

Undefined territory – desert.

There can be no question that I did NOT begin here, simultaneously plunging
into the deeper waters of *Mauve Desert* and *Ana Historic* – no, I began with a
circumscribe plumbing of the shallows of each individual source – separate entries
– my own line of ink following the submerged contours already printed darker
upon lighter blue in the theoretical atlas. Yet, when the imagination holds, simultaneously, as it can, the breaths from many dives, the oceans merge, the
waters/inks blend and the air bubbles of thought and idea surge to the surface with
little regard for the shore on which they were originally inhaled. The two currents
of my thought, my desire to impart, emerge here, wet (behind the ears) and adrift
from their textual banks. One: Brossard's tripartite work merges fiction and theory
– "FICTION/THEORY" – so that in my rewriting, I read *Cixous*, the writing of the
mother, of the body, the tongue, and *Kristeva* the rhythmic flow of the semiotic in
the multiple maternal voice. Two: in Marlatt's challenge to conventional his/story
(use the two s's) I perceive the need to reconstruct (not deconstruct) my own
critical language. The moment is critical and fictional – at once personal and
historical.

❧ ⊛ ☙

When I began before.... it was Sunday afternoon. I sat in a remote pub (I called it
"bar" in my mind, still commingled with the motel in Brossard's desert, "broad
daylight, hot and sweat," 28). It's wet here though, damp Welsh drizzle, The road
has been slow so slow, not the "fast so fast" (32) of Brossard's protagonist
Melanie. My friend got the drinks, put them on the table, turned to hear, to
confront, to challenge, what the two men were saying. Inevitable, what two
women alone in a public bar expect, rehearse on the road before they arrive....
LINK TO.... Marlatt, Mrs Richards, the titular Ana's fear of the two Indians on the
forest path:

> And then she felt rather than heard the tread, turned. Two Siwash in white men's
> clothes. Looking gloomy, dark even [...]. Perhaps they were furious and meant to do
> her harm. She should say Good day, something civil, but she froze on the path as
> they approached, sick with the stories she had heard: Stackeye axing Perry in his
> sleep, Mrs Sullivan menaced with a knife. It was the sickness of fear and they knew
> it as they crowded past her as if she were a bush, a fern shaking in their way. (41–42)

Common to women, and here my friend goes – Red-Riding-Hood-like, damn it –
refuting what they say.... what was it again?

Text and text, what I read and what I experience/write swirling in the same whirlpools of beginning. A recognition of/remembering of small events in a gendered existence, the passageways between men and women, the power, fear and sexuality of connecting. At the same time << D I S P L A C E M E N T >> the split away from circumstance and social/national identity towards the known, familiar, material construction of the subject.

Desire for unity and absorption of otherness
nostalgia for unity but welcoming of otherness
above all the intense
vortex of the
SELF

demanding a place within the reading of any text.

Brossard and Marlatt both acknowledge the feminine/ist drive towards the autobiographical. In *Mauve Desert* there are three layers. No. Rather, imagine the labial folds of a Georgia O'Keefe painting, the mauve flower at the sensual/sexual centre of a female self – the furrows of imploding narratives.

[INFOLD]

The First Part

A novel entitled simply *Mauve Desert*; not the outer skin, the enfolding organ of Brossard's fictional whole, but an inner, smaller layer – text within text. The account of Melanie.... "I was moving forward in life, wild-eyed with arrogance. I was fifteen" (11)....by Laure Angstelle who "was the author of a single book published in a small Arizona town" (57). Melanie's her/story – her self/story – her fast so fast account in a notebook of driving through the hot, dry, night of the desert in her mother's car. The mother, Kathy Kerouac (reverberations on the road – gender inversions/displacements igniting the imagination's motor-memory), of whom Melanie writes:

> "Mothers are as fragile as civilization. They must not be forgotten in front of their television sets. Mothers are spaces." (18)

Mothers in front of televisions, alone/neglected/lost/adrift. That touching flash, white-bright in the instant of recognition, then, moving fast along the dusty road of reality.... LINK TO.... Marlatt, to mothers. Imbibe two texts and they succour thirst every which way but....

Ana Historic then. Another her/story, another account by one woman of another woman of another woman – Marlatt unforming his/story in her creation of Annie, a late-twentieth-century woman who unforms his/story in her investigation of Ana Richards who arrived, in the records in the fall of 1873.

> *"Miss Sweney was shortly succeeded by Mrs Richards, who soon became Mrs Ben Springer and cast her lot with the struggling little hamlet, giving place to a Miss Redfern...great difficulty was experienced in keeping a teacher longer than six months."* (39)

Quote within quote, heteroglossia of information: my skin encircling, framing Marlatt's language; her adoption of Annie's voice; who in turn quotes from the "OFFICIAL HISTORY". Quickly, we're talking authority here >>>

back page >>

bold large letters indicate >

ACKNOWLEDGEMENTS

The genuflection to conventional insciptions – of texts, of the past, of ourselves. Yes, here it is:

> "grateful appreciation to the Vancouver City Archives...."

No pagination needed, we all know where to find the full stops of economic power, publisher's letters, money being handed over for one-line quotations. But, Vancouver? Family past? A personal past? The oral LINKS between mother and daughter are opened by these supposedly circumscibing signs. My family, going to Vancouver, a school teacher (memory of text and story merge), shocked by ice, lack of rooms, multiple occupations – "the doctor had to double up as the dentist" – familiarity of the other townsfolk. Follow the structural rhythm:

From outside in....

Critical fold, authorial fold, narratorial fold, archival fold, which does NOT deconstruct the others, but leads to the inner fold of self. Yet, if it too is a fold, may we move further up, further in – to mothers? Annie's mother, suspended like Melanie's in the late Fifties (but was it/is it so different?):

> all the housewives absent, their curlerheads, their still mops on their knees in the aftermath of storm. endless morning stretched before them, tendrils of quiet crept in their windows, hours of nothing slipped through their doors. bathrobe sleeping beauties gone in a trice, a trance, embalmed, waiting for a kiss to wake them when their kids, their men would finally come home. how peaceful i thought, how i longed for it. a woman's place. safe. suspended out of the swift race of the world.
> the monstrous lie of it: the lure of absence. self-effacing. (24)

Marlatt's anger, Brossard's ludic darkness – the sense of waste/not waste....passed on? Is this where the folds become one, unity of mother and daughter? Or do they ceaselessly furl and unfurl, denying a Utopian essentialism? Questions remained unanswered – the need is to posit. Turn back, then:

Unfolding from the centre....

Annie writes not only of Ana, but of her mother, Ina, who can be her source and her self Ina, even as Ana becomes, perhaps, at the end of the book, another Annie (Annie Richards or Richard's Annie, 152). The "Who's there? she was whispering. knock knock. in the dark" (9) is answered with "only me" – herself/ myself. Does this encompass Marlatt too? The trouble with and the delight of these labial petals, these mauve flowers, is that they always suck us and propel us in and out....friction and pleasure. So, to withdraw from the fold, from auto-biographical self to Ana, to Ina, to Annie, to Marlatt, to critical self which must, within expectations, be an autobiographical/an experiential/a reading subject self. Unfurling further, text out of text, from the historic to the elemental. *Mauve Desert.*

Melanie's autobiographical account of herself, her mother, her mother's lover – Lorna Myher – her mother's car – the white meteor – her mother's motel with its single acknowledged occupant – Longman ("I / am / become / Death"), the male symbolic bicipital bisector of Melanie's semiotic poetic prose. The fluid, fast – and loose – open language of the feminine (and, in this case, female) voice is paralleled, shadowed page by page, with the static, stultifying masculine (and in this case, male) chapters – headed numerically, contained within the motel-room of the page. The conscious – conscious of nuclear explosions, formulaic language, pornographic magazines – and unconscious coupling of sex and violence with impotence – Chandleresque insignia – hats and cigarettes – homoerotic male wrestling....intimacy carefully displaced:

> In the silence of the room the man eyes the genitals, their coloration. He does not see their faces. The faces, shadow of shadows, make white circles around the genitals. Then the circles make a noise like an explosion. (21)

He doesn't see their faces, but can we see his? The nuclear light shadows Longman's individuality as much as pornography objectifies women. Is this a deliberate obfuscation of the gendered subject? But there is another, more immediate, more compelling, more narratorial mystery:

Angels Parkins is
DEAD
Angels Parkins – Melanie's potential lover
a drinker in her mother's motel bar
the victim of her mother's single guest
– Longman –

[OUTFOLD]

The Second Part

No answers – the past becomes undecipherable. The closure, witholding of the inner pocket of flesh. Instead, *Mauve Desert* provokes the release of a second fold: the reading, interpreting, experiential writing of Maude Laures as she ingests Laure Angstelle's fiction. Maude Laures, the schoolteacher who never talked politics,

> She will never know why her whole being plunged into a book, why for two years she spent herself, stretched herself through the pages of this book written by a woman she knows nothing about except the presumed evidence of an existence cloistered in the time and space of a single book. (51)

Various notes scattered, free-floating on an unpaginated surface, interrupted by the islands of conventional critical analysis – Places and Things, Characters, Scenes, Dimensions. Yet, even these material swellings soften and metamorphose, glistening like newly-melted frost; what Brossard distills is the *RELATIONSHIP*. Who needs to hack out frozen chunks when the fingers of our imaginations warm the solid form into free-flowing channels between author, reader and text.

In one perfect moment of wish-fulfilment, Maud – the reader of *Mauve Desert* – is allowed to confront Laure the author:

> *The scene can be imagined by parting the curtain between author and translator. The distance is abolished by imagining the two women sitting in a cafe.* (131)

Maud wants to know – and so do we – why Angela Parkins was murdered and by who? The basic sucking force of a mystery novel, only this time, we actually get to ask – through Maud – "who dun it?" Laure begins:

> — What would you like to talk about?
> — One thing only: Angela Parkins' death. I'd like to talk to you exactly the way I imagine Angela Parkins would if she could get out of character, if she were its ultimate presence.
> — I'm listening.
> — *Why did you kill me?*
> — *You're going too fast, Angela, you're getting too directly to the heart of the essential. Wouldn't you rather we talk first about you or about me, that somewhere we find the familiar Arizona landsapes again? [Silence] So be it, if you like, we can talk about your death right now. But first, swear to me that you didn't see anything coming. Swear it.* (131–32)

Reader privileging character, allowing Angela to turn upon her creator/her mother/her Shelleyan doctor and ask why the plot had to work to her disadvantage. Maud turning upon Laure and asking why the fiction had to end, as it does on Angela's death. The same question may be replicated/reflected in my/our reading of Brossard's work: why doesn't *Mauve Desert* give us answers, a meaning? Why must it end so precipitously? Answers are predictably profuse and liquacious – the author allows the streams of self-conscious demand to flow freely, diamond like in the wake of the tide, a residue of the unconscious surprised by waking – Possibilities:

> 1. "You forgot about reality"
> 2. "It was you or him"
> 3. "You wanted to cross the threshold" (132–33)

Translation and interpretation of text goes thus.....possibly:

1. The restrictions that govern women and texts, and the punishment for breaking those taboos – in the immediate present, a crushing of homoerotic desire.

2. An eternal battle between men and women, power struggles in a hierarchical ideology, in which only one gender may emerge as victor/victrice.

3. And reality – a closure. A postmodern questioning and recognition of "how far can we go."

Look at the backdrop and suspend disbelief, here is a magic – a conjurer's hat – experience of re-embodying the author to ask her/his intention.The fiction of faith, the belief in one-dimensional realities.....satisfying?.....yes, but only until the lights go on. Instead, pull back the curtain and reveal, revel in, the multiplicity and diversity of both questions and answers. With the curtain drawn we can see the hands reversed, the serpent tail, the forbidden incestuous desires....all that Single Truth has shamefacedly tried to conceal, to pretend never existed. But this particularly fragile veil has been torn by more hands than Brossard's and Marlatt's. Unfolding from their texts to other FICTION/THEORIES. One labial curve uncovers Cixous speaking in Liverpool:

> There is no writing without reading. Writing is actually a kind of alliance between writer and reader. The reader within myself and the reader outside. Readers don't realise enough how much they are implied in the writing, how much they are at work, how much they write. They give rebirth.[2]

French feminism, *écriture féminine*, writing the body – a language which like Brossard's denies boundaries between the literary and the theoretical, between readers and writers.

A parallel agenda, this time allowing the social to swell above the sexual politics: Bruce Andrews (co-editor of L=A=N=G=U=A=G=E) speaking in New York –

> Define comprehension as something other than consumption. (*Other then*) So it's politicizing: a radical *reading* embodied in writing. A writing which is itself a "wild reading" *solicits* wild reading. The reading is a response, is a *dialogue with* the paradigms of sense – with *rhetoric* (which is a misreading in the writing itself): "We've been misread!" our job is to go beyond these norms and limits, to *read them*

---

[2] *The Body and the Text: Hélène Cixous, Reading and Teaching*, ed. Helen Wilcox, Keith McWatters, Ann Thompson & Linda Williams (London: Harvester Wheatsheaf, 1990): 26.

backwards, to offer up a different refraction of the circumstances. Let's let the status quo *read itself* being quarantined, scolded, frag'd & interrupted.[3]

Echoes of Brossard's undefined territory – allowance of dialogue. The democratization of text. Marlatt's insistent and pervasive dialogues. Maud and Maud-as-Angela talk to Laure. Annie talks to Ina, her mother, and to Zoe, her lover/friend. A welcoming of the hidden polemic, the massing of voices, a carnivalesque spirit, an abundant heteroglossia...all this scares the shit out of Single Truth when she pulls back her curtain, eyes so wide in panic, mouth agape. But then, radical language always did unnerve those with an investment in stasis.

Body reactions. Renaissance *"High Art"* to twentieth-century feminism (although I veer from essentialism) – the female orifice signifies horror to the anonymous artist (it has to be a "he") whose canvas *Allegory* magnetizes the punters in the National Gallery, as it does to the established art critic discussing Judy Chicago's *The Dinner Party*....this is Lola Lemire Tostevin's reworking/ refreshing of the article in *TIME* magazine:

calls it "static...cliche...hokey...
obsessive stereotype...mass devotional...
colors worthy of a Taiwanese souvenir factory...
evangelical...free of wit or irony..."
then goes on to label Chicago's explanation
for choosing the vagina as her mark
of otherness and identity
as "jargon"
and "femspeak."[4]

As Tostevin explains, it's perfectly acceptable to call female genitals an "amorphous shape," but it's crossing the boundaries, venturing into undefined territory, leaving the mapped out area of good taste, to say: women have vaginas and mothers have cunts (and I'm not quoting).

What Chicago moulds into a material sculpture, Brossard and Marlatt structure in their texts, squeezing the tubes of language onto the palette of form. And – as with Chicago and Tostevin – their aim is political: what is constructed can be changed. Brossard on radicalizing/feminizing language:

If you are careful with words, really try to stretch their meaning, arrange them in a certain way, each one can acquire a new aura, a new meaning.[5]

Changing auras in Brossard's words: a possibility of recolouring the seven chakras which envelop the body/word in an egg-like, womb-like halo. Quite unlike....totally unlike La Cicciolina's explanation of how she and Jeff Koons first

3 *The Politics of Poetic Form: Poetry and Public Policy*, ed. Charles Bernstein (New York: Roof, 1990): 28.

4 Lola Lemire Tostevin, *Color of Her Speech* (Toronto: Coach House, 1982): np.

5 *The Poetry Project* (December 1991–January 1992): 2.

"understood" one another, though this "understanding" was clearly not a permanent one: "It wasn't a problem. There was an *aura*. Everyone has an aura. It's
something you can't touch, but it exists, and you can relate, even to a stranger."
The gap between Canadian lesbian poet and Italian MP ex-porn queen exists not
only in their lifestyles, but in their rejection and acceptance of value-systems. La
Cicciolina makes a good living, even after leaving the oldest profession, out of
plying the trade of gender and linguistic conventionality – her provocative
posturings can only succeed in front of a mirror of shocked conservatism.
Brossard's self-aware shattering of that petrified mercury releases the globules of
reflecting silver to roll and slither without the constraints of a formal form, developing new auras in the diffuse light of movement.

This UNtelling, UNravelling, UNspeaking....UNites the Canadian feminist language poets, the US language poets and the French feminists, especially Cixous
and Kristeva.

The blurring of edges, the curling of the tongue about the linguistic geometrics
– **WORDS** – to suck   and   s o f t e n   c o r n e r s ,
b o r d e r s ,   d i v i d e d   –   U T T E R A N C E S –

Brossard, *Picture Theory* (1982):

Tango x 4. Lovhers/(w)rite: tireless borne alive.[6]

Daphne Marlatt and Betsy Warland, *Double Negative* (1988):

heads out of the door
i/s squint
the frame enlarged to sun and 360 degrees
language as billboards
feet unsteady
where to focus
life in 3-D
everything an inter/ruption.[7]

Ron Silliman, *The Age of Huts* (1986):

131 *Sad is faction*. That sounds alone are not precise meaning (in the referential) sense
means that before the listener can recognize content he/she must first have the
perception of the presence of words.[8]

Hélène Cixous, *The Newly Born Woman* (1975):

Text, my body: traversed by lilting flows; listen to me, it is not a captivating,
clinging "mother"; it is the equivoice that, touching you, affects you, pushes you
away from your breast to come to language, that summons *your* strength; it is the

---

[6] Nicole Brossard, *Picture Theory* (Montreal: Guernica, 1991): 103.
[7] Daphne Marlatt & Betsy Warland. *Double Negative* (Charlottetown: Gynergy, 1988): 33.
[8] Ron Silliman, *The Age of Huts* (New York: Roof, 1986): 56.

rhyth-me that laughs you....and pushes you to inscibe your woman's style in language.[9]

        "Lovhers"....."i/s"....."*Sad is faction*"....."rhythme"

[INFOLD]

The Third Part

Even so.....my choices cannot but inhibit the superfluity of linguistic rearrangement (use of hyphens/ parentheses/ puns/ parts of words/ broken sentences/ glosses/ words without translation/ fusions/ fragments/ recurrences/ isolations/ resemblances). Language is UNwritten, form is UNconstructed....we begin to explore the undefined territory. As Cixous writes, "When the line is crossed, contagion is produced. This phenomenon has been located and attested. Witches spread on the surface of the globe."[10] Marlatt's witches who have escaped from the ditch "on the far edge of town," and have spread themselves over the desert, fractured moments of self-conscious/self-unconscious energy.

Even so.....I have chosen. The heteroglossia of this text is not, cannot be, anarchic. I have allowed, filtered and translated the fractured moments of my own imagination. Like Annie reading Ana's journal, like Maud reading Laure's novel, like myself reading *Mauve Desert* and *Ana Historic*, I have interpreted, translated, for you and for me, what I have read/seen/understood in the texts. In *Mauve Desert* the third and final element of the fiction is Maud Laure's translation of Laure Angstelle's "Mauve Desert" into "Mauve the Horizon." Cover, title and text are altered, the language is close so close, but the meaning is far so far.

    1. Laure's version:

> My mother was on Lorna's lap, who was holding her by the waist with her right arm. With her left hand Lorna was scribbling. Their legs were all entwined and my mother's apron was folded over Lorna's thigh. I asked Lorna what she was writing. She hesitated and then spun out some sentence to the effect that she was unable to read the marks her hand had drawn. (20)

    2. Maud's translation:

> My mother was sitting on Lorna's lap and Lorna was absent-mindedly scribbling huge letters on her back. I asked for some paper and Lorna answered that writing served no purpose, that playing hard and screaming loud were more useful. (176)

    3. My interpretation: Maud, the teacher, the translator, the critic, immediately believes "scribbling" to be "absent-minded," to have "no purpose." For the

---

9 Hélène Cixous & Catherine Clement, *The Newly Born Woman* (Manchester: Manchester UP, 1986): 93.

10 Cixous & Clement, *The Newly Born Woman* , 34.

unknown writer Laure's scribbling may be unreadable, but its effect is nevertheless potent....sexually potent, bodily potent. Yet, like Maud's, my text is limiting, it E.L.U.C.I.D.A.T.E.S. = THEORY.

Even so.....this text, Maud's/Mauve's text, my text, your text is FICTION....allowing through the self, not denying the reading/writing inseparability. Brossard's tripartite form seduces us into a constant flicker of pages to and fro: "what did Laure say?" "what did Maud write?" "what was it again?"

[OUTFOLD]

The material action of a rhythmic text/ the material action of my rhythmic text, of my scribbling (infold/outfold)...."what was it again?"

What did those men say in the pub on that rainy Sunday afternoon?

WORKS CITED

BERNSTEIN, Charles, ed. *The Politics of Poetic Form: Poetry and Public Policy* (New York: Roof, 1990).

———— & Bruce ANDREWS, ed. *The L=A=N=G=U=A=G=E Book* (Carbondale & Edwardsville IL: Southern Illinois UP, 1984).

BROSSARD, Nicole. *Mauve Desert* (Toronto: Coach House, 1990).

————. *Picture Theory* (Montreal: Guernica, 1991).

CIXOUS, Hélène, & Catherine CLEMENT. *The Newly Born Woman* (Manchester: Manchester UP, 1986).

FITZGERALD, Judith, ed. *SP/ELLES. Poetry By Canadian Women* (Windsor, Ontario: Black Moss, 1986).

MARLATT, Daphne. *Ana Historic* (Toronto: Coach House, 1988).

———— & Betsy WARLAND. *Double Negative* (Charlottetown: Gynergy, 1988).

The Poetry Project (December 1991–January 1992).

SILLIMAN, Ron. *The Age of Huts* (New York: Roof, 1986).

TOSTEVIN, Lola Lemire. *Color of Her Speech* (Toronto: Coach House, 1982).

WILCOX, Helen, Keith MCWATTERS, Ann THOMPSON & Linda WILLIAMS, ed. *The Body and the Text: Hélène Cixous, Reading and Teaching* (London: Harvester Wheatsheaf, 1990).

☿ ✿ ☾

Freaks and Others
The Biggest Modern Woman *and the World*

JILL LeBIHAN

S USAN SWAN'S FIRST NOVEL, *The Biggest Modern Woman of the World* (1983) has been called "fictional biography" and a "flight of fantasy."[1] It has been called "one gigantic spiel" and "a freaky book."[2] One journalist suggests that the 340-page novel resembles some kind of outsized, elephantine progeny;[3] the implication is that the writer's project in some way mimics the life of the protagonist of the novel. The consensus would seem to be that this is an uncomfortable text, one which contains a variety of rhetorical turns and political ambitions, and which resists easy categorisation. Swan's novel demands of its reader that it be mapped into the world not only as a recovery-project from women's history, not only as a comic novel, not only as a work of myth-making, not only as a post-colonial critique of contemporary US imperialism, but also as an example of postmodern feminist allegory.

The Biggest Modern Woman of the World contains elements of both allegory and fantasy. These terms are sometimes deemed mutually exclusive, mainly on the basis of the argument that the former has a manifest relation to a presumably identifiable real, non-textual world, whereas the latter term refers to something which is attempting to exceed this presumed reality.[4] However, Swan's text employs features of both fantasy and allegory in her embellished narrative of a freak-show exhibit, a narrative which functions as a commentary on the Canadian experience as a post-colonial nation.

The fantasy elements of *The Biggest Modern Woman of the World* relate to the liberties Susan Swan has taken with nineteenth-century documentary evidence on Giant Anna, inventing a controversial, sexualised and politicised existence for her which extends beyond a mere commentary on the relics of her life. I have

---

[1] Linda Swan–Ryan, letter, *Maclean's* (29 October, 1984): 8.

[2] Douglas Barbour, "One Gigantic Spiel," *Essays on Canadian Writing* 33 (Fall 1986): 136–39, 136.

[3] Donna Guglielmin, "Susan Swan, Mythmaker," *Canadian Author and Bookman* 60.1 (Fall 1984).

[4] For a more detailed explanation of the problems surrounding the concept of these genres, see Lynette Hunter, *Modern Allegory and Fantasy: Rhetorical Stances of Contemporary Writing* (London & Basingstoke: Macmillan, 1991): 12–26.

discussed elsewhere the documents surrounding the historical figure of Anna Swan, doyenne of the nineteenth-century freak-show circuit and the reception of Susan Swan's narrative in its contemporary context.[5] My focus in this essay is on the possibilities for an allegorical mapping of the novel into the post-colonial politics of twentieth-century Canada.

As well as working as a narrative fantasy of a giant woman's isolation as a marketed commodity, then, the novel also operates on an allegorical level with the giant Canadian nation's sense of economic exploitation and its sense of Otherness as a post-colonial country. This kind of use of allegory is important for post-colonial literature in particular because of the opportunity it provides for re-reading and re-viewing history. Stephen Slemon argues that the presence of history in fictional texts is important for post-colonial literature because it produces an active reader: "The point for post-colonial allegory is that historical material must be read, and read in adjacency to a fictional re-enactment of it."[6]

The active reading of a historical document does not necessarily require the use of allegory.[7] However, Swan's use of Anna's body as an allegorical figure in her text demonstrates a similar mode of operation between the postmodern rewriting of the past and allegorical writing strategies. By making the woman's body so much the focus of her text, Swan is also drawing on feminist discourse. Her feminist discussion of a Victorian freak and the allegory of nationalism converge in my discussion of the representation of the cultural and gendered Other as a scrutinised figure of post-colonial subjectivity and colonial subjection.

The staging of Anna as a spectacle is done in such a way as to reflect the Victorian obsession with taxonomic knowledge. This focus on arbitrary, but extremely powerful, methodologies for organising knowledge is linked to postmodern interest in the exposure of metanarratives. The organisation of inform-ation abut the human body, like the organisation of documents through narrative, is a concern for Swan's novel because of the way in which the subject of the scientific discourses becomes objectified and disempowered. The documents or pieces of information have no powers of subjection in themselves: the emphasis is on the ways in which this information is organised and used.

Curiosity about the anatomy of the giant woman when she is in performance appears as unjustified and unjustifiable sexual voyeurism in the novel. Similarly, instances of the same kind of voyeurism in the guise of scientific enquiry are

---

5 See Chapter Five, Section (ii) of my unpublished doctoral dissertation, University of Leeds, 1993.

6 Stephen Slemon, "Post-Colonial Allegory and the Transformation of History," *Journal of Commonwealth Literature* 22.1 (1988): 157–68, 160.

7 Think, for instance, of the use made of Catharine Parr Traill in Laurence's *The Diviners* (1974), which is inventive and dialogic but certainly not allegorical.

abundant. By and large, the male inquisitors are exploited humorously by Susan Swan, but her exaggerated and parodic portrayal of these nineteenth-century men of science exposes their discourses as part of a system of domination.

The examples of the exposure of the giant woman to a sexualised gaze are numerous. They begin with Hubert, a dwarf, who, although an object of public curiosity himself, is one of the worst violaters of Anna's privacy, not to mention her maidenhood. It is Hubert, whose curiosity about the size of Anna's rectum and vagina prompts him to measure her intimate spaces with whatever instruments are at hand in the woods of Nova Scotia: an icicle and a willow twig. Such intimate exposures continue fairly relentlessly throughout the novel. Anna's first experience of sexual intercourse is with Angus McAskill, the Cape Breton Giant, and it takes place in a park near her Aunt's home, where she is staying while at college. The love-making of the two giants is viewed by several local boys lurking in the bushes. Anna also suffers the attentions of a peeping tom who hangs out in an oak-tree outside her window and "plays with himself," according to her Aunt, Mary Johnson.[8] Even Anna's eating is made into part of her performance by Barnum, who ropes off her table in a restaurant and allows other diners to gape (67).

The most appalling case of voyeurism occurs on board a ship when Anna is travelling to England with Martin Bates. The episode of "Bates at the Peep-hole" is quoted in Susan Swan's novel as being from his essay "Species Development, or a Tract Towards Continual Anatomical Wonders" (170). It is not part of one of Anna's spiels, and appears in the text as something which presumably the giant woman never saw, since the copy has *notionally* been amended and prepared for publication by Bates (332). The fiction of the editorial intervention of Bates is problematical, however, since it is unlikely that he would have allowed some of the details of his impotence to be published. This apparent inconsistency further throws into question the status of the narrative.

Bates, whose obsession with populating the United States with people as large as himself and Anna, his soon-to-be-wife, leads him to employ the services of the ship's doctor, who *performs* (literally) his internal examination of Anna near a window from which Bates has a view of the proceedings. Bates's belief in the progressive development of the human species by selective breeding is based on the (unjustified) assumption that size is a significant factor in building a country of international stature. Thus he lists in detail the approximate size, weight and state of perfection of Anna's genitalia and reproductive organs, based on the manual examination carried out by Dr Naughton.

The ritualised internal examination of Anna, which becomes a spectacle, with Bates as the lecherous audience and "scientific" documenter of the process, oper-

---

[8] Susan Swan, *The Biggest Modern Woman of the World* (Toronto: Lester & Orpen Dennys, 1983): 60. All subsequent quotations are from this edition.

ates on a complex system of power. There is something particularly horrifying about the complete subjection of a woman on the gynaecologist's table under usual circumstances, but this subjection is increased when the event is observed and recorded by an unseen man with ulterior motives. Bates's desire to obtain a perfect giant specimen of a woman for a partner, and his covert methods of ascertaining her state of physical perfection, is an exploitation of a far worse kind than the self-exhibition which Anna undergoes at theatres, fairs and museums. At least she is able to speak out in her lecturing voice when she knows she has an audience.

Martin Bates's view of the imperialist future of the United States hinges on the physical perfection, verified by internal examination, of his future bride and dreamed-of mother of a nation of giants. The partnership between the two giants is based on convenience, proximity and size. For Bates's project of a race of giants, the bigger the better, and Anna Swan just happens to be "the biggest modern woman of the world". But what is it that the gynaecological examination, as witnessed illicitly by Bates, is really seeking to verify? And what implications might this have for a project of nation-building, as well as for the theorising or metahistoriography of that project?

In feminist critiques of psychoanalytic theory, attention is focused on the construction of the crucial difference between the sexes on the basis of the sight of the woman's (lack of) genitalia: the penis is all that is recognised. As Jane Gallop writes, in male-centred psychoanalytic theory

> nothing to see becomes nothing of worth. The privilege of sight over other sense, oculocentrism, supports and unifies phallocentric, sexual theory (theory – from the Greek *theoria,* from *theoros,* "spectator", from *thea,* "a viewing").[9]

Gallop here positions the spectator and the theorist together, and this leaves a critical problem about the positioning of a non-oculocentric theorist. Another version of the problem that Gallop represents can be produced in an alternative discourse to that of psychoanalysis. This version is the one already formulated here: the difficult issues surrounding the selective processes of historical representation in postmodern literature.

The problem facing the historiographer is similar to that facing the gendered subject in psychoanalytic discourse: is it the case that "nothing to see" necessarily means "nothing of worth" in the textualised past? Nova Scotia's history has celebrated Angus McAskill often at the expense of Anna Swan. She does not even get a mention in P.T. Barnum's autobiography. Phyllis Blakely's conventional history and Susan Swan's novel both show that this has nothing to do with lack of interesting material on Anna; neither does it have anything to do with the inherent

---

9 Jane Gallop, *Feminism and Psychoanalysis: The Daughter's Seduction* (London: Macmillan, 1982): 58.

worth of recording freaks and giants, since Barnum's text and many others[10] are full of them. Contemporary theories of postmodernism, feminism and post-colonialism offer a set of perspectives from which we might judge what there is to see, while still taking into account the fact that the judgement is affected by gender, culture and historical standpoint. These theories also suggest that what can be seen is not all there is, and that access to information is mediated by many factors, including money and censorship. What none of these theories offers is an unproblematical position for the theorist, the spectator, the viewing subject.

The position of the reader/theorist in relation to *The Biggest Modern Woman of the World* is problematical for its readership. The novel causes difficulties of generic categorisation and historiographic taxonomies; it affronts moral codes and a particular culture's sense of personal privacy and decency;[11] and it challenges its readers to rethink their sense of the relationship between fact and fiction, gender and nationality, normalcy and difference. Smaro Kamboureli suggests that the "audience's ambivalent response" to Anna Swan within the text, and to the novel itself, is what grants *The Biggest Modern Woman of the World* its "high allegorical status." She continues:

> Allegory, in this respect, doesn't merely suggest the double semantic function of telling a story; it also suggests the semiotics of otherness, be it the otherness of discourse, gender or nation [...] Swan shows in this novel how within the markers of difference between history and fiction resides a logic of identity which authorises the postmodern writer to unveil a truth that demystifies its own absolute and terrifying status in human history.[12]

Attempts to unveil the "absolute and terrorising" truth of human history occur at several points in Swan's novel. There are the examinations of Anna by Bates and the doctor, the dwarf and the freak-show audiences already mentioned. There is the occasion when Angus McAskill is required to lift his kilt after taking bets on the size of his "cod" (45). And there is the occasion of "Victoria *en passant*," when the miserable, minuscule imperial monarch passes underneath Anna's petticoats and through the archway made by her legs in order to cheer herself up (196). What these various people are looking for beneath the undergarments of the over-sized Canadians could be described as giant genitalia and the sexual thrill it provides.

---

10 See Richard Altick, *The Shows of London* (Cambridge MA: Harvard UP, 1978); George Sanger, *Seventy Years A Showman: My Life and Adventures in Camp and Caravan the World Over* (London: Pearson, 1910); and Kellow Chesney, *The Victorian Underworld* (Harmondsworth: Penguin, 1970).

11 Elsewhere I have given a more detailed account of the Swan–Ryan controversy over the accusation by Giant Anna's inheritors that Susan Swan has taken liberties with her character. See my unpublished doctoral dissertation (University of Leeds, 1993) and also *Maclean's* (29 October 1984): 8.

12 Smaro Kamboureli, *"The Biggest Modern Woman in the World:* Canada as the Absent Spouse," *Australian–Canadian Studies* 6.1 (1988): 104.

What they are also looking for are the truthful signifiers of sexual difference. They are looking for the difference that genes and chromosomes make not only to gender but to size. They are looking for large, never-before-revealed passages, like questers for the Northwest Passage. Victoria, like the dwarf, is looking for a space over which she can claim to have domination. Bates, like Hubert and the little Queen, is looking for something sizeable and fertile on the products of which he can found an empire.

The most explicit figuring of Anna's body in relation to the great expanse of Canada is contained within the performance that she creates with the "Kentucky Giant" Martin Bates and the Australian Apollo Ingalls (178–83). This verse contains such momentous lines as Martin's address to Anna:

> the Near North is your shoulder
> draped with trade staples and immigrants
> who will learn to boast
> of your bitter winds and thousands
> of unproductive acres
> your breasts are cod canneries [...]
> Your lips are the north-west
> passage [...]
> O Anna, you are the American Dream.
> My will shall grow in your void. (180–82)

The heavy post-colonial irony in these verses is not exploiting Canada's relation to the British Empire, but rather the Canadian national paranoia with regard to the invasion of the culture and trading advantages of their neighbours across the US border and the imperialist domination that this is seen to represent. Although this novel was published before the Free Trade Agreement between the two countries was made law, it makes some incisive comments that remain relevant to current debates about contemporary trading relations across the US–Canadian borders.

Canada as the violated woman or exploitable resource is an allegorical representation which Anna's reply in verse refutes:

> I'll pull the continent
> about me to stop you
> from making more of yourself –
> The Wisconsin could freeze
> your grasping hand up my skirts
> before you respect my rights
> (let alone acknowledge them).
> I'll be damned, Martin,
> if I'll be crammed
> on the seat of your
> imperial fantasy. (183)

The position of the doubly colonised subject, woman and Canadian, is one that Anna Swan refuses to take up, at least in terms of the verse performance. But, as ever, Anna has more power on stage than off it. She is the enormous, empty Canadian landscape in the context of the stage-show, and speaks out about the attempted exploitation of the Yankee played by Bates. Off stage, Anna has known since the incident with the icicle that she is "human and vulnerable – a female who, like every other female, could be penetrated in a way that no man could" (35). Size is no guarantee of power, and being female is a positive disadvantage in such matters.

Richard Altick, in his discussion of *The Shows of London*, explains that it "was advantageous to ascribe foreign origin to a freak or a specialist in an extraordinary line of work", whether or not there was a "causal connection between putative country of origin and a freak's freakishness."[13] Altick claims that the exhibiting of colonial Others as freaks in the style of Barnum is the beginning of a kind of primitive ethnology, the kind illustrated by Bates perhaps, and the British doctors who pickle Anna's first infant for research purposes without her consent.

Barnum's five-storey New York museum is organised according to his own taxonomic rules, starting with "murky basement aquariums," moving up to murals and dioramas on the next floor, then trained mammals including the "LEARNED SEAL" and "Barnum's own display case with his writing desk." The third floor contains a selection of bizarre preserved remnants such as "a ball of hair from the stomach of a sow" and "a petrified piece of pork recovered from the water after sixty years" as well as various artifacts collected to represent, patronisingly, the skills of other cultures, which Barnum refers to as "unsightly sculptures" which are "highly revered by millions of ignorant Heathens" (43).

On the fourth floor there are "mineral and geological specimens" and "the GREAT MODEL OF NIAGARA FALLS." Finally, on the fifth floor of the museum, there is the "HAPPY FAMILY, a vast cage in which one owl, two pigeons, some guinea pigs, a nest of rats, one basset hound, and two kittens co-existed" (43). There is nothing "natural" about this strange conglomeration whose contented coexistence is helped along by laudanum, just as there is nothing natural about the golden pigeons and Zip, the man in the hairy suit, who are also on display at this evolutionary pinnacle of Barnum's strange hierarchy. It is the manufactured, the oddly combined hybrids, that erect Barnum's own evolutionary pinnacle. He, like Bates, believes in proving his own evolvedness by imposing his own "rational" and "scientific" schema on his collections.

Adam Kuper suggests that ethnology was in its very earliest stages in the 1860s and 1870s and that it was not necessarily affected in any way by the Darwinian notion of the arbitrariness of natural selection. Kuper goes on:

---

13 Altick, *The Shows of London*, 268.

The anthropologists took this primitive society as their special subject, but in practice primitive society proved to be their own society (as they understood it) seen in a distorting mirror. For them modern society was defined above all by the territorial state, the monogamous family and private property. Primitive society therefore must have been nomadic, ordered by blood ties, sexually promiscuous and communist. Primitive man was illogical and given to magic. In time he had developed more sophisticated religious ideas. Modern man, however, had invented science.[14]

Barnum, who is represented by Swan in this novel as the arch-capitalist and the essential Yankee, creates a museum which seems to have only a tangential relation to other explanations of the societal structure of the mid-nineteenth century. The museum nevertheless develops as an educational project, both in Swan's novel and in Barnum's own account of things. The question is really one of the relationship between this popular explanation of culture and the alternatives on offer. What kind of anchorage might Barnum's sort of science find in other histories or scientific analogies of the period? What kind of hold might this particular way of organising perceptions still exert?

Sander Gilman suggests that individuals can be made to create, by standing for, whole mythical classes of peoples. Barnum can come to stand for a Yankee capitalist class in the same way that Anna Swan can be made to stand for Nova Scotians/women/Canadians/giants, through the staging of them as icons. Gilman writes:

Specific individual realities are thus given mythic extension through association with the qualities of a class. These realities manifest as icons representing perceived attributes of the class into which the individual has been placed. The myths associated with the class, the myth of difference from the rest of humanity, is thus, to an extent, composed of fragments of the real world, perceived through the ideological bias of the observer.[15]

Anna's compact phrase for this "myth of difference" is that the "individual is a business gimmick" (156). Her difference is the feature that makes her an exploitable commodity, but she can still be made to operate metonymically for an assortment of things.

Gilman's essay is mainly concerned with the exhibition of Black women on the London freak-show circuit who were given the title "the Hottentot Venus." The one individual who first received the epithet, "Sarah Bartmann," was followed by a series of "Hottentot Venuses" whose shared feature was the "steatopygia" or "protruding buttocks" which were pathologised and fantasised over by the viewers and commentators. Gilman considers the metonymic functioning of parts of the

14 Adam Kuper, *The Invention of Primitive Society: Transformations of an Illusion* (London & New York: Routledge, 1988): 5.

15 Sander L. Gilman, "Black Bodies, White Bodies: Nineteenth-Century Art, Medicine and Literature," in *"Race", Writing and Difference*, ed. Henry Louis Gates, Jr. (Chicago: U of Chicago P, 1986): 223.

woman for the whole, as well as the iconographic status accorded to individual women that made them function on behalf of a whole mythical "race," to be a crucial aspect of the meaning of freak-shows:

> Sarah Bartmann's sexual parts, her genitalia and her buttocks, serve as the central image for the black female throughout the nineteenth century [...] To an extent, this reflects the general nineteenth-century understanding of female sexuality as pathological: the female genitalia were of interest partly as examples of the various pathologies which could befall them but also because the female genitalia came to define the female for the nineteenth century. When a specimen was to be preserved for an anatomical museum, more often than not the specimen was seen as a pathological summary of the entire individual. Thus the skeleton of a giant or a dwarf represented "giganticism" or "dwarfism" [...][16]

Anna Swan's "sexual parts" are put on display by Martin Bates, not to mention exposed by Hubert armed with his chunks of Nova Scotian wilderness, and by others who lift her skirt; Anna is made to operate on behalf of a whole group of non-specified "Others" in the same way as "Sarah Bartmann" and Gilman's other examples do. Like some of Gilman's prostitutes, Anna Swan is even said by Bates to be afflicted by "Darwin's ear," a lack of earlobes and a simplification of the convolutions, interpreted as a sign of female atavism (171).[17]

In some ways, then, Swan's novel itself replicates the exposure of Anna's sexuality and nationality and makes her stand for a variety of elements in a politicised discourse. This is the direct cause of the mysterious disease of "emblem fatigue" by which she is afflicted. Nevertheless, Anna Swan is given a very specific cultural and gendered identity which Susan Swan utilises in her text. The giant woman is not simply representative of a whole bunch of non-specific "Others." She is allowed to articulate quite clearly, and differentiate between, problems with her Canadianness, her femaleness, her freakishness.

In his recent discussion, "Post-Colonial Allegory and the Transformation of History," Stephen Slemon considers allegory a problematical mode in relation to post-colonial literatures.[18] Just as it would be possible to argue, as some of her opponents do, that Susan Swan replicates reductive and oppressive procedures through creating allegorical figurations for her characters, Slemon argues that all allegory may be read as part of an "imperial enterprise" rather than as resistance to it, if it is interpreted either "against a preexisting master code or typological system" which is presumed to be stable, or "in the manichean code" where "the 'other' is [...] fixed in a permanent position of subordination within a master code of binary thinking."[19] Slemon proposes that the solution to this conservative inter-

---

[16] Gilman, "Black Bodies, White Bodies," 235.
[17] Gilman, "Black Bodies, White Bodies," 243.
[18] Stephen Slemon, "Post-Colonial Allegory," 157–68.
[19] Slemon, "Post-Colonial Allegory," 162.

pretation of allegory lies in the lap of the reader, depending on her "binocular vision for the 'revisioning' process that allegory promotes," providing this reading is performed with scrupulous attention to the "cultural grounding" of the text.[20]

Lynette Hunter suggests that the "primary activity of allegory is to stimulate various forms of reading and writing, different ways of approach and interaction," and she notes Gay Clifford's argument "that modern allegory is sceptical, flexible and against social hierarchy."[21] Both Hunter and Slemon thus recognise the possibilities of reading and writing in allegorical forms for subversive effect, but they are careful to emphasise the risks involved. In particular, both stress the problems associated with "the passage of time [...] at the heart of allegory," wherein "ideologies of different chronological periods [...] twist and distort when reflected by our own."[22]

Hunter's and Slemon's contemporary analyses of allegory emphasise the uncertainty surrounding the project for readers and writers, returning us to the critical problem of the position of the spectator/theorist which I considered earlier, and which I wish to raise again with a suggestion of another insertion of *The Biggest Modern Woman of the World* into the late twentieth century. I refer here to a museum exhibit held at the Royal Ontario Museum in Toronto in the first half of 1990, which resulted in considerable controversy. The exhibition showed the results of Canadian involvement in colonial exploitation of Africa in the very late nineteenth and early twentieth centuries, displaying an assortment of artifacts not dissimilar to some of those on the third floor of Barnum's museum. The question of how the display could be read was raised, and the museum's defence was to suggest that it could be read ironically. The controversy partly focused on the captions attached to the exhibits, which were not found to be sufficiently conscious of the racist stereotyping involved in the exhibition (according to anti-racist protest groups, who regularly picketed the museum for the duration of the display). One key exhibit, for instance, positioned near the entrance of the display, was an enormously enlarged print showing the slaughter of a Southern African by a British soldier taken from the *Illustrated London News* of 1879. It was captioned "Lord Beresford's first encounter with a Zulu."

Marlene Nourbese Philip has produced incisive critiques of the ROM debacle, as it has become:

> For Africans, the museum has always been a significant site of their racial oppression. Within its walls reasons could be found for their being placed at the foot of the hierarchical ladder of human evolution designed by the European. Proof could

---

20 Slemon, "Post-Colonial Allegory," 165, 166.

21 Lynette Hunter, *Modern Allegory and Fantasy: Rhetorical Stances of Contemporary Writing* (Basingstoke & London: Macmillan, 1991): 131, 144.

22 Slemon, "Post-Colonial Allegory," 158. Hunter, *Modern Allegory and Fantasy*, 183.

also be found there of the "bizarre" nature and "primitive" anatomy of the African. Where else could you find the preserved genitalia of the black South African woman, Saarjtie Baartman [...] but in the *Musée de l'Homme* in Paris?23

Nourbese Philip points out that the significance of the protests against the ROM exhibition "lay in challenging the museum and its roles, particularly as it has affected African peoples." The ROM represents a particular, institutionalised staging of a spectacle. She continues:

> One reading saw these artifacts as being frozen in time and telling a story about white Canadian exploration of Africa; the other inserted the reader – the African Canadian reader – actively into the text, who then read those artifacts as the painful detritus of savage exploration and attempted genocide of their own people.24

The continuing of the stereotypical representation of an undifferentiated, non-specific Other through the display of metonymically functioning artifacts (such as spears, animal hides, beads and so on); the discussions still surrounding free-trade and US imperialism; the current exploitation of Canadian land; the continuing exposure of women's bodies to masculine oppression25 – these contextualising factors locate Susan Swan's novel in current-affairs commentary in an obvious way, and it is perhaps this rather too clear relation to contemporary reality that makes *The Biggest Modern Woman of the World* such as contentious text.

WORKS CITED

ALTICK, Richard. *The Shows of London* (Cambridge MA: Harvard UP, 1978).

BARBOUR, Douglas. "One Gigantic Spiel," *Essays on Canadian Writing* 33 (Fall 1986): 136–39.

BARNUM, Phineas Taylor. *The Struggles and Triumphs of P.T. Barnum As Told By Himself*, ed. John O'Leary (London: Macgibbon & Kee, 1967).

BLAKELY, Phyllis R. *Nova Scotia's Two Remarkable Giants* (Nova Scotia: Lancelot Press, 1970).

CHESNEY, Kellow. *The Victorian Underworld* (Harmondsworth: Penguin, 1970).

DISHER, M. Willson. *Fairs, Circuses and Music Halls* (London: Collins, 1942).

GALLOP, Jane. *Feminism and Psychoanalysis: The Daughter's Seduction* (London: Macmillan, 1982).

GILMAN, Sander L. "Black Bodies, White Bodies: Nineteenth-Century Art, Medicine and Literature," in *"Race", Writing and Difference*, ed. Henry Louis Gates Jr. (Chicago: U of Chicago P, 1986).

---

23 Marlene Nourbese Philip, *Frontiers: Selected Essays and Writings on Racism and Culture 1984–1992* (Stratford, Ontario: Mercury, 1992): 104.

24 Nourbese Philip, *Frontiers*, 105.

25 See, for example, Heather Robertson's article on the "Scarborough Rapist" (1990), and note that, bizarrely, the Miss Toronto Beauty Pageant was being held in Scarborough town centre in May 1990, at the time when the rapist was still attacking victims (see *Saturday Night*, June 1990: 19 for further details). Although there can, of course, be no direct parallel drawn between exploitative productions such as "beauty pageants" and rape, the irony of Scarborough as a choice of venue for Miss Toronto 1990 is rather bitter.

GUGLIELMIN, Donna. "Susan Swan, Mythmaker," *Canadian Author and Bookman* 60.1 (Fall 1984).

HEFFERMAN, Teresa. "Tracing the Travesty: Constructing the Female Subject in Susan Swan's *The Biggest Modern Woman of the World*," *Canadian Literature* 133 (Summer 1992): 24–37.

HUNTER, Lynette. *Modern Allegory and Fantasy: Rhetorical Stances of Contemporary Writing.* (London & Basingstoke: Macmillan, 1991).

KAMBOURELI, Smaro. "*The Biggest Modern Woman of the World*: Canada as the Absent Spouse," *Australian–Canadian Studies* 6.1 (1988): 103–10.

KUPER, Adam. *The Invention of Primitive Society: Transformations of an Illusion* (London & New York: Routledge, 1988).

NOURBESE PHILIP, Marlene. *Frontiers: Selected Essays and Writings on Racism and Culture 1984–1992* (Stratford, Ontario: Mercury, 1992).

———. "The White Soul of Canada," *Third Text* 14 (Spring 1991): 63–77.

ROBERTSON, Heather. "The Scarborough Rapist," *Canadian Forum* 69 (795, December 1990).

SANGER, George. *Seventy Years A Showman: My Life and Adventures in Camp and Caravan the World Over* (London: Pearson, 1910).

SLEMON, Stephen. "Monuments of Empire: Allegory/Counter-Discourse/Post-Colonial Writing," *Kunapipi* 9.3 (1987): 1–16.

———. "Post-Colonial Allegory and the Transformation of History," *Journal of Commonwealth Literature* 22.1 (1988): 157–68.

SMYTH, Donna E. *Giant Anna* (Toronto: Playwrights Canada, 1979).

SWAN, Susan. *The Biggest Modern Woman of the World* (Toronto: Lester & Orpen Denys, 1983).

SWAN–RYAN, Linda. Letter, *Maclean's* (29th October 1984): 8.

Representations of Crisis and Renewal

~❀~

Imaging the City
in Confederation Poetry

NORBERT H. PLATZ

"**O**UR ABILITY TO READ 'THE CITY' will continue to be concomitant with our ability to read the world." This is the concluding line of Steven Marcus's highly illuminating essay "Reading the Illegible: Modern Representations of Urban Experience."[1] As is demonstrated by Marcus's European and US examples, reading the city is an important task which cultural critics have set themselves. Among the observers of culture in the USA and Europe, literary critics have played a prominent part, availing themselves as they do of the rich material supplied by literature to explore questions central to the concept of the city.

When we turn to the Canadian scene, however, we encounter a striking paradox. Although, according to the statistical material available in the Seventies, "four out of five Canadians live in an urban area, with more than half of Canada's total population concentrated in the seventeen largest metropolitan areas,"[2] the city has been given short shrift in Canadian literary criticism. When I did bibliographical research to find material bearing on the city/literature relationship in Canada, the result proved rather disappointing. I could find neither survey guides to this topic nor any indication in the titles of books or articles that the city might be a major issue in Canadian literature. The small amount of relevant material consists of publications by Louis Dudek, Eli Mandel, Sherrill E. Grace, Hellmut Schroeder–Lanz, and Heinz Ickstadt.[3] On the other hand, urbanology is a thriving

---

[1] *Southern Review* 22.3 (1986), 464.

[2] *The Urban Experience*, ed. John Stevens (Themes in Canadian Literature; Toronto: Macmillan, 1975): 1.

[3] Louis Dudek, "The Poetry of the City," *English Quarterly* 1.2 (1969): 71–79; Eli Mandel, "The City in Canadian Poetry," in *An Anthology of Canadian Literature in English*, ed. Donna Bennett & Russell Brown (Toronto: Oxford UP, 1983), vol. 2: 128–37; Sherrill E. Grace, "Quest for the Peaceable Kingdom: Urban/Rural Codes in Roy, Laurence and Atwood," in *Women Writers and the City: Essays in Feminist Literary Criticism*, ed. Susan Merril Squier (Knoxville: U of Kentucky P, 1984): 193–205; Helmut Schroeder–Lanz, "Perception of Cities in Novel-Writing Compared to Mental Mapping Orientation in Cities," in *Shaping Telling Perspectives*, ed. Herbert Zirker & Johannes Michael Nebe (Schriftenreihe des Zentrums für Kanada-Studien an der Universität Trier 1; Trier, 1990): 71–90; Heinz Ickstadt, "The City in English Canadian and US-American Literature," *Zeitschrift der Gesellschaft für Kanada-Studien* 19–20 (1991): 163–73.

area of research in Canada today. Geographers, sociologists, political scientists, architects and, last but not least, economists and city-planners rally their intellectual forces to do substantial research in what recently has come to be called "the urban field."[4]

Is there an explanation for the literary critics' avoidance of the city? A tentative answer might run as follows: Under Northrop Frye's and Margaret Atwood's intellectual guidance,[5] Canadian literary criticism has shown a tendency to assign priority to a kind of literary experience which is rooted in the prairie and the wilderness. Susan Joan Wood, for example, looks upon Canadian literature "as a means of defining [...] values and assumptions – specifically Canadians' attitudes towards the land and to humanity's role within nature."[6] (There is an analogy to this phenomenon in Australia: there, too, roughly four-fifths of the total population live in the urban areas, yet in literature the values associated with the bush and bush life still seem to be of paramount significance.)

However, the seeming absence of the city in Canadian criticism does not, in reality, exclude the city's presence in imaginative literature. There are quite a few important novels dealing with Canadian city life such as Morley Callaghan's *Strange Fugitive* (1928), Mordecai Richler's *The Apprenticeship of Duddy Kravitz* (1959), Margaret Atwood's *The Edible Woman* (1969), *Bodily Harm* (1981) and *Cat's Eye* (1988), and Michael Ondaatje's *In the Skin of a Lion* (1987). More importantly, there is a substantial body of Canadian city-poems ranging from the period of the Confederation to the present day that have not been given the attention they deserve. Nearly all major Canadian poets have written about the city. Special mention ought to be made of Archibald Lampman, Charles G.D. Roberts, A.M. Klein, Earle Birney, Louis Dudek, Raymond Souster, Miriam Waddington, and Margaret Atwood. Although with some of them the city is perhaps not a dominant concern, a diachronic synopsis of their "city-poems" yields a rewarding reading experience insofar as the psychological dynamics of the Canadian city become accessible.

For reasons of space, I shall be dealing here exclusively with examples taken from Confederation poetry. In this connection it is well worth emphasising that the Confederation poets have generally been sensitive to the enigmatic character of the city and the ambivalent feelings which the latter might produce in its inhabitants.[7] My present concern, however, is not to offer a historiographic

---

4 For a list of more recent urban studies, see *Books on Canada / Livres sur le Canada* (1992): 82.

5 Northrop Frye, *The Bush Garden: Essays on the Canadian Imagination* (Toronto: Anansi, 1971); Frye emphasizes the "pastoral myth" (238). Margaret Atwood, *Survival: A Thematic Guide to Canadian Literature* (Toronto: Anansi, 1972).

6 Susan Joan Wood, *The Land in Canadian Prose 1840 to 1945* (Carleton Monographs in English Language and Literature 1; Ottawa: Carleton University, 1988): 2.

7 The imaginative presence of the city in Confederation poetry is demonstrated by the following writers and texts:

description of the development of Canadian city poetry from the late nineteenth century to the present day. What I am more interested in at the present stage of my research is the testing of a method that might be used for opening up Canadian city-poetry for critical inspection. Thus a few initial methodological consider-ations would seem to be apposite at this juncture.

Methodological Considerations

In a book published in 1977 by the Minister of Supply and Services Canada, we find the laudable attempt to use "the artists, poets, dramatists and writers" as the "still unsurpassed experts in the use of social indicators."[8] Consequently, passages from poems are quoted to highlight social issues under headings such as "the city is a place of inequality and felt injustice"[9] or "there is latent terror in a too mechanized city."[10] This is certainly not the kind of thing which I should like to pursue here. What I am more interested in is the symbolic meaning enshrined in what may be considered a symptomatic set of Canadian city-poems.

Central to my argument is the notion of *image*. I do *not* use the term *image* in the sense of figurative language, as it is commonly used by the literary critic. In my attempt to bridge the gulf between poetry and the kind of urbanology outlined in Rodwin and Hollister's inspiring book *Cities of the Mind*[11] I am, rather, using the term in the sense recorded in Webster's *Third New International Dictionary*: "a mental picture; impression; a mental conception held in common by members of a

---

Charles Sangster, "Quebec"; William McLennan, "Montreal"; William Douw Lighthall, "Montreal"; Duncan Campell Scott, "Ottawa"; all in William Douw Lighthall's anthology *Songs of the Great Dominion* (London: Walter Scott, 1889): 307–10, 314;

Isabella Valancy Crawford, "The City Tree", in *Canadian Poems 1850-1952*, ed. Louis Dudek & Irving Layton (Toronto: Contact Press, 1952): 24;

The Complete Poems of Pauline Johnson, ed. Theodore Watt (Toronto: Rousson Book Company, 1926), esp. "The City and the Sea" (121), "A Toast" (136), and "Calgary of the Plains" (160–61);

The Collected Poems of Sir Charles G.D. Roberts: A Critical Edition, ed. Desmond Pacey (Wombat Press, 1985), for: "The Deserted City" (129); "Quebec, 1757" (133–34), "Twilight on Sixth Avenue at Ninth Street" (191), "At the Railway Station" (243), "In the Solitude of the City" (243), "A Nocturne of Exile" (244), "In the Crowd" (245), "On the Elevated Railway at 110th Street" (247), "The Street Lamps" (256), "At the Drinking Fountain" (257), "A Street Song at Night (260–61), "Heat in the City" (282), and "The Unknown City" (294–95).

For Archibald Lampman, apart from the four poems that will be discussed below, also note "The City" and "Dead Cities" in *The Poems of Archibald Lampman*, ed. Duncan Campbell Scott (Toronto: Morang, 1913): 215, 269.

[8] *Changing Canadian Cities: The Next 25 Years*, ed. Leonard O. Gertler & Ronald W. Crowley (Toronto: McClelland & Stewart, 1979): 311.

[9] *Canadian Cities*, ed. Gertler & Crowley, 315.

[10] *Canadian Cities*, ed. Gertler & Crowley, 317.

[11] *Cities of the Mind: Images and Themes of the City in the Social Sciences*, ed. Lloyd Rodwin & Robert M. Hollister (New York: Plenum, 1984).

group and being symbolic of a basic attitude or orientation towards something." In this sense the term has been given given academic respectability by Boulding in his seminal study *The Image*.

According to Boulding, man's behaviour in his environment depends on the mental image he has produced of it; the image thus has an enormous impact on the practice of living. The basic structural features of the image are as follows:

i) The image has a history: "The image is built up as a result of all past experiences of the possessor of the image."[12]

ii) The image is constituted by facts and evaluations, the latter being impregnated by emotions.

iii) When new information "hits an image one of three things can happen":[13] either the image is confirmed, or it is enhanced, or it is questioned and needs revision.

In a nutshell, an image is a symbolic concept of an object of human attention containing a specific interpretation of the information which the image subsumes. It organises knowledge not in abstract and objective but in evaluative terms and influences human attitudes and ultimately behaviour. It satisfies the basic human need to comprehend reality in symbolic terms, in which the question of value is given proper attention.

Without the availability of images the complex system of the city could not be fully comprehended. Rodwin and Hollister have demonstrated that both the research aims and the research strategies of the various disciplines dealing with the city are determined by the basic mental images entertained by their practitioners. Thus if one wants to understand the city, its material and functional reality has to be translated into cognitive images of that reality. This is how "the total, objective, physical urban reality"[14] becomes a "city of the mind" or, to use a term that enables us to come closer to literature and literary criticism, this is how the city becomes a highly semanticised space.

When we deal with the way in which the city is imaged in a poem, we are well advised to consider questions like these:

i) Which traditional templates[15] provided and mediated by culture manifest themselves in the presentation of the city? How, and to what extent, do they influence the speaker's or persona's perception?

---

12 Kenneth E. Boulding, *The Image* (Ann Arbor: U of Michigan P, 1956): 6.

13 Boulding, *The Image*, 7.

14 *Cities of the Mind*, ed. Rodwin & Hollister, 9.

15 "Template" is used as an analytical term by Sam Bass Warner, Jr., "The Management of Multiple Urban Images," in *The Pursuit of Urban History*, ed. Derek Fraser & Anthony Sutcliff (London: Edward Arnold, 1983), 383–94.

ii) What are the actual visual manifestations or visual images characteristic of the city under consideration? How do they relate to the templates?

iii) What does this relationship reveal about the pattern of evaluation and basic ideological assumptions underlying the text?

Such questions promise to provide a basis on which to link the poets' insights to the issues debated in other fields of culturally oriented urban studies.

Five Early Examples of Canadian City Poetry

The poems which I should like to examine now were all written towards the end of the nineteenth century or at the beginning of the twentieth. With the exception of Bliss Carman's "Vancouver," Archibald Lampman is the author of all of them. The singular strength of the Lampman poems is that they serve the explanatory pattern which I envisage.

Archibald Lampman, "The City"[16]

In this sonnet, the speaker visualises a city from some distance, in the twilight of a beautiful sunset. His gaze wanders beyond the farms, following "the shallow stream / [...]Curved white and slender as a lady's wrist," until it arrives at "The bell-tongued city with its glorious towers." He sees this city arise as if "out of a dream." The city fits into the landscape quite naturally; it surges, as it were, out of a pastoral environment. The speaker is aware that he is rendering an impression which he has gained at a particular moment in time. Significantly, what he sees finds expression in adjectives which evoke quintessentially feminine qualities "quiet" (l. 3), "slender as a lady's wrist" (l. 4), "warmer" (l. 7), "lovelier" (l. 12). Instead of straight lines we get "curves" (see l. 4). The sharp edges of things are removed and softened, as we see in l. 6, where the "the pointed jewel" of the city becomes "softly set in clouds of colour warmer." The sun, quite often a symbol of male dominance and power, doesn't strike the city with its glaring light; instead, "the soft sun-touch of the yellowing hours" is recorded here. So the actual visual imagery through which the speaker renders his impressions define the city as a female offering warmth and softness, attractive because of its overwhelming beauty. It becomes the object of the speaker's desire, which manifests itself in his dreams.

The traditional template to which the poem refers is the "city as woman." This is a concept firmly inscribed in the system of the major European languages, for the grammatical gender of the terms corresponding to the English word *city* is usually feminine. (See, for example, *polis* in Greek, *urbs* in Latin, *la ville* in French, *la città* in Italian and *die Stadt* in German). If we go back to St John's *Revelation* we encounter two semantically opposed versions of the feminine character of the city.

---

16 Lampman, *Poems*, ed. Scott, 118.

The city is imagined either as the "Whore of Babylon" or as the "New Jerusalem". According to St John, "new Jerusalem, coming down out of heaven" is "made ready like a bride adorned for her husband" (*Rev.* 21:2). What we have in Lampman's sonnet is an epigonic, Romantic interpretation of the New Jerusalem template. The way the latter is reinterpreted, with the emphasis on the dreamlike quality of experiencing the city, puts this poem in the context of ideological beliefs sustained by nineteenth-century European aestheticism which asserted the desire for beauty as a basic human need. In the art of the time, this desire finds symbolic expression in the fact that woman becomes the painters' favourite icon. With respect to the city, it may more specifically be argued that the desire for beauty became mirrored in nineteenth-century attempts at beautifying and gentri-fying urban areas by paying special attention to "the auras emanating from the solid forms of the buildings and surfaces that enclose the urban space."[17] Thus the dirt and squalor of nineteenth-century industrial cities were increasingly counter-balanced by architectural design and craftsmanship. These often succeeded in both making the city an object of desire and offering gratification at an aesthetic level.

Archibald Lampman, "In the City"[18]

This again is a sonnet. Here the speaker wanders "in a city great and old," trying to capture its hidden historical significance. What makes this poem look different from the preceding sonnet is the absence of visual imagery recording an actual perception. Instead, notions like "splendour," "tumult," "gold" (l. 4) and "power," "passion" and "strife" (l. 6) occur – keywords typical of the nineteenth-century glorification of the past. Accordingly, it's the bygone intensity of life in that "mighty city" (l. 9) that stimulates a strong emotional response within the speaker. In line 12 we are given a cue to the traditional template that inspires the imaging of this particular city, whose name, however, is not mentioned. The phrase "all the spirit of humanity" evokes the cultural stereotype of the city as the expression of human civilisation and culture, in which the striving for power plays a predomi-nant part. To the speaker, the process of evoking the city's past thus becomes a thrilling imaginative encounter with man's civilising efforts; it is this encounter that strikes him "like a song" (l. 14)). The ideological content of this poem can be traced to nineteenth-century historicism and its tendency to foreground the heroic glamour of civilisation. At the time the poem was written, an imaginative revival of the past served the function of strengthening belief in human progress. This belief is the central ideological concept imposed on Lampman's "To Chicago" and Bliss Carman's "Vancouver."

---

17 Roger Kemble, *The Canadian City: St. John's to Victoria* (Montreal: Harvest House, 1989): 56.
18 Lampman, *Poems*, 259.

Archibald Lampman, "To Chicago"[19]

In Lampman's Chicago poem, the speaker again abstains from providing concrete visual details. Characteristic of his style of presentation is that he personifies and addresses the city as though it were a human being. This is particularly evident at the beginning: "You that with limitless daring and might of gold and decision / Have furnished the world for an hour with that gorgeous and vanishing vision." In l. 6, it is suggested that Chicago might behave as though it were a morally responsible agent capable of learning a lesson. But then the speaker proceeds to drive home his moral appeal by addressing the "men of the brave new land, the West, the impetuous City" (l. 10), exhorting them to find a "visible form of a life purged clean from the sins of the old" (l. 13) and to create a new society in which "weakness and want" (l. 14) are overcome and "freedom" and "brotherhood" (l. 16) realised.

Clearly, the biblical template of the New Jerusalem is linked here with the American Dream, which, in its mythological dimension, is nourished by the "Judeo-Christian millennial prophecy of new world and new earths."[20] Chicago, in the view of this poem, has the potential to become the epitome of human progress if the men of the west do the right thing by the city.

It is unclear why exactly Lampman chose Chicago as the city on which to project the dream of human progress and of an ideal society, for Chicago had by the 1890s become one of the ugliest cities in North America. The smoke-pollution produced by industry must have been enormous. Besides, visitors reported the disgusting smell produced by the slaughterhouses (whence the city's nickname of "Porkopolis"). The majority of the population lived in tenements that had begun to turn into slums. Rudyard Kipling wrote in 1889: "Having seen [Chicago], I urgently desire never to see it again. It is inhabited by savages."[21] It was the place in which social Darwinism's formula of "the survival of the fittest" was practised in its cruellest and most ruthless form. It may have been for this very reason – that the reality of Chicago was diametrically opposed to the ideals of the American Dream – that Lampman attempted to impose a lesson on this city, reminding its inhabitants of the dignity of the dream. Yet it is quite obvious that the ideological wishful thinking projected onto Chicago must have clashed considerably with this city's physical and social dimensions in 1893 (the year in which the poem was written). A city engulfed in smoke, stench, squalor and, increasingly, crime had little in common with the New Jerusalem, the archetypal blueprint on which Lampman developed his vision.[22]

---

19 Lampman, *Poems*, 118.

20 Warner, "Multiple Urban Images," 383–84

21 Quoted by Walter Göbel, "Schreckbild Stadt: Chicago im naturalistischen Roman," *Zeitschrift für Literaturwissenschaft und Linguistik* 48 (1982): 89.

22 That Chicago by that time must have been quite different from the vision Lampman offers in his "Chicago" poem is given poetic expression by Carl Sandburg in his *Chicago Poems* (1916).

Bliss Carman, "Vancouver"[23]

Whereas Lampman looks forward to human progress but doesn't seem to think that it will come automatically (ie, without the exertion of moral self-control), Carman has a less scrupulous way of handling his preoccupation with progress. In "Vancouver," he seems to have subscribed, on the ideological plane, to a bonanza view of historical evolution. The traditional perceptual mould in which he casts his vision of Vancouver is "the city as market-place" or "bazaar," offering cornucopic opportunities to its denizens. Significantly, in the final stanza he evokes Tyre, Sidon and Carthage for comparison, cities which had enjoyed a high reputation as centres of trade and commerce in classical antiquity. Wasn't it trade that brought people of different parts of the world together, activating a peaceful exchange of goods and commodities? Furthermore, didn't trade enhance human communication? That this was the case is instanced by the Phoenicians, who not only founded Tyre, Sidon and Carthage, but also invented the alphabet. What Carman is thus evoking is the economists' archetypal conception of the city. This view is based on the assumption that economic transactions constitute the basis for peace, meaningful human interaction, and cultural enrichment. Peter Langer writes about "the city as bazaar" that it "imagines the city as a place of astonishing richness of activity and diversity unparalleled in nonurban areas. It is a market, a fair, a place of almost infinite exploration and opportunity, a center of exchange. [...] There is a liberation from the one-dimensionality of the small town or the countryside."[24]

In the second stanza, mention is made of the goods that are shipped to and from Vancouver:

> There the adventurous ships come in
> With spices and silks of the East in hold,
> And coastwise liners down from the North
> With cargoes of furs and gold.

What should not be overlooked is the reference to the tales and symbols of foreign cultures in stanza 3. Ideally, in Carman's view, the template of the city as market or bazaar favours multiculturalism and leads to friendship among nations (see stanza 6). It was the German sociologists Georg Simmel and Max Weber[25] who spelt out the sociological and cultural implications of this template, which can be traced back to the epic of *Gilgamesh*.[26] Adam Smith, followed by the majority of

---

23 Bliss Carman, "Vancouver," in *Vancouver Poetry*, ed. Alan Safarik (Winlaw, B.C.: Polestar, 1986): 28. This poem was not included in *Windflower: Poems of Bliss Carman*, sel. & ed. Raymond Souster & Douglas Lochhead (Ottawa: Tecumseh, 1985).

24 Peter Langer, "Sociology – Four Images of Organized Diversity: Bazaar, Jungle, Organism, and Machine," in *Cities of the Mind*, ed. Rodwin & Hollister, 100.

25 Langer, "Four Images," 102.

26 Aaron Lichtenstein, "Impressions of the City from the Dawn of Civilization," *Journal of Evolutionary Psychology* 9.3–4 (1988): 190–99.

nineteenth-century British economists, succeeded in popularising the notion of the beneficial effect which the economy, as a dominant civilising factor, exercises on the relevant aspects of life. Thus, in Carman's poem, the archetypal template of the city as market and the period's predominant ideological conviction of the salutary effects produced by the economy reinforce each other. The final line, "With tomorrow's light on her brow," envisages Vancouver as a place where man may come into his own.

Archibald Lampman, "The City of the End of Things"[27]

Our last poem is Lampman's deservedly famous and frequently anthologised "The City of the End of Things" (1895). As far as this text is concerned, it looks as though all the templates by which the city has been conceived in the other poems examined so far are questioned or turned into their semantic opposite. Likewise, all the corresponding ideological positions seem to have lost their validity.

The speaker offers the reader an apocalyptic vision of an allegorised urban settlement named "the City of the End of Things" (l. 8). The first eight lines of the poem place the imagined city in a landscape reminiscent of the topography of hell as we find it in classical mythology. These introductory lines are followed by a shift of viewpoint, for the visual details evoked in lines 9–44 mark the city as a nineteenth-century industrial town. It would not be difficult to find similar depictions in Dickens, Disraeli and other mid-Victorian writers. The most obvious parallel is perhaps Coketown in Dickens's *Hard Times.* Typically, there are the "murky streets" (l. 11), the flaming chimneys and furnaces; an "inhuman music" (l. 24) makes itself heard as "beat," "thunder" and "hiss" (l. 27). The figures that people the scene are but "stalking shadows" (l. 13) obeying "a hideous routine" (l. 32). The degree to which they have become dehumanised can be seen in the following lines:

> They are not flesh, they are not bone,
> They see not with the human eye,
> And from their iron lips is blown
> A dreadful and monotonous cry. (33–36)

In the central part of the poem we learn that the city once did enjoy happier days:

> It was not always so, but once,
> In days that no man thinks upon,
> Fair voices echoed from its stones,
> The light above it leaped and shone (45–48)

But then, characterised by the gradual extinction of the "men / That [had] built that city in their pride" (50–51), its decay began. Only three specimens of the former race have survived "in an iron tower" (l. 54), remaining "masters" of the city's former "power" (l. 56). But they too are eventually doomed to death in the final

---

27 Lampman, *Poems*, 179–82.

cataclysm, described in ll. 65–75. Only a "grim Idiot" (l. 87) will be spared by "Time" (l. 86), testifying all alone and eternally to the city's "accursèd state" (l. 85).

How does the poem deny the traditional perceptual stereotypes we are familiar with? The visual imagery of lines 9–44 is set in stark contrast to the feminine coding which we encountered in the sonnet "In the city." What strikes us here is the relentlessly masculine rigour characterising the industrialised urban area. Thus the highly positive evaluation pattern inherent in the city-as-woman or New Jerusalem template is converted into its negative counterpart. The traditional equation of the rise of the city with the rise of civilisation and the advent of ever-better living conditions is equally negated. Furthermore, whatever is said about the city here contradicts all the possibilities covered by the concept of the city as marketplace or bazaar.

Correspondingly, all the evaluative and ideological implications expressed by these cultural stereotypes undergo transformation into the negative as well. In the city depicted in this poem, apart from the earlier stages of its history, there is no room for beauty. On the contrary, a horrifying ugliness prevails. Instead of progress and an immanent trend towards a new and perfect society, the determining forces manifestied by this city are regression and entropy. We are not graced by a view of a civilisation granting the boon of increased opportunities, but are confronted with the reduction of human action potential to machine-like functionalism. The idea of human self-realisation pursued under the assumed favourable conditions of the urban habitat is replaced by the notion of wholesale alienation. Instead of finally coming into his own, man is deprived of his deepest human qualities and reduced to a shadowy existence. Even at a physical level his survival is no longer possible.

This view goes along with a pessimistic evaluation of time. The teleological concept of time, with which the nineteenth-century idea of progress was so intimately connected, is inverted. A linear, upward progression of time aiming at maximum fulfilment is substituted for a linear, downward regression precipitating destruction and "the end of things." If, in the four preceding poems, the city has symbolically represented the climax of civilisation, here the downfall of the city stands for the breakdown of civilisation itself and for the extinction of mankind.

When he offered this pessimistic image of the city Lampman may have had second thoughts about what he really experienced in Chicago when he visited it. In "The City of the End of Things" he deconstructs the semantic content and the ideological assumptions concomitant with the predominant symbolic templates of his time. The city depicted here anticipates the way in which the German Expressionists were to handle the theme some two decades later. Georg Heym's famous poem *"Der Gott der Stadt,"* for example, offers a comparable apocalyptic vision of the city. The "god of the city" in Heym's poem is Baal, shaking his "butcher's fist" and devouring everything within a night.[28]

Conclusion

By moving back in time about one hundred years, I have tried to explore a method which could be used for analysing Canadian city-poetry. My contention is that there are insights to be gained from focusing on the interdependence of traditional template, actual visualisation, and ideological evaluation. The poems activate and "mobilise" the meaning inherent in the culturally semanticised space of the city *either* by concretising and reinforcing the connection between the traditional template and contemporary ideological preferences, *or* by deconstructing the semantics of the template as well as the validity of its corresponding ideology. Thus poetry can be shown to have the capacity not only to function as a depository of traditional views about the city but also – and this is the point that ought not to go unrecognised – to establish significant links between culturally inherited modes of perception and topical ideological and psychological concerns.

Having done some cursory reading in twentieth-century Canadian poetry, I can't resist the temptation to suggest that the city-poems of A.M. Klein, Louis Dudek, Earle Birney, Raymond Souster (who has been a prolific city-poet indeed), Miriam Waddington and Margaret Atwood would be worth studying along similar lines. Thus the emotional coherence and symbolic force of the Canadian urban experience could be brought into a historical perspective.

Such a broadly conceived humanistic exploration of urban space could also be understood as an approach to enlarging the scope of problem-solving research. If Goldberg and Mercer in *The Myth of the North American City* find approval for their claim that a "more complex way of thinking about cities" must emphasise "the city–culture relationship,"[29] then the humanistic insights gained by Canadian poetry should be integrated in, and made accessible to, current urbanological discussion. Because of its critical and quite often non-assertive character, the poets' local cultural expression could be deployed to question the widely practised "symbiotic relation between local authorities and development interests,"[30] which prefers to submit Canadian city-planning to an overall economistic perspective.

---

28 "Er streckt ins Dunkel seine Fleischerfaust. / Er schüttelt sie. Ein Meer von Feuer jagt / Durch eine Straße. Und der Blutqualm braust / Und frißt sie auf, bis spät der Morgen tagt" (Georg Heym, *Dichtungen und Schriften,* ed. Karl Ludwig Schneider [Hamburg: Ellermann, 1964]: 192).

29 *The Myth of the North American City: Continentalism Challenged*, ed. Michael A. Goldberg & John Mercer (Vancouver: U of British Columbia P, 1986): 5.

30 Eric E. Lampard, "The Nature of Urbanization," in *Visions of the Modern City: Essays in History, Art, and Literature*, ed. William Sharpe & Leonard Wallock (Baltimore MD: Johns Hopkins UP, 1987):72.

WORKS CITED

ATWOOD, Margaret. *Survival: A Thematic Guide to Canadian Literature* (Toronto: Anansi, 1972).

BOULDING, Kenneth E. *The Image* (Ann Arbor: U of Michigan P, 1956).

CARMAN, Bliss. *Windflower: Poems of Bliss Carman*, sel. & ed. Raymond Souster & Douglas Lochhead (Ottawa: Tecumseh, 1985).

DUDEK, Louis. "The Poetry of the City," *English Quarterly* 1.2 (1969): 71–79.

——— & Irving LAYTON, ed. *Canadian Poems 1850–1952* (Toronto: Contact Press, 1952).

FRYE, Northrop. *The Bush Garden: Essays on the Canadian Imagination* (Toronto: Anansi, 1971).

GERTLER, Leonard O., & Ronald W. CROWLEY, ed. *Changing Canadian Cities: The Next 25 Years* (Toronto: McClelland & Stewart, 1979).

GÖBEL, Walter. "Schreckbild Stadt: Chicago im naturalistischen Roman," *Zeitschrift für Literaturwissenschaft und Linguistik* 48 (1982): 89.

GOLDBERG, Michael A., & John MERCER. *The Myth of the North American City: Continentalism Challenged* (Vancouver: U of British Columbia P, 1986).

GRACE, Sherrill E. "Quest for the Peaceable Kingdom: Urban/Rural Codes in Roy, Laurence and Atwood," in *Women Writers and the City: Essays in Feminist Literary Criticism*, ed. Susan Merril Squier (Knoxville: U of Kentucky P, 1984): 193–205.

ICKSTADT, Heinz. "The City in English Canadian and US-American Literature," *Zeitschrift der Gesellschaft für Kanada-Studien* 19–20 (1991): 163–73.

JOHNSON, Pauline. *The Complete Poems of Pauline Johnson*, ed. Theodore Watt (Toronto: Rousson Book Company, 1926).

KEMBLE, Roger. *The Canadian City: St. John's to Victoria* (Montreal: Harvest House, 1989).

LAMPARD, Eric E. "The Nature of Urbanization," in *Visions of the Modern City: Essays in History, Art, and Literature*, ed. William Sharpe & Leonard Wallock (Baltimore MD: Johns Hopkins UP, 1987).

LAMPMAN, Archibald. *The Poems of Archibald Lampman*, ed. Duncan Campbell Scott (Toronto: Morang, 1913).

LANGER, Peter. "Sociology – Four Images of Organized Diversity: Bazaar, Jungle, Organism, and Machine," in RODWIN & HOLLISTER.

LICHTENSTEIN, Aaron. "Impressions of the City from the Dawn of Civilization," *Journal of Evolutionary Psychology* 9.3–4 (1988): 190–99.

LIGHTHALL, William Douw, ed. *Songs of the Great Dominion* (London: Walter Scott, 1889).

MANDEL, Eli. "The City in Canadian Poetry," in *An Anthology of Canadian Literature in English*, ed. Donna Bennett & Russell Brown (Toronto: Oxford UP, 1983), vol. 2: 128–37.

ROBERTS, Charles G.D. *The Collected Poems of Sir Charles G.D. Roberts: A Critical Edition*, ed. Desmond Pacey (Wombat Press, 1985).

RODWIN, Lloyd & Robert M. HOLLISTER, ed. *Cities of the Mind: Images and Themes of the City in the Social Sciences* (New York: Plenum, 1984).

SAFARIK, Alan, ed. *Vancouver Poetry* (Winlaw, B.C.: Polestar, 1986).

SCHROEDER–LANZ, Helmut. "Perception of Cities in Novel-Writing Compared to Mental Mapping Orientation in Cities," in *Shaping Telling Perspectives*, ed. Herbert Zirker & Johannes Michael Nebe (Schriftenreihe des Zentrums für Kanada-Studien an der Universität Trier 1; Trier, 1990): 71–90.

STEVENS, John, ed. *The Urban Experience: Themes in Canadian Literature* (Toronto: Macmillan, 1975).

WARNER, Jr., Sam Bass. "The Management of Multiple Urban Images," in *The Pursuit of Urban History*, ed. Derek Fraser & Anthony Sutcliff (London: Edward Arnold, 1983): 383–94.

WOOD, Susan Joan. *The Land in Canadian Prose 1840 to 1945* (Carleton Monographs in English Language and Literature 1; Ottawa: Carleton UP, 1988).

See also:

BUNTING, Trudy, & Pierre FILION. *Canadian Cities in Transition* (Toronto: Oxford UP, 1991).

BUTTIMER, Anne, & David SEAMON, ed. *The Human Experience of Space and Place* (London: Croom Helm, 1980).

CLARKE, Graham, ed. *The American City: Literary and Cultural Perspectives* (London: Vision, 1988).

GEERTZ, Clifford. *The Interpretation of Cultures* (New York: Basic Books, 1973).

HASSLÖCHER, Kerstin. "Die Stadt im kanadischen Roman des 20. Jahrhunderts," MA thesis (Berlin: John F. Kennedy Institut, 1990).

MECKSEPER, Cord, & Elisabeth SCHRAUT, ed. *Die Stadt in der Literatur* (Göttingen: Vandenhoeck & Ruprecht, 1983).

MOORE, Gary T., & Reginald G. GOLLEDGE, ed. *Environmental Knowing: Theories, Research and Methods* (Stroudsbourg PA, 1976).

POCOCK, Douglas C.D., ed. *Humanistic Geography and Literature: Essays on the Experience of Place* (London: Croom Helm, 1981).

ROTHE, Wolfgang, ed. *Deutsche Großstadtlyrik vom Naturalismus bis zur Gegenwart* (Stuttgart: Reclam, 1973).

THIELE, Herbert. "Die Stadt in der deutschen Lyrik," *Wirkendes Wort* 11 (1961): 103–11.

❧ ✺ ☙

"In Flanders fields the poppies blow"
Canada and the Great War

FRANZ K. STANZEL

W HEN WAR BROKE OUT ON 4 AUGUST 1914, Canada was the first
member of the Empire to respond to the mother-country's call for
help. Only ten days later Ottawa, despite some opposition (mainly
from Quebec), passed the War Measures Act, which authorised the government to
raise and train a fighting force of twenty-five thousand. Most people at the time
thought that this number would be sufficient to assist Britain in winning the war.
By November 1918 over six hundred thousand Canadians had served in the army
and more than sixty thousand had become casualties. In order to impress on Britain as well as Germany the size of the first Canadian contingent, it was shipped in
one convoy of thirty big passenger liners. The Canadian troops were given an
enthusiastic welcome in Portsmouth, where they arrived on 14 October 1914 –
only two months after the passing of the War Measures Act. Kaiser Wilhelm
pretended not to be impressed. When told about the thirty liners full of Canadian
troops he is reported to have sneered: "They will return in thirty row-boats."

The first great test of the military prowess of the Canadians came during the
second battle of Ypres, when the Germans, taking their opponents by surprise, for
the first time used poison gas. When the French–Moroccan troops stationed on the
Canadian left flank panicked and fled, the Canadians held on to their positions and
thus prevented a major German breakthrough. From then on Canadians were
involved in practically all the major battles on the Northern sector of the front,
including the Big Push, the disastrous Somme offensive in July and August 1916.
But the one military event which more than any other helped the Canadians to
attain a new sense of national pride was the storming of Vimy Ridge on Easter
Monday 1917. This first victory achieved by the Allied Forces after more than
thirty months of stationary warfare was an exclusively Canadian achievement,
involving in fact all four of the Canadian divisions in France.[1]

Literary historians who believe that powerful experience, individual or
national, will produce great poetry will look in vain in the annals and anthologies
of Canadian literature for works of distinction celebrating this national military
feat. In comparison to the British, French, German and Austrian literature of the

---

[1] Cf Pierre Berton, *Vimy* (Toronto: McClelland & Stewart, 1986).

Great War, Canadian war literature, with very few exceptions, is conventional and undistinguished. There is no Wilfred Owen or Isaac Rosenberg, no Edmund Blunden or Robert Graves among the poets, no Henri Barbusse or Ernst Jünger among the writers of war memoirs or novels, with perhaps the exception of Charles Yale Harrison's novel *Generals Die in Bed* (1929).

The reader will not expect me to enumerate those who tried and bravely failed to present either their combat experience or their imaginative reaction to the war. A more challenging task for the literary historian is to try and explain why Canada's literary response to the armageddon of 1914–18 was not more adequate to the experience of Canadians fighting in Flanders.

In Europe, the Great War was a great time for poetry. Never before and never since have so many poems been written on both sides during the first days, weeks and months of a war. Almost all of this poetic production was unabashedly war-affirmative, and poetically mediocre or worse. Canadian poets joined in this poetic crusade to overcome the foe. Ninety-nine percent of this poetic outburst in English, French and German has, mercifully, been consigned to oblivion.

In the second half of 1916 this unquestioning acceptance of the war as a revitalising, morally cleansing effort of the allied nations was gradually replaced by a more sober mood in which the rightfulness of the continued slaughter on the battlefields of France was at first covertly, then, after the disaster of the battle of the Somme, openly called in doubt – as by Siegfried Sassoon, in his manifesto against the continuation of the war, which was even read into the record of the House of Commons on 30 July 1917, and in his poems written thereafter, as well as in the later poems of Wilfred Owen, Isaac Rosenberg, Ivor Gurney and others.

No comparable shift in attitude is to be found in Canadian war-poetry. The reason for this unmodified perseverance of the "spirit of August 1914" in Canada must be sought in the geographical situation and sociocultural conditions of Canada at war, the country's remoteness from the field of slaughter, slow and incomplete communication, no experience of deprivation such as that undergone by the peoples of France and Britain. The main cause, however, is to be found in the general condition of Canadian literature at the time. Canadian poetry of the first decades of this century was traditionalist through and through, which thematically meant subservience to local patriotism and loyalty towards the Imperialism of the mother-country. This attitude still dominated Canadian poetry during the war. One could try to illustrate this by quoting from *Canadian Poetry of the Great War*, the only comprehensive anthology of Canadian war-poems, and published in the last year of the war.[2] But this would be a rather painful procedure (with the exception of a handful of poems written by Frank Prewett, Henry

---

2 *Canadian Poetry of the Great War*, ed. John W. Garvin (Toronto: McClelland & Stewart, 1918).

Smalley Sarson, F.G. Scott and a very few others). Let me, instead, single out the sole Canadian war-poem which has stood the test of time and which can be found even in such modern critical anthologies as the *Penguin Book of First World War Poetry*. Its editor, however, feels obliged to add a note warning the reader that this poem (and a few others) has been included against better judgement, as it were, because "a great many other people, have liked, even loved [it]."[3] It is precisely this circumstance which should make it particularly interesting for us.

Its author, John McCrae, was born in 1872 in Guelph, Ontario, as the son of Scottish pioneers, and was educated at the Guelph Collegiate Institute and the University of Toronto (Knox College). He developed an early interest in soldiering, which took him to the Boer War as a lieutenant in the artillery. Before leaving for South Africa he had studied medicine, graduating brilliantly from the University of Toronto Medical School in 1899. In 1914 he gave up a promising medical career in Montreal to join the First Brigade of the Canadian Field Artillery as a surgeon, but seems to have served also as a combatant officer with that unit during the first years of the war, taking part in the battles of Neuve Chapelle and Ypres. Later he was put in charge of the Canadian field hospital at Boulogne. He died there from meningitis and general exhaustion in January 1918.[4]

McCrae's "In Flanders Fields," the poem in question, is much indebted to the Georgian pastoral tradition which formed the mainstream of English poetry before and during the first part of the war. This partly explains the great popularity with a broad readership that it enjoyed immediately upon its first publication in 1915:

> In Flanders fields the poppies blow
> Between the crosses, row on row,
> That mark our place; and in the sky
> The larks, still bravely singing, fly
> Scarce heard amidst the guns below.
>
> We are the Dead. Short days ago
> We lived, felt dawn, saw sunset glow,
> Loved, and were loved, and now we lie,
> In Flanders fields.
>
> Take up our quarrel with the foe:
> To you from failing hands we throw
> The torch; be yours to hold it high.
> If you break faith with us who die
> We shall not sleep, though poppies grow
> In Flanders fields.[5]

---

3 Jon Silkin, "Introduction" to *The Penguin Book of First World War Poetry*, ed. Silkin (Harmondsworth: Penguin, 1981): 76.

4 Biographical data are taken from John F. Prescott, *In Flanders Fields: The Story of John McCrae* (Erin, Ontario: Boston Mills, 1985).

5 John McCrae, *In Flanders Fields and other Poems; With An Essay in Character by Sir Andrew Macphail* (Toronto: Briggs, 1919): 3.

The first strophe lives from the contrast between the serenity of undisturbed nature and the destruction wrought on man and nature by the war. Unlike the English war poets, who have made use of the same opposition (Edmund Blunden, for instance, in "The Zonnebeke Road" or "Third Ypres"), McCrae foregrounds the integrity preserved by nature and relegates the destructive effects of war to the background: the mutilated bodies have been moved out of sight, the fallen "slumber" under-neath the reassuringly orderly row of crosses, decorated by poppies, symbolically suggesting restful sleep. Perhaps there is also a faint echo of late-nineteenth-century decadent eroticism associated with poppies which also helps push to the back of the mind the knowledge that real blood was spilt on that ground. The elements of nature mentioned are highly selective. Only those things which have been codified by the aesthetic conventions of pastoral poetry are admitted: larks singing, sun rising and setting, and, of course, flowers blowing. The tendency towards the aestheticisation of trench reality is obvious. In the routine life of the trenches the hours of dawn and dusk, sacred to the imagination of romantic poets through the ages, were the periods of greatest danger when an enemy attack was most likely to happen. The order "stand to arms" regularly marked the beginning and ending of the day in the trenches.

The second strophe seems to echo Rupert Brooke's sonnet "Peace," though "the little emptiness of love" is given less emphasis. The irony of "lie" suggested by the possible reference of "lie" to both the love of "lying in bed with one's love" and to the death of "lying in the grave" is probably not intentional.

In the last strophe the poem takes a turn for which the reader has not been prepared. The dramatic appeal to patriotism is accompanied by a marked change in style. Now stock items of epic "high diction" obtrude in almost every line: "quarrel" for "war," "foe" for "enemy;" "failing hands" for "dying soldiers"; the torch, an emblem as conventional as it is vague in meaning, the archaism of the pronoun "ye" and the exhortative use of the present tense. Most critics have given short shrift to this last strophe. The American Paul Fussell in his widely acclaimed cultural and literary history of the Great War, *The Great War and Modern Memory*, is inclined to call these lines "*vicious* and *stupid*"[6] propaganda – a criticism which would not give sufficient consideration to the period and the circumstances of the poem's composition. A much more favourable view was recently presented by a Canadian critic, Thomas B. Vincent, who senses in the tension between the two parts of the poem an unresolved ambiguity characteristic of the attitude of some of the best of Canada's war poets – he specifically names Charles D.G. Roberts' "Going over" and F.G. Scott's "A Grave in Flanders": "[The last strophe] shifts the burden of responsibility for seeking a solution [to the intellectual and moral

6 Paul Fussell, *The Great War and Modern Memory* (New York: Oxford UP, 1975): 250.

crux presented by modern war] from the dead to the living, and in the process makes the issue a question of faith and action, not a question of logical comprehension."[7] National and cultural interests ultimately overrode the doubt. This is an interesting effort by a literary historian to salvage the one poem of his country eligible for canonisation among the memorable poems of the Great War by shifting the emphasis from patriotic support of the war to an ambiguous attitude towards the war-effort. From such a consideration we should, however, not exclude the historical fact that the first publication of the poem (in *Punch* on 6 December 1915 – it had been rejected by the *Spectator*[8]) comes at the end of the year in which the war had finally "deteriorated" into a war of attrition, with little immediate prospect of coming to a decisive conclusion. Hopes for a negotiated peace had been running high ever since President Wilson's peace initiative. In addition, Christmas was approaching, which would revive memories of the unprecedented fraternisation between German and British as well as French soldiers in No Man's Land on Christmas Day 1914. Seen in this historical perspective, the poem's ambiguity and irresolution, as suggested by Vincent, appear somewhat less convincing than its determined appeal to continue the "quarrel with the foe."

I shall leave the debate on the relative merits of Fussell's and Vincent's diametrically opposed readings of McCrae's poem for the time being, and turn to the phenomenal reception given to "In Flanders Fields" immediately upon publication and after the war.

At the time "In Flanders Fields" was published, it seems to have expressed sentiments to which every patriotic bosom returned an echo. It was recited, reprinted on posters, and quoted at war-loan and election campaigns, particularly in December 1917 when conscription was the main issue, and, of course, at commemoration services for the war dead. After the war, together with Laurence Binyon's "For the Fallen," it became the standard poem for recitation on Remembrance Day (later also called Poppy Day) services, and as such it is still used. As I have remarked already, it can be found in modern anthologies of war poems – it is in fact the only Canadian Great War poem regularly anthologised.

How can we explain the fact that a man who had, for over a decade, been writing poems of little or no promise, neither in thematic development nor in the art of versification, could produce a poem which had such a singular effect? One poem written in 1899, "Disarmament," is a response to proposals submitted by the Czar to stop the armaments race between the powers of Europe. It comes

---

7 Thomas B. Vincent, "Canadian Poetry of the Great War and the Effect of the Search for Nationhood," in *Intimate Enemies. English and German Literary Reactions to the Great War 1914-1918*, ed. Franz K. Stanzel & Martin Löschnigg (Heidelberg: Carl Winter, 1993): 169.

8 See Prescott, *In Flanders Fields*, 96.

thematically close to "In Flanders Fields." In a reply to the Czar's proposal, a British admiral had proclaimed that the best safeguard for peace in the world was a strong British fleet. On the eve of the outbreak of the Boer War, McCrae's poem reiterates the admiral's advice, exhorting its readers not to sheathe the sword as long as right does not prevail over evil everywhere:

> One spake amid the nations, "Let us cease
> From darkening with strife the fair
> World's light,
> We who are great in war be great in peace.
> No longer let us plead the cause by might."
>
> But from a million British graves took birth
> A silent voice – the million spake as one –
> "If ye have righted all the wrongs of earth
> Lay by the sword! Its work and ours is done."9

Here we already have the tenor of the third strophe of "In Flanders Fields"; here also, McCrae is already employing the device of having the dead speak. The voice from the grave will become a familiar motif in many war-poems, for instance in Hardy's "Channel Firing," in Owen's "Strange Meeting," and in Hans Leip's "Lili Marlen," which was written, contrary to common belief, not during the Second but the First World War.

After "In Flanders Fields," written in 1915, McCrae's poetic inspiration seems to have dried up. Only one further poem by him appeared in print in his lifetime. In June 1917, the *Spectator* published "The Anxious Dead," a poem received with reserve, if not disappointment, when compared with the success of "In Flanders Fields." Again its concern is the possible futility of the sacrifices made by the soldiers of the British and Canadian armed forces. Again it ends with lines exhorting the warriors not to give up before final victory is won. But compared with the happy balance of conventionality of theme and elegiac musicality of the first two strophes of "In Flanders Fields," this poem is flat and uninspired in diction and imagery. This takes us back to the original question: how can we explain that a writer of so much undistinguished verse could produce one of the most widely acclaimed poems of the Great War?

"In Flanders Fields" benefitted from the fortunate conjunction of a highly topical theme and the patriotic mood of the time, and from its diction and imagery, garnered from war poems in the prevailing manner of Georgianism. The poet obviously believed that this tradition was the right poetic mode for expressing the experience of war. The perseverance of this mode in McCrae is perhaps the most interesting aspect of the work of this soldier–poet. Georgianism had in fact, by the first year of the war, become obsolete as a poetic style for presenting the

---

9 John McCrae, *In Flanders Fields and Other Poems*, 29.

experience of modern warfare, even though most of the war poets continued to write poems in this manner. This becomes evident if we look at the actual combat experience of McCrae which forms the background of "In Flanders Fields."

A wide gulf separates the serene and reassuring image of war presented in the poem from the harrowing experience of the poet, who found himself in a Canadian artillery unit in the midst of tense fighting during the second Battle of Ypres, which began on 12 April 1915. As already indicated, on this day the Germans for the first time released poison gas against the British and French positions. The neighbouring French troops, Zouaves from Morocco, panicked and fled, thus leaving a wide gap in the front line. Thanks to the steadfastness of the Canadians, this gap was closed again and a major German breakthrough prevented.

We are relatively well informed about Major McCrae's share in this crucial action from his letters to his mother and to friends, extensive passages of which have been made available in John F. Prescott's *In Flanders Fields: The Story of John McCrae*. From this evidence we learn that "In Flanders Fields" was written at the centre of the storm, only hours after a fellow officer and friend of the poet had been killed by the direct hit of an eight-inch shell, which literally dismembered him, so that for burial the pieces of his body had to be collected in a sandbag.[10]

McCrae in fact records this incident in some detail, as he does the ordeal of those days of heavy fighting. In his letters, he also includes in his account the struggle of non-combatants, inhabitants of Ypres, "Women, old men, little children, hopeless, tearful, quiet or excited, tired or dodging the traffic, – and the wounded in singles or in groups,"[11] endlessly streaming by the Canadian gun positions with shells exploding, machine-guns rattling, houses on fire. McCrae, who then seems to have served both as a combatant officer and as a medical doctor in a dressing-station right at the front, felt quite helpless amidst this general misery. He does not spare us a close look at the ugly face of modern war in his letters. But the poem he writes in the midst of this havoc is "In Flanders Fields." This poem certainly does not fit the Wordsworthian formula of poetry as the "spontaneous overflow of powerful feelings." It is a poem which puts a great distance between itself and the experience of the soldier–poet. It is reliably reported by witnesses that McCrae wrote the poem soon after he had improvised some sort of burial-rites for his dismembered friend.[12] But nothing in the poem seems to refer directly to McCrae's experience in these days, except perhaps such an innocuous detail as the larks singing above the noise of the guns. In the letters written while the battle was still going on, he refers twice to birds singing in the

---

10 See Prescott, *In Flanders Fields*, 94–95.
11 Cited in Prescott, *In Flanders Fields*, 86.
12 See Prescott, *In Flanders Fields*, 95–96..

trees in spite of the continuous shell-fire coming down upon the area.[13] It deserves
to be noted that the unspecified "birds" of the letters in the poem become "larks,"
the favourite birds of pastoral poetry.

Let us turn back to the reading of "In Flanders Fields" offered by Vincent. The
content of McCrae's letters from the front at the time of writing the poem casts
serious doubt on Vincent's claim that "In Flanders Fields" expresses an
unresolved tension between a Georgian view of the natural world endangered by
the war and the harsh realities of modern war, death and destruction.[14] Nowhere in
his letters, as far as they are available, does McCrae question the rightfulness of
the war and the sacrifices it demands. And the poem accords with this attitude:
read in terms of the context of the letters, "In Flanders Fields," contrary to
Vincent's view, is a war-affirmative poem with no unresolved doubts. On the
other hand, Fussell's outright condemnation of the last strophe ignores the
historical frame of the assumptions held by most people in Britain and Canada at
the time of the poem's composition. A poem which in 1914 or 1915 expressed
such sentiments was neither "stupid" nor "vicious."

The important question concerning this poem, however, is not who is right,
Fussell or Vincent, but why McCrae himself, caught up in the maelstrom of some
of the fiercest battles of the war, did not write a poem which could have more
adequately revealed modern war for what it really was. The question has some
relevance beyond literary criticism. After all, the aestheticised image of war
presented by "In Flanders Fields" was exploited to the hilt in propaganda designed
to persuade thousands of young men in Canada and elsewhere to volunteer, which
for many of them meant mutilation or painful, undignified death.

Literary historians have to try literary explanations first before handing over
the case to sociologists, anthropologists, or moralists. My tentative explanation for
the inefficacy of Canadian war-poetry is that McCrae (and in this he seems to be
as representative as most other Canadian war poets) lacked a conception of poetry,
an appropriate model for the poetic presentation of the experience of mechanised
war. Modernism, with its rejection of the pastoral–heroic tradition of war poetry
and its corresponding "high diction," had hardly raised its voice in Britain, and
was virtually unknown in Canadian literary circles in 1915. Even in Britain it took
another year of the war and the horrific losses of 1916 before an Owen could say
in verse, of young soldiers being mowed down by machine-gun fire, that they
"died as cattle," or of a man asphyxiated by poison gas that "his blood came
gargling from the froth-corrupted lungs." Isaac Rosenberg, in referring to the
place where the dead were piled up for mass burials as "Dead Man's Dump," was
violating the Georgians' conventional piety towards the dead. It is true that Ezra

13 See Prescott, *In Flanders Fields*, 91, 93.
14 See Vincent, "Canadian Poetry of the Great War," 167–70.

Pound and T.S. Eliot had already begun their subversive poetic activities during the war, but these activities were known only to a small élite, from which the soldier–poets in the trenches were excluded. To the fellow soldier–poets of Wyndham Lewis, Vorticism seemed too wilfully eccentric. In fact, Sorley, Sassoon, Graves, Owen, Rosenberg brought about a change in war-poetry in Britain by jettisoning the traditional models of war-poetry but without accepting the revolutionary poetic creed of Futurism, Vorticism, Imagism or the modernism of Pound and Eliot. In Canada, the traditional model of pastoral–heroic war-poetry remained virtually unchallenged throughout the war. If Canada as a nation came of age, as has often been said, in the victorious battles fought by her troops in France, such as Second Ypres or the taking of Vimy Ridge two years later, then Canadian poetry still had to wait some years before finding its own identity.

In a sense, Canadians remained Imperialists during the war and for some time after. McCrae would have spontaneously agreed with Stephen Leacock's dictum: "Because I don't like to be a Colonial I am an Imperialist." In literature, however, colonialism and Imperialism are often hard to distinguish from each other, because they share one (and perhaps the most important) constituent: traditionalism.

The situation seems to have been different in the other arts – most clearly in painting, and in particular war paintings. Let me in conclusion take a quick comparative look at some war paintings done by Canadian artists. It so happens that such a comparison is made especially apposite by the fact that the second battle of Ypres, so important for McCrae, also caught the eye of painters in the service of Beaverbrook's Canadian War Memorial Fund.

When the Canadian Max Aitken, later Lord Beaverbrook, established the Canadian War Memorial Fund in November 1916 with the help of fellow newspaperman Lord Rothermere, one of the first tasks imposed on the painters who had offered their services was to reconstruct in painting some of the decisive events experienced by the Canadian Expeditionary Force in France. Thus the second battle of Ypres became one of the subjects painted by several of these artists.[15]

Richard Jack, a British academic portrait painter, had no combat experience himself, but had evidently studied the great tradition of battle painting very carefully. In his canvas *The Second Battle of Ypres*, he celebrates the successful defence of the salient, making use of practically all the familiar devices and motifs in older battle paintings: an officer with bandaged head is standing erect amidst a hail of German bullets; the attacking Germans have already come so close to the Canadian line that hand-to-hand combat with fixed bayonets – an almost indispensable motif in battle paintings – is here as inevitable as it is in heroic poetry. The

---

15 For the following, I am much indebted to Maria Tippett's *Art at the Service of War: Canada, Art and the Great War* (Toronto: U of Toronto P, 1984). See also her article on "British and Canadian Art and the Great War," in *Intimate Enemies*, ed. Stanzel & Löschnigg, 541–52.

faces of the Canadians are serene, almost happy, in their determination, those of the enemy, as far as they can be recognised, grim, almost villainous.

Arthur Nantel had had combat experience at Ypres before he joined the CWMF, yet his presentation of Second Ypres, titled *7 a.m., April 22, 1915*, is a hopeless attempt to pack everything into a panoramic view as seen from an elevated vantage-point (the conventional *Feldherrnhügel*), which gives the whole scene a picture-book unreality, suggesting a well-regulated army picnic rather than the chaotic turmoil of a battle. The case of Nantel clearly shows that, without an adequate artistic method, even personal experience of battle will not produce a near-authentic image of war.

The artistic adviser of the CWMF was a London art-critic of Hungarian descent, Paul G. Konody. He had the good sense to hire both traditionalists and modernists, a wise decision which enriched the CWMF's collection of paintings considerably. It also enables us to compare traditionalist and modernist renderings of the second battle of Ypres. Modernists, in particular the Futurists and Vorticists, were fascinated by machines, speed and power, and possessed a utopian vision of war as an agent of change and renewal. The most important of the British modernist war painters was Paul Nash. His influence is to be felt in William Roberts, an Englishman, and in A.Y. Jackson, a Canadian painter, who also painted the second battle of Ypres.

Roberts, in his painting *First German Gas Attack at Ypres*, rejects the panoramic view and concentrates on a single incident in the second battle. It is, in a way, the fertile moment of Lessing's aesthetic theory – that instant of an action from which the preceding and the following events can be deduced. Here the French–Moroccan troops seek safety from the gas in flight, the Canadians in the midst of the confusion trying to keep operating their guns. Roberts, in limiting himself to a small section of the events, already shows a modernist awareness of the impossibility of presenting a modern battle in a panoramic painting. By crowding his canvas with figures, all in a state of great agitation and tension, he manages at least to convey a sense of what it might have meant for a man to be caught in this situation.

TOP PICTURE: A.Y. Jackson, *A Copse: Evening* (Canadian War Museum, Ottawa). BOTTOM PICTURE: William Patrick Roberts, *First German Gas Attack at Ypres* (National Gallery of Canada, Ottawa).

TOP PICTURE: Richard Jack, *The Second Battle of Ypres* (Canadian War Museum, Ottawa). BOTTOM PICTURE: Arthur Nantel, *7 a.m., April 22, 1915* (Canadian War Museum, Ottawa).

In *A Copse: Evening*, A.Y. Jackson chooses another solution offered by modernism. He focuses his painting not on the soldiers in action but on the devastated landscape pockmarked by innumerable shell-holes, forming craters filled with foul water, and blistered with gigantic molehill-like earth-mounds. The most striking detail of all are the trees shorn of their foliage and branches by having been exposed to heavy gunfire. The geometrical searchlight beams, reminding us of the still present war-machine, intersect ominously in the sky with the ruined trunks of the trees. Here birds will never sing again. The tiny figures, Tommies walking among the débris, hardly count. The shell-torn landscape in this painting becomes a metonymic trope for the destructiveness of modern warfare. Suggesting rather than depicting, this is a method characteristic of modernism. The Laurentian Shield landscapes painted after the war by Jackson and the Group of Seven painters are clearly anticipated in Jackson's pictures of the war-torn terrain of Flanders.

In a cartoon published in *Punch*, a soldier in the trenches complains to his companion: "'I shouldn't really be here, you know, I've never written a poem in my life'."[16] The Great War in European art was mainly a poets' war, as Paul Fussell has emphasised. In Canada, things took a somewhat different turn. Painting the war, as it was encouraged by the CWMF, has left a more lasting imprint on the modern consciousness of the war than Canadian poetry. Painting, by the very nature of its medium, has always been more open to international exchange and influence than poetry, whose language is national. Canada, at the beginning of the war in many respects still a colony of Britain, was one step further removed than Britain from the centres of the pre-war avantgarde, Paris and Berlin, where experimental techniques in music, ballet and literature were being tried out. The Canadian historian Modris Eksteins titles the first two chapters of his book *Rites of Spring: The Great War and the Birth of the Modern Age* (1989) "Paris" and "Berlin" respectively.

Elizabeth Marsland in her Edmonton dissertation published in 1991, *The Nation's Cause* (a comparative study of French, English and German poetry of the Great War, and as such a pioneering work), subsumes Canadian war-poems under "English" because she finds little to distinguish the one from the other. This ignores the absence of modernism, which is so much more conspicuous in Canadian than in English war-poetry. That McCrae keeps the larks singing above the deafening thunder of the guns seems to me symbolic of this situation. With the advent of modernism in war literature, the birds fall silent. Farley Mowat's account of the Sicilian and Italian campaign of the Eighth Army in the Second World War carries the emblematic title *And No Bird Sang*. To qualify my much too schematic picture of Canadian war poetry I hasten to add that I did find one war

---

16 Quoted from Elizabeth A. Marsland, *The Nation's Cause: French, English and German Poetry of the First World War* (London & New York: Routledge, 1991): 191.

poem, written by a Canadian in 1915, in which the birds are already silenced. It is Henry Smalley Sarson's "The Village II,"[17] a poem regrettably ignored by anthologists. Smalley Sarson, in contrast to McCrae, is able to look squarely at the "sovereign cruelty of war," but poetically his lines lack the bite which a brief exposure to modernism might have supplied.

WORKS CITED

BERTON, Pierre. *Vimy* (Toronto: McClelland & Stewart, 1986).

FUSSELL, Paul. *The Great War and Modern Memory* (New York: Oxford UP, 1975).

GARVIN, John W., ed. *Canadian Poetry of the Great War* (Toronto: McClelland & Stewart, 1918).

MCCRAE, John. *In Flanders Fields and other Poems. With An Essay in Character by Sir Andrew Macphail* (Toronto: Briggs, 1919).

MARSLAND, Elizabeth A. *The Nation's Cause. French, English and German Poetry of the First World War* (London & New York: Routledge, 1991).

PRESCOTT, John F. *In Flanders Fields: The Story of John McCrae* (Erin, Ontario: Boston Mills, 1985).

SARSON, Henry Smalley. "The Village II," in *Soldier Poets. Songs of the Fighting Men*, ed. Galloway Kyle (London: Erskine MacDonald, 1916), vol. 1.

SILKIN, Jon, ed. *The Penguin Book of First World War Poetry* (Harmondsworth: Penguin, 1981).

TIPPETT, Maria. *Art at the Service of War. Canada, Art and the Great War* (Toronto: U of Toronto P, 1984).

———. "British and Canadian Art and the Great War," in *Intimate Enemies, English and German Literary Reactions to the Great War 1914–1918*, ed. Franz K. Stanzel & Martin Löschnigg (Heidelberg: Carl Winter, 1993).

VINCENT, Thomas B. "Canadian Poetry of the Great War and the Effect of the Search for Nationhood," in *Intimate Enemies. English and German Literary Reactions to the Great War 1914–1918*, ed. Franz K. Stanzel & Martin Löschnigg (Heidelberg: Carl Winter, 1993).

❦ ✿ ❧

---

[17] In *Soldier Poets: Songs of the Fighting Men*, ed. Galloway Kyle (London: Erskine MacDonald, 1916), vol. 1: 83 ff.

The Appeal of Failure
Lewis's Self Condemned *and* Lowry's October Ferry to Gabriola

PETER EASINGWOOD

"We went from agrarian to post-industrial in a leap that excluded high modern from our experience." (Robert Kroetsch)

THIS WELL-KNOWN STATEMENT by Robert Kroetsch[1] reflects not only on the aesthetics of Canadian writing but also on matters of difference and community, since it applies to Canadian "experience" as well as to the issue of representation. But this view of "our experience" is too exclusive: it writes off a vital part of the history of Canada's connection with Europe. The gradual assimilation of artistic technique, as well as the shared recognition of general crisis, are recorded in Canadian art and literature from the Twenties onward.[2] Lewis's *Self Condemned* (1954) and Lowry's *October Ferry to Gabriola* (unfinished when the author died in 1954) are dystopian novels which set Canada in a modernist perspective.[3]

Lewis and Lowry were both resident in Canada throughout the Second World War. No contact occurred and no sign of awareness is given by either writer of the other's existence. They are antipathetic types: the early Lewis shows a political tendency which Fredric Jameson carefully defines as "proto-fascist";[4] while Lowry might be condemned in Lewis's terms as a "revolutionary simpleton" and as the kind of bohemian artist whose survival always depended on a private income, however small.[5]

---

[1] Robert Kroetsch, "Death is a Happy Ending," in *Figures in a Ground: Canadian Essays on Modern Literature Collected in Honor of Sheila Watson*, ed. Diane Bessai & David Jackel (Saskatoon: Western Producer Prairie Books, 1978): 206–207.

[2] For extensive evidence of this, see *Forum: Canadian Life and Letters 1920–70; Selections from "The Canadian Forum"*, ed. J.L. Granatstein & Peter Stevens (Toronto: U of Toronto P, 1972).

[3] Wyndham Lewis, *Self Condemned* (Chicago: Henry Regnery, 1955); Malcolm Lowry, *October Ferry to Gabriola* (1970; Harmondsworth: Penguin, 1971). Page references are given in the text of the essay. Pagination in the New Canadian Library edition of *Self Condemned* is the same as in the first edition.

[4] See Fredric Jameson, *Fables of Aggression: Wyndham Lewis; The Modernist as Fascist* (Berkeley: U of California P, 1979).

[5] See John Lent, "Wyndham Lewis and Malcolm Lowry: Contexts of Style and Subject Matter in the Modern Novel," in *Figures in a Ground*, ed. Bessai & Jackel, 61–75.

For both writers, the text in question has autobiographical as well as fictional significance. The circumstances of production entail acute physical and mental stress. Lewis endures poverty in exile and loses his sight by the time of writing *Self Condemned*. Lowry complains continually of the agony of writing: manuscript sheets of *October Ferry* are headed with a prayer to St Jude, patron of desperate causes. Admittedly, the circumstantial details are irrelevant unless one accepts Lowry's claim that "the bloody agony of the writer writing is so patently extreme that it creates a kind of power in itself."[6] Roland Barthes writes in 1953 that "every writer born opens within himself the trial of literature."[7] The two cases in question are exemplary trials of writing which presuppose a distinctively modern context for the representation of Canadian experience. Commenting on *Self Condemned* with its Momaco/Toronto setting, Hugh Kenner reflects on

> the continuous disorientation of the political prisoner, the man displaced, the survivor (there have been millions) of a community elsewhere in space or mislaid in time. Everyone alive knows something about this. The breakup of familiar order transposes whole peoples into a sort of lifelong Toronto.[8]

In this description, the general crisis takes on a familiar, almost domesticated aspect. The statement, however, suggests a consensus that did not apply to the actual situation of Lewis and Lowry at the time. Both wrote from a position in which they experienced acute isolation. The situation of the English writer in Canada is problematical. Both novels are constructed from the point of view that to be perceived as English in Canada is a problem in itself. The external relations between English and Canadian, as well as the internal strains of difference and community, would seem to be aggravated rather than improved by the double-edged criticism of the Momaco Canadians in *Self Condemned*:

> If you criticize them you criticize the average population of Belfast, of Bradford and Leeds, and of Glasgow. If you deplore the materialism and the humble cultural level, you are merely criticizing anglo-saxon civilisation.
>   Canadians have all the good qualities as well as the bad, of the Ulsterman, the Scot, the Englishman: and among them, of course, are about the same percentage of gifted people as you would find in these islands. (196)

The characters in both novels feel threatened by the exclusiveness of the community and by the occasionally brutal exploitation of differences. Lewis's main character, Rene Harding, is half-French by parentage: he maintains that "'No

---

6 Malcolm Lowry, letter to Albert Erskine (Dollarton, early summer, 1953), in *Selected Letters of Malcolm Lowry*, ed. Harvey Breit & Margerie Bonner Lowry (Harmondsworth: Penguin, 1985): 335, 339.

7 Roland Barthes, *Writing Degree Zero and Elements of Semiology*, tr. Annette Lavers & Colin Smith (London: Jonathan Cape, 1984): 72.

8 Hugh Kenner, *The Pound Era: The Age of Ezra Pound, T.S. Eliot, James Joyce and Wyndham Lewis* (London: Faber & Faber, 1975): 503.

Nazi could feel more racial superiority than the English Canucks of Upper Canada'." When he attempts conversation in French with a taxi-driver and is repulsed "in pidgin English," he takes the snub with good grace, since "the driver's face was almost purely Indian, and with traces of the 'nobility' of the Redskin" (330). Lewis attacks racism yet at the same time antagonises liberal opinion. The style of the novel throughout betrays strong tension on the subject of differences – racial, national, sexual – and it can be read, from a Canadian or liberal standpoint, as a constant provocation. Nevertheless, in the scene just mentioned, the patronising comments are framed as those of Rene himself, who pays a high price for his critical attitude.

Lowry's Ethan Llewelyn explains his problem to the partner he meets "one afternoon of thunder and snow in 1938 within the foyer of a suburban Toronto cinema, where they were showing Douglas Fairbanks, Jr, in *Outward Bound*":

> "I feel lonely," he said. "Everybody takes me for an Englishman and they seem to
> hate the English like the devil. Myself, I take pride in saying I'm English even
> though I'm half Welsh, even though strictly speaking I'm a Canadian."
> "I'm Scottish."
> " – but are we going to heaven, or hell?" the great voice of one of the characters in
> the show boomed through into the foyer [...] (17)

Both stories recognise the enormous attraction of American society as well as showing the centrifugal forces unleashed from Europe. Both express the same apocalyptic fear of the disintegration of European and, specifically, English culture. The Lewis couple sail to Canada in 1939 on what a fellow-passenger describes as "the last boat out of Europe" (146).

Though they do not otherwise share in a consensus view of contemporary reality, both novels assume a realistic basis, which is constituted by a plot-development of a fairly minimal kind and by a style of *récit* which at least appears to conform to realistic conventions. *Self Condemned* is sometimes too bluntly described as a "realistic" or "psychological" novel, though this is to undervalue Lewis's investment in style. Lowry himself commented on *October Ferry* in a sentence that itself suggests a procedure somewhat more convoluted than straight realism:

> some of the writing seems slack or matey in places or redundant (though sometimes
> later it is meant to appear redundant on purpose – as to give the effect of a man
> caught, washed to and fro in the tides of his mind) and can stand tightening.[9]

Both texts reveal a secondary, reflective order of significance which competes with the realistic development. The immediate individual problems of cultural dis-location and intellectual despair are allegorised as part of the scene of global conflict.

---

9 *Selected Letters of Malcolm Lowry*, 347.

The "trial of literature" which the author opens within himself appears in the
text in the difference between a neutral language and a self-consciously literary
language. In terms of mode, the contest is between realistic presentation and
allegory. Both novelists thematise the problem of representation quite extensively.
According to Lowry's Ethan Llewelyn, "Nothing was more unreal than a novel,
even a realistic novel" (183). The theme of the representation of reality is
interwoven with the theme of community, as the characters in both novels find
their sense of reality threatened by the suspension of normal social relationships.
To their perception and that of both authorial narrators, society is represented by a
stream of bad news and propaganda in favour of "the social lie" (*OF* 38), "the
compromise of normal living" (*SC* 163). They live as if under a malign spell. The
concern with literary representation enters into the proposition "as if," which is
articulated to uncanny effect by both texts. Lewis's Rene is morbidly convinced
that he can forsee his fate: "The general shape of the future was starkly outlined,
for him, as if by some supernatural hand." The logic of the situation seems
inescapable: "An individual who has repudiated publicly the compromise of
normal living must thereafter be careful never to use compromise, or half-
compromise, under whatever circumstances" (*SC* 163). Both writers are
committed, to the point of obsession, to outlining an aesthetic of alienation as part
of the story they have to tell.

   The stories both concern the situation of a married couple who find themselves
sharing the general crisis of the time in keenly degrading but still conventionally
domestic circumstances. The couples attempt to resist the pressure of a society in
which stereotypical and conformist views are advertised with punitive zeal.
Stylistically, both texts show their resistance to the form of realism that articulates
and reproduces a conformist culture of this kind: the style takes on a special
brilliance, an allegorical radiance. In *Self Condemned* and in *October Ferry*, the
leading character regards himself as an heroic intellectual type and is presented
ironically as a figure badly out of tune with the Zeitgeist. The allegorical
significance of both narratives appears in a cluster of themes they have in
common, including the struggle to survive in bad times, the identification of
difference as a curse, and the pain of social rejection. Singled out as different and
therefore cursed, Lewis's and Lowry's figures are projected against a symbolic
environment polluted by black magic, littered with shells and husks, and inhabited
by demons.

   "The Cemetery of Shells" is the final chapter of *Self Condemned*. Shell-
metaphors have particular resonance in Lewis's theoretical writings: they illustrate
"the external approach" to writing that produces the satire which is always the
basis of representation for Lewis: "satire is all constructed out of the dry shells
and pelts of things. The surface of the visible machinery of life alone is used [...].

All is metallic – all is external." Taking issue with other modernist styles of writing, Lewis adds that "the bustling manners of the satiric art do not lend themselves to swamp-effects, and to the smudgings of aura-lined spirit-pictures."[10] The extreme divergence between Lewis and Lowry must be noted at this point, since *October Ferry* specialises in the blurring of focus between internal and external presentation here dismissed as "swamp-effects." In contrast, the hard satiric definition of *Self Condemned* is shown in the figure of Rene, who by the end of the novel is reduced to "a shell," "a half-crazed replica of his former self," "an automaton." His academic colleague McKenzie, "a sober man, not prone to feyness," experiences "the presence of the supernatural" when he recognises Rene's condition (400–404). This is a Canadian dystopia where Toronto is a city a bit like hell; where impressions of freezing and burning are easily naturalised.

Rene's Momaco/Toronto is the destination he arrives at as a result of his own "furious analysis," which "began disintegrating many relationships and attitudes which only an exceptionally creative spirit, under very favourable conditions, can afford to dispense with" (401). The irony of the novel is consistent with a theory of the absurd that Lewis had propounded in 1927. According to this view, "We are not constructed to be absolute observers." The essay entitled "The Meaning of the Wild Body," in the process of defining "the absurd," cites Schopenhauer on the subject of national differences. In the essay, Lewis reflects on the most intimate problems of personal relationship and self-perception. His conclusion is that "it is comparatively easy to see that another man, as an animal, is absurd; but it is far more difficult to observe oneself in that hard and exquisite light."[11] *Self Condemned* addresses itself to the reader as a peculiarly stringent analysis of the relations between self and other in the circumstances of a world crisis.

Self Condemned brings that hard and exquisite light to bear on the self which is its subject. Rene, a historian who by 1939 has published a controversial book called *The Secret History of World War Two*, finds to his cost that there is no neutral position from which to observe the crisis. He insists that "It is the circumstances of the time in which we live that have made it impossible for me to mistake my road: there have been signposts or rather lurid beacons all the way along it, leading only to one end, to one conclusion" (18). Rene's conviction that he can see through the motives of others subjects him in turn to an unbearable degree of exposure, to the point where the idea of an inner life no longer carries any meaning:

---

10 *Enemy Salvoes: Selected Literary Criticism by Wyndham Lewis*, ed. C.J. Fox (London: Vision, 1975): 35–37 (from *Men Without Art*, 1934: 126–28).
11 Wyndham Lewis, *The Complete Wild Body*, ed. Bernard Lafourcade (Santa Barbara: Black Sparrow, 1982): 150–60.

> If the personality is emptied of mother-love, emptied of wife-love, emptied of all the
> illusions upon which sex-in-society depends, and finally emptied of the illusions
> upon which the will to create depends, then the personality becomes a shell. (400)

The strategy of Lewis's novel is to confront the issue of a world drained of
meaning. Lowry, on the other hand, imagines dystopia as an environment in which
the subject-self is oppressed by a plethora of meanings.

Lowry's representation of Canadian experience also encodes an allegorical
level of meaning to which shell-metaphors provide access. Lowry envisages a
problematical relationship between surface and depth. In his remarkable defence
of *Under the Volcano* in a letter to Jonathan Cape, Lowry comments on certain
references to the Cabala that are relevant to that novel's "deeper meanings": "The
Consul's spiritual domain in this regard is probably the Qliphoth, the world of
shells and demons, represented by the Tree of Life upside down." Lowry tries to
reassure Cape: "all this is not important at all to an understanding of the book; I
just mention it in passing to hint that, as Henry James says, 'There are depths'."[12]
The reference to Qliphoth as "the world of shells and demons" is taken up again in
October Ferry (148) and is implied throughout in the symbolic code of the
narrative. These comments suggest that Lowry handles the topic with a certain
detachment. Any doubts about the realisation of such "depths" can, in the case of
Under the Volcano, largely be overcome by reference to the letter and to the novel
itself. However, the comments which Lowry makes on *October Ferry* are less
persuasive. The latter work more closely corresponds to Lewis's hostile evocation
of the "smudgings of aura-lined spirit-pictures." *Self Condemned*, with its external
approach, is by implication a critique of the lurid technique of internalisation in
October Ferry. Yet it is evident that, for Lowry, the exploration of these "depths" of
consciousness is the main interest of writing.

Reference to this world of magic in both novels provides an index to the split
between the characters' natural and social selves. The hero–intellectual appears in
an ambivalent light: he is gifted but is also the target of ridicule. "The affiliation
of the sublime and the ridiculous" is a constant principle in Lewis's aesthetic
theory.[13] Lowry insisted that *October Ferry* was both "satanically horrendous" and
"incredibly funny."[14] From an authorial point of view, reference to magic also
stands in both cases for the writer's own commitment: "Art at its fullest is a very
great force indeed, a magical force," according to Lewis.[15] Magic is not only a
metaphor for the risk that attends the hero's self-imposed quest in the course of

---

12 *Selected Letters*, 65.

13 *Wyndham Lewis: An Anthology of His Prose*, ed. E.W.F. Tomlin (London: Methuen, 1969): 274
(from the "Introduction" to *Men Without Art*).

14 *Selected Letters*, 339.

15 *Wyndham Lewis: An Anthology*, ed. Tomlin, 272 (from "The Political Exploitation of the
Magical Power of Art," in Part 2 of *The Diabolical Principle* [1931]).

the story but also a sign of the precarious nature of the writer's actual project, since there is an obvious conflict with realism. In his correspondence, Lowry refers with a mixture of loathing and humour to his "daemon."[16] That a demonic aspect also underlies Lewis's apparently more rational approach is suggested by Jameson:

> *Self Condemned* suggests that the question of the magic or origins of satire must now be reviewed in a new light. It is often suggested that contemporary life – far from being rationalized – is riddled with prelogical and superstitious thought modes which are so many survivals of older types of social behaviour [...].

Jameson goes on to speculate on the persistence, in modern culture, of "types of alienation specific to more archaic modes." According to this argument,

> the commodity reification of capitalism does not supersede, but is rather laid over and coexists with the power systems of precapitalist societies – as, for instance, in machismo and sexism – as well as the most archaic division of labour of tribal society itself, in the form of the inequality between man and woman and between youth and elder.[17]

This speculation is relevant here because it enables one to identify a similar kind of speculation in both the novels under discussion. This relates to the intuition, compelling in both texts, of a collapse of civilised standards extending far beyond the theatre of war.

Both stories concern a couple not only living in a single room but reduced to a situation where all the shared values derived from love and work are undermined. In Momaco, Rene and his wife Hester, trapped by "the magic of total war," face privation. Rene insists on making a joke of their life as exiles in a hotel room:

> "No. This is a joke, he said." He got up. "The fat from our food collects in the bottom of the oven. If we scraped it out and ate it on our bread, that would be hard times – though in hard times there would be no fat in the bottom of the oven." (175)

There are strategic references to the suicide of Stefan Zweig, to the Ghetto in Cracow, and to the option of gassing oneself in the same oven. Lowry's couple, faced with the threat of eviction from their cabin home, take an apartment in Vancouver. To them the postwar world appears in a hostile and estranging light, where social intercourse seems entirely conventional and fragile:

> The first thing that happens in a city is that the weather dies in the soul, though people may talk of nothing else, using it as the only medium for conversation, much as people will talk idly, gossip in the terms of long-forgotten heresies, mysterious codes of honor, not knowing the significance of their own metaphors. (183)

Lowry's reflection on metaphor precisely records the complex experience of alienation recognised by Jameson in Lewis's text.

---

16 *Selected Letters*, 338.
17 Jameson, *Fables of Aggression*, 140.

Rene and Ethan are both credited with the ability to interrogate the world of conventional appearances more closely than others can. To Ethan it seems that, even in an overheard casual conversation, "almost every phrase had another meaning, perhaps many meanings intended for his ears alone" (231). Rene announces his resignation as a history professor in the following terms: "I am no longer able to teach a story of the world which they would find acceptable: they would not let me teach my students the things which I now know, so I have had to tell them that there is no longer anything that I can teach" (16). But Rene's mother's response is the question: "You are not by any chance a fool, my son?" (26). The mood of interrogation persists in both novels in a characteristically modernist way, in a post-Kafka North America.

The writer himself has to pay a price for his resistance to social convention. Jameson has a distinctive view on the deliberate perverseness of Lewis's satiric role:

> the prelogical force of all the fears associated with the magical curse and satiric onslaught is perhaps better understood in terms of the aggressor than of his targets. Not the victim, but rather the satirist himself still obscurely believes in the annihilating force of his incantation. He is indeed the only one in an adequate position to measure the whole range and potency of the destructive impulses he bears within himself [...] The satirist is his own first victim; and his misanthropy is accompanied with an ineradicable sense of guilt no less intense for the purely symbolic or imaginary nature of his gesture.[18]

Jameson's emphasis seems just too literal, though it is true that Lewis occasionally seems to take his role almost as seriously as Jameson does. Lewis remarks: "though you would scarcely believe it, satirists suffer much as a class from an uneasy conscience." Lewis cheerfully accepts that the satirist is "a sort of Cain among craftsmen."[19] These comments are pleasantly cool, but Eliot described *Self Condemned* as "a book of almost unbearable spiritual agony."[20] Lowry wrote of the "guilt-laden" and unfinished *October Ferry* that he regarded it as an ultimate challenge: "a matter of life and death, or rebirth for its author, not to say sanity or otherwise."[21] Yet both narratives avoid the impasse of a situation in which the author is merely the medium of spiritual agony with the reader merely the witness to it.

Both texts advertise their performance to the reader with a grin of pleasure. The delight in representation is manifest. The novels can be read as social satire

---

18 Jameson, *Fables of Aggression*, 140.

19 *Wyndham Lewis: An Anthology*, ed. Tomlin, 272 (from the "Introduction" to *Men Without Art*). Lowry's poem "Cain Shall Not Slay Abel Today on Our Good Ground" also reveals an interest in the figure of Cain.

20 Cited by Jeffrey Meyers, *The Enemy: A Biography of Wyndham Lewis* (London: Routledge & Kegan Paul, 1980): 312.

21 *Selected Letters*, 339.

but also as a kind of parody in relation to conventionally realistic fiction. Lowry pleads with his publisher, who he thinks is about to prejudge the work unfavourably: "*Gabriola* won't admit of any stock responses to it, as a novel of situation, character, etc. It's probably hard to read, as the *Volcano* was."[22]

"Satire" is of course Lewis's own preferred term for his fiction. The implication of satire is less familiar in Lowry's case, but the connection can be made through Lowry's interest in German expressionism. Sherrill Grace argues for a "quality of expressive emphasis and distortion" in Lowry's style which, from the present point of view, relates him to Lewis.[23] *October Ferry* makes ironic and reflexive use of Ethan Llewelyn's enjoyment of German expressionist cinema:

> Films had more reality to him than life [...] But novels possessed secretly no reality for him at all. Or almost none. A novelist presents less of life the more closely he approaches what he thinks of as his realism. (64)

It has been suggested that "in cinema technique, Lowry finds not only a method but a metaphor to express the tormented, surrealistic world of his characters."[24] "Surrealistic" is an exaggeration; nevertheless, Lowry's self-reflexive technique, like Lewis's satire, is there to subvert conventional perceptions of reality. Throughout both narratives, deliberately banal realistic effects are relieved by textual patterning and intertextual play.

In *Self Condemned*, the range of allusion includes Dante, Henry James, and Proust. There is also a sardonic glance at the kind of Thirties reading found in a liberal London household: "Shaw, G.D.H. Cole, Priestley, Katherine Mansfield, Wystan Auden, *The Road to Wigan Pier*, Father Brown" (46). The novel's self-consciousness and mockery save it from the clichés of immigrant fiction. The range of intertextual reference in *October Ferry* defies brief summary, but another allusion to film shows the intensive style of reference and the authorial humour:

> Ethan wondered if this wasn't an almost universal experience, when life was going desperately, and you dropped into some lousy movie to get away for an hour from yourself, only to discover that [...] this movie might as well have been a sort of symbolic projection, a phantasmagoria, of that life of yours, into which you'd come halfway through. (132)

The play of representation is overt in Lowry's text and more covert in Lewis's. By any realistic standard, Lowry's writing appears grotesquely self-indulgent: Albert

---

22 *Selected Letters*, 360.

23 This key phrase originates in John Willett, *Expressionism* (1970): 8. Cited by Sherrill E. Grace, "Malcolm Lowry and the Expressionist Vision," in *The Art of Malcolm Lowry*, ed. Anne Smith (London: Vision, 1978): 94.

24 Paul G. Tiessen, "Malcolm Lowry and the Cinema," *Canadian Literature* 44 (Spring, 1970): 48.

Erskine, Lowry's editor, eventually called a halt to the project.[25] As a conventional novel, *October Ferry* seems hopeless, though Lowry was not prepared to admit it. The story can be valued now precisely for the way in which it engages with the problem of representation.

The crisis in experience is a crisis in representation. Issues of experience and of representation are brought into focus through the constant, intricate interplay between utopian and dystopian imaginings within the texts. Both novels may be described as "dystopian," but both suggest that dystopia (like utopia) usually secretes within itself the sign of its opposite. This interplay illustrates the latent appeal of Lewis's text as well as the more flamboyant appeal of Lowry's. *Self Condemned* introduces Rene's friend Parkinson in the little paradise of his London study: "This was 1939, the last year, or as good as, in which such a life was to be lived" (76). But even the room in Momaco, which Rene and Hester sometimes regard as a "lethal chamber," is capable of a more benign construction. Within the hell of the space that measures twenty-five feet by twelve, there is still the hope that "a more intelligent society may be in the making" (182). In Lowry's story, the corresponding play of meanings is caught in the ultimate shell-image of the waterside hermitage, the idyllic refuge where Ethan and Jacqueline used to live like Ferdinand and Miranda, faced by the SHELL oil refinery which has lost the "S" from its sign (159). From his stranded situation, Ethan, like Rene, tries to make out the signs of the times: "Quite against his better judgement he believed that some final wisdom would arise out of Canada, that would save not only Canada herself but perhaps the world. The trouble is, the world never looks as though it's going to be saved in one's own lifetime" (202). The project of utopian reconstruction is extensively thematised in both novels, in articulating the relationship between Europe and Canada. Both texts rehearse the opposition between utopian and dystopian elements as a problem of discourse which, crucially, reflects the internal predicament of the characters themselves and suggests the splitting of identity within the subject. Thus the very assertion of "Englishness" by Rene and Ethan, which is reassuring and flattering to their sense of culture and identity, is also a problematical point for both characters and one which, in the new world of their choice, further contributes to the experience of marginality and estrangement.

In Lewis's novel, the presence of utopian/dystopian alternatives is apparent even though the ending, in realistic terms, is so uncompromisingly severe. In Lowry's novel, the actual ending elaborately defers the due arrival of the couple on Gabriola Island: the arrangement of signs does not absolutely foreclose on a utopian construction of the story. But the immediate destination of these

---

25 See Albert Erskine, "The Disappointed Editor," in *Malcolm Lowry Remembered*, ed. Gordon Bowker (London: BBC, 1985): 189.

characters in transit is not utopia. In the present, what links Canada with Europe is the crisis of contemporary culture that makes it necessary to renegotiate the terms of difference and community, even, or especially, for the English in Canada. Norman Levine, a Canadian writer resident in England, whose book *Canada Made Me* conveys an exceptionally sharp impression of the period, weights his conclusion with a remark he himself made in conversation: "I said that failure in Canada is something that appeals to me."[26] Levine's handling of this topic traces complex procedures of adjustment within Canada itself and extensive transactions between Canada and Europe, following the events of world war, social revolution, and forced migration. The interest in failure opens a wide field of exploration for an observer in Levine's position: he can reflect on the need for diversity, on the blandness or repressiveness of conventional attitudes when faced with difference, and on the question of the integrity of his own response to the Canadian scene. These fictional and autobiographical narratives of failure by Lewis and Lowry construct that scene as one of the sites of modernism. A place that has been written about like this comes closer to realising the different possibilities within itself.

WORKS CITED

BARTHES, Roland. *Writing Degree Zero and Elements of Semiology*, tr. Annette Lavers & Colin Smith (London: Jonathan Cape, 1984).

BREIT, Harvey & Margerie Bonner LOWRY, ed. *Selected Letters of Malcolm Lowry* (Harmondsworth: Penguin Books, 1985).

ERSKINE, Albert. "The Disappointed Editor," in *Malcolm Lowry Remembered*, ed. Gordon Bowker (London: BBC, 1985).

FOX, C.J., ed. *Enemy Salvoes: Selected Literary Criticism by Wyndham Lewis* (London: Vision, 1975).

GRACE, Sherrill E. "Malcolm Lowry and the Expressionist Vision," in *The Art of Malcolm Lowry*, ed. Anne Smith (London: Vision, 1978).

GRANATSTEIN, J.L., & Peter STEVENS, ed. *Forum: Canadian Life and Letters 1920–70; Selections from "The Canadian Forum"* (Toronto; U of Toronto P, 1972).

JAMESON, Fredric. *Fables of Aggression: Wyndham Lewis, The Modernist as Fascist* (Berkeley: U of California P, 1979).

KENNER, Hugh. *The Pound Era: the age of Ezra Pound, T.S. Eliot, James Joyce and Wyndham Lewis* (London: Faber & Faber, 1975).

KROETSCH, Robert. "Death is a Happy Ending," in *Figures in a Ground: Canadian Essays on Modern Literature Collected in Honor of Sheila Watson*, ed. Diane Bessai & David Jackel (Saskatoon: Western Producer Prairie Books, 1978): 206–207.

LENT, John. "Wyndham Lewis and Malcolm Lowry: contexts of style and subject matter in the modern novel," in *Figures in a Ground: Canadian Essays on Modern Literature Collected in Honor of*

---

26 Norman Levine, *Canada Made Me* (1958; Toronto: Deneau, 1982): 276.

Sheila Watson, ed. Diane Bessai & David Jackel (Saskatoon: Western Producer Prairie Books, 1978): 61–75.

LEVINE, Norman. *Canada Made Me* (1958; Toronto: Deneau, 1982).

LEWIS, Wyndham. *The Complete Wild Body*, ed. Bernard Lafourcade (Santa Barbara: Black Sparrow, 1982).

———. *Self Condemned* (Chicago: Henry Regnery, 1955)

LOWRY, Malcolm. *October Ferry to Gabriola* (1970; Harmondsworth: Penguin Books, 1971).

MEYERS, Jeffrey. *The Enemy: A Biography of Wyndham Lewis* (London: Routledge & Kegan Paul, 1980).

TIESSEN, Paul G. "Malcolm Lowry and the Cinema," *Canadian Literature* 44 (Spring, 1970): 48.

TOMLIN, E.W.F., ed. *Wyndham Lewis: An Anthology of His Prose* (London: Methuen, 1969).

❧ ❀ ☙

Traces of Europe
in Robert Kroetsch's Fiction
or: *"I wish I'd had a crack
at that Henry the Eighth"*

MARTIN KUESTER

I WOULD LIKE TO START WITH AN ANECDOTE, a suitable enough way of dealing with an author who, more than any other Canadian writer, has emphasised the importance of oral anecdotes and tales in his writing. When I mentioned my present topic in a letter to the Canadian novelist and critic David Williams, he wrote back with the following comments:

> "Traces of Europe in RK's Fiction" might be qualified by what RK said to me just after we had parted from an afternoon of drinking [...] at the Fort Garry Hotel. "We've got to get rid of Europe," he growled on the way to Garbonzo's Pizza. "Rub it out once and for all. Without a trace." I don't think it was anything [one of us] said. Just the usual weight of literary history and tradition. Or maybe Robert getting apocalyptic after a few beers.

This is certainly the typically deconstructionist Kroetschian stance that we have come to know from his uncompromising narrators in novels such as *The Words of My Roaring* or from his radical theoretical statements: "Rub it out once and for all. Without a trace." Am I then totally misguided in looking for remaining traces of Europe in Robert Kroetsch's work? Has it been rubbed out without any trace? I would (and will) claim that this is not so, that there are still quite a few traces of Europe left in his work – that these traces are in fact one of its most important features.

On a superficial level one might say that a trace is any direct mention or indirect influence that can be spotted in a text: in this case, references to European things, places, earlier texts. But trace does of course have strong Derridean overtones, on which I will draw here in a rather eclectic fashion. Derrida's concept of *trace* depends on his dual concept of *différance*: (1) a word is used in a certain communicative situation – at a certain time, involving a certain relationship to a certain referent – which can never again be reconstructed in exactly the same way and is thus *different* from any other communicative situation. This difference is of course even more obvious in a new environment such as Canada where things, inadequately named after European concepts, are automatically *different* from their counterparts in Europe, a fact that had already shocked early immigrants to Canada such as Susanna Moodie, who had to come to terms with the fact that her romantic concept of nature was not necessarily adequate when roughing it in the bush. But (2) *différance* also has to do with the action being *deferred* or delayed. In addition to there being a time-lag, if not a jet-lag, between Canada and Europe, a sign or word of course refers to something which – at the moment of verbal communication – is not necessarily any longer there. As Jacques Derrida puts it in *Speech and Phenomena*,

> Differance is what makes the movement of signification possible only if each element that is said to be "present," appearing on the stage of presence, is related to something other than itself but retains the mark of a past element and lets itself be hollowed out by the mark of its relation to a future element. This trace relates no less to what is called the future than to what is called the past, and it constitutes what is called the present by this very relation to what it is not, to what it absolutely is not.[1]

Or, as Derrida writes in further developing Saussure's concept of the sign in *Of Grammatology*: "Without a retention in the minimal unit of temporal experience, without a trace retaining the other as other in the same, no difference would do its work and no meaning would appear."[2] We need traces, that is, in order to communicate. Gayatri Spivak points out that *trace*, "the French word carr[ying] strong implications of track, footprint, imprint," is a word "that presents itself as the mark of an anterior presence, origin, master." She claims that Derrida is thus "asking us to change certain habits of mind: the authority of the text is provisional, the origin is a trace; contradicting logic, we must learn to use and erase our language at the same time."[3] Traces of Europe are thus, on the one hand, easily identifiable elements to be spotted in Kroetsch's novels, and, on the other, these slippery Derridean concepts that are identifiable only through their absence. It will be my argument that (1) we can observe a steady progression from the one, topographical–historical type of trace to the other, intertextual one from Kroetsch's early novels such as *But We Are Exiles* to the later *Alibi*, and that (2) for all his alibis to the contrary, Kroetsch has not been able (or, I would claim, willing) really to wipe out all the traces of Europe in his writing. Rather, as David Creelman puts it in a recent essay on Kroetsch's stance, he "simply refuses to use the *différance* of language to deconstruct texts and leave them unassembled: he must begin his own theoretical and fictional reconstructions."[4]

---

[1] Jacques Derrida, "Différance," in Derrida, *Speech and Phenomena And Other Essays on Husserl's Theory of Signs*, tr. David B. Allison (Evanston: Northwestern UP, 1973): 142–43.

[2] Derrida, *Of Grammatology*, tr. & intro. Gayatri Chakravorty Spivak (Baltimore MD: Johns Hopkins UP, 1976): 62.

[3] Gayatri Chakravorty Spivak, "Translator's Preface," in Derrida, *Of Grammatology*, xv, xviii.

[4] David Creelman, "Robert Kroetsch: Criticism in the Middle Ground," *Studies in Canadian Literature/Études en littérature canadienne* 16.1 (1991): 77.

An obvious place to start for any trace hunter is Kroetsch's theoretical and essayistic work, but the studious critic is frustrated by the fact that neither the index of Kroetsch's selected essays, *The Lovely Treachery of Words*, nor that of his book-length conversation with Shirley Neuman and Robert Wilson, *Labyrinths of Voice*, contains any reference to either Europe or traces. But a whole section of *Labyrinths* is entitled "Influence" – obviously almost as good a place to start; and here Shirley Neuman picks up the Derridean notion of a text being "a differential network, a fabric of traces referring endlessly to something other than itself, to other differential traces."[5] Traces, we are once again reminded here, may be references to European actuality; but, much more often, traces in literature are also intertextual references to earlier – in this case, European – texts. But in one context, in his fascinating personal essays in *The Lovely Treachery of Words*, Kroetsch himself starts out from the actual traces of the past, traces that haunt him. He describes a situation from his own home base in Alberta: his father had allowed dam-builders to take away stones that had belonged to a historical and supposedly magical site, an Indian tipi ring. He goes on:

> If history betrayed us, we too betrayed it. I remember my father one night at supper, saying out of nowhere that he'd made a mistake, letting those men pick up those stones. For reasons he couldn't understand, he felt guilty. Where I had learned the idea of absence, I was beginning to learn the idea of trace. There is always something left behind. That is the essential paradox. Even abandonment gives us memory.[6]

But the absence and traces he talks about here are obviously the absence and traces of an Amerindian past. What about Europe? "Our inherited literature, the literature of our European past and of eastern North America, is emphatically the literature of a people who have not lived on prairies," Kroetsch argues, and claims that Western Canadians had to uninvent or reinvent the language of which the new literature is composed. "Canadian prairie fiction," he quotes from Dick Harrison, "is about a basically European society spreading itself across a very un-European landscape. It is rooted in that first settlement process in which the pioneer faced two main obstacles: the new land and the old culture."[7] The old words are put – in Derridean terms – *sous rature*, "under erasure," as Gayatri Spivak conveniently and fittingly translates it. The concepts of European culture are exploded: Kroetsch chooses Timothy Findley as an example of a writer who "acts out for the colonial society the destruction and loss of its European centres, cultural, political, economic." As a result, "what we witness is the collapse, for North American

---

5 Shirley Neuman & Robert Wilson, *Labyrinths of Voice: Conversations with Robert Kroetsch* (Edmonton: NeWest, 1982):10.

6 Robert Kroetsch, *The Lovely Treachery of Words: Essays Selected and New* (Toronto: Oxford UP, 1989): 2.

7 Kroetsch, *Lovely Treachery*, 5, 15.

eyes, of the meta-narrative that once went by the name Europe." Kroetsch's paradigmatic model of this collapse of the European meta-narrative is Frederick Philip Grove, who left Germany under the name Felix Paul Greve and seems to have changed identities, to have unnamed and renamed himself, in mid-Atlantic:

> This erasure of names is a part of the experience of migrating peoples, and part of the narrative of that experience. And that erasure becomes palimpsest, it leaves its trace – as it did when Greve changed his name to Grove, at once concealing and changing who he was and leaving a trace that would enable us to complete the task of renaming that he had initiated.[8]

So what about Europe in Kroetsch's novels? What role does the Old World play in the works of somebody who is credited with having been among the creators of a new literary language in a young country? Not much about Europe in his first novel, *But We are Exiles*[9] – at least at first sight. Peter Guy, the hero, decides to go north and work on a boat on the Mackenzie River after his girl-friend has left him for his friend Michael Hornyak. Hornyak later gets killed in an accident that his rival might have prevented, and thus a feeling of guilt persecutes Peter until he is left behind in Hornyak's canoe-*cum*-coffin in a snowstorm on Great Slave Lake. Should the water-imagery not have become clear enough, the epigraph of the novel, which unfortunately is missing from my paperback version, is from Ovid's *Metamorphoses* and deals with Narcissus. In Peter Thomas's words, "Narcissus on Narcissus could almost describe the narrative perspective of the novel, expressed as it is through the consciousness of Peter Guy."[10] In an interview, Kroetsch claims that it was only a review that made him aware of another intertextual trace in *Exiles*, that of Coleridge's *Ancient Mariner*:

> The reviewer said that the parallels [...] were so close that it was downright embarrassing. When I read the review I thought, well, actually that's pretty damn ingenious [...] but I had never once thought of Coleridge while I was writing the novel. On the other hand, I *had* been teaching *The Rime of the Ancient Mariner* at least once a year for four or five years and I'm fascinated by the poem. So I think that he was right, that on an unconscious level I was using the poem.[11]

Although the Mackenzie River and Canada's northern territories seem to be as far away from Europe as one can get, Kroetsch the writer has not been able to liberate himself from European literary influences and the traces of such writers as Coleridge and Conrad.

---

8 Kroetsch, *Lovely Treachery*, 23, 92.

9 Kroetsch, *But We Are Exiles* (1965; Toronto: Macmillan, 1977).

10 Peter Thomas, *Robert Kroetsch* (Vancouver: Douglas & McIntyre, 1980): 33.

11 Russell M. Brown, "An Interview with Robert Kroetsch," *University of Windsor Review* 7.2 (1972): 17.

Kroetsch's second novel, *The Words of My Roaring*,[12] is the first instalment of the *Out West* trilogy, set in rural Alberta. *Words* takes place in the Thirties depression and shows us aspects of the rise of the Social Credit movement, here represented by the undertaker and later MLA, John J. Backstrom. Backstrom, too, fights against a tradition, but the tradition that he is up against is that of Eastern Canada, the high muckie-mucks in Toronto, rather than a European past. Still, memories – or should I say traces – of the Great War and Passchendaele linger, while the references to Greek mythology are kept alive in the name of Helen Persephone, the daughter of Backstrom's surrogate father, Doc Murdoch. And, just as Hades had kidnapped Persephone, Johnnie Backstrom tempts her Depression counterpart in the garden of her father's home.

In *The Studhorse Man*, the same Albertan region is presented at the time of the Second World War, and here Europe figures importantly, if not prominently, not only in the war that is going on there but also in the memories that Hazard Lepage, the last studhorse man in Alberta, has of his European experiences in the Great War. In a wider context, one can of course, as Peter Thomas does, see Hazard's travels through Alberta as an effort to "'retell the *Odyssey* on dry land so to speak' while exploding the whole epic presumption."[13] Greek mythology, however, is turned upside down or inside out, when we meet the mad narrator sitting in a bath-tub. His name is Demeter, a rather unfortunate name deriving from his mother's somewhat unfounded aspirations to higher learning: "my dear mother, pretending to knowledge and believing Demeter to be a masculine name, affixed it to my birth certificate."[14] In an amusing kind of Canadian *différance*, here the European name is not exactly rubbed out, but the signifier is applied to an unsuitable signified, resulting in a palimpsestuous name for an androgynous narrator.

Gone Indian,[15] the last instalment, which takes the *Out West* trilogy up to Kroetsch's present in the Seventies, once more puts more emphasis on the textual-ised form of European traces. This is not surprising in a novel that deals not only with a doctoral student's eternal quest for his thesis topic but also with the conversion of "the possibilities of tragic love and death in *Tristram and Isolde* to [Professor] Mark Madham sending forth [his student] Jeremy Sadness."[16] Jeremy Sadness, whose first name links him to the English philosopher Bentham, tries to emulate intertextually the Englishman George Stansfield Belaney, who refashioned himself as the native Canadian Grey Owl, and then disappears into the Alberta winter.

---

12 Kroetsch, *The Words of My Roaring* (1966; Markham, Ontario: PaperJacks, 1977).
13 Thomas, *Robert Kroetsch*, 6.
14 Kroetsch, *The Studhorse Man* (1969; Markham, Ontario: PaperJacks, 1980): 65.
15 Kroetsch, *Gone Indian* (1973; Nanaimo, B.C.: Theytus, 1981).
16 Thomas, *Robert Kroetsch*, 5.

Badlands[17] is a confrontation of the Canadian present with its archaeological past and of the male version of historiography with its female counterpart. In his search for dinosaur fossils, the palaeontologist William Dawe is not at all interested in European traces but in the real traces that earlier, pre-human inhabitants of the North American continent had left, while his daughter tries to reconstruct her father's personality from the entries in his journal. Still, the novel also abounds in intertextual references to "the narrative quests of Odysseus, Orpheus, the knight errant, Conrad's Marlow."[18] Gus Liebhaber, the hero of Kroetsch's flirt with magic realism in *What the Crow Said*,[19] is once again haunted by European spectres such as Gutenberg, whose concept of the printing press he explodes. Even in textual and intertextual respects, the Canadian seems to reject his European inheritance and prefers the world of magic realism.

The most interesting novel that Kroetsch has given us – at least as far as the use or deconstruction of European traces is concerned – is his second-latest, *Alibi*, and so I will be dwelling on this work, which has come in for some heavy criticism. William William Dorfen, the hero of this novel, is an Albertan like Robert Kroetsch himself. He is sent not only to Europe but around the world by the mysterious nouveau-riche Calgary oil baron Jack Deemer in order to gather up traces of all kinds of things, including the European heritage of Canadians. His job in this case is to find a spa, ie, a bathing and healing place, for the aging Deemer. (I have wondered sometimes how Kroetsch hit upon the idea of a spa, and at the risk of sounding a bit like Demeter Proudfoot, the mad biographer in *The Studhorse Man*, I am sure that his source of inspiration was a place on Pembina Highway in Winnipeg selling and advertising spas – the smaller kind for home use. Kroetsch must have driven by this shop every day on his way to the University of Manitoba, as I did when I was a student there.) Looking for a redeeming spa in England, Wales, Germany, Hungary, Portugal, and Greece, Dorf thus becomes the first of Kroetsch's Canadians whom we accompany to Europe on a non-military mission. On his trip, he is writing the first and original entries into his journal, which *Alibi* turns out to be; in retrospective, the journal's purpose is to be Dorf's alibi, proving that he cannot be responsible for the death of Julie Magnuson. Julie had been his own and Deemer's lover, and it was she, he claims, who had told him right from the start that she would kill him as soon as he found Deemer a spa.

At first sight, the Europe we see in *Alibi* does not seem to have that much to do with the Europe the traces of which Kroetsch wants to erase, but the various scenes at which Dorf arrives in search of a spa prove to have interesting

---

17 Kroetsch, *Badlands* (1975; Toronto: General, 1982).

18 Linda Hutcheon, *The Canadian Postmodern: A Study of Contemporary English–Canadian Fiction* (Toronto: Oxford UP, 1988):164.

19 Kroetsch, *What the Crow Said* (1978; Markham, Ontario: PaperJacks, 1979).

connotations, or traces. Once again, the traces are not so much, or at least not only, real historical or topographical traces but, rather, intertextual ones. A model case of such intertextual traces is the journal form of the novel itself. The intriguing feature of this journal is its metafictionality, the fact that Dorf often includes comments on his own activity of writing. This aspect of writing about the writing of a journal, of the act of transcribing incoherent notes into a supposedly coherent text, is brought to light also through the epilogue to *Alibi*, which gives us some of those original notes Dorf was writing while transcribing earlier notes. Traces of Joyce's strategy of writing and rewriting in *A Portrait of the Artist as a Young Man*? Probably. But then Kroetsch goes one step further than Joyce in introducing yet another frame to the narrative by giving us chapter-headings to the entries in the reworked journal, and these obviously are not Dorf's. In their style, they seem to be going back – another intertextual trace? – to the omniscient narrators of eighteenth-century novelists such as Henry Fielding, who taunt the reader with titles such as "DORF'S PRESENTIMENT (A CHAPTER IN WHICH MUCH IS FORE-TOLD, BUT –)"[20] The novel encourages us to read these titles as comments written by Dorf's sometime girlfriend, the film-maker Karen Strike, who had given him the journal in the first place, as a birthday gift, and who now acts as an editor – or, at least, that is the function Dorf seems to have intended her to perform.

It is with Karen Strike that Dorf discovers his first spa, at Banff, not at all far from Calgary. Here Linda Hutcheon glimpses another "deliberate intertextual echo"[21] of Joyce's work in *Alibi*, this time a reference to the short story "The Dead": "Snow was general on the eastern slope of the Rockies" (11). One wonders to what extent the situation in the hotel room, in which Dorf and Karen do not make love and in which he tells her about Julie, the woman he had copulated with in the spa, is an inverted echo of the memory of Gretta's romance with Michael Furey which she shares with Gabriel in "The Dead." But then, Dorf and Karen would not be able to have sex anyway, because Dorf has scalded his penis in the shower. In her excellent short study of Kroetsch's "Deconstructive Narratology" in *Alibi*, Susan Rudy Dorscht traces the central problem of the novel back to where Derrida, too, had started – Saussurean semiotics: "It seems not insignificant," she writes, "that it was a trusting of the relation between signified and signifier (the hot and cold water taps were misnamed) that began both the written event and the written critique of the written event."[22] Karen also draws the reader's attention to a certain European aspect of the Banff Springs Hotel, a print of "Robert Burns ... Reading His Poem of the 'Winter Night'" (44), which is not necessarily very

---

20 Kroetsch, *Alibi* (Toronto: Stoddart, 1983): 6. Further references to this novel are in the text.

21 Hutcheon, *The Canadian Postmodern*, 78.

22 Susan Rudy Dorscht, "A Deconstructive Narratology: Reading Robert Kroetsch's *Alibi*," *Open Letter* 6.8 (1987): 80.

suitable in a North American environment, even if it may be suitable in this very hotel. While still in Canada, Dorf himself establishes a line of tradition from European to North American spas that does not catch the interest of Karen's cameraman:

> I [...] distracted poor Randy by talking about R.G. Brett, the spa doctor who went on to become lieutenant–governor of Alberta; [...] I sort of got wound up on the subject of spas. In Roman times, I explained. Before that, in Greece. The use of water to cure disease: "Look at your Hippocrates. Look at Celsus. Look at Galen [...]. Sir John Floyer, [...] the English physician, believed and demonstrated that a cold bath will cure damned everything that's wrong with you." (53)

On his way to England, however, Dorf becomes more sceptical of the assembly of traces that the old continent has become:

> Europe is a dream too. But not of silk and spice. Maybe, I thought, maybe Deemer's mad collecting is just that, and that only, a calling up of ghosts from a million ancestral pasts. It is only that, a hailing and a hollering too, a head in the rain barrel listening to its own echo, a lost voice hearing a voice from the far cliff. The cry that comes banging back from the barn wall. The creaking sound from the attic. (74)

The first spa town that Dorf visits in England is an obvious choice: Bath, a place in which many literary works, ranging from Defoe's *Moll Flanders* to Jane Austen's *Northanger Abbey*, have left their intertextual traces. Surprisingly, it is Dorf's chicken-farmer sister, whom he had met on his Wardair flight to London and who joins him on the British leg of his tour of European spas, who reminds him "that the Allens had themselves taken lodgings on our street." And these Allens are not, as Dorf had feared, "neighbors of the Thorns in Edenwolf," Alberta, but "it turned out they were eminent persons in the world of Jane Austen. Sylvia was thrilled to death" (84). Dorf, on the contrary, would have preferred a Thomas Hardy intertext with "fictional characters, more robust, more genuinely honest about desire" (84). And finally Dorf, the pragmatist, the handyman, confronted with the "architectural triumph of lunacy based on the bleeding of an entire empire," has to realize that "Deemer, with all his oilfields, couldn't quite have this. I felt sad" (85). His sister, however, has some of that New World optimism left: "I wish I'd had a crack at that Henry the Eighth," she remarks, to the amazement of her brother (93).

But Dorf does not find his spa in England, nor does he in Wales or in Portugal, where he meets with Julie Magnuson and her dwarfish lover and doctor, Manuel de Medeiros. While Julie mysteriously disappears, Dorf follows Medeiros' advice, looks for and finds a smelly hermaphroditic woman and her spa in Greece, is joined by his daughters, and is finally caught up with by Interpol, who want to question him about Julie's death in a car accident in Portugal. Back in Calgary after his excursion is cut short by Interpol, Dorf

> was beginning to understand the plot that connives the world into visible being; the
> necessary plot that makes us seek each other, if only to do violence to the meeting.
> Deemer thinks he can take the law into his own hands, and that just because he's
> managed to collect a trace of the discarded world into his warehouses: he thinks it's
> his money and his silent manipulation that make the collection. Too bad for him is all
> I can say; it's my scrounging and my snooping and my talking, talking, talking that
> make his famous collection [...]. The collection itself only confirms the discontinuity
> of this scattered world; it's my talk that puts it together [...] (195)

It's Dorf's talk that puts it all together; but then, his story is far from coherent or
even complete. He is unable to finish transcribing all his notes into the final
version of his alibi, because he seems to be responsible for De Medeiros' death.
But before this incident he discovers – or, rather, he is guided to – and runs
Deemer's spa, and becomes somewhat of a healer himself. In an act reminiscent
of, but more felicitous than, Demeter's mother's misnaming of her son in *The
Studhorse Man*, he – who has two identical Christian names – gives one of them to
a man who suffers because he does not have any name; he is a human *tabula rasa*,
somebody who does not seem to be haunted by any traces, by any name given to
him by others. Both the giver and the receiver of a new name feel much better
after this quasi-divine act of naming. Dorf's "creation" thus becomes the ideal
Canadian with a new name in a new country; he is not haunted, as Frederick Philip
Grove had been when he arrived in America, by a palimpsestuous name
reminiscent of an earlier and different environment.

Does this mean, after all, that everything – even the trace of something
foreign, even European possibly – is better than no name, no trace, at all? Perhaps,
because "no name" equals "no trace" equals "no meaning." But the traces, also the
traces of Europe, that Dorf – or should I say Kroetsch – leaves us with, are far
removed from factual truths and tangible archaeological finds. The original
European experiences have been lost in the process of writing and rewriting, of
framing and reframing. In Robert Lecker's words, "the text becomes an alibi
concerning an act that has taken place – the destruction (the death) of Dorf's
journal – and with it any semblance of narrative position or coherence."[23] Like the
truth behind Dorf's alibi, Dorf's Europe is inscrutable and absent whenever we
want to have a closer look at it.

❧ ❀ ❧

I think I have shown in this brief overview that Robert Kroetsch, far from erasing
Europe without a trace, as he once threatened, has been using Europe and its traces
– intertextual as well as archival – to great profit in his novelistic work. Europe is
still there, even if it is often *sous rature*, even if it is as difficult to grasp and

---

23 Robert Lecker, *Robert Kroetsch* (Boston: Twayne, 1986): 110.

pinpoint as the crime for which Dorf has felt obliged to create his alibi. The only illusion one may have of catching up with these traces is to write them out of one's system, but then, as Dorf's unsuccessful, or at least unfinished, attempt at coming to terms with his European notes by transcribing them has shown, even by writing we leave new traces.

WORKS CITED

BROWN, Russell M. "An Interview with Robert Kroetsch," *University of Windsor Review* 7.2 (1972): 1–18.

CREELMAN, David. "Robert Kroetsch: Criticism in the Middle Ground," *Studies in Canadian Literature/Études en littérature canadienne* 16.1 (1991): 63–81.

DERRIDA, Jacques. "Différance," in Derrida, *Speech and Phenomena And Other Essays on Husserl's Theory of Signs*, tr. David B. Allison (Evanston: Northwestern UP, 1973): 121–60.

——. *Of Grammatology*, tr. & intro. Gayatri Chakravorty Spivak (Baltimore MD: Johns Hopkins UP, 1976).

DORSCHT, Susan Rudy. "A Deconstructive Narratology: Reading Robert Kroetsch's *Alibi*," *Open Letter* 6.8 (1987): 78–83.

HUTCHEON, Linda. *The Canadian Postmodern: A Study of Contemporary English–Canadian Fiction* (Toronto: Oxford UP, 1988).

KROETSCH, Robert. *Alibi* (Toronto: Stoddart, 1983).

——. *Badlands* (1975; Toronto: General, 1982).

——. *But We Are Exiles* (1965; Toronto: Macmillan, 1977).

——. *Gone Indian* (1973; Nanaimo, B.C.: Theytus, 1981).

——. *The Lovely Treachery of Words: Essays Selected and New* (Toronto: Oxford UP, 1989).

——. *The Studhorse Man* (1969; Markham, Ontario: PaperJacks, 1980).

——. *What the Crow Said* (1978; Markham, Ontario: PaperJacks, 1979).

——. *The Words of My Roaring* (1966; Markham, Ontario: PaperJacks, 1977).

LECKER, Robert. *Robert Kroetsch* (Boston: Twayne, 1986).

NEUMAN, Shirley, & Robert WILSON. *Labyrinths of Voice: Conversations with Robert Kroetsch* (Edmonton: NeWest, 1982).

SPIVAK, Gayatri Chakravorty. "Translator's Preface" to *Of Grammatology* (Baltimore MD: Johns Hopkins UP, 1976): ix–lxxxvii.

THOMAS, Peter. *Robert Kroetsch* (Vancouver: Douglas & McIntyre, 1980).

❦ ✾ ❧

Experienced Travellers
in Jack Hodgins's Recent Fiction
Exploration of Inner Landscapes

WALDEMAR ZACHARASIEWICZ

I N HIS STIMULATING SURVEY of canonical Canadian novels from the last twenty-five years, Frank Davey points out the abrupt and sometimes random transfer of the setting in many of these novels to other continents and reads this as a sign of "post-national" orientation, regarding "transnational mapping" in Canadian fiction as a reflection of the problems, or even the absence of a national discourse. My hypothesis in trying to contextualise Jack Hodgins's inclusion of foreign settings is somewhat different. I am inclined to see his procedure as connected with a national condition and as part of its discourse.

Considering the collective experience of Canadians, for many of whom (as inhabitants of a vast country and heirs of a colonial legacy with its orientation towards Europe) long-distance travel has always been a geographical necessity, it is perhaps not surprising that journeys across wide expanses and an awareness of remote landscapes have been recurrent fictional motifs in Canadian literature. In addition, the memory of immigration and of individual and communal odysseys has inspired not only expatriate writers, ethnic and "transcultural" authors.[1] However, few contemporary Canadian authors with strong regional roots have shown as keen an interest in the fictional potential of distant or even inter-continental travel as Jack Hodgins. From the outset much less inclined towards avantgarde goals than, say, Robert Kroetsch, who has similarly employed (but parodied) the motif of the quest journey,[2] and ready to retain consistent characters and not subject them to bizarre metamorphoses as some postmodernists have done, Hodgins has allowed an attenuation of the experimental vein in favour of

---

1 Cf Rudy Wiebe's epic story of the Mennonites in *The Blue Mountains of China*, which depicts several continents. See also Margaret Laurence's novels, especially her depiction of the stages in the lives of her female protagonists (in *The Diviners*, Morag's temporary residence in the UK; earlier, in *The Stone Angel*, the presentation of Hagar's reminiscences of her past, with the memory of her move from the prairies to the West Coast). For the concept of transcultural writers see Janice Kulyk Keefer, "From Mosaic to Kaleidoscope: Out of the multicultural past comes a vision of a transcultural future," *Books in Canada* 20.6 (1991): 13–16.

2 See especially his novels *The Studhorse Man* and *Gone Indian*; also *Badlands*, and especially *Alibi*.

more traditional narrative stances. Thus he has availed himself of the established motif of the quest. Though he made his mark in his first novel and his first collection of stories by recording and reconstructing individual and communal life in and by graphically depicting a section of Pacific Canada, thus achieving his status as the principal (white) chronicler of Vancouver Island of the Seventies and early Eighties, his self-imposed task of map-making – through and in his fiction – was not restricted to his native island, but also included visits to Ireland, the homeland of quite a few settlers. Since this debut he has increasingly taken his characters on journeys to faraway regions and has shown the impact of these foreign landscapes on them. It is with the manifestations of such adventure and discovery, and their consequences for the traveller, that I should like to deal.

In Hodgins's early texts, significant experiences are already triggered off by a confrontation with landscapes which seem to stimulate reflection and prompt attempts to fathom a fundamental inner reality. This does not apply to the world trip in "Separating" (the story with which Hodgins's first collection opens), which is spoiled for Spit's family by his inability to refrain from listening to the taped noise of his Old Number One at historic spots; but it holds good for the memorable scene at Wickanninish Bay on the Pacific Rim which furnishes the intriguing symbolism of the question about "the dividing line," with all its epistemological implications.[3] It is true, this short trip and the journeys of one of the many eccentrics who populate Hodgins's fiction (Madmother Thomas, in *The Invention of the World*, who indefatigably searches for her own birthplace) do not extend beyond Vancouver Island. Yet the restless meanderings of this victim of the disastrous utopian enterprise lorded over by Donal Keneally imply the conviction that a close relationship exists between environment and human personality, and stress the tacit assumption that the discovery of a place may lead to a moment of recognition for the individual. Despite the scepticism of much-travelled Julius Champney and his (sour) conviction of the fruitlessness of distant journeys,[4] such an epiphany is also granted to Maggie Kyle while she visits Ireland in the company of Wade Powers and Strabo Becker in order to execute Lily Hayworth's last will. When they are about to return the ashes of Donal Keneally to the spot where he was allegedly born, intense emotions are evoked in her when she finally reaches the top of the steep, windswept hill with its neolithic stone circle.

> It was too immense to be experienced alone, without crying, or mistaking the cold for fear. She called to the men.
>   The view from this edge was too wide to be taken in all at once, it was like seeing the whole world laid out and not knowing where to look. Ocean and mountains and

---

[3] See *Spit Delaney's Island* (1976; Toronto: Macmillan, 1978): 7, 18–19 & 23.

[4] Cf the sentiment expressed in the Julius section of *The Invention of the World* (1977; Toronto: Macmillan, 1978): 234.

valleys and church spires and roads and patchwork farms and animals and moving cars. To the right, to the north, hills like giant blue and purple domes pushed against each other, folded and fell, crowded across the top end of the valley. Down the valley, which was a long sharp gash slanting like a pried-open chute to the sea, the silver road ran loose and lazy, disappearing behind a clump of trees, swinging up around farms and their little white houses, twisting along the hedges, nipping past grey ruins of houses and one crumbling tower of a castle. Along the opposite slope, farms climbed up as high as they dared, laid their green and blue and yellow fields, framed by darker ruffled hedges, right up nearly vertical and then stopped so that the rest of the hill, a wide expanse, was only a dark green patchy dome freckled with sheep.[5]

Hodgins, who in one of his many interviews described his own artistic task as a "discovering [of] place and the meaning of place,"[6] employed the literary device of the "prospect" from the historic spot, reminiscent of a scheme used in eighteenth-century topographical, sublime and romantic poems, to inspire a moment of soul-searching and profound insight.[7] Allan Pritchard and other experts on the literature of the Canadian Pacific Rim have demonstrated that B.C. authors are not really conscious of "a struggle between man and nature," or of "characters as victims of their environment."[8] Consequently, Hodgins does not present the landscape as an antagonistic force, but allows the natural Old-World setting associated with the mythic origin of the dubious founder of the Revelations Colony of Truth to have a positive emotional influence on her. While excitedly trying to cling to one of the maps which receive considerable attention in the novel as tools to give pattern to seemingly unstructured phenomena, but whose straight lines are also shown to be incommensurate with the reality of the world, Maggie is made to realise on this elevation, from which she has an unobstructed

---

5 The relevant passage is preceded by the following paragraph: "But if there was magic here it wasn't in the stones, it was in the command they had of the earth, which fell away below them and ringed them round as far as she could see. *Dominion* was the word that nagged to be said. Dominion over the sun, even, whose fire had already sunk beneath the hills but whose rays like horizontal bands of light streaked out of cloud to cross the valley and find themselves absorbed in stone. Absorbed and then thrown out again, against themselves" (Jack Hodgins, *The Invention of the World*, section "Pilgrimage," 315).

6 See his interview with Geoff Hancock in *Canadian Fiction Magazine* 32–33 (1979–80): 33–63, especially 38.

7 A plausible theory which accounts for the psychological effects of panoramatic views in terms of a "landscape's hazard potential" and its reduction by its potential for prospects and refuge has been provided by Jay Appleton in *The Experience of Landscape* (Chichester: Wiley, 1975). Barbara Korte has applied this theory in her instructive essay "English–Canadian Perspectives of Landscape," *International Journal of Canadian Studies* 6 (Fall 1992), 9–24, which came to the attention of the author of this essay long after its completion.

8 See Hodgins himself in his interview with Geoff Hancock, 41–42, and Allan Pritchard, "West of the Great Divide: A View of the Literature of British Columbia," *Canadian Literature* 94 (Autumn 1982): 96–112, and "West of the Great Divide: Man & Nature in the Literature of British Columbia," *Canadian Literature* 102 (Autumn 1984): 36–53.

view,[9] that in her eagerness to rise from her lowly beginnings[10] she has overlooked what was nearest to her, the proximity of Wade Powers, her dedicated
though often perplexed friend and cousin.

This insight into her own shortcomings gained at the climax of her
"pilgrimage" on a steep Irish hill imbued with a sense of history shapes her future
behaviour, though this moment is immediately shattered by the intrusion of
vandals. Considering Hodgins's emphasis on the sense of community, it is no
coincidence that the salutary effect of this setting is not experienced in isolation
but, as it were, shared with those close to her, especially Wade, who gains an
insight into his fears about his "buried twin," as Frank Davey has put it.[11] This
moment of revelation determines Maggie's prompt reaction – after the additional
excitement of the journey and the breathtaking panorama of the island and the
Strait of Georgia from the small aeroplane – on her return home. Her decision on
her arrival to drive up the coast to seek her roots in the shack in Hed where she
spent her youth is part of the necessary preparation for the solution celebrated and
consummated in "Second Growth," the final section of the novel. It was initiated
by her experience on her European journey, which thus appears to function as a
catalyst for the (romance-like) *dénouement* in this chapter.

In Hodgins's later stories and novels this pattern recurs, and the light
cosmopolitan hue discernible in *The Invention of the World* is enhanced. Different
characters similarly react to impressions abroad, and there is more scope for the
potential impact of both rural and urban panoramas. It is obvious that Hodgins's
personal visits to and longer sojourns far from his native island – in Ottawa, Japan
and then in Europe, and finally in Australia – inspired his fictional treatment of the
confrontation of various members of the Barclay clan with remote places and the
formative experiences they gain from foreign settings and culture-specific life-styles
and art-forms.[12] The shift in emphasis from the vivid re-creation of regional
material, which Hodgins, of course, had always tried to transcend and which he had
sought to suffuse with universal implications, to a much wider dimension was no

---

9 Cf Appleton's plausible claim that the opportunity for prospect diminishes the environment
hazard, while the excess of prospect transforms it in a "landscape of exposure" and also of the
mixed feeling which characterizes the experience of the sublime.

10 Cf her yearning to rise "until she could see right into the centre of things" (*The Invention of the
World*, 13).

11 Frank Davey, "Disbelieving Story: A Reading of *The Invention of the World*," in *Present Tense.
The Canadian Novel*, vol. 4, ed. John Moss (Toronto: NC Press, 1985): 30–44.

12 See *The Barclay Family Theatre* (1981; Toronto: Macmillan, 1983): 181–261 (eg, Jacob Weins'
observations on the kabuki theatre and his insights into the dilemmas of ageing sumo wrestlers in
Japan and the inferences he draws for himself).

doubt also prompted by Hodgins's discovery and emulation of literary masters both Canadian and foreign, and his creative adoption of their cosmopolitan influence.[13]

In his early semi-autobiographical story "The Leper's Squint," his substitute Philip Desmond had still proudly maintained to the fellow writer and temptress Mary Brennan that although he was staying in Ireland (in Frank O'Connor's country, in fact) there was no need for him to use or borrow material from his host country: "I have my own place."[14] The difficulties resulting from his change of heart in this matter and from the inclusion of a much wider territory, one in which he is not yet as much at home as in his native world, are suggested by Hodgins's inability to complete a projected novel (with the working title "The Master of Happy Endings," or "Lost Villages") involving the Vancouver Island logger Topolski, whom romantic attachments take him to remote places such as Ottawa and New Orleans.[15] Some of Hodgins's problems also derive from his ambition to focus on very sophisticated characters and levels of experience, which seems to have tested his admirers. Together with the lessening of a specific element of his early fiction, the infusion of the marvellous in vividly visualised scenes, usually labeled "magic realism," this shift in interest and tone may account for the fact that Hodgins has not yet been able to repeat the successes of his first books.

It was in *The Honorary Patron*,[16] originally projected as a novella, that the author took even greater risks in choosing a retired professor of art history as the protagonist and in moving a considerable part of the action away from his home ground to Europe – in fact, opening and closing the novel in Zurich, but also including important scenes in Vienna (and offering allusions to and glimpses of other European cities, such as Copenhagen). The hero of this novel, which uses a circular structure and largely employs a figural narrative situation with long passages in quoted and narrated monologue, originally fled from Vancouver Island after a tragic and illicit love-affair in his youth. At the beginning of the novel – which in its structure combines an analytic impulse with the story of another temptation, a relationship with another passionate, young married woman, and the threat of disaster – ageing expatriate Jeffrey Crane is disconcerted by the suggestion that he should return to his home town as the "honorary patron" of a drama festival, the Pacific Coast Festival of the Arts.

---

13 One may recall his allusions to, and echoes of, Robertson Davies, or of "Faulknerian" writers from South America – who replaced his earlier models.

14 "The Lepers' Squint," in *The Barclay Family Theatre*, 160–80, especially 173.

15 An excerpt from this text was printed in *True North/Down Under: A Journal of Canadian and Australian Literature* 1 (Lantzville, B.C.: Eletheria, 1985): 34–53. On this abandoned text, see David Jeffrey, "Jack Hodgins (1938–)," in *Canadian Writers and Their Work*, vol. 10 (Toronto: ECW, 1989): esp. 226–27.

16 *The Honorary Patron* (1987; Toronto: McClelland & Stewart, 1989). Later references in the text under *HP* are to the paperback edition.

Crane, who has meanwhile achieved a placid if uneventful life-style, is correct in assuming that if he accepts the invitation after an absence of forty years he would have to face the realities which have gradually faded from his memory or have been suppressed. As in *The Invention*, a prospect scheme, in this case the panorama of the city of Vienna seen from the height of the Upper Belvedere Palace, serves partly as a catalyst, partly as a backdrop for some soul-searching on the part of the protagonist.

> A great profusion of trees had grown up since Bellotto had done his famous painting from this location, but the essential landmarks were still clearly visible: St. Stephen's tall black spire, the cupola of St. Charles. And monuments, it seemed, from edge to edge – [...] Here you were in the presence of History – and could believe that even the birds that came down to the garden pool had witnessed events you'd always half believed the writers of textbooks had invented. [...] Looking out across the rooftops of this imperial city in the direction of the pale-blue hills of the Vienna Woods, he discovered that he could remember almost nothing of the town to which she wanted him to return. A harbour town. Coal mines beneath the streets. (*HP* 52–54)

A much more sophisticated and articulate person than Maggie, Crane is in a position to analyse his own dilemma early on in the book. He is ready to confide hitherto concealed facts from his tragic past to his two European friends during one of their regular reunions in Vienna. Before he hazards the journey back to the harbour town, with the coal mines beneath its streets faded from his memory, he shows his awareness of the risks of an unavoidable exploration of his inner state of being back on his native island. Vienna seems the proper ambience for an analysis of the dreams which have again disturbed him since the invitation to return home. One of his two seemingly ironic (but in reality sympathetic) friends, Karl, a philanderer and man-of-letters (also taking his cue from one of the paintings by Egon Schiele which drew Jeffrey regularly to the gallery in the Belvedere palace) offers a semi-serious assessment of Jeffrey's projected return home as a "mythic journey, an old man in search of his dream children, deep into the caverns beneath the unfabled city at the edge of the Western world" (*HP* 66).

To a surprising extent this grandiloquent and slightly ironic comment is to prove true in Crane's case. The journey reluctantly undertaken turns out to be a kind of quest, though not of a novice but of an experienced traveller. It is true that the abrupt return to the initial setting in Zurich in the last chapter, together with the reunion with his friend Franz, makes the reader wonder whether Jeffrey ever undertook this odyssey or whether his journey to the chaotic world on the western fringe only took place in his imagination. The reactions of Franz, the addressee of several confessions and the silent participant in an imaginary conversation in the preceding sections of the book, as well as the reappearance of other – Canadian – figures such as Blackie would, however, suggest that the fathoming of the inner landscape and the past really occurred in the New World, and not in the cosiness of Jeffrey's retirement in Zurich.

On his home ground, Jeffrey's nightmares, which tormented him for many years after the suicide of Edward Argent, the betrayed husband of his love Elizabeth, recur, and his insomnia gets worse, but eventually he confronts the physical setting of the tragedy and sounds the depths of the inner conflict of his youth, before coming to terms with it in a sequence of ultimately cathartic scenes.

Brief allusions to Jeffrey's former marriages and memories of other disappointments and dashed aspirations account for his resignation. But it is on his native island that he is made to realise that he has not completely abandoned his yearning for totally absorbing experience and is eager for rejuvenation. He allows himself to be recruited by a young group of amateur actors for their "Shake-spearean Hash" and performs with them all over the island, thus neglecting some of his official duties and functions as honorary patron. Attracted and teased by the moody Nordic beauty Anna–Marie, whose fancy he seems to have taken as he did her mother's, he eventually gives up his passivity and reticence and engages in an attempt, doomed from the outset, to make up for time lost. It should be noted that Hodgins, in exploring Jeffrey's irrational drives in the past and the present yearnings of the ageing protagonist, fused the story of a reluctant confrontation with the burden of the past with a tale of passionate, if untimely desire, for which Thomas Mann's *Death in Venice* provided the acknowledged pattern.[17]

In his attempt to recover the passionate involvement of his youth, Jeffrey temporarily ignores the claims of the past, and does not spare the sensibilities of his former love Elizabeth Argent. But he is crudely reminded of this onus by Blackie Blackstone, the epitome of the earthy and somewhat freakish character from the western fringe of the continent. Blackie's annoyance at being unable to recruit and patronise the prominent expatriate prompts his blunt references to Jeffrey's earlier entanglements, to Edward Argent's fate and his, Blackie's, knowledge of the disastrous adulterous affair. Faced with Blackie's bullying, Jeffrey's imaginative reconstruction of past events, and even of the feelings of his former rival prior to his suicide, is triggered off while he and Blackie are paddling their canoe past drowned cedars and the skeletons of other dead trees:

> Soon they'd begun to thread themselves through the stand of drowned cedars. All around, thick trunks soared up, skinned naked of bark and weather-flailed of softwood to pale-grey standing pillars of ribs – they might be bone, with their twisted and blunted branches a tangled skeletal canopy beneath the sky. Had Edward Argent passed by here, along that shoreline, on the last day of his life – his crammed head clanging with the impossibility of going on with his existence? With the urgency of

---

17 Cf the hint offered by Joann McCaig, "Lines and Circles: Structure in *The Honorary Patron*," *Canadian Literature* 128 (Spring 1991): 65–73.

finding that hidden spot where he could put an end to it, to everything – the humiliation, the self-pity, the blinding rage? Call it what it was: the broken heart.
It must not be thought of. Not in this shadowy cold. There was nothing he could do for Edward Argent now, beyond experiencing this profound thumping gob of regret, of too-late sympathy, which he had been careful all these years to avoid. (*HP* 152)

In tune with the psychological realism which the author has adopted and cultivated, the archaic landscape of the lake thus functions at times as a kind of objective correlative of states of mind, at others even evoking and amplifying the mood of the protagonists.

Later on, Hodgins sets the stage for Jeffrey's dangerous confrontation with the deeply frustrated Blackie in front of Jeffrey's own childhood shack, which is now doomed to destruction from two quarters, from Blackie's bulldozer and from subsidence into the mine-shafts below. This encounter with the choleric Blackie forces Jeffrey Crane to face those concrete, dangerous galleries, corridors and caverns which, in Blackie's malicious allusion, are linked with the distant place of Edward Argent's suicide. They also symbolically represent the hidden desires and irresponsible drives in Jeffrey's soul, which he has tried to forget. With another author the intensity of emotion felt by the antagonists – rage on the part of Blackie and sadness overwhelming Jeffrey – might have led to a violent end, but Jack Hodgins's own outlook and deeply ingrained optimism prompted an affirmative ending to this culminating episode. Not only Jeffrey's long residence in Europe, through which he seems to have (partly) atoned for the guilt of his youth, but especially the more recent painful disappointment with Anna–Marie which terminated his emotional paralysis but failed to provide a positive (re)-solution to the deficiencies of his emotional life, enable him to cope with the disclosure and full recognition of the destructive forces. These facts reflect Hodgins's willingness to depart from the literary pattern which he had in mind when he first worked on the novel, Thomas Mann's rendition of the tragic obsession of Gustav von Aschenbach (with youthful beauty) in *Death in Venice*.[18]

As if to elaborate on the symbolic significance of the system of caverns and shafts underneath Jeffrey's native town, Hodgins allows a subsidiary character to describe a painting by a promising young local artist, which seems to encapsulate the human dilemma in general and Jeffrey's in particular. A young parachutist, "an angel 'vo[m] himmel'," offers his puzzled comment on the painting of a "naked family, [H]uddled together in the dark like they're waiting for someone to let them out" (*HP* 392). The local painting has an obvious iconographic link with the aforementioned canvas by Schiele in the Upper Beleveder entitled *Die Familie*, and thus underlines its application to his case.

---

18 Cf the subdued allusions to Gustav von Aschenbach (*HP* 22) and the ironic phrase "Death in Zürich was a matter of global envy" (*HP* 17).

> A uniformed guard had the Egon Schieles to himself. [...] no one at all had gathered to admire *Die Familie*, though it deserved, in Crane's opinion, the constant admiring attention of busloads. [...] Here, despite the tension that existed within the work, the mottled yellow and orange flesh of its three interlocking figures – separated by the bold outlining from the blurred confusion of dark blankets and darker wall behind them – achieved a sense of the collective life that was being celebrated. (*HP* 54–55)

It is appropriate to mention the fact that for the hardcover edition Hodgins used a reproduction of Schiele's painting, thus emphasising the centrality of this motif through paratextual means.[19] The connection to Jeffrey's fate had already been anticipated by his friend Karl, but the parachutist's remark goes further than the earlier assessment in disclosing the unfulfilled dream of the childless protagonist and its association with the concrete uncanny landscape in which the libidinal desires usually expressed through such imagery foundered.[20]

The young parachutist talking about the paintings of the local artist also vaguely suggests an antidote to the anxiety modern man is heir to, and the trajectory of Jeffrey's private journey suggests that some reconciliation is possible. Though the ghosts from Jeffrey's past are eventually laid to rest, the novel, which contains an ironic, metafictional reference to man's "persistent hope for the occasional happy ending" (*HP* 399), does not literally and ultimately satisfy this wish, yet leaves such possibilities open.

In his more recent novel, *Innocent Cities*,[21] Hodgins again employs Vancouver Island as the more important of two major settings, though this time he has chosen not the region round or north of Nanaimo, but the capital of the province. In this historical novel set largely in B.C. in the 1880s, Hodgins again introduces characters who are widely travelled, and depicts their experiences in landscapes which reveal deeper unacknowledged urges in them and a threatening reality. In this instance, the key episodes involve the female protagonist of the book, an initially mysterious Australian widow, Kate Jordan–McConnell, originally from the vicinity of Manchester. Her reactions to sense-impressions on two continents are presented twice, revealing a great deal about her inner life and the workings of her soul. Although there are other figures in the book who are well-travelled and experienced, like Lady Riven–Blythe, the absence of a deeper dimension in this supercilious

---

19 The paperback edition, however, has a different, inconspicuous cover, depicting a visitor with a suitcase, ostensibly in a gallery looking at a landscape painting showing a fjord.

20 I do not want to go as far as Leonard Lutwack, who, in his relatively recent study of *The Role of Place in Literature* (Syracuse NY: Syracuse UP, 1984), has proposed psychoanalytic readings of all kinds of landscape presented in literature.

21 Jack Hodgins, *Innocent Cities* (1990; Toronto: McClelland & Stewart, 1991). References in the text under *IC* are to the paperback edition.

aristocratic gossip, who constantly compares provincial matters with conditions at
the centre of the Empire, precludes any insight, as she is not confronted with any
landscape beyond the severely restricted social sphere in which she moves. The
scenes just mentioned involving Kate were also central episodes in the genesis of
the book, which has its imaginative roots in Hodgins's first sojourn in Australia and
his discovery of historical material linking B.C. with that continent.[22]

In spite of some anachronistic details concerning audacious experiments with
an airborne contraption designed by a native Canadian, the novel is set apart from
Hodgins's other recent fiction by its relatively close adherence to historical facts.
While the book includes a revalued, distinct ethnic voice in the talented and
rebellious Zachary Jack, who is Logan's foster-brother, and generally shows an
awareness of the problematics of the codes of language and communication, self-
consciously referring to conventions operating in verbal constructs, Hodgins is
again primarily concerned with the "comedy and tragedy of human life," and the
mysteries of human beings.

Thus the novel offers (primarily) a fictionalised account of the exposure of a
notorious case of bigamy in nineteenth-century Victoria, B.C., by a lady from
Ballarat in Victoria, Australia, and her struggle to get her rights. Though *Innocent
Cities* employs a more traditional narrative technique than *The Invention of the
World*, lacking the latter's polyphonic range of voices and the dedication of an
authorial substitute like Strabo Becker to an archaeological reconstruction of the
past, the later novel takes the reader relatively close to the minds of several
characters: passages of direct first-person narration, and of quoted and narrated
monologue are interspersed in the narrative, which predominantly blends authorial
and figural narration.

After some delay, which builds up suspense, the quality of the complex
experience of the visitor from the antipodes is conveyed to the reader. Kate's single-
minded attempt to win back her lawful mate, James Horncastle, does not at first
undermine the charm she radiates, though the ingenuity and persistence with which
she pursues her goal puzzle not only melancholy Logan Sumner, who enjoys the
second focus of interest. The various weaknesses, excessive Old-World reticence
and ill-fortune in love of this "rather ineffectual romantic"[23] evoke a mixture of
sympathy and pity in the reader and are the source of some humour. The young
widowed architect and builder, a "furnisher of fake façades," in colonial Victoria,

---

22 See Hodgins's own statement in the interview with Alan Lawson and Stephen Slemon: "Out
on the Verandah: A Conversation with Jack Hodgins," *Australian–Canadian Studies* 5.1 (1987): esp.
41–42. The author has spoken about archival material he found in Victoria and in Ballarat which
provided the subject matter for the main strand of action in the book. See the conversation with the
author of this essay in September 1991 and a personal letter dated February 3, 1992.

23 See Hodgins's assessment of this figure in letter of February 3, 1992.

entrusts his moods and later his visions and utopian dreams to the stone-cutter, who has to chisel them on the tombstone of Logan's deceased wife. This yields an opportunity for some metafictional discourse (without transforming the novel as a whole into an example of "historical metafiction"). It is no coincidence that this character, who lacks wider experience abroad and whose initial naiveté manifests itself in his early ritual of climbing a Garry oak and welcoming the sunrise (*IC* 89–90), is not granted major revelation in the landscape. His later despair at rejection by Adeline Horncastle, however, marks his initiation and shatters his Victorian reserve, and his hallucinatory communion with his dead mother near the site of the cottage of his childhood is already a sign of a beginning development (*IC* 185–86). It is not surprising that the participants in the experiments with the flying machine, the métis Zachary Jack and his associates including a Chinese cook and opium smuggler, who use the slope of the present Beacon Park in Victoria for their venture, are not particularly keen on, and responsive to, the spectacular panorama of the Strait and the Olympic mountains beyond.

But let me return to Kate. It is slightly disconcerting for the reader to discover signs of intense irritation and unjustified harshness in the experienced widow, who at first seemed to belong to the lineage of attractive heroines in Hodgins's fiction. Later, one also notes that her behaviour is marked by insincerity, frustration and eventually neurotic tension, for which the episodes recounted earlier have not sufficiently prepared the reader. One is intrigued by the description of her outbursts in Ballarat and her shooting at the cockatoos (*IC* 53–54, 83–84), while one's attention is taken up more by the graphic delineation of this colorful multicultural Australian mining town, prominent during the nineteenth century, and for which Hodgins draws on an exhaustive modern study.[24] Her increasingly pathological state of mind, which finds expression in her violent temper and in various quarrels with James Horncastle on account of his reckless gambling and spendthrift habits, and which results in her destruction of pottery and finally her setting fire to the furniture in his Great Blue Heron Hotel, forces the reader to revise his opinion of her. This fact is, of course, in keeping with Hodgins's own description of the novel as a story about the revising of stories.[25] This need is indirectly suggested earlier in Kate's slightly paranoiac response to the lush vegetation on her brother-in-law's estate near Brisbane. The young woman is both attracted and repelled by the exotic opulence of the Queensland jungle flora and the sensuous quality of the environment, as well as by Paul Longspur's male

---

24 It is interesting to observe how closely Hodgins has followed the full historical document-ation offered in Weston Arthur Bate, *Lucky City: The First Generation at Ballarat, 1851–1901* (Carleton South, Victoria: Melbourne UP, 1978).

25 See Hodgins's interview with Lawson and Slemon, 41–42, also the interview with Jeanne Delbaere in *Kunapipi* 9.2 (1987): 84–89.

delight in domination by naming every plant and confusing her by his sensual relish in pronouncing a profusion of names.[26]

She seemingly regards this as a "male plot," a kind of attempt at hypnosis through endless naming, and a threat to her liberty and sense of identity. This anxiety, which she shares with the author, who has attributed to the heroine some of his own Australian experiences, ambivalent feelings about phenomena in tropical rainforests and metalinguistic worries in botanical gardens,[27] is made worse by her fears for her children playing in the tall jungle trees, especially a huge giant strangler vine, which had choked the original trees.

> [...] the trunk of the most peculiar tree she had ever seen, even in this continent of eccentric vegetation.
>
> Though it was perhaps six feet across at its base, it seemed not to have what was normally thought of as a trunk, but to have been woven and knotted out of a variety of twisting smaller trunks. A great soaring braided tube, a long, long tower that sprouted both leaves and children from all its orifices. The children had climbed up inside where it was hollow, Paul showed her – a round ventilated spire, a soaring turret. "There was a tree here once. But what we are looking at is really just a giant vine that strangled the life out of the tree long ago." What he called a vine was sometimes as thick as her arm, she saw, or even thicker, and sometimes a snarl of little snakes. "The tree itself has long since rotted away in the steamy heat."
>
> Paul's hand at the small of her back urged her closer, to enter through a large opening in the base. This meant approaching the tree between two of the flying buttresses it had thrown out – a foundation of narrow upright grey blades that swept out from as high as her waist to go knifing down into the soil amongst the less spectacular trees. She shrank from brushing against these, which might have been made from the hip-bones of giants, the shoulder-blades of mammoths, upholstered with tough stretched hides peeled from a herd of strangled elephants who had somehow wandered onto the wrong continent and been ingested into this monster's twisted internal ducts.
>
> But when she looked up – a dark, round, soaring tunnel populated by the headless bodies of all their children, her own children and her sister's children, all those children to whom she was expected to devote her life – her knees weakened, and she found it necessary to throw out a hand and hold onto some part of that twisting vine. Paul's hand moved along her waist, so that his arm could support her. (*IC* 74)

It is relevant to note that Kate experiences a sense of alienation while surrounded by huge objects in a seemingly suffocating landscape, in which she is placed without

---

[26] See also: "At mealtimes, Lilian's husband continued to plant his forest of names around her. He taught them all how the tree-fern grows, building a trunk out of its own dead fronds. He spoke as though to the children [...] 'The grass-tree we call 'black boy' thrusts a spear up higher than this ceiling.' He demonstrated the force of the black boy's thrust with his fork, and smiled into her eyes, so that she felt the thrust somewhere inside. [...] Though she continued to resist the children's attempt to lure her out into the forest world, Paul Longspur was determined that she not get away with this for long" (*IC* 72–73).

[27] See letter dated February 3, 1992.

being able to survey the region from above (as Maggie had).[28] Her first directly
narrated speculation relates this uncanny experience so explicitly to male
preferences and habit (for instance, the urge to give everything a name) that there is
no need for psychoanalytic training to connect this alleged practice to the phallic
objects surrounding her in the jungle. This experienced link between the tropical
botanical fertility and the pull of human sexuality is also suggested in Paul's
suspicious interest in her (*IC* 72–74, 76), and prompts her hasty return to Ballarat.

But it is in the proximity of the Canadian city of Victoria that the inner landscape of Kate's anxieties and desires is made even more palpable, in one of the
many episodes for which there are parallels between Australia and B.C. It occurs
after the failure of her private ambitions, after the destruction of her high hopes and
the gradual erosion of the initially harmonious relationship with James Horncastle.
This happens despite her (unsuccessful) attempt to include her younger sister Annie,
a protofeminist and later partner to a willing Logan Sumner, in their ménage.

Wandering away from her group near Lizzie Sheepshank's farm on the day of
the fateful races arranged on the occasion of the royal visit, and anxiously looking
for her children in the Vancouverian rainforest, she again encounters "Old
Stonybrow," one of her rejected suitors. Mr Hawks's shack in a huge hollow tree
now becomes a focus for her fears and desires:

> "You have them up in your – "
> Braided tower.
> "Them brats? No thank you." He did not step aside, but seemed to let all his
> weight hang from his hands while he leaned towards her.
> "Then, do you know where they might – ?"
> No! We shan't fall. Uncle Paul, do take her away!
> "You come to offer me a drink? It's about time we had a little talk."
> The owl again: Hoo–hoo! Hoo–hoo!
> "Mr. Hawks, we have already had all the conversation you and I were meant to
> have. Please, step aside and let me join the others." Her hands were wet, and cold.
> Rain had run up her wrist to dampen her sleeve. Would it be enough to raise the
> umbrella against him, if she should need to protect herself?
> "We could go up." This was said with a crooked smile. "Them rungs'll hold a
> lady, easy enough." He added, with a grin, "I know that for a fact." (*IC* 350–51)

It is not coincidental that the memory of the Queensland experience pervades and
punctuates her thoughts, while she seems both to resist and to surrender gradually
to the influence of this most persistent male admirer. There are distinct parallels
between the scenes, though the hysterical tone in Kate's articulated or silent
communication with Mr Hawks suggests a loss of self-discipline, a decline in

---

28 On the psychological effects of a limitation of the potential for prospect, which according to
Jay Appleton increases the landscape's hazard potential cf Barbara Korte's illustration of the forest
experience of claustrophobia in nineteenth-century English–Canadian texts, especially Korte,
"English–Canadian Perspectives of Landscape," 12–13.

Kate's self-control, which have in the meantime also become apparent in her frequent use of laudanum to control her headaches. It is difficult for the reader to decide whether the words related are truly spoken or only thought.

> "Come! Up you go! The ladder!"
>
> "Step out of my way, sir! I shall scream!"
>
> *You cried out. I shall stay until I am content that you are safely asleep again.*
>
> "One rung at a time. You've been prancin' and side-steppin' and sashayin' your way towards my little shack for a year now or more. Anybody can see you made a bad choice. It's time you finished the journey. Up! Your skirts will be no hindrance once you've started. Let me help you place your foot on the bottom rung."
>
> He would try to *talk* her up, as though the sounds and shapes of his words could serve as stairs to put your feet upon. One more man had built a universe out of words. His charred hollow tower was not wrapped in salvaged brand names like the Indian's barn, or inscribed with accounts of a fictitious career like Logan Sumner's tomb, or held upright like the Blue Heron by the sound of barroom tales, but the idea was much the same. When in her life had she bid farewell to the world of things and entered a world created out of nothing more than sounds and printed shapes? Was it something that happened, she wondered, to everyone?
>
> One hand had reached as though to take an arm but she pulled back and began to protest. She would not go up! But she was, she found, no longer able to speak. Everything had tightened in her throat, there might have been hands around her neck, choking off the words at their source. Choking off her breathing as well. She would be strangled here without this fellow even touching her! (*IC* 352)

Outer and inner reality seem to merge and their borderlines seem to become blurred. Kate is rescued from this temptation, in which the inner landscape is laid bare, by the voices of her friends. But the ensuing riding accident which befalls James Horncastle burdens her with the duty of caring for the paralysed invalid and with the nightmarish task of sharing this care with her hated elder sister and her most ardent and relentless male persecutor.

Unlike Maggie in *The Invention* and Jeffrey Crane in *The Honorary Patron*, Kate, this much-travelled heroine, whose inner landscape has been explored and revealed, seems not to have undergone a cathartic experience. Eventually she fades from our view, first as a part of a grim constellation of figures involved in a speechless confrontation with rivals and enemies, her existence meaning hardly much more than mere survival, and later after Horncastle's burial regularly frequenting a coffee house, and involved in a "ritual of silence" (*IC* 389–91).

Such a (re)solution is not fully balanced by the happiness in store for Logan Sumner and Anne McConnell, the youngest of the Manchester clan who makes good in the colonies. Such an ending is apparently an exception in Hodgins's fictional work, which has often employed significant moments of experience on vantage points in landscapes as high-points in the lives of his characters. These scenes are components of the psychological realism used to convey a fundamentally optimistic view of man's role and position. Such epiphanies, often in foreign settings, have so far usually been related to and have borne fruit in the perceptions and actions of figures in Hodgins's "local backyard."[29] It will be interesting to see how the author will render his own experience of a more remote and harsher setting than his own familiar Vancouver Island. His response to the Australian outback on a more recent second journey (in 1991) is contained in a forthcoming travel book by him punningly entitled "Over Forty at Broken Hill."

WORKS CITED

APPLETON, Jay H. *The Experience of Landscape* (Chichester: Wiley, 1975).

BATE, Weston Arthur. *Lucky City: The First Generation at Ballarat, 1851–1901* (Carleton South, Victoria: Melbourne UP, 1978).

MCCAIG, Joann. "Lines and Circles: Structure in *The Honorary Patron*," *Canadian Literature* 128 (Spring 1991): 65–73.

DAVEY, Frank. "Disbelieving Story: A Reading of *The Invention of the World*," in *Present Tense: The Canadian Novel*, vol. 4, ed. John Moss (Toronto: NC Press, 1985): 30–44.

HODGINS, Jack. *The Barclay Family Theatre* (1981; Toronto: Macmillan, 1983).

————. *The Honorary Patron* (1987; Toronto: McClelland & Stewart, 1989).

————. *Innocent Cities* (1990; Toronto: McClelland & Stewart, 1991).

————. *The Invention of the World* (1977; Toronto: McClelland & Stewart, 1978).

————. *Spit Delaney's Island* (1976; Toronto: Macmillan, 1978).

JEFFREY, David. "Jack Hodgins (1938–)," in *Canadian Writers and Their Work*, vol. 10 (Toronto: ECW, 1989): 187–239.

KEITH, Bill. *A Sense of Style: Studies in the Art of Fiction in English-Speaking Canada* (Toronto: ECW, 1989).

KULYK KEEFER, Janice. "From Mosaic to Kaleidoscope: Out of the multicultural past comes a vision of a transcultural future," *Books in Canada* 20.6 (1991): 13–16.

LAWSON, Alan, & Stephen SLEMON. "Out on the Verandah: A Conversation with Jack Hodgins," *Australian–Canadian Studies* 5.1 (1987): 31–47.

LUTWACK, Leonard. *The Role of Place in Literature* (Syracuse NY: Syracuse UP, 1984).

PRITCHARD, Alan. "West of the Great Divide: A View of the Literature of British Columbia," *Canadian Literature* 94 (Autumn 1982): 96–112.

————."West of the Great Divide: Man & Nature in the Literature of British Columbia," *Canadian Literature* 102 (Autumn 1984): 36–53.

~ ❀ ~

---

29 See Bill Keith's review of Hodgins's second novel in *Canadian Forum* (September–October 1981): 30, and his appreciation of Hodgins's art in *A Sense of Style: Studies in the Art of Fiction in English-Speaking Canada* (Toronto: ECW, 1989): 195–213.

LIST OF CONTRIBUTORS

RICHARD COLLINS is Head of the Department of Communications and Music Technology at London Guildhall University. His research interests centre on the role of the communications media (broadcasting in particular) in making and breaking collective identities. His work on these questions has been published in academic journals in Canada, Germany and the United Kingdom. He is the author of *Culture Communications and National Identity: The Case of Canadian Television* (1990) and *Broadcasting and Audio-Visual Policy in the European Single Market* (1994). He is a member of the British Association for Canadian Studies and of the Editorial Advisory Committee of the *Canadian Journal of Communication*.

FRANK DAVEY, Carl F. Klinck Professor of Canadian Literature at the University of Western Ontario, is a well-known editor, poet and literary critic. He was a founding editor in 1962 of the controversial literary magazine *Tish*. He currently edits the journal *Open Letter*. Among his critical works are *Surviving the Paraphrase* (1983), *Reading Canadian Reading* (1988), *Post-National Arguments: The Politics of the Anglophone Canadian Novel Since 1967* (1993), and *Canadian Literary Power* (1994).

PETER EASINGWOOD lectures in English and American Studies at the University of Dundee, and is a founder-member of the Literature Group in the British Association for Canadian Studies. He is co-editor of *Probing Canadian Culture* (1991) with Konrad Groß and Wolfgang Klooss.

KONRAD GROSS, a founding member of the Gesellschaft für Kanada-Studien, lectures in American and Canadian Studies at the University of Kiel. He has written on Victorian fiction, British drama, native and Afro-American literature. His Canadianist publications range from Western Canadian fiction, early travel reports, Margaret Laurence, E.J. Pratt, ethnicity and literature, to the development of Canadian Studies in Germany, Canadian Identity, David French, and popular fiction.

CORAL ANN HOWELLS, former President of the British Association for Canadian Studies (1992–94), is Reader in Canadian Literature at the University of Reading. Her books include *Private and Fictional Words: Canadian Women Novelists of the 1970s and 1980s* (1987) and *Jean Rhys* (1991). She is co-editor with Lynette Hunter of *Narrative Strategies in Canadian Literature: Feminism and Postcolonialism* (1991). Her critical study *Margaret Atwood* (1996) has just been published, and she is also working on a book on Alice Munro.

LYNETTE HUNTER is a Senior Lecturer in the School of English, University of Leeds, where she teaches Canadian Literature and Publishing History, and researches on post-medieval rhetoric. She has written extensively on Canadian cultural topics and is the author of *Outsider Notes*, a monograph on Canadian literary issues.

DAVID HUTCHISON is Senior Lecturer in Communication Studies at Glasgow Caledonian University. His published work has been in the areas of media policy, the media and national identity and the Scottish theatre.

WOLFGANG KLOOSS is a professor of English and director of the interdisciplinary Centre for Canadian Studies at the University of Trier, having previously taught at the University of Kiel and the University of Marburg. With Konrad Gross he has co-edited *English Literature of the Dominions. Writings on Australia, Canada and New Zealand* (1981) and *Voices from Distant Lands. Poetry in the Commonwealth* (1983). Since 1980 his research interests have focused on Canadian studies, as reflected in his post-doctoral dissertation, *Geschichte und Mythos in der Literatur Kanadas: Die englischsprachige Métis- und Riel-Rezeption* (History and Myth in Canadian Literature: Métis and Riel as Reflected in Literature in English; 1989). Further publications include a special Canadian issue of the German–English yearbook *Gulliver* (co-edited with Hartmut Lutz; 1986), *Probing Canadian Culture* (co-edited with Peter Easingwood and Konrad Gross; 1991), and *Kanada: Eine interdisziplinäre Einführung* (Canada: An Interdisciplinary Introduction; co-edited with Hans Braun; 1992). Wolfgang Klooss is also co-editor of the series *Grundlagen der Anglistik und Amerikanistik*.

BARBARA KORTE is a professor of English Literature at the Technical University of Chemnitz–Zwickau. Her recent publications include *Körpersprache in der Literatur: Theorie und Geschichte am Beispiel des englischsprachigen Romans* (Theory and History of Body-Language: The English Novel; 1993), "English–Canadian Perspectives of Landscape," *International Journal of Canadian Studies*, (1992), and "In Quest of an Arctic Past: Mordecai Richler's *Solomon Gursky Was Here*," in *Historiographical Metafiction in Modern American and Canadian Literature*, ed. Bernd Engler & Kurt Müller.

MARTIN KUESTER studied English and French at the Universities of Aachen, British Columbia, Trier and Manitoba. He teaches in the Department of English and the Institute for Canadian Studies at the University of Augsburg. He has published numerous articles and a book (*Framing Truths: Parodic Structures in Contemporary English–Canadian Historical Novels*) on Canadian Literature, and is the editor of the introductory reader *Canadian Studies: A Literary Approach* (1995).

JANICE KULYK KEEFER was born in Toronto to a Ukrainian–Polish family, and was educated at the Universities of Toronto and Sussex. Her published works include a volume of poetry *White of the Lesser Angels*, three books of short fiction, *The Paris–Napoli Express*, *Transfigurations* and *Travelling Ladies*, two novels, *Constellations* and *Rest Harrow*, and critical studies of Canadian literature, *Under Eastern Eyes: A Critical Reading of Maritime Fiction* and *Reading Mavis Gallant*. She has won numerous prizes for her writing, including the CBC Radio Literary Competition and the National Magazine Award, and has lectured on Canadian writing and read from her own work across Canada and Europe. She is currently Professor of English at the University of Guelph, Ontario, where she teaches transcultural Canadian literature and creative writing.

JILL LeBIHAN lectures in English Studies and Women's Studies at Sheffield Hallam University. She is a graduate of the University of Leeds, although she did doctoral research at the University of Alberta, researching contemporary Canadian women writers. She has written articles on Margaret Atwood, Daphne Marlatt, the position of women in the literary-theory classroom, travel literature and women primatologists. She is co-author, with Keith Green, of *Critical Theory and Practice* (forthcoming). Her current projects include a critical edition of Anna Jameson's *Winter Studies and Summer Rambles in Canada*.

LEON LITVACK lectures in Canadian studies and nineteenth-century literature at the School of English, Queen's University, Belfast. Born and raised in Toronto, he is a graduate of the University of Edinburgh. He has worked and published extensively on ethnicity and multi-culturalism in Canada, in both literary and sociological contexts. From 1987 to 1990 he was Visiting Professor at Kwansei Gakuin University in Nishinomiya, Japan, where he coordinated Canadian studies for Western Japan. Currently he is a member of the British Association for Canadian Studies Council, and edits the Association's newsletter; he is also Vice-Director of the Centre for Canadian Studies at Queen's University. His publications on multiculturalism and post-colonialism include the section on Canadian literature for the *Handbook of English Post-Coloniality* (forthcoming) and a chapter on multicultural methodology in *Global Cultures, Local Classrooms: Theoretical Essays on Teaching Nonwestern and Postcolonial Literatures*. He is the author of *John Mason Neale and the Quest for Sobornost* and the forthcoming *Dombey and Son: An Annotated Bibliography*.

IAN LOCKERBIE is Professor and Head of Department in Educational Policy and Development at Stirling University. He also works in the areas of Québec Studies and film studies.

HARTMUT LUTZ, born in Rendsburg, Schleswig–Holstein, has taught at the University of Cologne, the University of California at Davis, Deganawidah–Quetzalcoatl University, the Saskatchewan Indian Federated College (University of Regina) and the University of Osnabrück. He holds the chair in North American Literature and Cultures at the Ernst-Moritz-Arndt Universität, Greifswald. Among his publications are *"Indianer" und "Native Americans"* (1985), *Minority Literatures in North America* (together with Wolfgang Karrer; 1990), and *Contemporary Challenges* (1991). Since 1989 he has been the founding editor of the *OBEMA* series, publishing bilingual editions of Minority Authors.

NORBERT PLATZ is a professor of English Literature at the University of Trier. He previously worked in the English Department of Mannheim University. His main teaching and research interests are the drama of the English Renaissance, the literature and culture of the Victorian period, modern drama, and the New Literatures in English (with a focus on Australia and New Zealand). Subsidiary interests include the teaching of literature and creative writing. His main publications are *Ethik und Rhetorik in Ben Jonsons Dramen* (Ethics and Rhetoric in the Plays of Ben Jonson; 1976) and *Die Beeinflussung des Lesers: Untersuchungen zum pragmatischen Wirkungspotential viktorianischer Romane zwischen 1844 und 1872* (Influencing the Reader: Pragmatic Potential in Victorian Novels 1844–1872; 1986); he is also the editor of the essay-collection *Mediating Cultures: Probleme des Kulturtransfers* (Problems of Cultural Transfer; 1991–92).

SUSAN SPEAREY is currently completing a doctorate at the University of Leeds, on postcolonial migrant writing (including V.S. Naipaul, Bharati Mukherjee, Michael Ondaatje and Salman Rushdie).

FRANZ K. STANZEL, Professor Emeritus from the University of Graz, is best known for his contributions to literary theory *Die typischen Erzählsituationen im Roman* (1955; tr. *Narrative Situations in the Novel* 1971) and *Theorie des Erzählens* (1979; tr. *A Theory of Narrative,* 1984). A former Vice-President of the Gesellschaft für Kanada-Studien, he is the co-editor of *Encounters and Explorations. Canadian Writers and Euopean Critics* (with Waldemar Zacharasiewicz; 1986).

KIT STEAD completed her doctoral thesis on contemporary women's writing at the University of Reading. She is a sub-editor with the *Observer* newspaper.

MARION WYNNE–DAVIES is a lecturer in English Literature at the University of Keele, England, where she teaches medieval, Renaissance and Canadian literature. She has published several books, including *The Bloomsbury Guide to English Literature* and *Gloriana's Face: Women, Public and Private, in the English Renaissance.*

WALDEMAR ZACHARASIEWICZ has been professor of English and American Studies at the University of Vienna since 1974. He has been a Visiting Scholar at the Universities of Oxford and Birmingham (England), Charlottesville (Virginia), Duke (Chapel Hill), and Stanford. His interest in Southern literature is mirrored in *Die Erzählkunst des amerikanischen Südens* (Narrative of the American South; 1990) and in his editorship of *Faulkner, His Contemporaries, and His Posterity* (1993). He has also been the recipient of several grants in the field of Canadian Studies and is co-editor of *Encounters and Explorations: Canadian Writers and European Critics* (1986). He has published on the literature of the Canadian regions, Canadian short fiction, Jack Hodgins, Henry Kreisel, and auto- and heterostereotypes in Canadian texts.

◦❀◦

Cross Cultures
Readings in the Post/Colonial
Literatures in English
Series Editors:
Gordon Collier, Hena Maes-Jelinek, Geoffrey Davis

Vol. 1: ISBN: 90-5183-135-8   Bound Hfl. 150.-/US-$ 100.-
CRISIS AND CREATIVITY IN THE NEW LITERATURES IN ENGLISH. Ed. by Geoffrey Davis and Hena Maes-Jelinek. Amsterdam/Atlanta, GA 1989. 541 pp.
Vol. 2: ISBN: 90-5183-136-6   Hfl. 70.-/US-$ 46.50
CRISIS AND CREATIVITY IN THE NEW LITERATURES IN ENGLISH: CANADA. Ed. by Geoffrey Davis. Amsterdam/Atlanta, GA 1990. 253 pp.
Vol. 3: ISBN: 90-5183-196-X   Hfl. 50.-/US-$ 33.-
ALBERT GÉRARD: Contexts of African Literature. Amsterdam/Atlanta, GA 1990. 169 pp.
Vol. 4: ISBN: 90-5183-197-8   Hfl. 70.-/US-$ 46.50
CHANTAL ZABUS: The African Palimpsest: Indigenization of Language in the West African Europhone Novel. Amsterdam/Atlanta, GA 1991. 224 pp.
Vol. 5: ISBN: 90-5183-393-8   Bound Hfl. 150,-/US-$ 100.-
GORDON COLLIER: The Rocks and Sticks of Words. Style, Discourse and Narrative Structure in the Fiction of Patrick White. Amsterdam/Atlanta, GA 1992. xi,499 pp.
Vol. 6: ISBN: 90-5183-394-6   Bound Hfl. 125,-/US-$ 83.-
US / THEM. Translation, Transcription and Identity in Post-Colonial Literary Cultures. Ed. by Gordon Collier. Amsterdam/Atlanta, GA 1992. ix,416 pp.
Vol. 7: ISBN: 90-5183-395-4   Hfl. 60.-/US-$ 403-
RE-SITING QUEEN'S ENGLISH. TEXT AND TRADITION IN POST-COLONIAL LITERATURES. Essays Presented to John Pengwerne Matthews. Ed. by Gillian Whitlock and Helen Tiffin. Amsterdam/Atlanta, GA 1992. vii,203pp.
Vol. 8: ISBN: 90-5183-404-7   Hfl. 55.-/US-$ 36.50
THE POLITICS OF ART: ELI MANDEL'S POETRY AND CRITICISM. Ed. by Ed Jewinski and Andrew Stubbs. Amsterdam/Atlanta, GA 1992. xviii,156 pp.
Vol. 9: ISBN: 90-5183-310-5   Hfl. 90,-/US-$ 60.-
IMAGINATION AND THE CREATIVE IMPULSE IN THE NEW LITERATURES IN ENGLISH. Ed. by M.-T. Bindella and G.V. Davis. Amsterdam/Atlanta, GA 1993. 297 pp.
Vol. 10: ISBN: 90-5183-549-3   Hfl. 75,-/US-$ 50.-
CHRISTIAN HABEKOST: Verbal Riddim. The Politics and Aesthetics of African-Caribbean Dub Poetry. Amsterdam/Atlanta, GA 1993. 262 pp.
Vol. 11: ISBN: 90-5183-559-0   Hfl. 60,-/US-$ 40.-
MAJOR MINORITIES. ENGLISH LITERATURES IN TRANSIT Ed.by Raoul Granqvist.Amsterdam/Atlanta, GA 1993. 198 pp.
Vol. 12: ISBN: 90-5183-648-1   Hfl. 60,-/US-$ 40.-
"RETURNS" IN POST-COLONIAL WRITING. A Cultural Labyrinth. Ed. by Vera Mihailovich-Dickman. Amsterdam/Atlanta, GA 1994. XV,173 pp.
Vol. 13: ISBN: 90-5183-743-7   Hfl. 60,-/US-$ 40.-
HILDEGARD KUESTER: The Crafting of Chaos. Narrative Structure in Margaret

Laurence's *The Stone Angel* and *The Diviners*. Amsterdam/Atlanta, GA 1994. 212 pp.
Vol. 14: ISBN: 90-5183-616-3   Hfl. 48,-/US-$ 32.-
BERNTH LINDFORS: Comparative Approaches to African Literatures.Amsterdam/Atlanta,GA 1994.160pp.
Vol. 15: ISBN: 90-5183-723-2   Hfl. 55,-/US-$ 36.50
PETER HORN: Writing my Reading. Essays on Literary Politics in South Africa. Amsterdam/Atlanta, GA 1994. XI,172 pp.
Vol. 16: ISBN: 90-5183-742-9   Bound Hfl. 160,-/US-$ 107.-
ISBN: 90-5183-765-8   Paper Hfl. 50,-/US-$ 33.-
READING RUSHDIE. PERSPECTIVES ON THE FICTION OF SALMAN RUSHDIE. Ed. by M.D. Fletcher. Amsterdam/Atlanta, GA 1994. 400 pp.
Vol. 17: ISBN: 90-5183-731-3   Hfl. 120,-/US-$ 80.-
CHRISTIANE FIOUPOU: La Route. Réalité et représentation dans l'œuvre de Wole Soyinka. Amsterdam/Atlanta, GA 1994. 390 pp.
Vol. 18: ISBN: 90-5183-814-X   Hfl. 75,-/US-$ 46.50
DAVID FAUSETT: Images of the Antipodes in the Eighteenth Century. A Study in Stereotyping. Amsterdam/Atlanta, GA 1995. VIII,231 pp.
Vol. 19: ISBN: 90-5183-879-4   Bound Hfl. 140,-/US-$ 93,-
ISBN: 90-5183-863-8   Paper Hfl. 45,-/US-$ 30.-
THE GUISES OF CANADIAN DIVERSITY / LES MASQUES DE LA DIVERSITÉ CANADIENNE. New European Perspectives/Nouvelles perspectives européennes. Ed. by Serge Jaumain & Marc Maufort
Amsterdam/Atlanta, GA 1995. 288 pp.
Vol. 20: ISBN: 90-5183-964-2   Bound Hfl. 250,-/US-$ 165.-
ISBN: 90-5183-953-7   Paper Hfl. 55,-/US-$ 36.50
A TALENT(ED) DIGGER. Creations, Cameos, and Essays in honour of Anna Rutherford. Ed. by Hena Maes-Jelinek, Gordon Collier, Geoffrey V. Davis. Amsterdam/Atlanta, GA 1996. XIX,519 pp.
Vol. 21: ISBN: 90-5183-972-3   Hfl. 60,-/US-$ 40.-
ALBERT GÉRARD: Afrique plurielle. Études de littérature comparée. Amsterdam/Atlanta, GA 1996. 199 pp.
Vol. 22: ISBN: 90-5183-984-7   Bound Hfl. 175,-/US-$ 116.50
ISBN: 90-5183-967-7   Paper Hfl. 45,-/US-$ 30.-
"AND THE BIRDS BEGAN TO SING". Religion and Literature in Post-Colonial Cultures. Ed. by Jamie S. Scott. Amsterdam/Atlanta, GA 1996. XXVII,327 pp.
Vol. 23: ISBN: 90-420-0021-X   Bound Hfl. 150,-/US-$ 100.-
ISBN: 90-420-0013-9   Paper Hfl. 45,-/US-$ 30,-
DEFINING NEW IDIOMS AND ALTERNATIVE FORMS OF EXPRESSION. Ed. by Eckhard Breitinger. Asnel Papers 1
Amsterdam/Atlanta, GA 1996. XXVI,282 pp.